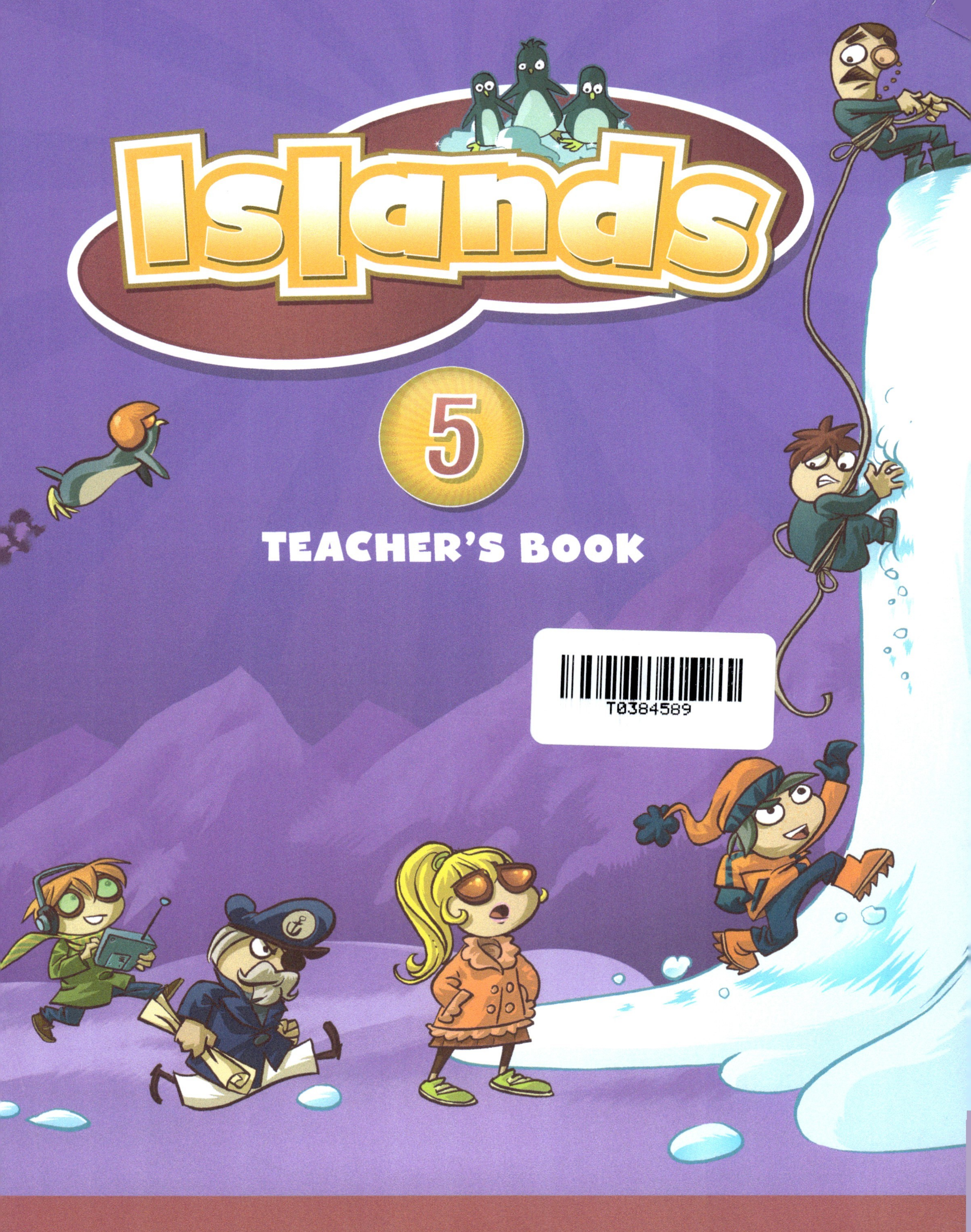
Islands
5
TEACHER'S BOOK
T0384589

Contents

5

Scope and sequence

Welcome

Grammar structures	New vocabulary	Additional language	Phonics
G1: He likes (playing). / They like (running).	V1: listened, played, practised, studied, watched, went, fell, took		
G2: How about (going to the cinema)?	V2: two days ago, yesterday, now, today, tomorrow		
G3: I (played) (tennis) on (Monday morning). He/She (danced) at the (party) on (Friday evening). They (went to) the (cinema) on (Saturday afternoon).			

1 Friends

Grammar structures	New vocabulary	Additional language	Phonics
G1: What does he/she look like? He's (good looking). / She's (beautiful). / He's/She's got (straight dark hair) and (brown eyes). He/She hasn't got (blond(e) hair). What do they look like? They're (tall) and (handsome). / They've got (short blond(e) hair) and (blue eyes). / They haven't got (dark hair).	V1: *Physical characteristics:* dark hair, spiky hair, handsome, good-looking, moustache, blond(e) hair, beautiful, cute, beard, straight hair, curly hair, bald	CLIL: Art (Personal descriptions) Wider World: Families of the world Values: Help your friends in class.	–er / –or ending
G2: What's he/she like? He's (sporty) and he's (clever). / She's (bossy) but (hard-working). I like him because he's (kind).	V2: *Adjectives (personality):* bossy, kind, sporty, lazy, clever, shy, talkative, helpful, friendly, hard-working		
G3: She is (taller) than (her brother). She is the (tallest) (in her family). They are (more handsome) than (their friends). They are the (most handsome). I think that … / I believe that …	V3: CLIL: intelligent, bored, excited, important, lovely, little		

2 My life

Grammar structures	New vocabulary	Additional language	Phonics
G1: You must (brush your teeth). *(Order)* You should (brush your teeth). *(Advice)*	V1: *Activities:* brush my teeth, make my bed, wash my face, tidy my room, do my homework, take out the rubbish, revise for a test, take notes in class, meet my friends, be on time	CLIL: Science (Digestion) Wider World: Shopping for food Values: Giving is great!	Present simple 3rd person singular /s/ /z/ /ɪz/
G2: I never (brush my teeth). He sometimes (brushes his teeth). She usually (brushes her teeth). They often (brush their teeth). We always (brush our teeth). Should + not = Shouldn't	V2: *Adverbs of frequency:* never, sometimes, usually, often, always		
G3: Infinitive of purpose Your tongue helps you to taste the food.	V3: CLIL: butter, chocolate, flour, sugar, salt, smell, taste, plate, snack, digestion		

3 Free time

Grammar structures	New vocabulary	Additional language	Phonics
G1: What is she good at? She's good at (hitting) but she isn't good at (catching). What are they good at? They're good at (hitting) but they're not good at (catching).	V1: Activities: hitting, kicking, throwing, catching, diving, going shopping, telling jokes, reading poetry, playing video games	CLIL: Maths (Graphing favourite hobbies) Wider World: Funny sports Values: Try new things. Have a hobby.	Raising and falling intonation: questions and answers.
G2: What were you doing (yesterday at 7:00)? I was (going to school). What was he/she doing (yesterday at 7.00)? He/She was (going to school). What were they doing (yesterday at 7.00)? They were (going to school). Were you (going to school)? Yes, I was. / No, I wasn't. Was he/she (going to school)? Yes, he/she was. / No, he/she wasn't. Were they (going to school)? Yes, they were. / No, they weren't.	V2: trampolining, playing chess, playing the drums, acting, rollerblading, running races, singing karaoke, skateboarding, reading magazines, drawing		
G3: What would you prefer, dancing or singing? I'd rather sing than dance. / I'd prefer singing to dancing.	V3: CLIL: score, graph, highest, lowest, range, calculate, team		

4 Around the world

Grammar structures	New vocabulary	Additional language	Phonics
G1: There's a rainforest in Brazil. / There isn't a rainforest in Spain. There are some penguins in Argentina. / There aren't any penguins in Italy.	V1: *Countries:* China, Korea, Japan, Australia, the United States, Mexico, Poland, Brazil, Argentina, the United Kingdom, Spain, Italy, Egypt, Turkey	CLIL: Science (The Solar System) Wider World: The weather Values: Working as a team.	Negative contractions (isn't, aren't, wasn't, weren't, hasn't, haven't, don't, doesn't, didn't)
G2: Is there a volcano? Yes, there is. / No, there isn't. Are there any volcanoes? Yes, there are. / No, there aren't.	V2: *Places:* forest, desert, pyramid, statue, city, cave, volcano, lake (regular/irregular plurals)		
G3: How much water is there in the lake? Not much / a little / a lot. How many lakes are there in that country? Not many / a few / a lot.	V3: CLIL: air, future, planet, hill, sky, space		

5 Clothes

Grammar structures	New vocabulary	Additional language	Phonics
G1: How much is that (wallet)? It's £20 (twenty pounds). How much are those gloves? They are £24.50 (twenty-four pounds fifty). It's too expensive. / They're too expensive.	V1: *Clothing and accessories:* tracksuit, swimsuit, watch, bracelet, wallet, umbrella, gloves, belt, pocket, label	CLIL: Social sciences (Shopping) Wider World: Charity shops Values: Dress correctly for each occasion.	Intonation: Exclamations
G2: Whose (hat) is this? It's Dan's/mine/yours/his/hers/its/ours/theirs. Whose (glasses) are these? They're Louis's/mine/yours/his/hers/its/ours/theirs	V2: *Clothing and accessories:* tight, baggy, cheap, expensive, old-fashioned, modern *Numbers 100 – 1000:* 101, 102, … 999 and 1000		
G3: I'll buy this belt. I am going to save money this year.	V3: CLIL: shop assistant, advertisement, receipt, change, customer, department store, money		

6 Party time

Grammar structures	New vocabulary	Additional language	Phonics
G1: I (brought) a (present). / They didn't (bring) any (presents). They could (come to the party). / They couldn't (eat everything).	V1: *Simple past tense verbs:* make/made, have/had, come/came, give/gave, get/got, sing/sang, bring/brought, meet/met, eat/ate, see/saw	CLIL: History (The First Thanksgiving) Wider World: New Year's Eve around the world Values: Be a creative problem solver.	Intonation: Closed (or Yes/No) questions and Information (or Wh-) questions
G2: Where did you go? I went to (Ghana). When did you go to (Ghana)? I went on (August 1st). What did you see? I saw (giant butterflies). Who did you meet? I met (my uncle).	V2: *Ordinals 1st–31st:* first second, third, fourth, fifth, sixth, seventh, eighth, ninth, tenth, eleventh, twelfth, thirteenth, fourteenth, fifteenth, sixteenth, seventeenth, eighteenth, nineteenth, twentieth, twenty-first, twenty-second, twenty-third, twenty-fourth, twenty-fifth, twenty-sixth, twenty-seventh, twenty-eighth, twenty-ninth, thirtieth, thirty-first		
G3: I must … / I have to …	V3: CLIL: month, diary, native American, settler, voyage		

7 School

Grammar structures	New vocabulary	Additional language	Phonics
G1: Was it interesting? Yes, it was. / No, it wasn't. Was there an alien in it? Yes, there was. / No, there wasn't. Were there any exciting stories? Yes, there were. / No, there weren't.	V1: *Adjectives:* interesting, boring, exciting, scary, funny, difficult, easy, romantic	CLIL: Art: (Writing a storyboard) Wider World: Unusual schools Values: Learn about your older family members' youth.	Long and short vowels
G2: Did you have Maths on Tuesday? Yes, I did. / No, I didn't. Did she have History on Friday? Yes, she did. / No, she didn't.	V2: *School subjects:* Computer Studies, Maths, Geography, Science, History, Art, Music, Sport, Design, Drama		
G3: I have finished. / I haven't finished. He has drawn the pictures. / He hasn't drawn the pictures.	V3: CLIL: glue, scissors, storyboard, character, scene		

8 All about us

Grammar structures	New vocabulary	Additional language	Phonics
G1: Is he from the United States? Yes, he is. / No, he isn't. Where's she from? She's from Argentina. / She's Argentinean. Where are they from? They're from Australia. / They're Australian.	V1: *Nationalities:* American, Colombian, Brazilian, Argentinian, British, Spanish, Italian, Egyptian, Chinese, Australian, Canadian, Irish, Greek, Polish, Turkish, Japanese, Irish	CLIL: Science (Time) Wider World: Video games Values: Be a good role model for others.	Simple past of regular verbs –ed: /t/ /d/ /ɪd/
G2: He's an artist who likes playing the guitar. It's an American film that is very famous.	V2: *Occupations:* artist, photographer, painter, astronaut, businessman, cook, firefighter, dentist, waiter, actor, engineer, mechanic, footballer, journalist		
G3: This is the gym where I go twice a week. Those oranges, which I bought yesterday, are delicious. in – the morning, June, spring, 2008 on – Thursday, January 16th at – five o'clock, night	V3: CLIL: time, a.m., p.m., midday, midnight, hour, minute, date, year		

Goodbye

Festivals

Halloween: apple bobbing, pumpkin bread, caramel corn, devil, ghost story, gravestone, spooky food
Christmas: Christmas tree, Father Christmas, mistletoe, Christmas cards, stocking, turkey, Brussels sprouts, Christmas pudding
Pancake day: Shrove Tuesday, recipe, pour, beat, heat, toss, batter, syrup, topping, syrup, mashed
April Fool's Day: prize, contest, prank

Introduction

Islands is a multiple-level course for children learning English as a foreign language in Primary schools. The level, content and pace make it suitable for use in primary schools with typically five or more lessons of English per week. *Islands* offers best practice methodology in the classroom while also offering teachers and pupils an innovative digital environment.

The key course features are:

High level content – *Islands'* vocabulary and grammar syllabus has been developed in line with external exam topics, vocabulary and grammar to help pupils who are preparing for external English exams for young learners (*CYL, Trinity* and *KET for schools*).

Phonics/Literacy syllabus – *Islands* offers an integrated phonics programme across the whole series.

CLIL and cultural references – Integrated within each unit, this provides links to other school subjects and offers the opportunity to study children's lives and culture in other parts of the world.

Enriched digital offer – An Online World, Active Teach Interactive Whiteboard Software and Digital Activity Book provide opportunities to enrich pupils' learning both in school and at home.

Islands can be used as a blended learning course and takes into account the current movement towards using an increased amount of technology in the classroom and also at home as more and more families have home computers and want safe, effective, educational material for their children.

Islands motivates children by introducing them to a group of characters in an Online Island that mirrors the island in their English book. Pupils follow the characters on a quest through their book whilst listening to stories, singing songs, communicating and playing games along the way. Most importantly, pupils will enjoy themselves and make their own discoveries in English. In *Islands* learning is an adventure!

On *Ice Island*, the main characters, Finn, Dylan, Jenny and Dr Al, live in a lush winter wonderland. The adventure begins when a valuable treasure map, showing the location of a Golden Penguin statue, is stolen from Captain Formosa's submarine. Our heroes follow the thieves, Rufus and Ivan and recover the statue much to the delight of two cheeky penguins, Penn and Gywn, who help but get into mischief along the way.

Methodology and skills

Islands', methodology builds on the traditional '3P' (Presentation, Practice, Production) approach. This is a tried and tested approach which is favoured by many teachers in the Primary classroom. The lesson sequence is clear and easy to follow and works in a structured way. The *Islands'* '5Ps' approach adds also Personalisation and Pronunciation.

Presentation is the first stage. In each unit there are two grammar points and three vocabulary presentations – two sets of key topic words and an additional set of CLIL and culture-related content. The teacher demonstrates the key language (often in illustrated form or using gesture) while providing a model (on Audio CD or Active Teach) for pupils to hear the correct pronunciation. Teachers can use the flashcards and Wordcards at this stage of the lesson.

Practice is provided in the form of controlled and more open activities using the presented language. Within each level skills are worked on from unit to unit and across the various components (with a focus on oral in the Pupil's Book and written in the Activity Book) and then built up gradually from level to level. Reading skills are further developed with a range of texts increasing in length and variety to offer pupils 'real' reading opportunities.

Production activities encourage pupils to use the language either to speak or write something. These activities encourage pupils to become more autonomous and to manipulate the language in order to communicate.

Personalisation activities are also included in the lesson structure to engage the pupils further with the unit language and to help them with language recall. At the end of each unit there is an opportunity for pupils' self evaluation.

Pronunciation and spelling of English sounds is a key literacy area which is addressed in the phonics and spelling lessons (Lesson 6). *Islands* Level 5 introduces a wide variety of practice around prefixes, suffixes, intonation and sounds oriented to strengthen pupils' productive skills: speaking and writing.

LITERACY

Islands introduces pupils to reading and writing from the beginning of the course. In Level 5, reading is introduced in the Pupil's Book and Activity Book in the form of paragraphs and short texts. In the Activity Book pupils practise writing sentences and short paragraphs to reinforce the new language. Vocabulary labels, speech bubbles, songs and reading texts are included in the Pupil's Book. Specific reading tasks such as matching, circling, drawing and colouring are included in the Activity Book. At this level pupils are also encouraged to write short texts in the CLIL and Wider World lessons.

The phonics lessons in *Islands* provide a comprehensive and complete phonics syllabus, designed to aid literacy. In Level 5, these lessons are also focused on spelling and, thus, called *Phonics and Spelling* lesson. Pupils are introduced to a sound or spelling rule in each unit. Each sound or spelling is presented in the Pupil's Book, then blended together into simple words or sentences and finally practised orally in pairs. Then in the Activity Book pupils are provided with extensive practice likely to reinforce both productive and receptive skills around that sound or spelling aspect of the English language.

Components for the pupil

PUPIL'S BOOK

The Pupil's Book provides materials to effectively present and practise the target language. It introduces new language in lively and engaging contexts. A wide variety of practice tasks lead from controlled language activities through to production and personalisation activities. Extensive further practice is provided in the Activity Book. Each unit includes listening, speaking, reading and writing activities, ensuring that pupils develop their skills and are able to practise new language in a broad range of contexts. There is also a high level of cross-curricular and cultural content, so that language learning can be integrated into the Primary curriculum (CLIL). Additionally the Pupil's Book contains songs, chants, stories, games, listening and reading texts and communicative activities to ensure lessons are varied, motivating and effective. The Pupil's Book is organised as follows:

- A **Welcome unit** of four lessons. This introduces pupils to the group of characters and the island, as well as some key introductory language.
- **Eight units** divided into **ten distinct lessons**.
- A **Goodbye unit** of four lessons. This rounds up the quest as well as offering plenty of recycling opportunities.
- **Four festival lessons** at the back of the book for use at Halloween, Christmas, Pancake Day and April Fools' Day.
- A **Grammar summary** of each unit for pupils' reference.
- Eight **Extensive readings** related to each unit.

The **Access code** printed at the back of the book gives pupils and parents unique and safe access to *Ice Island Online* via the internet.

ACTIVITY BOOK

The Activity Book provides reinforcement and consolidation of the language presented in the Pupil's Book. It contains controlled and freer practice plus personalisation and further listening and reading texts. It is organised as follows:

- A **Welcome unit** of four lessons, for use after the corresponding Pupil's Book pages.
- **Eight units** divided into ten lessons (as in the Pupil's Book).
- A **Goodbye unit** of four lessons (as in the Pupil's Book).
- **Four festival lessons** at the back of the book for use at Halloween, Christmas, Pancake Day and April Fools' Day.
- **Unit review activities**. These are linked to the corresponding grammar points in the Pupil's Book and can be used for evaluation or additional practice.
- A **Picture dictionary** at the back of the book to help pupils to review and remember the target language.

Full details of when to use the Activity Book are given in the teaching notes.

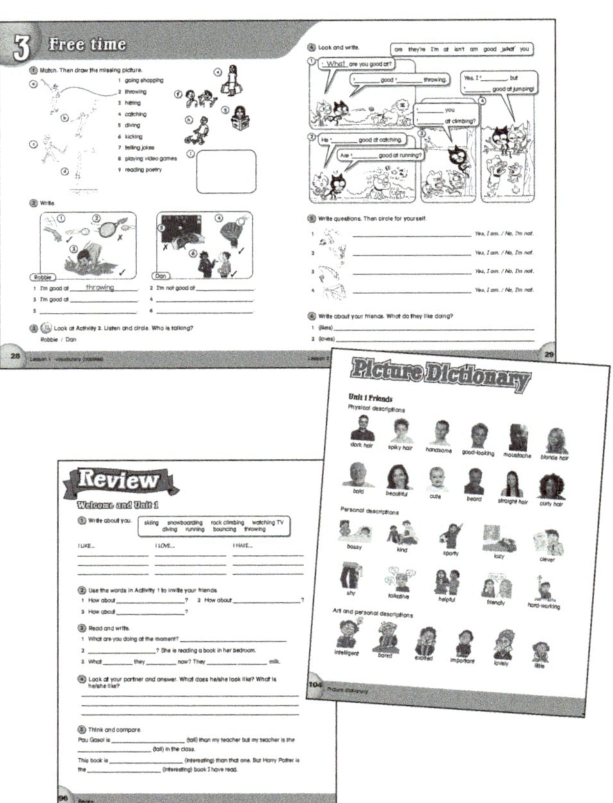

DIGITAL ACTIVITY BOOK

The Digital Activity Book is a version of the Activity Book that contains all the activities from the printed book with some additional interactive exercises and games. It also has interactive versions of the flash cards, story cards, picture dictionary and the songs and chants for the relevant level of the course (with karaoke versions).

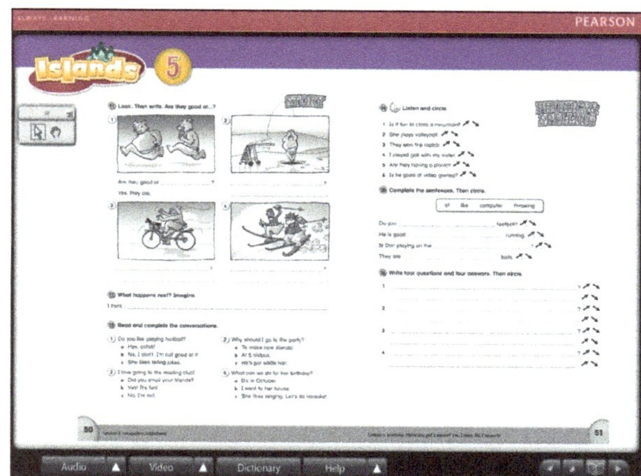

ONLINE WORLD

Islands includes a unique Online World component. This provides a safe, engaging, highly-motivating environment where the pupils meet the characters from the Pupil's Book plus a host of other exciting characters and follow them on an adventure. Pupils encounter and practise target language from the course in a stimulating environment. They will engage in safe 'closed-chat' dialogues with the characters they meet and follow instructions and guidance to help them solve clues and puzzles and engage in supplementary language games along the way. It's a great way to make learning happen in an interactive environment and further consolidates and extends the language-learning process. Most of all, pupils will enjoy the experience of learning through play and will absorb English without realising it!

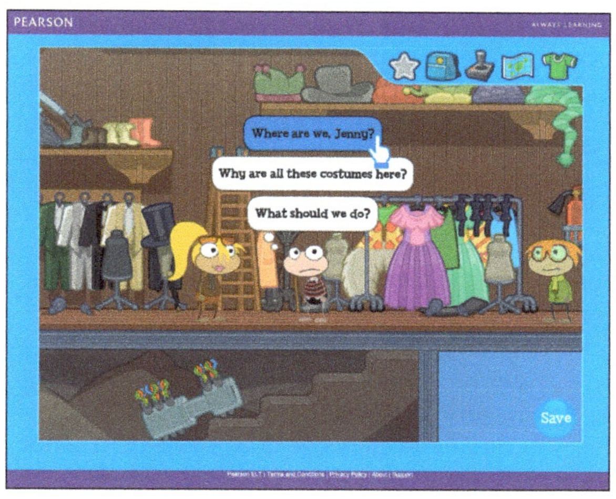

READING AND WRITING BOOKLET

The Reading and Writing Booklet includes four pages per unit to target these specific skills. The first page focuses on reading and the second on comprehension with a range of texts more than those offered in the CLIL and Wider World pages of the Pupil's Book. The third page offers reading and writing activities based on revision of key vocabulary and, using the fourth page, pupils have the opportunity to write texts which practice punctuation, syntax and structure. An answer key is provided at the back of the Teacher's Book. Details of when to use this booklet are given in the teaching notes.

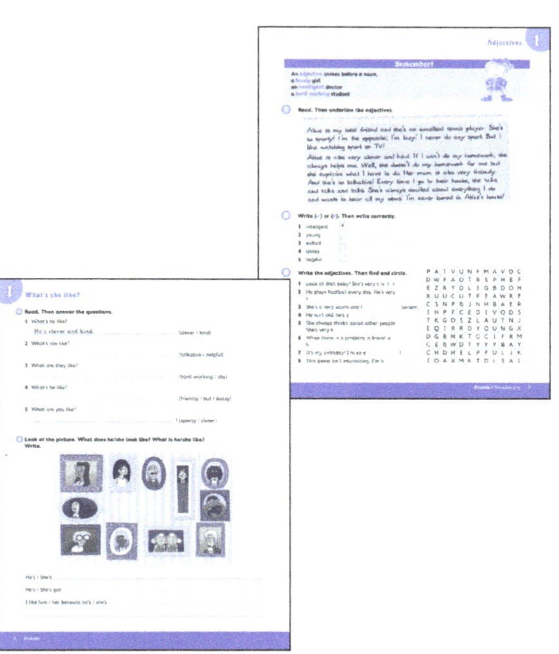

GRAMMAR BOOKLET

The Grammar Booklet offers four pages per unit to further practice the grammar points covered in the corresponding Pupil's Book unit. Tip boxes are provided for exercises and key vocabulary is reinforced. The last page of each unit provides opportunities for consolidation and review of all key grammar points. An answer key is provided at the back of the Teacher's Book where required. Details of when to use this booklet are given in the teaching notes.

Components for the teacher

TEACHER'S BOOK

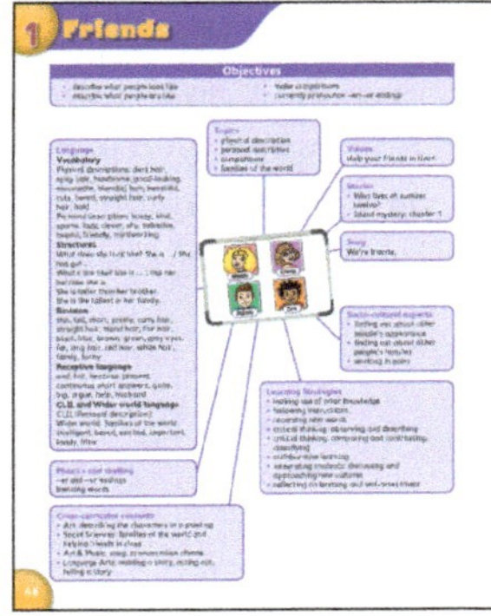

The Teacher's Book provides the following:

- An introduction highlighting the main features of the course. It includes a 'tour' of a unit, giving advice for how the different features and components are woven into each unit. Advice is also provided for how to use the digital components, the Digital Activity Book and the Online World effectively in class.
- A summary map for each unit. As well as highlighting the linguistic content of the unit, this lists the cross-curricular, cultural and phonological elements, as well as summarising how the eight basic competences have been integrated.
- Step-by-step lesson plans covering all the course material. Each lesson is clearly structured into stages, with activities included for starting and ending the lesson. There are further optional activities suggested for fast finishers or extension work. The recording script and answer key is provided at the end of each unit.
- Teaching notes and answers for using the Reading and Writing Booklet, the Grammar Booklet, the Photocopiables and the Test Booklet. There is also a page for recording pupils' test scores.
- A games bank providing procedure for all the games suggested in the lesson notes. There is also a useful summary of classroom language at the back of the book.

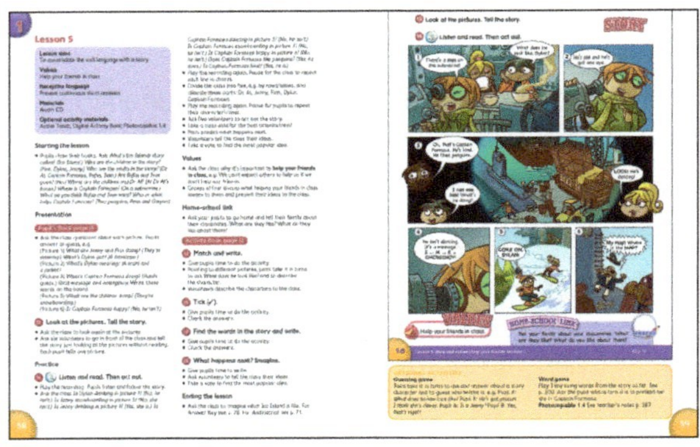

Access codes printed at the back of the book give the teacher special access to *Ice Island Online*, the Active Teach and the Digital Activity Book.

TEST BOOKLET

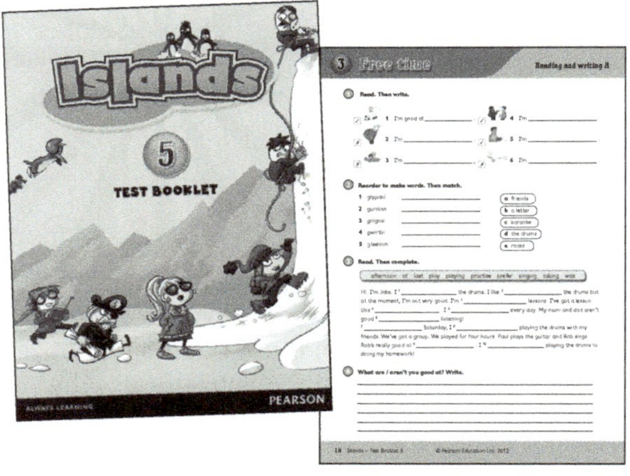

The Test Booklet contains initial placement tests, progress tests for each unit and practice tests, testing all four skills – reading, writing, listening, speaking – using question types from external exams (*CYL, Trinity* and *KET for schools)*. Audio recordings are provided on the Class audio CDs, an answer key and page to record test results are provided in the Teacher's Book. The audioscript for all the listening activities is available in the Active Teach.

ONLINE WORLD

Teachers have special access to the *Online World* using the Access code provided in the Teacher's Book. This takes them into *Ice Island Online* with the pupils and gives access to an easy to use Progress Review System (PRS) where the teacher can monitor the progress of their pupils. There are step-by-step help guides detailing all aspects of game play, plus log in and classroom management through the PRS. These are available both on screen and as a download to print. Teachers will also find report cards showing each pupil's progress that they can print out for the class and parents. Teachers will find further information on pages 31–35.

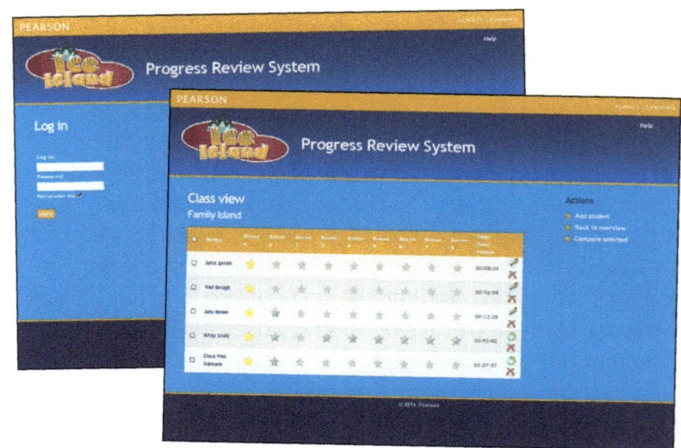

AUDIO CDs

The CDs contain all the songs, stories and listening comprehension activities. Karaoke versions of the songs are available via the Active Teach.

ACTIVE TEACH

Islands Active Teach provides software for use on any Interactive Whiteboard (IWB) with integrated tools and a 'How to …' video demonstration of use. It eases classroom management as it contains direct links to all of the Pupil's and Activity Book pages, digitally transformed to create more opportunities for interaction between the pupil, teacher and the material. It includes 'hide' and 'reveal' answers, links to further practice activities and games that recycle the language of the unit and previous units and links to audio and video content without the need of a separate CD or DVD player. It has stimulating and engaging digital board games with electronic spinners and flashcards and posters.

On each level of *Islands* Active Teach there are four animated stories episodes. Each episode can be used to reinforce and extend the language of the course, focusing on the topics and language of two units. There are songs presented by three young presenters, Sally, Jack and Albert. And there are animated stories, showing further adventures of the Ice Island characters. Teachers will find further information on pages 28–31.

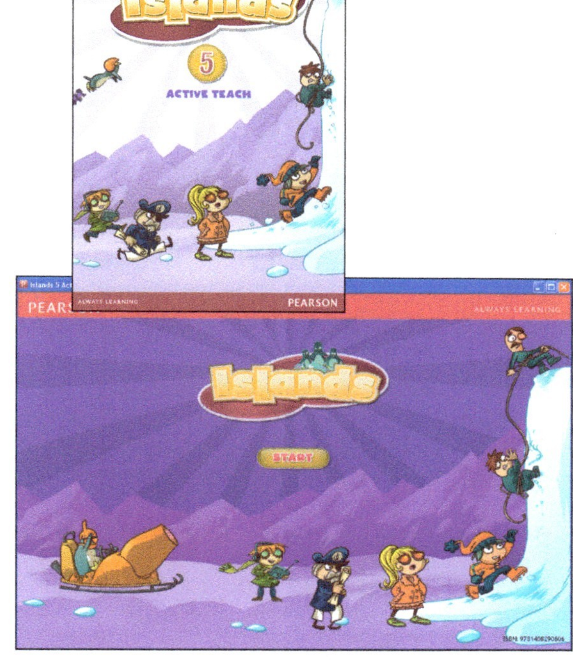

PHOTOCOPIABLES

Sixty-two pages of photocopiable material are offered via the Active Teach to give maximum flexibility and variety throughout the teaching year. The material includes:

- Seven photocopiables for use in each unit. This includes extra practice of the vocabulary presented in the unit, the song and the story, as well as material for reinforcing the phonics and spelling skills consolidating the CLIL and cultural themes in the unit.
- Three photocopiables for use with the festival lessons.
- A template for a letter that can be written to parents.
- A course certificate.
- A cover pupils can use for their portfolio.

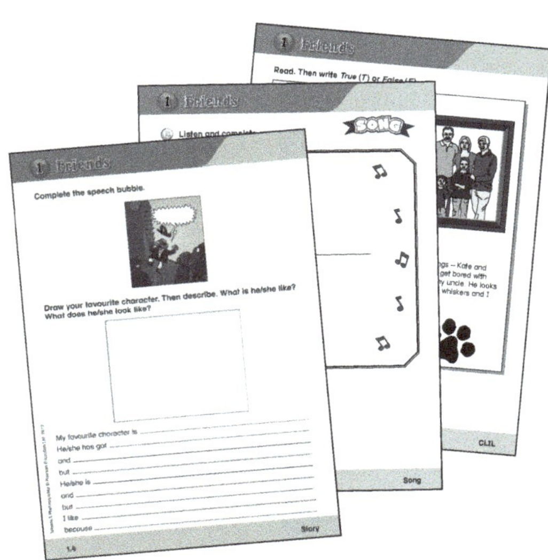

FLASHCARDS

There are 175 flashcards at Level 5 illustrating the two main target vocabulary sets for each unit. The lesson plan and Games section in the Teacher's Book clearly explain how the flashcards can be used to present, practise and consolidate language through games and activities.

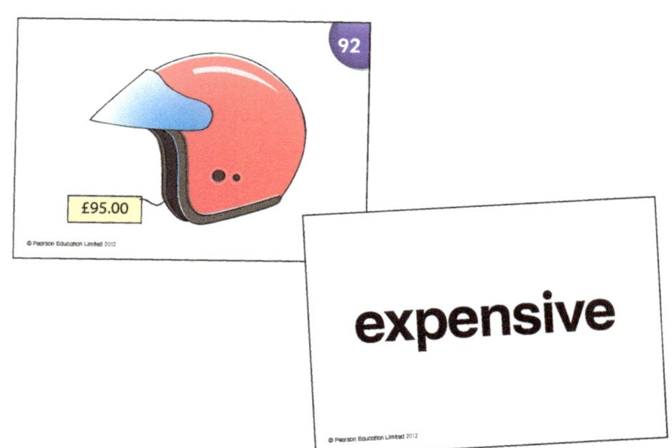

WORDCARDS

A set of wordcards matching the flashcards are provided at each level. The lesson plan and Games section in the Teacher's Book clearly explain how these can be used for helping with reading and literacy, through games and activities.

POSTERS

There are four posters to accompany each level of *Islands.* The posters provide an additional resource for the Vocabulary, Phonics and spelling, CLIL and cultural elements of each unit. There is also a generic poster at each level which helps students with vocabulary they will need for external exams. Teachers will find information on how best to use posters on pages 26–27 and in the main lesson notes.

Join us at the Great Teachers' Primary Place

Find inspiring ideas for your primary classroom, discover new techniques and solutions that work, connect with other primary teachers, and share your own stories and creativity.

The Great Teachers' Primary Place is the place to go for free classroom resources and countless activities for primary teachers everywhere.

Go to www.pearsonelt.com/primaryplace and register for membership.

Members of The Great Teachers' Primary Place will receive exclusive access to:

- Free articles on current trends in the primary classroom!
- Free reproducible activity sheets to download and use in your classroom!
- Free Teacher Primary Packs filled with posters, story cards, and games to use in your classroom!
- Exclusive access to professional development via print materials and web conferences.

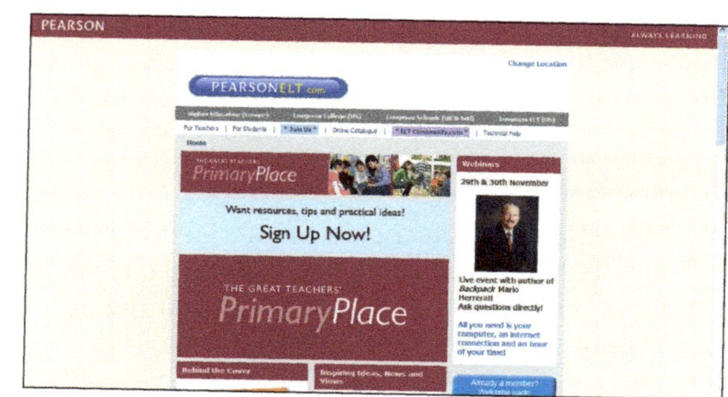

Pronunciation table

Consonants		Vowels		
Symbol	Keyword		Symbol	Keyword
p	pen	short	ɪ	bit
b	back		e	bed
t	ten		æ	cat
d	day		ɒ	dog
k	key		ʌ	cut
ɡ	get		ʊ	put
f	fat		ə	about
v	view		i	happy
θ	thing		u	actuality
ð	then	long	iː	sheep
s	soon		ɑː	father
z	zero		ɔː	four
ʃ	ship		uː	boot
ʒ	pleasure		ɜː	bird
h	hot	diphthongs	eɪ	make
x	loch		aɪ	lie
tʃ	cheer		ɔɪ	boy
dʒ	jump		əʊ	note
m	sum		aʊ	now
n	sun		ɪə	real
ŋ	sung		eə	hair
w	wet		ʊə	sure
l	let		uə	actual
r	red		iə	peculiar
j	yet			

Evaluation

Islands provides three different ways of assessing pupils' progress.

1 Formative (or informal) evaluation
The teacher monitors pupils' progress throughout the unit as they carry out the activities in class. This guide includes an Evaluation Chart (also available in the *Islands* Active Teach) which the teacher can use to evaluate pupils' performance in the different classroom activities.

2 Summative (or formal) evaluation
Eight Progress Check lessons are provided, one at the end of each unit.
In addition, the Test Booklet contains: a placement test for the beginning of the school year; three end-of-term tests which enable the teacher to carry out a cumulative assessment if the teacher considers it necessary; and an end-of-year test. The tests are classified as A and B to cater for mixed-ability classrooms.

3 Self evaluation
At the end of each unit in the Activity Book pupils evaluate their own participation in the different classroom activities. This helps them to become aware of how they are progressing and to start to develop a realistic appreciation of their own skills, knowledge and learning objectives.

Portfolio

The Council of Europe promotes the use of a *European Language Portfolio* as a means of encouraging language learning and of providing an internationally recognised record of language achievement.

Islands adapts the European Language Portfolio so that pupils can keep a record of what they are learning in class in a way that is appropriate to their age and their stage of cognitive development.

The portfolio for *Islands* consists of a selection of the work which pupils have carried out throughout the year. It is the pupils themselves who decide which pieces of work they want to include (for example, the ones they think represent their best work). Pupils' portfolios should preferably be kept in the classroom; pupils can take them home to show to their parents when they wish.

Pupils will need a box or a large folder to store the work which they have done throughout the year. They should put their name on the portfolio cover included in the Photocopiables on the Active Teach and decorate it as they wish, then stick it onto the outside of their box or folder. Pupils can include some of the following in their portfolio:

- The Portfolio project for each unit.
- The posters they have made, their All About Me projects and photocopiable worksheets, cards and other material that they have completed during the year.
- Their end-of-unit and end-of-term tests.

Pupil's evaluation

Unit ______________________________ Topic ______________________________

Term ______________________________ Number of sessions/teaching hours __________

Objectives	Degree of Achievement	Notes/comments
Lesson 1	Low/Medium/High	
Lesson 2	Low/Medium/High	
Lesson 3	Low/Medium/High	
Lesson 4	Low/Medium/High	
Lesson 5	Low/Medium/High	
Lesson 6	Low/Medium/High	
Lesson 7	Low/Medium/High	
Lesson 8	Low/Medium/High	
Lesson 9	Low/Medium/High	
Lesson 10	Low/Medium/High	

Primary school work areas			
Reading		Listening	
Writing		Speaking	

Material used	in the classroom	delivered to the family
Pupil's Book		
Activity Book		
Photocopiables		
Flashcards & Wordcards		
Posters		
Digital Activity Book		
Active Teach		
Other		

Connections with tutor
Comments:

Unit evaluation	liked most	liked least
Teacher		
Pupils		

Tour of a unit

At Level 5, there is an introductory unit of four lessons *(Welcome)* followed by eight main teaching units, each divided into ten lessons. Consolidation and round up is then provided in a four-lesson *Goodbye* unit. The *Festival* lessons can be used at Halloween, Christmas, Pancake Day and April Fools' Day. There are also grammar summaries and extensive readings at the back of the Pupil's Book.

As well as linguistic and skills practice, the Activity Book provides opportunities for self evaluation and personalisation. There are also Unit review activities at the back of the Activity Book, a Picture dictionary and four pages of activities about festivals.

The eight main teaching units consist of ten lessons as follows:

Lesson 1
Presentation and practice of vocabulary with audio support.

Pupils listen to the key topic vocabulary in context, e.g. a dialogue between the characters for this level: Maddy, Emma, Dan and Robbie. They also listen and repeat the new vocabulary. The target vocabulary is clearly labelled on each page. The penguins appear once in each unit with an item from Ice Island. Pupils find the item online and click on it to access a supplementary language task.

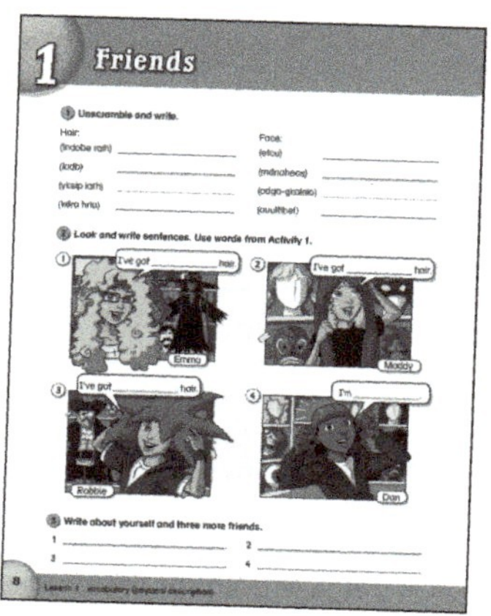

1 Friends

1 Unscramble and write.

Hair:
(lndobe rahi) ______
(lodb) ______
(ykisp iarh) ______
(krda hrai) ______

Face:
(etcu) ______
(mdnaheos) ______
(odgo-gkolni) ______
(auulftbe) ______

2 Look and write sentences. Use words from Activity 1.

3 Write about yourself and three more friends.

1 ______ 2 ______
3 ______ 4 ______

8

Pupils practice new vocabulary in the Activity Book.

1 Friends

1 Listen and read. Who lives at number 12?

2 Listen and repeat.

1 dark hair 2 spiky hair 3 handsome 4 good-looking 5 moustache 6 blonde hair
7 bald 8 beautiful 9 cute 10 beard 11 straight hair 12 curly hair

3 Who's who? Listen and point to the correct picture in Activity 2.

12

The penguins, Penn and Gwyn, appear on one of the Pupil's Book pages in each unit, holding a picture of an item from *Ice Island Online*. Pupils have to find the item online, click on it and complete the supplementary language activity based on the vocabulary of the unit. The lesson notes in the Teacher's Book give the precise location of each online clue.

Flashcards and wordcards can be used to present new words and practise them in a variety of games.

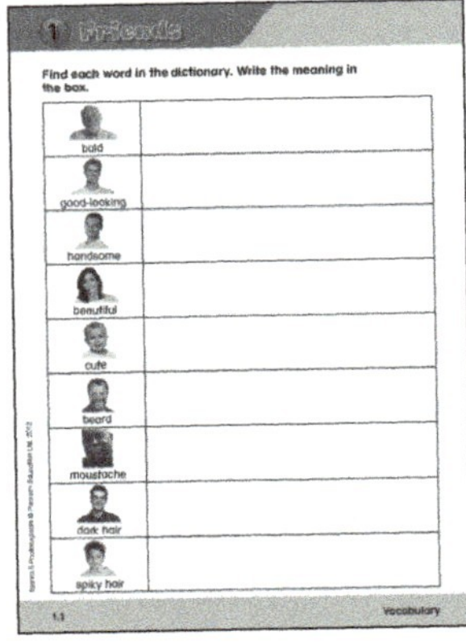

Find each word in the dictionary. Write the meaning in the box.

bald	
good-looking	
handsome	
beautiful	
cute	
beard	
moustache	
dark hair	
spiky hair	

Vocabulary

Extra practice of vocabulary is offered through the photocopiable available on the Active Teach.

Lesson 2
Presentation and practice of grammar with audio support.

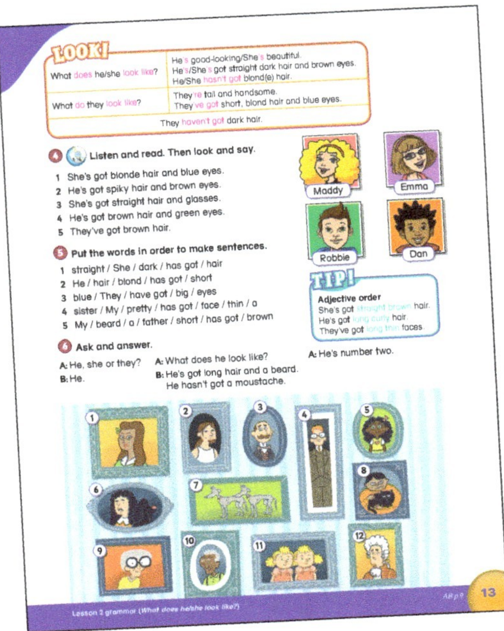
LOOK!

What does he/she look like?	He's good-looking/She's beautiful. He's/She's got straight dark hair and brown eyes. He/She hasn't got blond(e) hair.
What do they look like?	They're tall and handsome. They've got short, blond hair and blue eyes. They haven't got dark hair.

4 Listen and read. Then look and say.

1 She's got blonde hair and blue eyes.
2 He's got spiky hair and brown eyes.
3 She's got straight hair and glasses.
4 He's got brown hair and green eyes.
5 They've got brown hair.

Maddy Emma Robbie Dan

5 Put the words in order to make sentences.

1 straight / She / dark / has got / hair
2 He / hair / blond / has got / short
3 blue / They / have got / big / eyes
4 sister / My / pretty / has got / face / thin / a
5 My / beard / a / father / short / has got / brown

TIP! Adjective order
She's got straight brown hair.
He's got long curly hair.
They've got long thin faces.

6 Ask and answer.

A: He, she or they?
B: He.
A: What does he look like?
B: He's got long hair and a beard. He hasn't got a moustache.
A: He's number two.

Lesson 2 grammar (What does he/she look like?) 13

The new structure is presented in a Look! box and there is further practice of vocabulary. The new grammar content of the lesson is practised through both listening and oral activities.

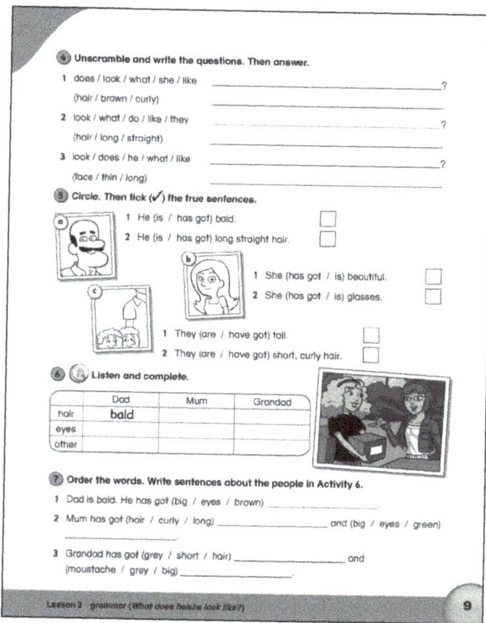
4 Unscramble and write the questions. Then answer.

1 does / look / what / she / like ____________?
(hair / brown / curly) ____________
2 look / what / do / like / they ____________?
(hair / long / straight) ____________
3 look / does / he / what / like ____________?
(face / thin / long) ____________

5 Circle. Then tick (✓) the true sentences.

a
1 He (is / has got) bald.
2 He (is / has got) long straight hair.

b
1 She (has got / is) beautiful.
2 She (has got / is) glasses.

c
1 They (are / have got) tall.
2 They (are / have got) short, curly hair.

6 Listen and complete.

	Dad	Mum	Grandad
hair	bald		
eyes			
other			

7 Order the words. Write sentences about the people in Activity 6.

1 Dad is bald. He has got (big / eyes / brown) ____________
2 Mum has got (hair / curly / long) ____________ and (big / eyes / green) ____________
3 Grandad has got (grey / short / hair) ____________ and (moustache / grey / big) ____________.

Lesson 2 grammar (What does he/she look like?) 9

The Activity Book provides additional written practice for pupils with the new grammar structures.

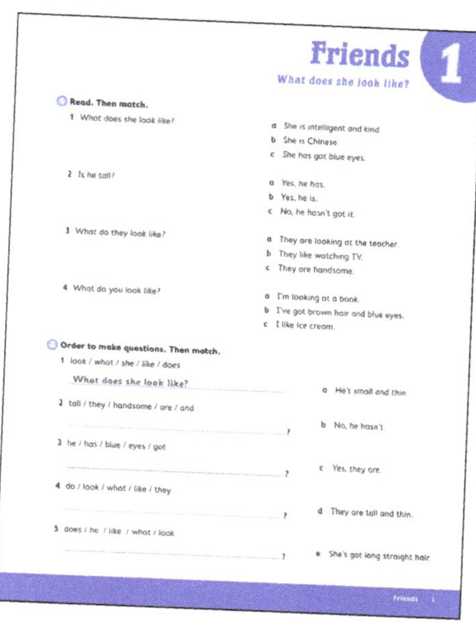
Friends 1
What does she look like?

Read. Then match.

1 What does she look like?
a She is intelligent and kind.
b She is Chinese.
c She has got blue eyes.

2 Is he tall?
a Yes, he has.
b Yes, he is.
c No, he hasn't got it.

3 What do they look like?
a They are looking at the teacher.
b They like watching TV.
c They are handsome.

4 What do you look like?
a I'm looking at a book.
b I've got brown hair and blue eyes.
c I like ice cream.

Order to make questions. Then match.

1 look / what / she / like / does
What does she look like? ____ a He's small and thin.
2 tall / they / handsome / are / and
____________? b No, he hasn't.
3 he / has / blue / eyes / got
____________? c Yes, they are.
4 do / look / what / like / they
____________? d They are tall and thin.
5 does / he / like / what / look
____________? e She's got long straight hair.

Friends 1

Additional grammar practice is offered through the Grammar Booklet.

Active Teach uses digital editions of the flashcards and wordcards to reinforce the language.

Lesson 3
Presentation and practice of vocabulary with audio support.

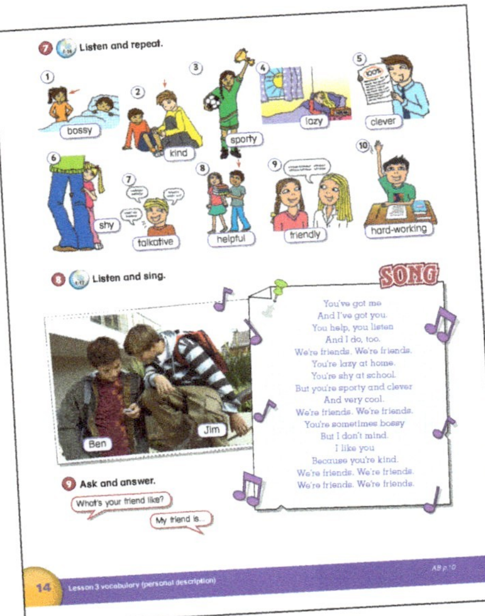
7 Listen and repeat.
1 bossy
2 kind
3 sporty
4 lazy
5 clever
6 shy
7 talkative
8 helpful
9 friendly
10 hard-working

8 Listen and sing.

SONG

You've got me
And I've got you.
You help, you listen
And I do, too.
We're friends. We're friends.
You're lazy at home.
You're shy at school.
But you're sporty and clever
And very cool.
We're friends. We're friends.
You're sometimes bossy
But I don't mind.
I like you
Because you're kind.
We're friends. We're friends.
We're friends. We're friends.

9 Ask and answer.

What's your friend like?
My friend is...

Pupils learn a second set of target vocabulary, which is linked to the unit topic. This may be additional words or it may be a separate vocabulary set. The language of the unit is then presented and practised in a song. Karaoke versions of the songs are included in the audio files on the Active Teach.

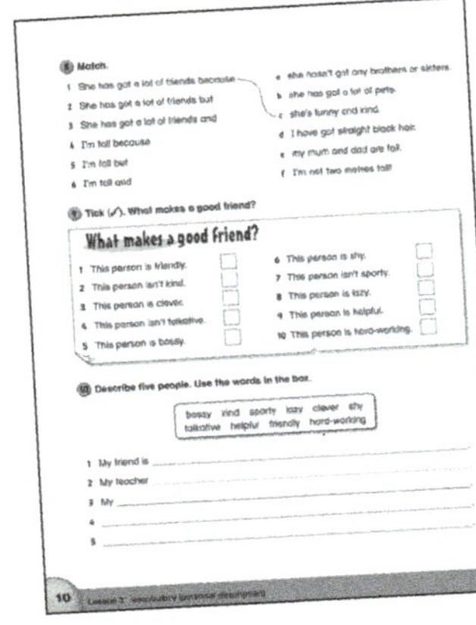

Written practice of both vocabulary sets is provided via the Activity Book activities and also on two photocopiables available on the Active Teach.

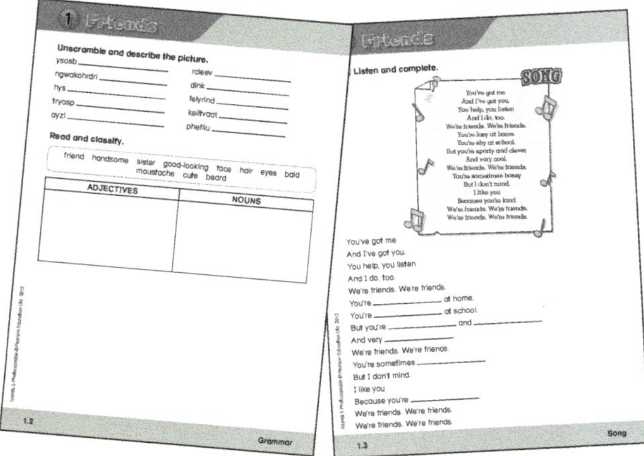

Photocopiables to practise the grammar and the song are available in the Active Teach.

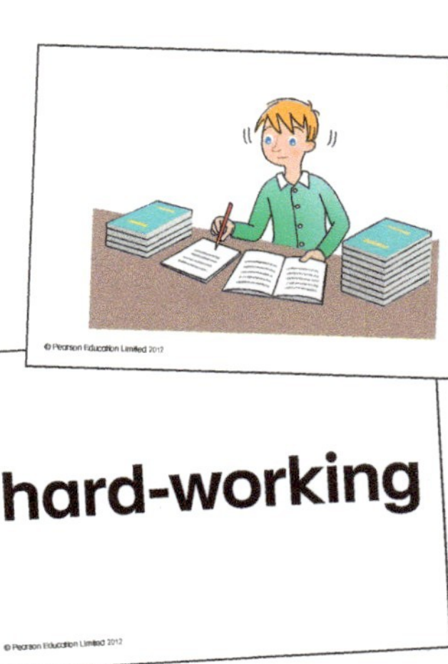

A second group of flashcards and wordcards is provided for the new vocabulary set.

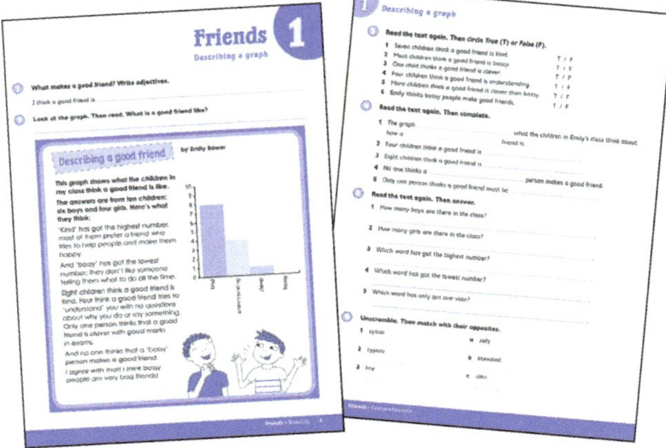

Pupils can further practise the key vocabulary and grammar through the reading and comprehension activities offered in the Reading and Writing Booklet.

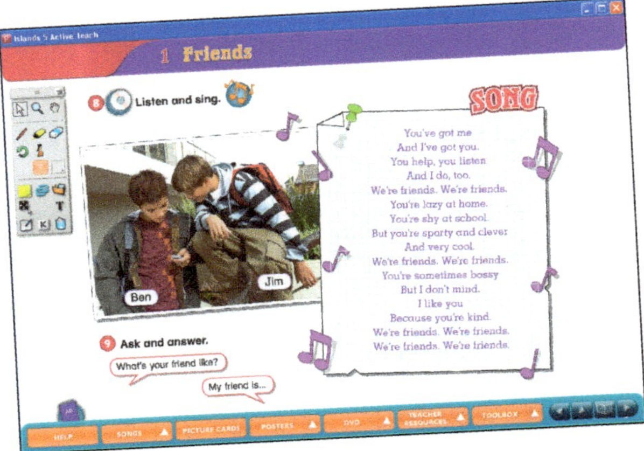

Pupils can sing the karaoke version of the song and use the photocopiable available on the Active Teach.

Lesson 4
Presentation and practice of grammar with audio support.

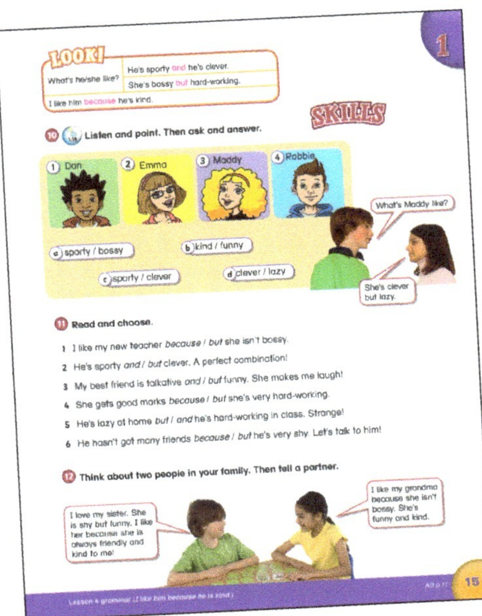

LOOK!

What's he/she like? | He's sporty and he's clever. / She's bossy but hard-working.

I like him because he's kind.

SKILLS

10 Listen and point. Then ask and answer.

1 Dan 2 Emma 3 Maddy 4 Robbie

a sporty / bossy b kind / funny c sporty / clever d clever / lazy

What's Maddy like?

She's clever but lazy.

11 Read and choose.

1 I like my new teacher *because / but* she isn't bossy.
2 He's sporty *and / but* clever. A perfect combination!
3 My best friend is talkative *and / but* funny. She makes me laugh!
4 She gets good marks *because / but* she's very hard-working.
5 He's lazy at home *but / and* he's hard-working in class. Strange!
6 He hasn't got many friends *because / but* he's very shy. Let's talk to him!

12 Think about two people in your family. Then tell a partner.

I love my sister. She is shy but funny. I like her because she is always friendly and kind to me!

I like my grandma because she isn't bossy. She's funny and kind.

Lesson 4 grammar (I like him because he is kind.) 15

The new structure is presented with a task listening activity and practised with a skills activity. Further practice is included of all the vocabulary and grammar. The new grammar content for this lesson is summarised in a Look! box at the top of the Pupil's Book page.

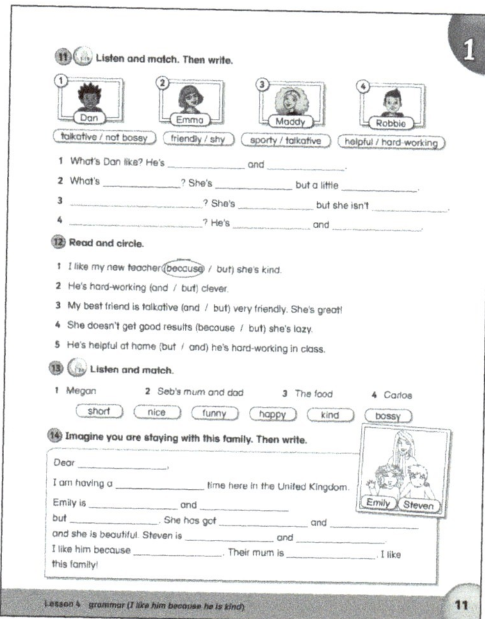

11 Listen and match. Then write.

1 Dan 2 Emma 3 Maddy 4 Robbie

talkative / not bossy | friendly / shy | sporty / talkative | helpful / hard-working

1 What's Dan like? He's _____ and _____.
2 What's _____? She's _____ but a little _____.
3 _____? She's _____ but she isn't _____.
4 _____? He's _____ and _____.

12 Read and circle.

1 I like my new teacher (because / but) she's kind.
2 He's hard-working (and / but) clever.
3 My best friend is talkative (and / but) very friendly. She's great!
4 She doesn't get good results (because / but) she's lazy.
5 He's helpful at home (but / and) he's hard-working in class.

13 Listen and match.

1 Megan 2 Seb's mum and dad 3 The food 4 Carlos

short | nice | funny | happy | kind | bossy

14 Imagine you are staying with this family. Then write.

Dear _____,
I am having a _____ time here in the United Kingdom.
Emily is _____ and _____
but _____. She has got _____ and _____
and she is beautiful. Steven is _____ and _____.
I like him because _____. Their mum is _____. I like this family!

Emily Steven

Lesson 4 grammar (I like him because he is kind.) 11

The Activity Book provides pupils with further practice of the new grammar structures with a literacy focus on reading and writing.

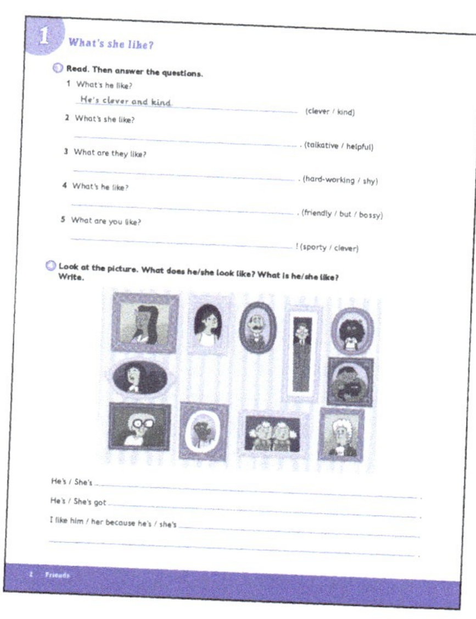

What's she like?

Read. Then answer the questions.

1 What's he like?
He's clever and kind. (clever / kind)
2 What's she like?
_____ (talkative / helpful)
3 What are they like?
_____ (hard-working / shy)
4 What's he like?
_____ (friendly / but / bossy)
5 What are you like?
_____ I (sporty / clever)

Look at the picture. What does he/she look like? What is he/she like? Write.

He's / She's _____
He's / She's got _____
I like him / her because he's / she's _____

1 Friends

Additional practice of grammar is offered through the Grammar Booklet.

Lesson 5
Story and values.

13 Look at the pictures. Tell the story.

STORY

14 Listen and read. Then act out.

VALUES
Help your friends in class.

HOME-SCHOOL LINK
Tell your family about your classmates. What are they like? What do you like about them?

PARENT

AB p.12

16 Lesson 5 story and values (help your friends in class)

The story is provided as a cartoon strip with speech bubbles and audio support. It recycles vocabulary and structures from previous lessons and introduces some new language.

The values topic for the unit is usually linked to the story and is summarised in the Values box on the Pupil's Book page. There is also a Home-School Link suggestion connected with the values topic to encourage parental involvement.

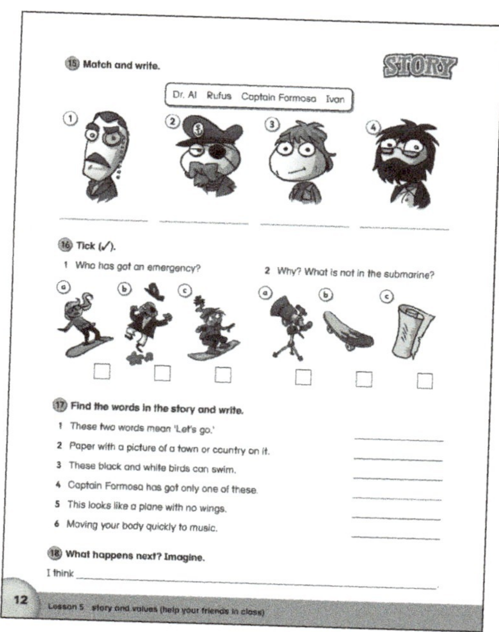
15 Match and write.

STORY

Dr. Al Rufus Captain Formosa Ivan

1 ______ 2 ______ 3 ______ 4 ______

16 Tick (✓).

1 Who has got an emergency? a ☐ b ☐ c ☐

2 Why? What is not in the submarine? a ☐ b ☐ c ☐

17 Find the words in the story and write.

1 These two words mean 'Let's go.' ______
2 Paper with a picture of a town or country on it. ______
3 These black and white birds can swim. ______
4 Captain Formosa has got only one of these. ______
5 This looks like a plane with no wings. ______
6 Moving your body quickly to music. ______

18 What happens next? Imagine.

I think ______

12 Lesson 5 story and values (help your friends in class)

The Activity Book provides activities for both story comprehension and for the values content of the lesson.

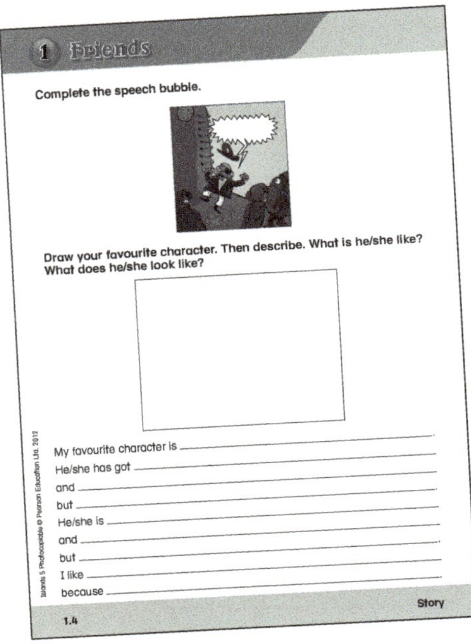
1 Friends

Complete the speech bubble.

Draw your favourite character. Then describe. What is he/she like? What does he/she look like?

My favourite character is ______
He/she has got ______
and ______
but ______
He/she is ______
and ______
but ______
I like ______
because ______

Islands 5 Photocopiable © Pearson Education Ltd. 2012

1.4 Story

A photocopiable available on the Active Teach supports further work on the story.

Lesson 6
Phonics and spelling with audio support.

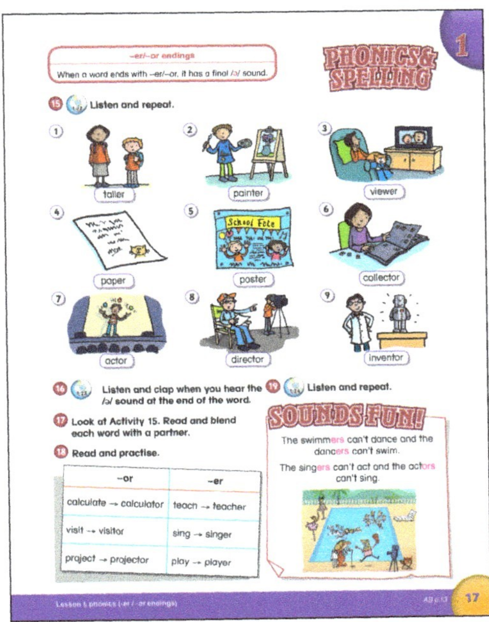
PHONICS & SPELLING 1

-er/-or endings

When a word ends with -er/-or, it has a final /ə/ sound.

15 Listen and repeat.

1 taller 2 painter 3 viewer
4 paper 5 poster 6 collector
7 actor 8 director 9 inventor

16 Listen and clap when you hear the /ə/ sound at the end of the word.

17 Look at Activity 15. Read and blend each word with a partner.

18 Read and practise.

-or	-er
calculate → calculator	teach → teacher
visit → visitor	sing → singer
project → projector	play → player

19 Listen and repeat.

SOUNDS FUN!

The swimmers can't dance and the dancers can't swim.
The singers can't act and the actors can't sing.

Lesson 5 phonics (-er / -or endings) 17

In Level 5, pupils are introduced to a sound or spelling rule in each unit. Each sound or spelling is presented in the Pupil's Book, then blended together into simple words or sentences and finally practised orally in pairs. Then in the Activity Book pupils are provided with extensive practice likely to reinforce both productive and receptive skills around that sound or spelling aspect of the English language.

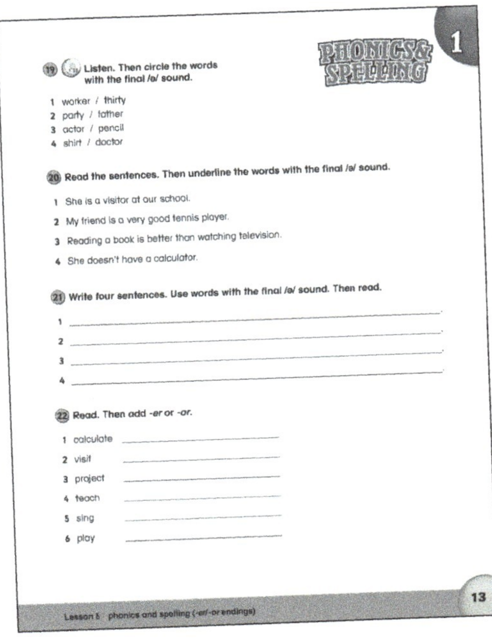
PHONICS & SPELLING 1

19 Listen. Then circle the words with the final /ə/ sound.

1 worker / thirty
2 party / father
3 actor / pencil
4 shirt / doctor

20 Read the sentences. Then underline the words with the final /ə/ sound.

1 She is a visitor at our school.
2 My friend is a very good tennis player.
3 Reading a book is better than watching television.
4 She doesn't have a calculator.

21 Write four sentences. Use words with the final /ə/ sound. Then read.

1 ______
2 ______
3 ______
4 ______

22 Read. Then add -er or -or.

1 calculate ______
2 visit ______
3 project ______
4 teach ______
5 sing ______
6 play ______

Lesson 5 phonics and spelling (-er/-or endings) 13

Written practice is available in the Activity Book.

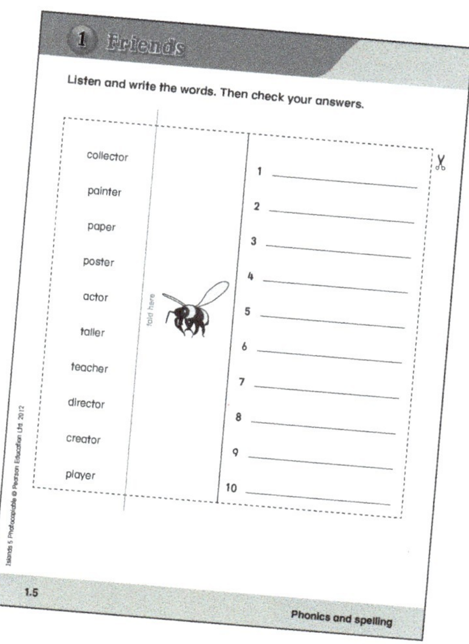
1 Friends

Listen and write the words. Then check your answers.

collector 1 ______
painter 2 ______
paper 3 ______
poster 4 ______
actor 5 ______
taller 6 ______
teacher 7 ______
director 8 ______
creator 9 ______
player 10 ______

Islands 5 Photocopiable © Pearson Education Ltd 2012

1.5 Phonics and spelling

A phonics and spelling photocopiable is provided on the Active Teach.

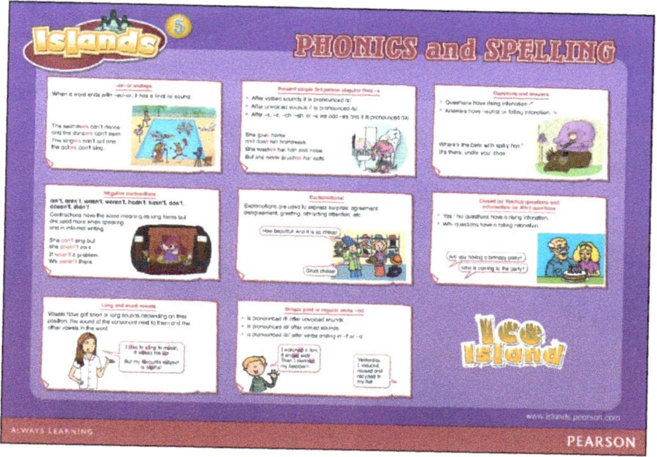

The Phonics and spelling poster presents the key phonics sounds or spelling for each unit.

Lesson 7
CLIL (cross-curricular content).

CLIL

20 Read and match.

Katy is visiting a museum in Madrid. She is looking at a painting of the royal family in 1656. Have a look at her notebook. Can you match her notes with the characters in the painting?

1. He's the youngest and he's got short blond hair. He doesn't look excited, he looks bored.
2. He is older than the others. He looks intelligent and likes to think about things a lot.
3. She's got long blonde hair and looks bossy. She doesn't look very hard-working.
4. He's got brown hair and is the youngest. He gets very excited about things and is very talkative.
5. She's the smallest and has got red hair. She looks kind and helpful.
6. He's got dark hair. He doesn't look very friendly. He thinks that he is very important.

intelligent bored excited important lovely little

LOOK!
Comparatives and Superlatives
She is taller than me
He is lazier than his brother
I am more talkative than my sister
She is the tallest
He is the laziest
I am the most talkative

I think that... I believe that...

21 Ask and Answer.

1 Who is taller than the boy?
2 Who is older than the other people?
3 Who is the friendliest character?
4 Who is the most important character?

22 Think about your family. Talk to your partner.

Who is taller and older than you in your family?
Who is the friendliest?
Who is the most interesting member of your family? Why?

Mini-PROJECT
Find a painting you like and write about it.

18 Lesson 7 art (personal description and comparatives)

New language and grammar is presented through a cross-curricular topic in English. It also practises new and recycled language from previous lessons. The material may be related to science, the social sciences, maths, arts and crafts, P.E. or music. In this way, a range of topics which the pupils are learning about in other curricular subjects are revised and developed. A Mini-project encourages further exploration of the CLIL topic and production of the unit language.

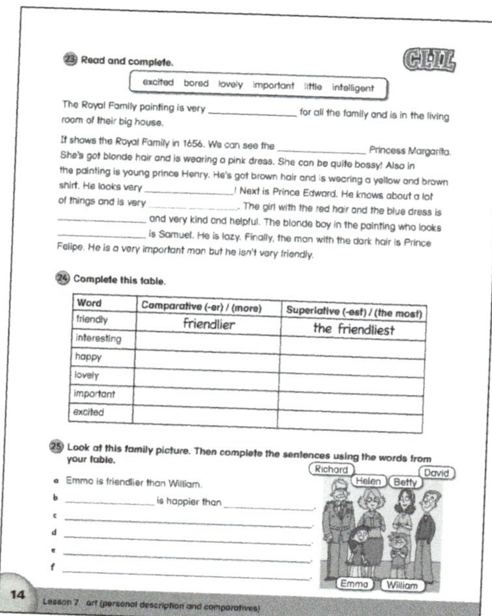
CLIL

23 Read and complete.

excited bored lovely important little intelligent

The Royal Family painting is very __________ for all the family and is in the living room of their big house.

It shows the Royal Family in 1656. We can see the __________ Princess Margarita. She's got blonde hair and is wearing a pink dress. She can be quite bossy! Also in the painting is young prince Henry. He's got brown hair and is wearing a yellow and brown shirt. He looks very __________! Next is Prince Edward. He knows about a lot of things and is very __________. The girl with the red hair and the blue dress is __________ and very kind and helpful. The blonde boy in the painting who looks __________ is Samuel. He is lazy. Finally, the man with the dark hair is Prince Felipe. He is a very important man but he isn't very friendly.

24 Complete this table.

Word	Comparative (-er) / (more)	Superlative (-est) / (the most)
friendly	friendlier	the friendliest
interesting		
happy		
lovely		
important		
excited		

25 Look at this family picture. Then complete the sentences using the words from your table.

a Emma is friendlier than William.
b __________ is happier than __________
c __________
d __________
e __________
f __________

Richard Helen Betty David Emma William

14 Lesson 7 art (personal description and comparatives)

The Activity Book offers reading and writing practice of new vocabulary and grammar.

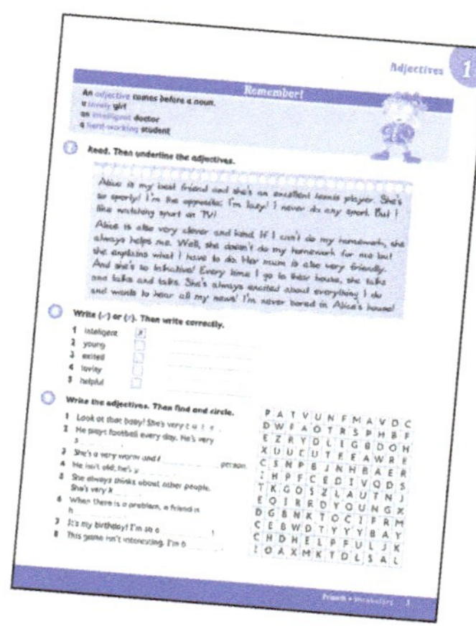

Extra reading and writing practice activities focused on the vocabulary are offered in the Reading and Writing Booklet.

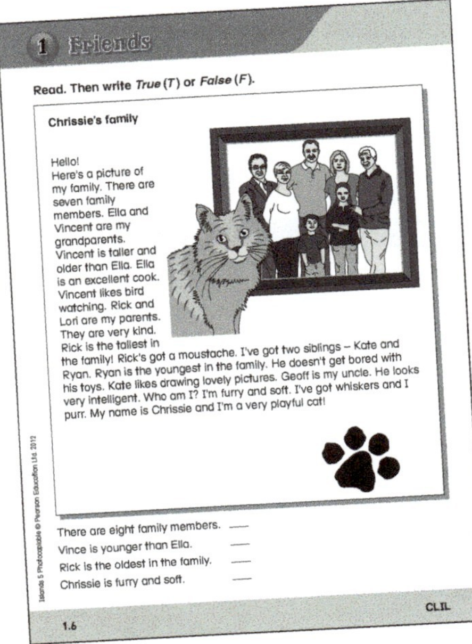
1 Friends

Read. Then write *True* (T) or *False* (F).

Chrissie's family

Hello!
Here's a picture of my family. There are seven family members. Ella and Vincent are my grandparents. Vincent is taller and older than Ella. Ella is an excellent cook. Vincent likes bird watching. Rick and Lori are my parents. They are very kind. Rick is the tallest in the family! Rick's got a moustache. I've got two siblings – Kate and Ryan. Ryan is the youngest in the family. He doesn't get bored with his toys. Kate likes drawing lovely pictures. Geoff is my uncle. He looks very intelligent. Who am I? I'm furry and soft. I've got whiskers and I purr. My name is Chrissie and I'm a very playful cat!

There are eight family members. ___
Vince is younger than Ella. ___
Rick is the oldest in the family. ___
Chrissie is furry and soft. ___

Islands 5 Photocopiable © Pearson Education Ltd. 2012

1.6 CLIL

A photocopiable is provided on the Active Teach which offers additional practice of CLIL vocabulary.

The CLIL poster presents cross-curricular vocabulary and consolidates the key vocabulary seen in the unit.

Lesson 8
Wider World (Cultural focus).

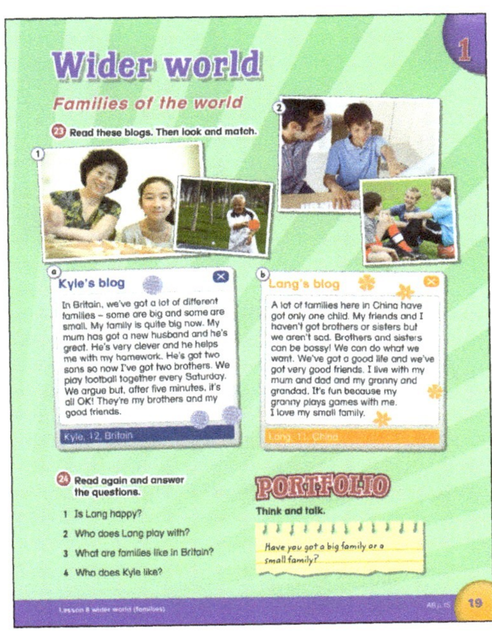

1

Wider world

Families of the world

23 Read these blogs. Then look and match.

a **Kyle's blog**

In Britain, we've got a lot of different families – some are big and some are small. My family is quite big now. My mum has got a new husband and he's great. He's very clever and he helps me with my homework. He's got two sons so now I've got two brothers. We play football together every Saturday. We argue but, after five minutes, it's all OK! They're my brothers and my good friends.

Kyle, 12, Britain

b **Lang's blog**

A lot of families here in China have got only one child. My friends and I haven't got brothers or sisters but we aren't sad. Brothers and sisters can be bossy! We can do what we want. We've got a good life and we've got very good friends. I live with my mum and dad and my granny and grandad. It's fun because my granny plays games with me. I love my small family.

Lang, 11, China

24 Read again and answer the questions.

1 Is Long happy?
2 Who does Long play with?
3 What are families like in Britain?
4 Who does Kyle like?

PORTFOLIO

Think and talk.

Have you got a big family or a small family?

Lesson 8 wider world (families) AB p.15 19

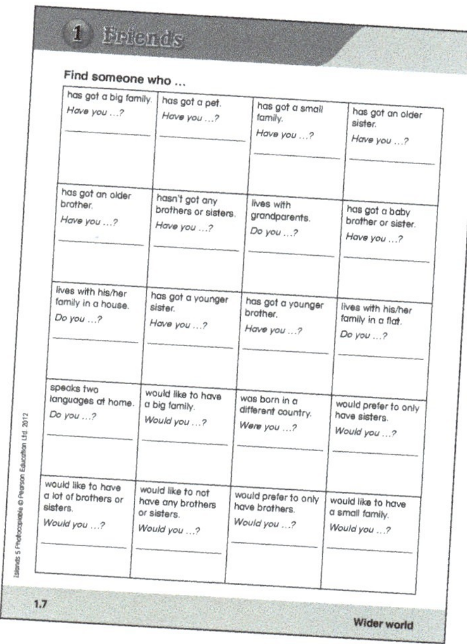

1 Friends

Find someone who ...

has got a big family. *Have you …?*	has got a pet. *Have you …?*	has got a small family. *Have you …?*	has got an older sister. *Have you …?*
has got an older brother. *Have you …?*	hasn't got any brothers or sisters. *Have you …?*	lives with grandparents. *Do you …?*	has got a baby brother or sister. *Have you …?*
lives with his/her family in a house. *Do you …?*	has got a younger sister. *Have you …?*	has got a younger brother. *Have you …?*	lives with his/her family in a flat. *Do you …?*
speaks two languages at home. *Do you …?*	would like to have a big family. *Would you …?*	was born in a different country. *Were you …?*	would prefer to only have sisters. *Would you …?*
would like to have a lot of brothers or sisters. *Would you …?*	would like to not have any brothers or sisters. *Would you …?*	would prefer to only have brothers. *Would you …?*	would like to have a small family. *Would you …?*

Islands 5 Photocopiable © Pearson Education Ltd 2012

1.7 Wider world

A photocopiable is provided on the Active Teach which offers additional practice of cultural-focus vocabulary.

Pupils read a text that explores an element of international culture linked to the unit topic, often through the eyes of a child of their own age. Vocabulary and language is recycled and there is sometimes additional new language which is taught in the context of the text. The Portfolio encourages pupils to explore the cultural topic further and apply it to themselves.

26 Read Activity 23, page 19, in the Pupil's Book again. Then complete.

WIDER WORLD 1

In Britain, some families are big [1] ________ some are small. My family is quite [2] ________ now [3] ________ my mum has got a new [4] ________. I have got two [5] ________ brothers. They are [6] ________ sons. We play football together every Saturday. We argue [7] ________, after five minutes, it's all OK! They're my brothers [8] ________ my good friends.

[9] ________ child families are very common in China. I [10] ________ and brothers or sisters [11] ________ I'm not sad. Brothers and sisters can be [12] ________! We can do what we want [13] ________ we've got very good friends. I live with my mum and dad and my granny and grandad. I can [14] ________ with my granny. I love my [15] ________ family.

27 Think and write.

BIG FAMILY		SMALL FAMILY	
advantages	disadvantages	advantages	disadvantages

28 Answer the questions.

1 How big is your family?

2 Which type of family do you prefer?
I think I like a ________ family
because ________

MINI-PROJECT
Bring photographs of your family to make a poster. Pets are welcome!

Lesson 8 wider world (families) 15

The Activity Book offers reading and writing practice of new vocabulary.

Lesson 9
Review and consolidation.

HAVE FUN!

25 Look at the characters. Then spot the differences.

a b

26 Draw. What does he/she look like? What is he/she like? Use your notebook.

helpful	talkative	kind
sporty	clever	dark hair
funny	friendly	spiky hair
bossy	hard-working	cute
shy	lazy	

He is tall and handsome. He's got short dark hair and green eyes. He's shy but helpful.

Picture dictionary AB p.104

20 Lesson 9 review and consolidation

Pupils practise the unit language through a fun language game. At the end of the lesson pupils are invited to look at the Picture dictionary in the Activity Book.

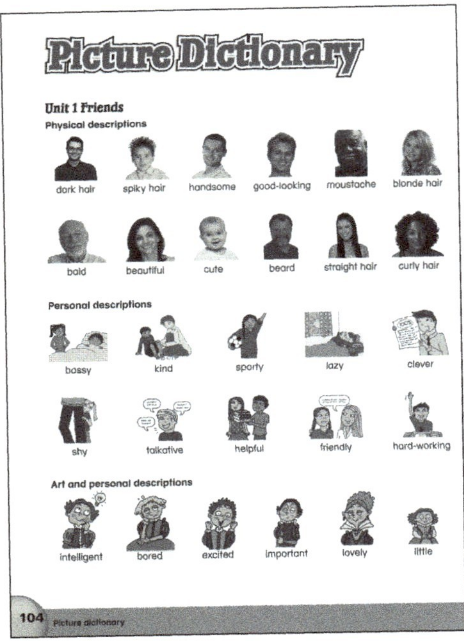

Picture Dictionary

Unit 1 Friends

Physical descriptions

dark hair, spiky hair, handsome, good-looking, moustache, blonde hair

bald, beautiful, cute, beard, straight hair, curly hair

Personal descriptions

bossy, kind, sporty, lazy, clever

shy, talkative, helpful, friendly, hard-working

Art and personal descriptions

intelligent, bored, excited, important, lovely, little

104 Picture dictionary

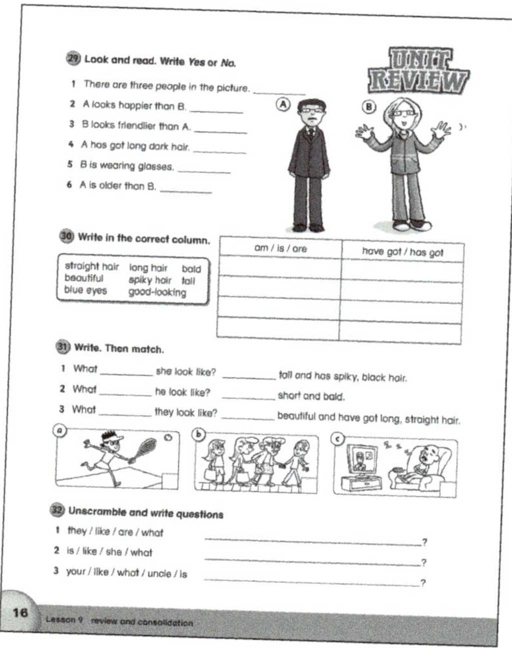

UNIT REVIEW

29 Look and read. Write *Yes* or *No*.

1 There are three people in the picture. ________
2 A looks happier than B. ________
3 B looks friendlier than A. ________
4 A has got long dark hair. ________
5 B is wearing glasses. ________
6 A is older than B. ________

A B

30 Write in the correct column.

straight hair, long hair, bald, beautiful, spiky hair, tall, blue eyes, good-looking

am / is / are	have got / has got

31 Write. Then match.

1 What ________ she look like? ________ tall and has spiky, black hair.
2 What ________ he look like? ________ short and bald.
3 What ________ they look like? ________ beautiful and have got long, straight hair.

a b c

32 Unscramble and write questions.

1 they / like / are / what ________________?
2 is / like / she / what ________________?
3 your / like / what / uncle / is ________________?

16 Lesson 9 review and consolidation

The Activity Book provides reading and writing activities to review the whole unit.

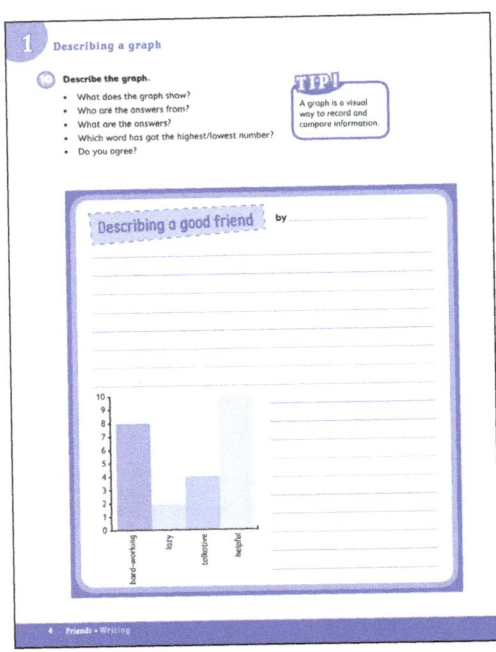

1 Describing a graph

10 Describe the graph.

- What does the graph show?
- Who are the answers from?
- What are the answers?
- Which word has got the highest/lowest number?
- Do you agree?

TIP! A graph is a visual way to record and compare information.

Describing a good friend by ________

4 Friends • Writing

Extra writing practice activities are offered in the Reading and Writing Booklet.

Lesson 10
Self assessment and evaluation.

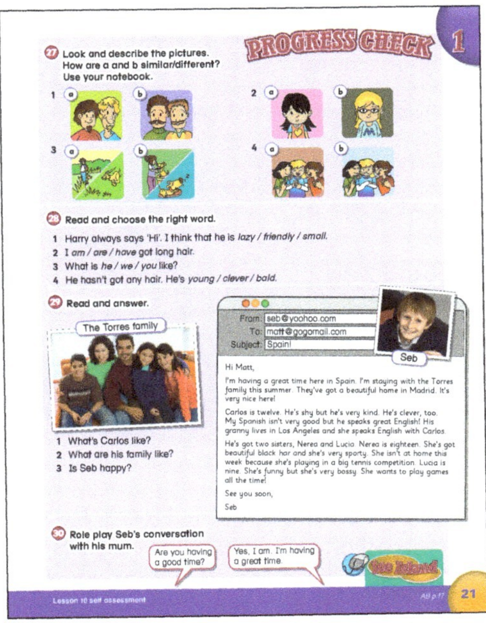

PROGRESS CHECK 1

27 Look and describe the pictures. How are a and b similar/different? Use your notebook.

28 Read and choose the right word.

1 Harry always says 'Hi'. I think that he is lazy / friendly / small.
2 I am / are / have got long hair.
3 What is he / we / you like?
4 He hasn't got any hair. He's young / clever / bald.

29 Read and answer.

The Torres family

1 What's Carlos like?
2 What are his family like?
3 Is Seb happy?

From: seb@yoohoo.com
To: matt@gogomail.com
Subject: Spain!

Seb

Hi Matt,

I'm having a great time here in Spain. I'm staying with the Torres family this summer. They've got a beautiful home in Madrid. It's very nice here!

Carlos is twelve. He's shy but he's very kind. He's clever, too. My Spanish isn't very good but he speaks great English! His granny lives in Los Angeles and she speaks English with Carlos.

He's got two sisters, Nerea and Lucia. Nerea is eighteen. She's got beautiful black hair and she's very sporty. She isn't at home this week because she's playing in a big tennis competition. Lucia is nine. She's funny but she's very bossy. She wants to play games all the time!

See you soon,

Seb

30 Role play Seb's conversation with his mum.

Are you having a good time?

Yes, I am. I'm having a great time.

Ice Island

Lesson 10 self assessment AB p 17 21

Pupils complete a Progress Check activity in the Pupil's Book. The unit ends with a link to show teachers when to take pupils to *Ice Island World.*

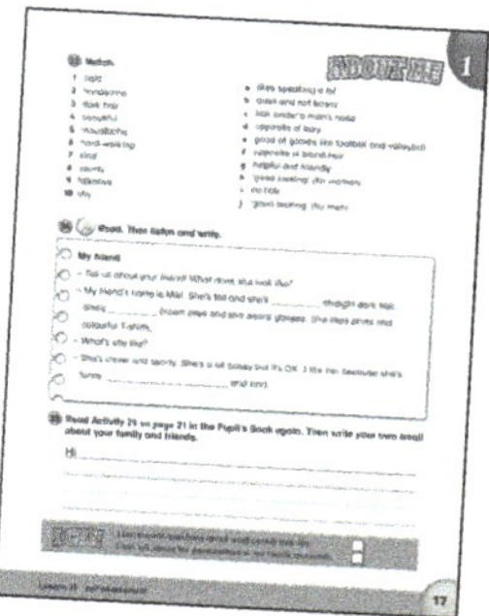

The Activity Book provides an opportunity for pupils to personalise the language of the unit with listening and writing activities and to self evaluate what they now can do in English after the unit.

In addition there is a Unit review which revises the key unit contents.

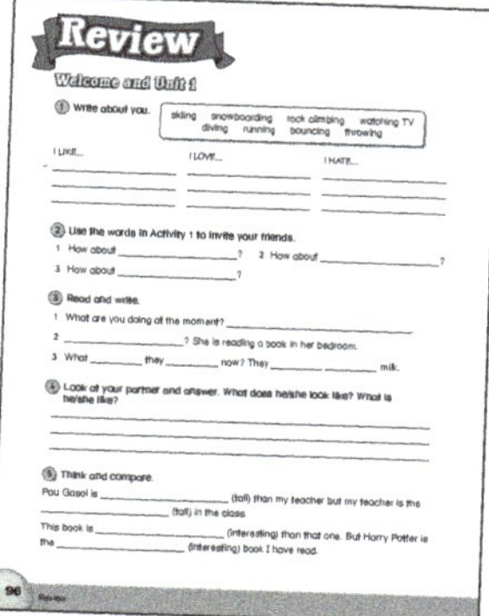

Review

Welcome and Unit 1

1 Write about you.

skiing snowboarding rock climbing watching TV diving running bouncing throwing

I LIKE... I LOVE... I HATE...

2 Use the words in Activity 1 to invite your friends.

1 How about ___? 2 How about ___?
3 How about ___?

3 Read and write.

1 What are you doing at the moment? ___
2 ___? She is reading a book in her bedroom.
3 What ___ they ___ now? They ___ milk.

4 Look at your partner and answer. What does he/she look like? What is he/she like?

5 Think and compare.

Pau Gasol is ___ (tall) than my teacher but my teacher is the ___ (tall) in the class.
This book is ___ (interesting) than that one. But Harry Potter is the ___ (interesting) book I have read.

96 Review

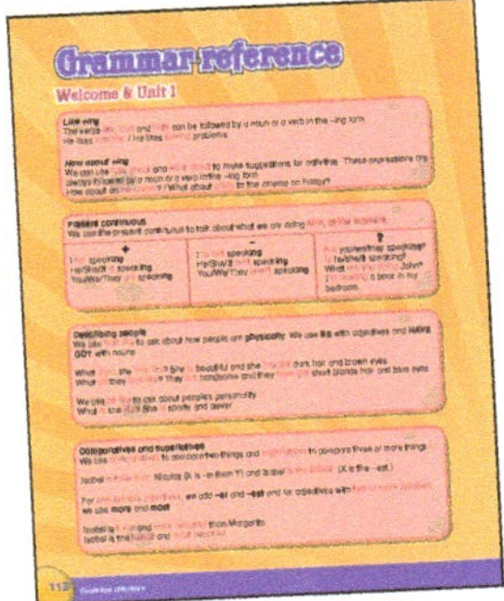

Grammar reference

Welcome & Unit 1

The key grammar points covered in the unit are provided as a clear reference for pupils in the Grammar reference section.

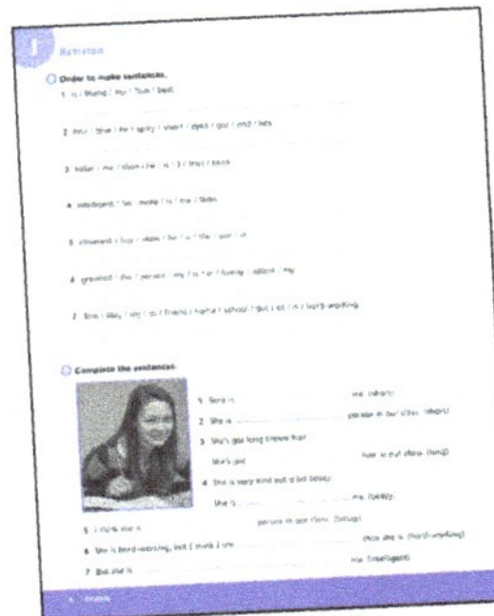

Additional grammar practice of grammar and revision is offered through the Grammar Booklet.

End-of-unit reading, writing, listening and speaking tests are provided in the Test Booklet.

How to use posters

Posters can play a key role in the English language lesson as they are such a powerful visual tool. They can be a valuable way to focus pupils' attention, allowing for pupils to consolidate and extend the language already learnt. In addition, the *Islands* posters help develop a pupil's speaking ability as they interact with visually appealing characters, authentic 'real-world' photos and captivating scenes. The interactive posters provide even greater scope as the interactive elements can be moved around and a wider variety of language can therefore be practised.

General poster activities

- Before displaying the poster for the first time, pupils can anticipate and predict who and what they will see within a topic area and then see how many items they guessed correctly once the poster is visible.
- Pupils can create their own posters, based on a similar topic.
- Using a large piece of paper placed over the top of the poster (with a 5 cm hole cut out), pupils can be asked to identify what they can see through the hole.
- Through description, pupils can identify objects that are being described orally, e.g. *It's orange. It's a food. Yum, it's tasty.*
- With a time limit, pupils can look at the posters and try to remember as much language and content as possible and then, in pairs or led by the teacher, they can try to recall the content through questions and answers, e.g. *Is there a flower? What colour is it?*
- By pointing to an object and making a statement, pupils can reply *Yes* or *No* if the information is correct or incorrect, e.g. *This is my bedroom.*
- In teams or pairs, pupils can write down as many words as possible for the items in each poster.

Poster 1 Ice Island Map

This is a visual representation of the Online Island for Level 5. It can be used to check pupils' progress through *Ice Island Online*, to check where they have located the items presented in each unit of the Pupil's Book in order to play the supplementary vocabulary game and to stimulate language production. Pupils are taken further into Ice Island as they meet new characters in new settings not represented in the stories in the Pupil's Book.

Specific poster activity

- At the beginning of each lesson, unit or term, ask pupils where they are in *Ice Island Online* asking them to point on the map. This allows instant feedback as to which pupils are engaging with the Online Island and which pupils are perhaps progressing at a different speed to others.

Poster 2 Phonics and Spelling

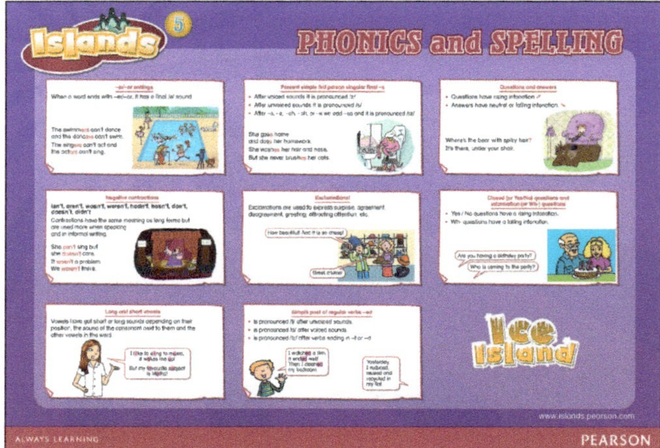

The Phonics and spelling poster shows a summary of all sounds covered for the level broken down unit by unit.

Specific poster activity

- Give pupils time to look at the Phonics and Spelling poster. Read aloud some examples from Activity 1.
- Ask pupils to repeat after you some words from Activity 1. Write these words on the board.
- Encourage pupils to find a pattern.

Poster 3 CLIL

This poster offers a summary of all the CLIL content areas offered within a level and represents key CLIL vocabulary.

Specific poster activity

- Give pupils time to look at the poster. Read aloud the vocabulary or grammar related to the CLIL lesson.
- Ask pupils to repeat after you some words or sentences. Write these words or sentences on the board.
- Encourage pupils to describe the photos presented in the lesson using the words or sentences on the board.

Poster 4 Questions and Answers

This poster offers supporting information that can be useful throughout the year and offers a comprehensive summary of all the Pupil's Book oral activities.

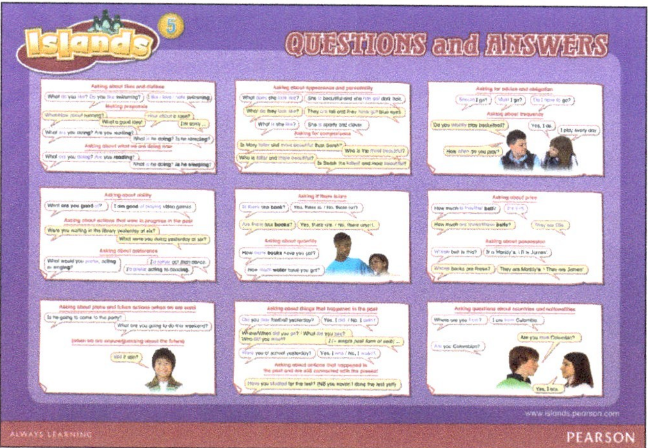

General poster activities

Draw attention to the relevant picture on the poster (depending on the content of your unit). Ask pupils to describe it. Use the poster to emphasise the key content of the lesson. After stating the goal of your lesson, read aloud the skill to be learnt. Use the examples on the poster to model that skill. (For Unit 6 you can reuse the Unit 3 content to revise knowledge of rising and falling intonation. For Unit 8 you can reuse the Unit 1 content to revise knowledge of pronouncing suffixes.)

During guided practice, allow pupils to look at the poster for reference. Use the poster to end the lesson – pupils can read the skill and self evaluate their progress. They could place sticky notes on it with examples of what they understood or additional things that they would like to know related to the lesson. Use the poster to allow pupils to show what they know, e.g. they could explain the poster to a partner or the rest of the class.

How to use the Active Teach

New technologies in the classroom

The use of new technologies can considerably improve the learning and teaching experience in the English classroom. *Islands* Active Teach is a software package for computers and interactive whiteboards. Active Teach is very easy to use, and allows the teacher to get the most out of the possibilities afforded by new technologies in the English classroom.

***Active Teach* includes:**

- Interactive versions of both the Pupil's Book and the Activity Book, which makes it possible to teach the material using an interactive whiteboard. In this way, the teacher can monitor the attention and progress of the class at all times.
- All the listening material in the course plus karaoke versions of the songs (not on the class audio CD) which can be easily accessed – either directly from the songs section, or by clicking on the pages of the interactive Pupil's Book.
- Digital versions of the flashcards and wordcards which can be used with the interactive whiteboard in a more flexible way than the physical cards; an added advantage is that the recording can be played at the same time as the cards are displayed on the interactive whiteboard.
- Animated stories to reinforce the target language.
- PDFs of all the posters for each level.
- A section of downloadable PDFs which include editable versions of all the course tests and photocopiables for the supplementary activities suggested in the teaching notes.

How to use the animated stories

Episode	Target Language
1	always, often, sometimes, never, usually; brush my teeth, eat bananas, go swimming, play football, have a shower, climb mountains, ski, snowboard, make my bed, meet my friends
2	I/We love/like (playing basketball / skateboarding / karate / dancing / cooking / singing / snowboarding). I can (throw a basketball / skateboard / jump / do karate / kick). I'm good at (kicking). Watch me dance. Can you cook? Egypt, Brazil, the USA, mountain, forest, volcano, cave
3	Where are you going? I'm going shopping. Hat, scarf, socks, coat, suit, jacket, wetsuit, shorts, sunglasses, sandals; this/that; too (big, small, long, short, loose, tight); valley
4	Whose camera is this? yours, mine, ours; toys, radio, books, mobile phone, skateboard

The animated stories give the language of *Islands* a new context. Sally, Jack and Albert provide a song and there is an animated story from Ice Island. Each episode also contains a Language Moment – a short focus on one language point.

- **Song** Pupils watch, listen and follow the actions. As they grow more confident, they can join in with the song.
- **Story** Watch the story. Ask pupils (in L1) what happened in the story. Watch again, stopping at key points, and ask them about the language, the images or the story. Ask pupils to act out the story. Assign the roles of the characters to confident speakers and let other pupils play the other parts. Encourage them to say as much of the dialogue as they can and prompt them where necessary.
- **Language moments** These reinforce a common language point with short, humorous animation.

Episode 1

Song – Do you ever?
Extra activity
Ask pupils about things they *always, usually, often, sometimes* and *never* do. Make sure they understand the differences in frequency given by these adverbs. If necessary draw a line on the board and use percentages to indicate the differences. Use the formula *Do you ever ...?* and insist that the reply must contain one of the adverbs of frequency. When you have been round the class asking questions, encourage the pupils to take turns asking each other.
Story – Meet Finn and Jenny.
Language moment – Curly red hair.

Episode 2

Song – I love playing basketball
Extra activity
Put the pupils into pairs and ask them to decide on one thing that they both like doing and one thing that they like doing but their partner doesn't. Then get them to tell the class, using the structures: *I like ... He/She doesn't like ... We like ...* .
Story – He wants to freeze the world!
Language moment – Spelling with –ing.

Episode 3

Song – Do you like this hat?
Extra activity
In pairs, pupils take turns miming the scene at the market where Jack asks Sally if she likes various items of clothing. They can choose any clothes. The pupil playing Jack should say *Do you like this sweater/coat/ T-shirt, etc?* or *Do you like these socks/shoes/trousers/ shorts/sunglasses, etc?* and the pupil playing Sally should say *No, I don't* and give a reason: *It's/They're too big, too small, too long, too short, etc.* Demonstrate first in front of the class with a confident pupil.
Story – Get the machine!
Language moment – Find the word.

Episode 4

Song – Whose camera is this?
Extra activity
Collect some items from the class and then return them by asking *Whose book/pen/bag, etc. is this? Is it yours?* The pupils should answer either *No, it's not mine* or *Yes, that's my book/pen/bag, etc. Thank you.* Do this with singular items first and then move on to plurals.
Story – He's escaping!
Language moment – Word order.

How to use the Digital Activity Book

New technologies at home

The *Digital Activity Book* is a version of the Activity Book that contains all the activities from the printed book with some additional interactive exercises and games. It has been designed to be used by pupils at home, so that parents can take part in their learning experience.

An access code for this is supplied in the Activity Book.

The *Digital Activity Book* allows pupils to:

- work interactively with their *Activity Book*.
- play at recognising words with the flashcards and wordcards.
- practise songs.
- revise language with the *Picture dictionary* for each unit.

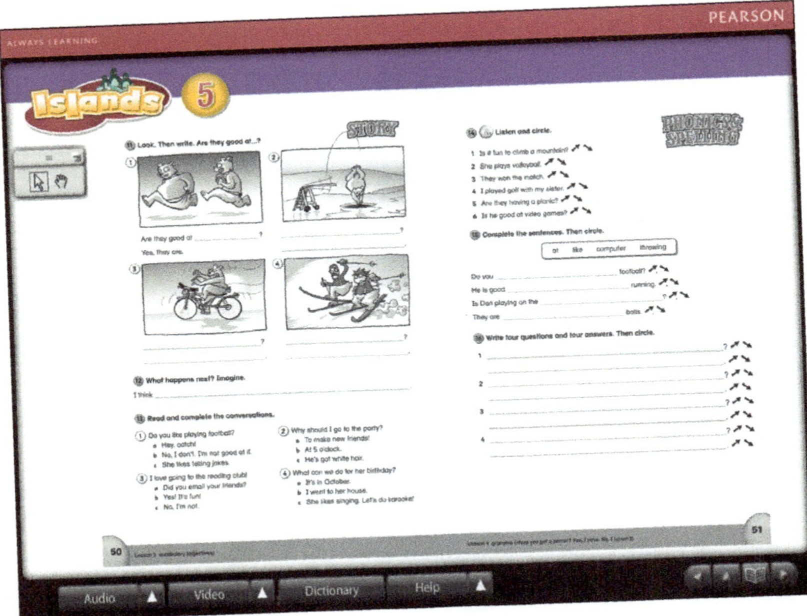

Young learners and technology

Research shows that appropriate use of computer technology in education is beneficial for pupils (Clements and Sarama, 2003; Waxman, Connell, and Gray, 2002; Byrom and Bingham, 2001). Broadly speaking, pupils can learn *from* computers and *with* computers. Pupils learn *from* computers when the computer assumes the role of a tutor, with the goal of imparting and increasing basic knowledge and skills. Pupils learn *with* computers when the computer serves in the role of a facilitating tool, with the goal of developing critical thinking skills, research skills and the creative imagination (Ringstaff and Kelley, 2002).

Computer activities should be age-appropriate and foster instruction in ways that increase learning, motivation, personal productivity and creativity. For example, Perry (2009) noted that "Children three to five years old are natural 'manipulators' of the world – they learn through controlling the movement and interactions between objects in their world – dolls, blocks, toy cars and their own bodies." Children are naturally curious and willing to interact with computers and they enjoy their ability to control the type, pace and repetition of an activity. In some cases, children have even managed to learn how to use a computer with no instruction at all, through their own curiosity, fearlessness and persistence (Mitra, 1999).

Computers in the English language classroom

The decision to use computers in the language classroom, including the English language classroom, requires the establishment of both technological goals and language-learning goals. For young children, goals such as the following facilitate a path to focused learning.

Technology objectives	Language objectives
To become familiar with the parts of a computer (screen, keyboard, mouse, cursor, printer and so on).	To use English to interact in the classroom and to communicate in social situations.
To become familiar with approved software programs for the classroom.	To use English to describe self, family, community and country.
To become familiar with operations (select, drag, save, delete and so on).	To use learning strategies to increase communicative competence.
To become familiar with finding, filing, tracking and organising information.	To develop the four skills: listening, speaking, reading and writing.
To share information and collaborate with others.	To pronounce English words, phrases and sentences intelligibly.
To develop learner autonomy.	To use appropriate register.

International Society for Technology in Education (2000). *National Educational Technology Standards for Students: Connecting Curriculum and Technology.*

Teachers of English to Speakers of Other Languages, Inc. (1997). *ESL Standards for Pre-K–12 Students.*

References

Byrom, E., and Bingham, M. (2001). "Factors Influencing the Effective Use of Technology for Teaching and Learning: Lessons Learned from SEIR-TEC Intensive Site Schools, 2nd Edition." Greensboro, NC: SERVE.

Clements, D. H., and Sarama, J. (2003). "Strip Mining for Gold: Research and Policy in Educational Technology – A Response to 'Fool's Gold.'" *Educational Technology Review,* 11(1), 7–69.

Kneas, K. M., and Perry, B. D. (2009). "Using Technology in the Early Childhood Classroom." *Early Childhood Today.* (Retrieved 5 November 2009 from the World Wide Web.) Scholastic.

Mitra, S. (1999). "Hole in the wall – can kids learn computer literacy by themselves?" Generation YES Blog. (Retrieved 5 November 2009 from the World Wide Web.)

Ringstaff, C., and Kelley, L. (2002). "The Learning Return on Our Educational Technology Investment." San Francisco, CA: WestEd.

Waxman, H. C., Connell, M. L., and Gray, J. (2002). "A Quantitative Synthesis of Recent Research on the Effects of Teaching and Learning with Technology on Student Outcomes." Naperville, IL: North Central Regional Educational Laboratory.

Islands Online World is an immersive world which accompanies the *Islands* series. It is a ground-breaking digital product, combining the methodologies of classroom-based ELT and games-based learning and is a safe learning environment, suitable for young learners, which can be:

- used on individual computers at school or at home
- used in groups at school
- used through the Active Teach IWB software.

It provides immediate feedback on performance and contains features that appeal to young learners, such as colourful attractive visuals, clear audio providing excellent pronunciation models, animation and game-like activities, all of which play a part in pupil motivation. It is carefully calibrated to appeal to children between the ages of 4 and 11. The target vocabulary and grammar directly reinforce the syllabus of the course. Because tasks are intuitive and clear, and because students receive immediate audio and visual feedback on their progress, the programme builds learner confidence and independence.

Islands Online World was authored by a team of ELT specialists and multimedia games developers and offers rich and engaging digital worlds which build on the language and aims contained within the books. The main emphasis is on expanding vocabulary while the pupils learn through playing language games and achieving tasks. New language is introduced gradually and contextualised so that pupils feel confident and motivated to complete each level. The key concepts which have guided the design are:

- **Immersion**. The Online World takes pupils out of their classroom or home environment and immerses them in a coherent and believable context. Engaging content and beautiful design hold the pupils' interest and motivate them to continue with the game. Research conducted with the Online World indicates that even very young children are able to maintain concentration and enthusiasm for long periods of time.
- **Stealth learning**. The Online World is enjoyable and learning takes place almost without the pupils being aware of it. Rather than mirroring the type of tasks in the Pupil's Book, pupils learn via interactions with characters in the adventure. They are presented with real-world-like tasks, giving them a sense of responsibility and active involvement which is extremely motivating. Learning takes place through listening and reading comprehension of speech bubbles, and through exposure to the target lexical sets via speech bubbles, dialogues, the picture dictionary and supplementary language games.
- **Mastery.** Striking the right balance of challenge and achievability is a key component in any game. The online world has been carefully designed to introduce the key skills needed to complete the task at the start of each level, and then continue by slowly building the complexity of the language pupils encounter. It is important that pupils find the tasks within the game sufficiently challenging. Pupils with prior exposure to digital games expect to fail at complex tasks several times before achieving them. This makes the tasks more, not less, satisfying, once achieved. The model of 'try, fail, repeat, succeed' is also important because it gives repeated exposure to the target language, ensuring that pupils comprehend the language before they move on.
- **Control.** Pupils love immersive worlds because they feel free within them. They can move their avatar around at their own speed and in their own chosen direction. They are also free to experiment and to fail without censure or observation. This gives them confidence and motivation. *Islands Online World* has been designed to allow children sufficient freedom to enjoy the game but at the same time to carefully channel them towards the learning outcomes and to expose them gradually to the target language. A carefully controlled gating system means they must achieve certain tasks before progressing into new parts of the game. A starred report card system motivates them to complete all the tasks within a scene but gives them some freedom to determine when and how they do this.
- **Reward.** The Online World includes many of the most popular features of existing games, such as collectible items, costumisation, avatar design and 'hidden' rewards such as new characters who appear once certain tasks are complete as well as audio and visual feedback to a task.

Skills

The Online World is designed first and foremost to be a vocabulary booster. Although it could be completed in isolation, it is designed to complement and extend the language presented in the Pupil's Book. Extra vocabulary pertinent to the context of each level is presented and such items are included in the Picture dictionary to give extra support.

Pupils interact with characters in the game by reading speech bubble text and hearing a corresponding audio file. Listening and reading comprehension are key skills required in order to progress through the game. Children do not type or write anything, but for some tasks they use the mouse to manipulate text or tick boxes to create simple documents such as emails.

Children do not need to speak in order to complete any tasks within the game, but in some tests we have observed children speaking spontaneously to the characters on screen, either repeating what they said or attempting to anticipate what they will say next. This type of outcome demonstrates the motivational and confidence-building aspects of immersive online environments.

Task types

There is a large variety of different task types within the Online World. These can be broken down into the following types:

- **Following instructions.** A character within the World may tell the player to perform a task, such as finding people with certain skills or items. In order to complete such a task, the player will need to comprehend the target language in each instruction, which may be a gerund *(Find someone who likes skateboarding.)* or a noun *(Please get me an apple.).*
- **Choosing the correct response.** A character within the World may ask the pupil a question. They will then be presented with a variety of answers to choose from. In order to complete the task, they need to understand the target language in both the question and answer, and they most often have to explore the scene in order to find the answer. For example, a character might ask the player what another character is doing. The pupil must then look through some binoculars to find out what activity the character in question is performing. To discourage pupils from clicking random answers, answer selections can be randomised, or the pupil may be forced to restart the whole task if they get three answers in a row wrong.
- **Manipulating items within the game.** These tasks add a physical aspect to the game. For example, the pupil may have to collect certain items to fix a broken machine. Once they have done this, a character may direct them on how to use the machine. They must comprehend the language and then manipulate their avatar in the right way (for example, by jumping on a red lever instead of a blue lever).
- **Traditional games.** These can be accessed as multi-player games in the chatroom, or at various points in each scene as 'hidden' games which the child can find by looking at a picture clue in their Pupil's Book. These include spelling games such as Hungry Shark (a version of Hangman) and Spelldrop (a version of Tetris). There are a number of picture matching games such as Photoshoot and Matchcard. There is also a Quiz game with a multiple-choice or True/False version. These language games sometimes form a major task within a scene, but more often they are supplementary or reward activities which are designed to be completed after the main tasks.

Progression through the game

The game is designed to encourage pupils to work through each scene in a linear fashion, building their vocabulary and language comprehension as they do so. Support includes visual, as well as verbal, clues, and the Picture dictionary, which is available at all times in the top right corner of the screen, and allows pupils to check the meaning of any unfamiliar vocabulary. Once they have completed all of the tasks in a scene, they are given a silver star in their progress chart. Upon completion of all of the supplementary activities and the tasks in a scene, they are given a gold star.

Teacher support

We recognise that many teachers are likely to be unfamiliar with this type of component and have developed a series of help guides both online and as a download to be printed to help teachers gain confidence in using *Islands Online World* in the classroom, assisting pupils with queries about the tasks, or setting parts of the game for home study.

In conjunction with this there are video walkthroughs of each level to answer queries about specific sections of the adventure. These videos can also act as an introduction or provide quick support for teachers who can't spare the time to work through the Online World themselves.

All teachers will receive an individual PIN code to *Islands Online* and, unlike the pupil version it will contain a map, allowing them to skip back and forward between scenes.

For ease of classroom management we have included a Progress Review System (PRS) where teachers can register their classes and monitor their progress. Parents can also view pupils' progress via the Report Card online.

ICE ISLAND WORLD

Ice Island Online is set on a cold, snowy island, where pupils visit a training camp to learn wilderness survival skills, visit Dr Al's observatory, Professor Ice's secret lair and rescue Jenny who is trapped on the edge of an ice cliff among other adventures. Pupils will recognise Dr Al and Jenny as well as Dylan and Finn from their Pupil's Book. Pupils must help find the villain, Professor Ice, who has stolen an Ice Laser and some yetis from a Science Laboratory. They need to discover Professor Ice's plans and acquire the skills they need to trek across the icy wilderness and stop him before it is too late!

The adventure begins with an introductory tutorial Scene Zero with a simple activity. The aim is to familiarise the pupil with the layout and computer controls, and to provide some context for the following scenes. This also contains the chatroom, where the pupil can interact and play games with other pupils such as Spell Drop, etc. The chatroom contains sample dialogue matching the language aims of each unit at this level. The pupils can return to the chatroom at any stage during the adventure to test their mastery of the language.

The pupil then progresses to the first scene. Each scene contains one, two or three tasks (such as moving an object out of the way or finding the parts of a broken machine). Within each scene there are some supplementary activities such as Match Card or Hungry Shark to further test vocabulary. One of the supplementary activities in each scene is flagged by an image in the Pupil's Book, held by Penn and Gwyn, the penguins. This is not linked in with the task and pupils can complete this at any time. Players can move freely through Scenes 1–3, but they cannot progress to Scenes 4–6 until they have completed all the tasks from Scenes 1–3. Progression to Scenes 7–8 is similarly dependent on the pupil having completed all the tasks in Scenes 4–6. The Level ends with an *Exit Scene*, which occurs automatically and doesn't require interaction from the pupil. The purpose of this scene is to 'round off' the Level and to reward the pupil for completing all the tasks.

Ice Island Unit 3 Lesson Plan

If you wish to incorporate Ice Island Online into your lessons, below is an easy-to-follow lesson plan which shows how simple it is to manage it in class.

Learning aim

- To distinguish between different activities: *(ice-skating, trampolining, playing chess, drawing, hitting, kicking)* and to understand statements about likes and dislikes *(I like playing the drums.)*
- Receptive language: *Professor Ice has sent a lot of yetis. They're coming towards my observatory! I'm scared! Look through my binoculars. Tell me what the yetis are doing. How can we stop the yetis? Maybe we should try talking to them.*
  Can yetis speak English? There's only one way to find out.

- Carry this out as part of Lesson 10, after the pupils have completed the Pupil's Book activities. Pupils may have already found the book/online link item that Penn and Gwyn are holding up on the Pupil's Book page at the end of Lesson 1 (ski poles) and may have therefore completed the supplementary language activity based on the vocabulary in this unit. If not, the teacher can 'walk' the pupils through this now. The ski poles are in the snow to the right-hand side of the door to Dr Al's observatory .
- Online: Using the IWB or a computer screen visible to the class, go to *Ice Island Online* and access Scene 3, Dr Al's observatory.

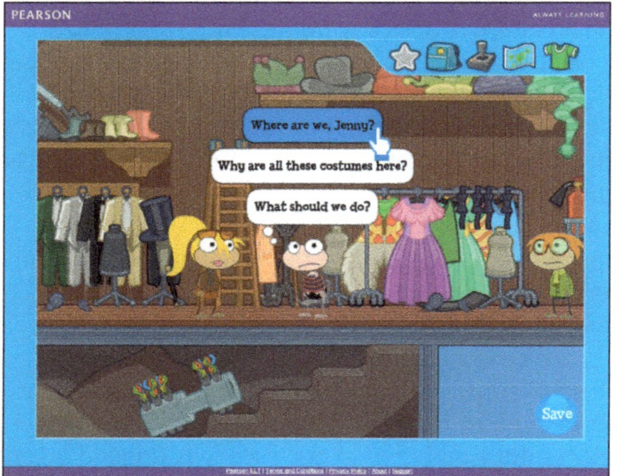

- Walk pupils through the first part of the task. Enter Dr Al's observatory through the door and find and talk to Dr Al (he's on the top floor near the telescope). Look through Dr Al's binoculars and tell him what the escaped yetis are doing. Complete the first one. (Pink yeti is throwing some rocks.)
- Divide the class into four groups. Choose a pupil from each group to take over with the mouse, looking through the binoculars and answering one of Dr Al's questions. (Red yeti is catching a ball. Green yeti is kicking some rocks. Blue yeti is hitting the ground with a stick. Brown yeti is hitting some rocks with a stick.)
- Exit the observatory and talk to Dylan, (pupils will recognise him from their Pupil's Books) who will tell you to talk to the yetis. Choose five pupils in turn to come to the computer and take over the mouse. They must each click on one of the yetis and find out what they like doing (e.g the green yeti likes trampolining). They must then search around the scene (inside and outside the observatory) to find the item that the yeti needs to do its favourite activity (e.g. trampoline is on ground floor of the observatory on the extreme lefthand side near some boxes). Click on the trampoline and a trampoline card is delivered into your inventory backpack. Go outside and find the green yeti, open your inventory backpack and click on the trampoline card and click USE. The card will be delivered to the green yeti and he will be happy. Allow the class to shout out suggestions as to where each pupil should go to look for the items. (Blue yeti likes drawing pictures – collect pencils and paper from top floor of observatory near the telescope. Brown yeti likes playing the drums – collect drum from top floor on top of machine extreme righthand side. Pink yeti likes ice-skating – collect ice skates hanging up inside observatory on the ground floor righthand side of the door. Red yeti likes playing chess – collect chess board from top floor lefthand side near the telescope)
- When they have found each item, they must return to the yeti and give it to them. If it is the wrong thing, the yeti will be angry and they must try again.
- When the second quest is complete, Dr Al will appear to congratulate them on talking to animals and give them a stamp on their training card.
- Choose pupils to complete the supplementary tasks: talk to Jacob (outside the observatory on the lefthand side) and read aloud the joke card he delivers, find a page from Amelia Explorealot's diary (top floor of observatory righthand side above the machine) and read it aloud to the class.
- Alternatively, once you have completed an example online with the whole class, direct pupils to individual or shared computers, or have them access the task at home for homework.
- End the lesson as detailed in the main lesson notes.

Online Island access code record

Class: ______________________________

Pupil's name	Access code

Welcome

Island presentation

Lesson aims
To revise vocabulary and the present continuous

Receptive language
star, planet, penguin, submarine

Materials
Audio CD; Ice Island poster

Optional activity materials
Active Teach; Digital Activity Book

Starting the lesson

- Pre-teach the word *penguin* and find out what pupils know about penguins. Ask, e.g. *Can penguins swim? (Yes, they can.) Can they walk? (Yes, they can.) Can they fly? (No, they can't.) Do they live in hot places or in cold places? (Cold places.)*
- Elicit anything else pupils know about penguins. Then ask them to open their books and find two penguins in the story. Tell pupils that one of them is called Penn and ask them to guess what the other one is called (Gwyn).
- Use the Ice Island Poster. Explain to the children that this is where the Island mystery story takes place.

Presentation

Pupil's Book pages 6–7

- Ask the class questions about each picture in turn. Pupils answer or guess, e.g.
(Picture 1) *Who is the man? Who are the children?* Point to the clock. Ask *What time is it? (It's four o'clock.)*
(Picture 2) Ask *Where are they? What's the man doing?*
(Pictures 3, 4, 5 and 6) *What can you see?*
(Pupils say what they can see in the moon.)
(Picture 7) Ask *What/who can you see on the submarine?*
(Pictures 9 and 10) *Where are they?* Point to Captain Formosa. Ask *What's he doing? (He's sleeping.)* Point to Rufus and Ivan. Ask *What are they doing?*
(Pictures 11, 12 and 13) Pointing to Rufus and Ivan, ask *Do they like the penguins? (No, they don't!)*

Practice

  **Listen and read.**

- Play the recording. Pupils listen and read the story.
- Ask the class questions about the story.
(Picture 1) *What's the man's name? (Dr Al.) Do the children like mornings? (No, they don't!)*
(Picture 2) *What's Dr Al doing? (He's studying the moon.)*
(Pictures 1 and 2) Point to Jenny and Finn. Ask *What's her/his name?*
(Pictures 3 to 6) *What can they see in the moon? (The man in the moon, a rabbit, a snail and cheese.)*
(Picture 9) *Who's sleeping? (Captain Formosa.)*
(Pictures 9 to 13) *What are the bad men's names? (Rufus and Ivan.)*
(Picture 13) *Can the penguins see Rufus and Ivan? (Yes, they can.) Can Captain Formosa? (No, he can't.)*

- Play the recording again. Pause for the class to repeat each line in chorus.
- Divide the class into nine, e.g. by rows/tables, and allocate these parts: Dr Al, Jenny, Finn, Dylan, Rufus, Ivan, Captain Formosa, two penguins.
- Play the recording again. Pause for pupils to repeat their character's lines. Encourage the penguins to snore!
- Ask nine volunteers to act out the story.
- Take a class vote for the best actors/actresses!
- Pairs predict what happens next.
- Volunteers tell the class their ideas.
- Take a vote to find the most popular idea.

Ending the lesson

- Ask if pupils would like to live on a submarine. *Why (not)?*
- In turns one pupil mimes one action and asks the class *What am I doing?* The one who guesses the answer takes the turn, e.g. *Are you reading? (Yes, I am. / No, I'm not.)*
- Play a memory game. One pupil says, *I'm speaking English*, the next says, *You're speaking English and I'm reading a book* and so on.
- Ask the class what they found easy and more difficult, and what they liked the most, to help you get to know pupils.
- For Audioscript see p. 47.

OPTIONAL ACTIVITIES

True or false?
Pupils say true or false sentences about the story and ask a friend, e.g. *Dr Al is studying the moon in picture 2.* (True.)

Tell the story!
Pupils mix the story cards and put them in a different order. Then they tell a new story.

Pair work
Pupils draw the moon and objects 'hidden' on it following the instructions of their classmates. Provide them with examples in the imperative, e.g. *Draw a penguin .../Put 5 stars .../Include a small submarine ... .* Then they compare their drawings, e.g. *In my picture there is a ... /I can see ... and in your picture ... .*

Writing a story
Ask pupils to write a piece of a story using one of the story cards. Then put them together and read the story. Divide the class according to the number of cards.

Guessing game
Say what a pupil is wearing and doing but don't say their name, e.g. *He's wearing black jeans and a yellow T-shirt. He's writing the date.* Ask *Who is it?* The first pupil to guess correctly describes another pupil for the class to guess.

Lesson 1

Lesson aims
To revise vocabulary and use the *+ing* form with *like*

Target language
skiing, snowboarding, rock climbing, watching, diving, running
He likes *+ing*

Materials
Audio CD

Optional activity materials
Active Teach; Digital Activity Book

Starting the lesson

- Tell pupils things you like doing. Then ask them whether they like doing those things.

Presentation

- Present the vocabulary miming each action. Say the word for the children to repeat. Mime the actions in a different order for pupils to repeat again.

Pupil's Book page 8

Skills

2  Listen and point.

- Give the class time to look at the pictures.
- Play the recording. Pause after each description to let pupils say the correct name.
- Play the recording again, pausing for pupils to repeat the sentences.
- Ask the class to silently read the Look! box.
- Read the Look! box. Pause for pupils to repeat.
- Remind pupils we use the verbs in the *+ing* form after *like, love* and *hate*.

3 Read and say.

- Ask pupils to read the sentences aloud.
- Allow pupils time to identify the character for each sentence.
- Pairs talk about themselves, e.g. *I am* ..., *I like* or *I love* ..., *I hate* ... and *I* ... .

Practice

Activity Book pages 2–3

1 Read the story again. Write the names of the characters.

- Give pupils time to do the activity.
- Check answers.

2 Look at Activity 1. Then read and number the sentences.

- Remind pupils of the structure *like* + verb *+ing*.
- Give pupils time to do the activity.
- Check answers.

3 Look and tick (✓) the correct picture.

- Allow pupils time to look at the pictures.
- Check answers.

4 Read and circle *T* (true) or *F* (false).

- Give pupils time to do the activity.
- Check the answers.

5 Match and answer the questions.

- Remind pupils of the structure of the present continuous *subject* + *be* + *verb +ing*.
- Give pupils time to do the activity.
- Check the answers.

Ending the lesson

- Draw three faces on the board, one smiling, one neutral and one grumpy. Then ask the pupils to say *I like* ..., *I love* ... and *I hate* ... *+ing*.
- Mime an activity, e.g. running and ask pupils *Do you like running? Yes, I do. / No, I don't.* If the answer is *yes*, then ask *How about running in the playground after school?*
- Ask pupils to continue the activity in pairs.
- For Answer Key see p. 46. For Audioscript see p. 47.

SKILLS

2 1:03 **Listen and point.**

3 **Read and say.**

He likes thinking and solving problems.

Dylan

1 She likes adventure and has got a backpack full of useful things.

2 He likes skiing, snowboarding and rock climbing.

3 He likes watching the stars and planets.

4 He likes penguins and he lives in an old submarine.

5 He likes diving and he is strong.

6 He likes running and wants to find the treasure.

OPTIONAL ACTIVITIES

Guessing game

Pupils work in groups of four or five. They choose one of them to be described, e.g. *He likes running and speaking English but he hates doing homework.* They write a description of him/her and read it to the other groups, who guess. (*Is It ...?*) Then they take the turn.

Lesson 2

Lesson aims
To revise vocabulary and the use of the *+ing* form

Target language
skiing, snowboarding, rock climbing, watching, diving, running, bouncing, throwing
Present continuous
He likes *+ing*
How about *+ing?*

Materials
Audio CD

Optional activity materials
Active Teach; Digital Activity Book

Starting the lesson

- Assign actions to some pupils. Then write on the board: *What are you doing?* Pupils with no assigned actions ask pupils with actions, e.g. *What are you doing? I'm skiing.*

Presentation

- Remind pupils we use the verbs in the *+ing* form after *like, love* and *hate*, in the present continuous and after propositions.
- Write on the board:
  I am **reading** a book now/at the moment.
  I like/love/hate **reading** books.
  How about **reading** a book?

Pupil's Book page 9

4  Listen and point. Then answer the questions.

- Give the class time to look at the pictures.
- Play the recording. Pause after each description to let pupils say the correct name.
- Play the recording again, pausing for pupils to repeat the sentences. Check the answers.

KEY 1 swimming **2** studying **3** snowboarding

5 Look and say.

- Give pupils time to look at the picture and read the words.
- Read the example aloud, preceded by the question: *What is he doing now? e) He is playing the violin.*
- Pupils ask and answer, e.g. *What is he/she/are they/ doing now? He/She is …* or *They are …* .
- Ask the class to silently read the Tip! box.
- Remind pupils we use the verbs in the *+ing* form after *How about +ing?* to invite someone to do something.

Practice

6 Ask and answer.

- Give pupils time to read the questions.
- Draw a happy face on the board and write next to it: *Yes, that's a good idea!* Then draw a sad face and write next to it: *I'm sorry, I can't.*
- In pairs, pupils ask and answer, e.g. *How about playing in the park after school? Yes, that's a good idea!*

Activity Book pages 4–5

6 Read and write the missing words to complete the sentences.

- Give pupils time to read the words.
- Check the answers.

7 Read and match.

- Give pupils time to look at the two columns.
- Ask five pupils to say sentences 1–5 and five pupils to ask questions A–E accordingly.
- Give pupils time to match.
- Check the answers.

8 Look and write to complete the questions.

- Give pupils time to look at the pictures and write the questions. Check the answers.

9 Look and write sentences.

- Give pupils time to look at the picture and write sentences. Check the answers.

10 Ask a classmate and tick (✓) *yes* or *no*.

- Give pairs time to ask questions and tick answer.
- Ask volunteers to talk about their friend.

11 Look at Activity 10. Write questions if the answer is *yes*.

- Give pupils time to write questions.
- Check the answers.

Ending the lesson

- Ask one pupil *What are you doing? Do you like studying English? How about reading the story of the unit?*
- Volunteers can ask and answer looking at the three structures you wrote on the board at the beginning of the lesson.
- For Answer Key see p. 46. For Audioscript see p. 47.

4 Listen and point. Then answer the questions.

a 

b 

c 

1 What is Finn doing?

2 What is Dylan doing?

3 What is Jenny doing?

5 Look and say.

reading kicking running ~~playing~~
drinking swimming sleeping

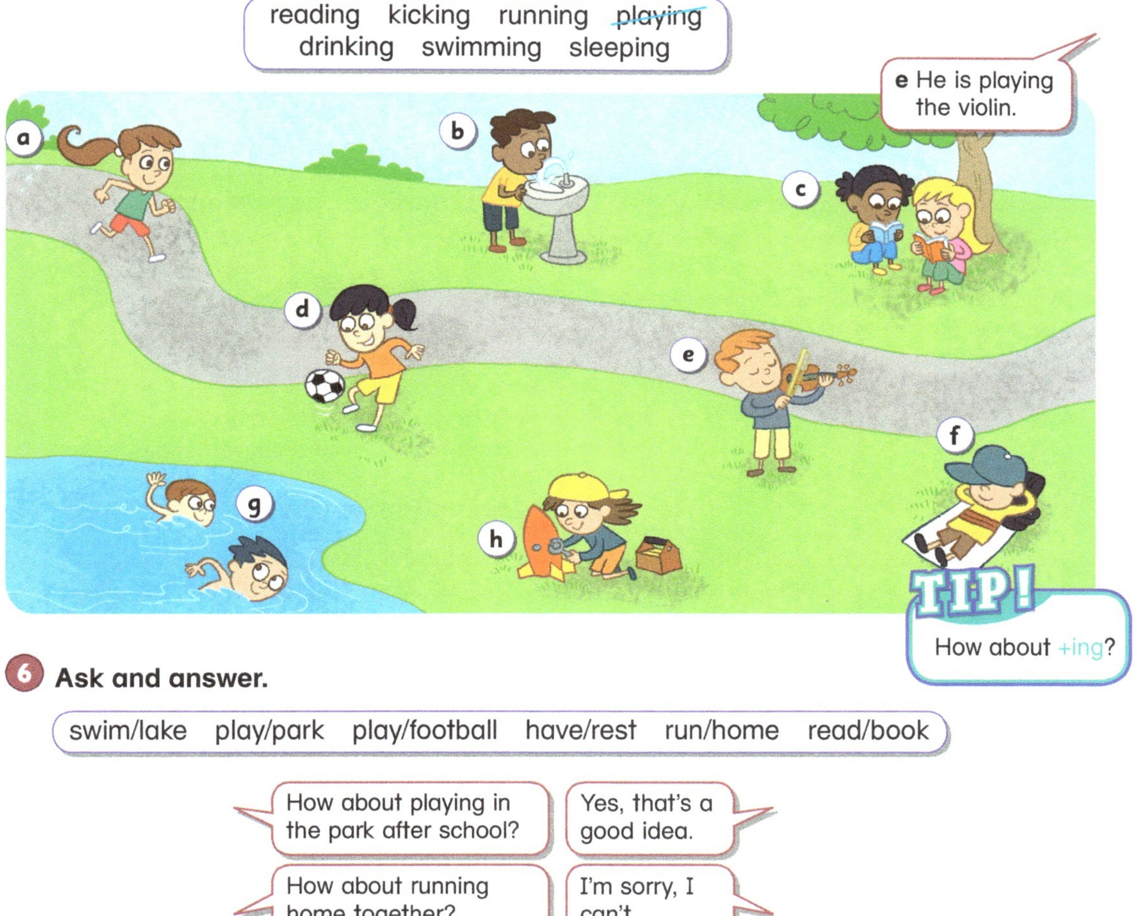

TIP!

How about +ing?

6 Ask and answer.

swim/lake play/park play/football have/rest run/home read/book

How about playing in the park after school?

Yes, that's a good idea.

How about running home together?

I'm sorry, I can't.

OPTIONAL ACTIVITIES

Guessing game

Pupils draw themselves doing one of the actions on the vocabulary flashcards and write one sentence like this: *I am rock climbing because I like going to the mountains!* Or *I am playing football because I love doing sports!* Or *I am skiing because I like doing snow sports!* Collect all the cards and put them in a bag. Take one and show and read it to the class. The one who guesses first takes another card.

Lesson 3

Lesson aims
To practise past simple tense forms

Target language
listened, played, practised, studied, watched, went, fell, took

Materials
Audio CD

Optional activity materials
Active Teach; Digital Activity Book

Starting the lesson

- Ask volunteers to tell you what they did yesterday morning, afternoon and evening.

Presentation

- Introduce the new words using mime and then by using each word in a sentence, e.g. I played football. Ask pupils to repeat each new word.
- Write the words on the board. Point to the different words and ask the class to say the words.

Pupil's Book page 10

Skills

- Ask the class to silently read the Look! box.
- Then pupils read the sentences after you in chorus. As you say each sentence, mime the action and use gesture to indicate the past, e.g. point back over your shoulder.

7 Look at Jenny's diary and say. What did she do last week?

- Give pupils time to read the diary.
- Ask *What did Jenny do on Monday morning? What did she do on Tuesday afternoon? And what did she do on Wednesday evening?*
- Pupils work in pairs: one asks, the other answers and vice versa.

KEY
Monday: studied and practised the piano
Tuesday: studied, played computer games and watched TV
Wednesday: studied, played tennis and listened to music
Thursday: studied, practised the piano and went to the cinema
Friday: studied and watched TV

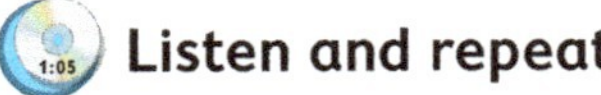

8 Listen and repeat.

- Read the verbs in the Tip! box. Check understanding by saying *Yesterday I ...* and miming a verb: pupils say the verb.
- Give pupils time to look at the pictures.
- Play the recording.
- Read the sentences and the class repeats them after you.

Practice

Activity Book page 6

12 Listen and match.

- Give pupils time to look at the pictures.
- Play the recording. Pupils do the activity.
- Check the answers.

13 Look at Activity 12. Then write to complete the sentences.

- Give pupils time to read the sentences and write.
- Pupils read them aloud for checking.

14 What did you do last week? Write sentences using the words from Activity 13.

- Give pupils time to write.
- Volunteers read their sentences.

Ending the lesson

- Divide the class into four or five groups. Choose one action word and ask all the members of each group to write one sentence with this past action. Groups have one minute to write. If all the members of each group have written a correct sentence, the group wins one point. Repeat three or four times with other words.
- For Answer Key see p. 46. For Audioscript see p. 47.

LOOK!

I played tennis on Monday morning.
He/She danced at the party on Friday evening.
They went to the cinema on Saturday afternoon.

7 **Look at Jenny's diary and say. What did she do last week?**

	Monday	Tuesday	Wednesday	Thursday	Friday
morning	study	study	study	study with Dylan	study
afternoon	study	play computer games	play tennis with Finn	practise the piano	study
evening	practise the piano	watch TV	listen to music	go to the cinema	watch TV

She practised the piano on Monday evening and Thursday afternoon.

TIP!

listen	listened	watch	watched
play	played	go	went
practise	practised	fall	fell
study	studied	take	took

8  1:05 **Listen and repeat.**

1 

2 

3 

4 

5 

6 

7 

8 

9 

OPTIONAL ACTIVITIES

Word games Play *Hangman* with the whole class using the new words. Divide the class in two groups. Write the verbs in infinitive form on the board and ask each group in turn to give you the past form. Each right answer is one point. The group with more points wins.

Lesson 4

Lesson aims
To revise structures and learn new vocabulary

Target language
two days ago, yesterday, last month
listened, played, practised, studied, watched, went, fell, took

Materials
Audio CD; school timetables

Optional activity materials
Active Teach; Digital Activity Book

Starting the lesson

- Draw a time line on the board and write the days of the week on it. Read it with the pupils. Today is ..., Yesterday was ..., Two days ago was ....

Presentation

Pupil's Book page 11

  9 Listen and repeat.

- Play the recording. Pause after each expression and point to the time line on the board.
- Play the recording again, pausing for pupils to repeat the expressions.

 10 Listen and read.

- Give pupils time to read.
- Play the recording.
- Play the recording again, pausing for pupils to read aloud.

 11 Listen and find. Then read.

- Give pupils time to look at the pictures and read the labels. Read them aloud.
- Play the recording.
- Play the recording again, pausing for pupils to read complete sentences aloud.

KEY **1** b **2** d **3** c **4** a

Practice

12 Talk about yourself.

- Ask a volunteer to say what he/she did yesterday, two days ago and last year.
- Pupils give you examples about themselves.
- In pairs, pupils talk about what they did in the past. Write on the board past time expressions such *as three months ago, two days ago, last year, last weekend*, etc. Circulate, correcting and prompting.

13 Look at the pictures. Ask and answer.

- Tell a volunteer that you went to the cinema last week and enjoyed it a lot. Then ask him/her *How about going to the cinema today/tomorrow?*
- Some pupils give you examples about themselves, e.g. *I studied in the library two days ago and it was very nice. How about studying in the library today/tomorrow?*

Activity Book page 7

15 Write the days.

- Give pupils time to write.
- Check the answers.

16 Write the years.

- Give pupils time to write.
- Check the answers.

17 Listen and match. Then write.

- Give pupils time to look at the pictures.
- Play the recording.
- Give pupils time to write.
- Volunteers read their sentences for checking.

18 Write about yourself.

- Give pupils time to write.
- Volunteers read their works.

Ending the lesson

- Ask pupils to read their school timetables. Then ask them:
  If today is Wednesday, when did you have Maths this week? Possible answers are *yesterday, last Monday, two days ago.*
  If today is Wednesday, when do you have Maths this week? Possible answers are *today, tomorrow, on Friday.*
- For Answer Key see p. 46. For Audioscript see p. 47.

9 Listen and repeat.

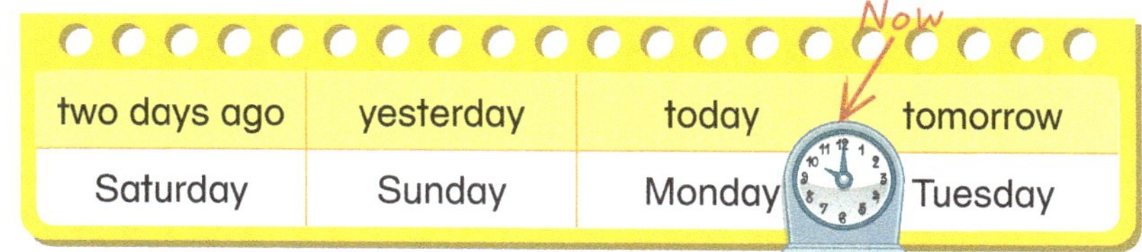

two days ago	yesterday	today	tomorrow
Saturday	Sunday	Monday	Tuesday

10 Listen and read.

Now it's 10 o'clock.
Today is Monday.
Tomorrow is Tuesday.
Yesterday was Sunday.
Two days ago was Saturday.

11 Listen and find. Then read.

1 

2 

3 

4 

a two weeks ago
b three years ago
c yesterday
d two days ago

1 I watched that film…
2 I practised the trumpet…
3 We played tennis…
4 I tidied my room…

12 **Talk about yourself.**

I walked to school yesterday.

13 **Look at the pictures. Ask and answer.**

OPTIONAL ACTIVITIES

True or false?
Pupils say sentences to the class looking at their timetables, e.g. *Yesterday, we did sports in the morning. True or false? We studied English in the afternoon two days ago. True or false?*

The time line Divide the class in two groups. Write a time line on the board with the days of the week. Then say one subject and choose one pupil from each group. They have to say when they studied that subject without looking at the timetable. Each right answer is one point. The group with more points wins!

Activity Book Answer Key

p. 2, Activity 1
1 Dr Al
2 Rufus
3 Jenny
4 Dylan
5 Ivan
6 Finn
7 Captain Formosa

p. 2, Activity 2
a 4
b 3
c 6
d 1
e 7
f 5
g 2

p. 3, Activity 3
1 c
2 c

p. 3, Activity 4
1 T
2 F
3 T
4 T
5 T
6 T

p. 3, Activity 5
1 (2.00 pm) Finn is swimming.
2 (9.00 pm) Dylan is studying.
3 (10.00 am) Jenny is snowboarding.

p. 4, Activity 6
1 reading
2 kicking
3 playing
4 diving/swimming
5 running

p. 4, Activity 7
1 d
2 e
3 b
4 c
5 a

p. 4, Activity 8
1 Jenny is playing with her PS3.
2 Jenny is playing football.
3 Jenny is listening to music on her MP3 player.
4 Jenny is swimming.
5 Jenny is snowboarding.

p. 5, Activity 9
a She is running.
b He is drinking water.
c They are reading.
d She is kicking a ball.
e He is playing the violin.
f He is sleeping.
g They are swimming.
h She is playing.

p. 6, Activity 12
1 c
2 e
3 b
4 f
5 a
6 d

p. 6, Activity 13
1 listened
2 studied
3 played
4 watched
5 went
6 practised

p. 7, Activity 15
1 Monday
2 Sunday
3 Tuesday

p. 7, Activity 16
Answers will depend on current year.

p. 7, Activity 17
1 She danced at school on Monday morning.
2 He played baseball yesterday.
3 They tidied the classroom two weeks ago.
4 She watched that film two years ago.
5 They went to the library three days ago.

Audioscript

Activity 1, pp. 6–7 CD1:02

D = Dr. Al J = Jenny F = Finn D = Dylan
I = Ivan R = Rufus C = Captain

Ice Island. Four o'clock in the morning.

D Come on. Wake up, kids!
J Wake up?! It's the middle of the night, Dr Al!
D I know, Jenny. Come and see the moon.
F What are you doing?
D I'm studying the moon, Finn. Look! What can you see?
F I can see the man in the moon.
F No, it isn't a man. It's a rabbit!
D Well, I think it's a snail!
J You're all wrong. It's a big piece of cheese and I'm hungry!
D It's breakfast time!

Meanwhile, down in the harbour ...

I It's here, Rufus!
R Ssh! Captain Formosa's sleeping!
R Hurry up, Ivan. And be quiet!
C What's that? Who's there?
R The Captain's coming! Quick! Hide in here!
R Go away!

Lesson 1, Activity 2, p. 8 CD1:03

1 This is Dylan. He likes to think and solve problems.
2 This is Jenny. She likes adventure and has a backpack full of useful things.
3 This is Finn. He likes skiing, snowboarding and rock climbing.
4 This is Dr Al. He likes watching the stars and planets.
5 This is Captain Formosa. He likes penguins and he lives in an old submarine.
6 This is Ivan. He likes diving and he is strong.
7 This is Rufus. He likes running and wants to find the treasure.

Lesson 2, Activity 4, p. 9 CD1:04

1 This is Finn. At two o'clock he's swimming in the swimming pool. He's not good at swimming so he has a swimming class.
2 This is Dylan. At nine o'clock he's studying. He gets up early and studies, so in the afternoon he can surf the Internet.
3 This is Jenny. At ten o'clock she's snowboarding. She likes it – it's fun!

Lesson 3, Activity 8, p. 10 CD1:05

1 She practised the piano.
2 They danced at school.
3 They watched TV.
4 She tidied her room.
5 He walked to school.
6 They played badminton.
7 She fell in the park.
8 They took a bus to go to the cinema.
9 He listened to music.

Lesson 3, Activity 12, p. 6 (AB) CD1:06

1 She listened to some music on Monday morning.
2 He studied English on Thursday morning.
3 They played volleyball on Saturday afternoon.
4 She watched a football game on Wednesday evening.
5 They went to the park on Sunday afternoon.
6 He practised the guitar on Tuesday evening.

Lesson 4, Activity 9, p. 11 CD1:07

two days ago
yesterday
today
now
tomorrow

Lesson 4, Activity 10, p. 11 CD1:08

Now it's ten o'clock.
Today is Monday.
Tomorrow is Tuesday.
Yesterday was Sunday.
Two days ago was Saturday.

Lesson 4, Activity 11, p. 11 CD1:09

1 I watched that film three years ago.
2 I practised the trumpet two days ago.
3 We played tennis yesterday.
4 I tidied my room two weeks ago.

Lesson 4, Activity 17, p. 7 (AB) CD1:10

1 She danced at school on Monday morning.
2 He played baseball yesterday.
3 They tidied the classroom two weeks ago.
4 She watched that film two years ago.
5 They went to the library three days ago.

1 Friends

Objectives

- describe what people look like
- describe what people are like
- make comparisons
- correctly pronounce *–er*/*–or* endings

Topics
- physical description
- personal description
- comparisons
- families of the world

Language
Vocabulary
Physical descriptions: dark hair, spiky hair, handsome, good-looking, moustache, blond(e) hair, beautiful, cute, beard, straight hair, curly hair, bald
Personal descriptions: bossy, kind, sporty, lazy, clever, shy, talkative, helpful, friendly, hardworking

Structures
What does she look like? She is .../
She has got ...
What's she like? She is ...
I like her because she is ...
She is taller than her brother.
She is the tallest in her family.

Revision
thin, tall, short, pretty, curly hair, straight hair, blond(e) hair, fair hair, black, blue, brown, green, grey eyes, fat, long hair, red hair, white hair, family, funny

Receptive language
and, but, because,
present continuous, short answers, quite big, argue, help, husband

CLIL and Wider world language
Art (Personal description): intelligent, bored, excited, important, lovely, little
Wider world: Families of the world.

Values
Help your friends in class.

Stories
- Who lives at number 12?
- Island mystery: chapter 1

Song
We're friends.

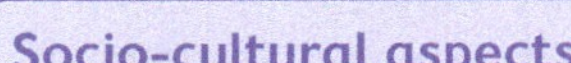

Socio-cultural aspects
- finding out about other people's appearance
- finding out about other people's families
- working in pairs

Learning Strategies
- making use of prior knowledge
- following instructions
- recording new words
- critical thinking: observing and describing
- critical thinking: comparing and contrasting, classifying
- collaborative learning
- integrating contents: discussing and approaching new cultures
- reflecting on learning and self assessment

Phonics and spelling
- *–er* and *–or* endings
- blending words

Cross-curricular contents
- Art: describing the characters in a painting
- Social Sciences: families of the world and helping friends in class
- Music: song, pronunciation rhyme
- Language skills: reading a story, acting out, telling a story

Basic competences

Linguistic communication: Use language as an instrument for communication (L.1 to L.10).
Knowledge and interaction with the physical world: Learn about cultural differences and families (L.8).
Mathematical competence: Compare and contrast age, height and size (L.7 to L.8).
Processing information and digital competence: Use Active Teach, Digital Activity Book and Ice Island Online World

Social and civic competence: Talk about friendship (L.3). Help your friends in class (L.5).
Cultural and artistic competence: Discuss paintings and art (L.18).
Learning to learn: Reflect on what has been learnt and self evaluate progress (L.10).
Autonomy and personal initiative: Use own judgement and ideas and further develop social skills (L.1 to L.10).

Skills

Listening

- can understand people talking about their physical and personal appearance
- can understand a dialogue about physical and personal appearance
- can understand questions about physical and personal appearance
- can understand a description of a group of people
- can understand a song about a friend's personality
- can understand a pronunciation rhyme

Speaking

- can give information about physical appearance and personality
- can sing the *We're friends* song
- can compare two or more people
- can introduce themselves
- can say the pronunciation rhyme

Taking part in conversations

- can ask and respond to questions about physical appearance and personality
- can ask and respond to questions about other people's families
- can take part in a dialogue about physical appearance
- can ask and respond to factual questions about the characters in a painting

Reading

- can read and understand personal information (about physical appearance and personality and families) in sentences, short paragraphs and texts
- can read and understand a cartoon strip story, captions and speech bubbles
- can read and understand factual information about families around the world
- can read and understand a paragraph-length description of a person

Writing

- can write physical appearance and personality words correctly
- can use comparatives and superlatives correctly in sentences
- can complete sentences about physical appearance and personality
- can write sentences about their own physical appearance and personality
- can write questions about physical appearance and personality
- can write a short text to describe someone's physical appearance and personality

Classroom ideas

- Make posters to decorate the class with photos of pupils' families. Use the CLIL poster of the unit.
- Ask pupils to bring family photos to class and to present their families to the class. They can describe their physical appearance and personality.
- If you have pupils from other countries in your class, ask them to make flags to decorate the classroom.
- You or your pupils could use the websites below to access more information about the lives and families of children who live in different countries around the world:
  http://www.oxfam.org.uk/coolplanet/kidsweb/children.htm
  http://www.timeforkids.com/around-the-world
- Play games from the Games Bank.
- Photocopiables 1.1–1.7.

Take-home English

- Letters for parents. When you begin Unit 1, complete and give pupils a copy of the letter for the unit (Active Teach). This explains what pupils are going to learn in this unit.
- Home-School Link. Encourage pupils to talk to their families about their classmates. (L.5)
- Grammar Booklet and Reading and Writing Booklet. Pupils take these home to show their parents.
- Pupils' Digital Activity Books.
- Portfolios. Encourage pupils to take their portfolio files home to show their parents when they finish Unit 1.

Evaluation

Self assessment

- Pupils can answer questions about what people look like
- Pupils can talk about the personalities of their friends and family
- Pupil's Book page 21
- Activity Book page 17

Resources

- Grammar reference (Pupil's Book page 104)
- Unit review (Activity Book page 96)
- Picture dictionary (Activity Book page 104)
- Test Booklet – Unit 1 (pages 6–9)
- Grammar Booklet pages 1–4, Reading and Writing Booklet – Unit 1 (pages 1–4)

1 Friends

Lesson 1

Lesson aims
To present and practise new vocabulary: personal appearance

Target language
dark hair, spiky hair, handsome, good-looking, moustache, blond(e) hair, bald, beautiful, cute, beard, straight hair, curly hair

Receptive language
What does it look like? What do they look like?

Materials
Audio CD; Flashcards and Wordcards (Physical descriptions)

Optional activity materials
Magazine or internet photos of people to illustrate the appearance adjectives; Active Teach; Digital Activity Book; Photocopiable 1.1

Starting the lesson

- Write *friends* on the board jumbled up *(drefisn)*. Elicit the word.
- Ask the class if they think it's better to have lots of friends or to have fewer, very good friends. Why?

Presentation

- Present the vocabulary using flashcards (physical descriptions). Hold up each in turn and say the word for pupils to repeat. Hold up the flashcards in a different order for pupils to repeat again.

Pupil's Book page 12

1 Listen and read. Who lives at number 12?

- Ask the class *Where are the children? (At home/in the garden.)*
- Ask *Who lives at number twelve?* Play the recording. Pupils listen, follow the story and find the answer to the question. Elicit the answer.
- Play the recording again. Mime *tall, bald, curly, spiky* as pupils listen, and encourage the class to copy you, e.g. *tall* (stretch and hold a hand up), *bald* (cover the top of your head with your hands).

KEY Maddy, her family and Kipper the cat.

2 Listen and repeat.

- Give pupils time to look at the pictures.
- Play the recording. Pause for pupils to find the correct picture and repeat.
- Play the recording again, pausing after each word so that pupils can say and point to classmates or themselves where possible. Encourage pupils to point to themselves for *good-looking/beautiful!* Tell them *good-looking* can describe a boy or girl, but *beautiful* is only for girls.

Practice

3 Who's who? Listen and point to the correct picture in Activity 2.

- Give pupils time to look at the pictures again and read 1–12.
- Play the recording. Pause for pupils to find and point to the correct pictures.
- Play the recording again, pausing after each paragraph so that pupils can check.

KEY a 1 b 2 c 8 d 7 e 4 f 3 g 9 h 6

Activity Book page 8

1 Unscramble and write.

- Give pupils time to do the activity.
- To check answers, you could ask volunteers to write the words on the board.

2 Look and write sentences. Use words from Activity 1.

- Point to each picture and ask *Who is it? What are they doing? (They're trying on wigs.)*
- Give pupils time to do the activity. Tell them they can use other words as well as those in Activity 1.
- If your class needs support, elicit the answers before pupils write.

3 Write about yourself and three more friends.

- Give pupils time to do the activity.
- Volunteers read out their answers.

Pupils can now, or at the end of this unit, go online to Ice Island and find the ice cream that Penn and Gwyn are holding. It is inside the Ice Palace, on display in the stall called 'Frosty Ice', to the left of the entrance. Once pupils click on the ice cream they are taken to a supplementary language game based on the vocabulary in this unit.

Ending the lesson

- Stick the photos you've brought on the board. Divide the class into two teams. Describe one picture at a time. One runner from each team runs to the board and touches the correct picture.
- For the next lesson, ask pupils to bring a magazine or internet photo of a hero. For Answer Key see p. 70. For Audioscript see p. 72.

OPTIONAL ACTIVITIES

Matching pairs Use the wordcards and the photos you've prepared. See p. 301.
Descriptions In pairs pupils describe famous people.
Photocopiable 1.1 See teacher's notes p. 287.

Lesson 2

Lesson aims
To revise Lesson 1 vocabulary; to learn and practise question forms with *look like*

Target language
What does he/she look like? What do they look like?

Materials
Audio CD; Flashcards and Wordcards (Physical descriptions)

Optional activity materials
Pupils' magazine/internet photos of their hero; Active Teach; Digital Activity Book; Grammar Booklet

Starting the lesson

- Say *You've got curly/spiky/straight hair, stand up!* (Only pupils with curly/spiky/straight hair stand up.) Repeat the sentence changing the adjectives.

Presentation

- Display the flashcards (physical descriptions), learnt in Lesson 1, around the room and play *I spy* (see p. 300). Ask individual pupils to come and write the words on the board.
- Ask the class to silently read the Look! box.
- Remind pupils we use *do* to form questions with *I*, *you*, *we* and *they*, but *does* in third person singular questions.
- Remind pupils that the contractions *she's/he's/it's* + adjective mean *she/he/it is*, e.g. *She's beautiful. She's got* means *She has got*.
- Tell pupils when we use *have got* and *be*. (We use *have got* for describing physical details, e.g. hair and eyes, and *be* for describing a person in general, e.g. *beautiful, bald*.)

Pupil's Book page 13

4  Listen and read. Then look and say.

- Give the class time to look at the pictures.
- Play the recording. Pause after each description to let pupils say the correct name.
- Play the recording again, pausing for pupils to repeat the questions and answers.

KEY **2** Dan **3** Emma **4** Robbie **5** Robbie and Emma

5 Put the words in order to make sentences.

- Give pupils time to read the words.
- Ask pupils to read the Tip! box.
- Give pupils time to do the activity in their notebooks.
- Check the answers.

KEY
1 She has got straight dark hair.
2 He has got short blond hair.
3 They have got big blue eyes.
4 My sister has got a thin, pretty face.
5 My father has got a short, brown beard.

Practice

6 Ask and answer.

- Ask two confident pupils to read the example dialogue. The class looks at the pictures and identifies which portrait is being described.
- Pairs continue, asking and answering about the pictures.
- Remind pupils the importance of adjective order in English. *The usual order is* value + size + shape + colour + noun, e.g. beautiful long curly blonde hair.

Activity Book page 9

4 Unscramble and write the questions. Then answer.

- Give pupils time to rearrange the words to make questions.

5 Circle. Then tick (✓) the true sentences.

- Ask a volunteer to describe picture a. Ask *Has he got long hair? (No, he hasn't. He's bald.)* Look at the examples together and make sure everyone understands the two parts of the activity.
- Give pupils time to do the activity.

6 Listen and complete.

- Give pupils time to look at the table before you play the recording. Explain that they are going to hear Emma asking Maddy about her family.
- Play the recording. Give pupils time to complete the table.
- Play the recording again, pausing to elicit answers.

7 Order the words. Write sentences about the people in Activity 6.

- Give pupils time to write. Note common mistakes with order and *be/have got*.
- Write the sentences on the board to check adjective order in the sentences. Pupils can use their notebooks.

LOOK!

What does he/she look like?	He's good-looking/She's beautiful. He's/She's got straight dark hair and brown eyes. He/She hasn't got blond(e) hair.
What do they look like?	They're tall and handsome. They've got short, blond hair and blue eyes.
They haven't got dark hair.	

4 Listen and read. Then look and say.

1 She's got blonde hair and blue eyes.
2 He's got spiky hair and brown eyes.
3 She's got straight hair and glasses.
4 He's got brown hair and green eyes.
5 They've got brown hair.

5 Put the words in order to make sentences.

1 straight / She / dark / has got / hair
2 He / hair / blond / has got / short
3 blue / They / have got / big / eyes
4 sister / My / pretty / has got / face / thin / a
5 My / beard / a / father / short / has got / brown

TIP!

Adjective order
She's got straight brown hair.
He's got long curly hair.
They've got long thin faces.

6 Ask and answer.

A: He, she or they?
B: He.

A: What does he look like?
B: He's got long hair and a beard. He hasn't got a moustache.

A: He's number two.

Ending the lesson

- Using your notes from AB Activity 7, write three or four common mistakes on the board, e.g. *He has good-looking*. Ask volunteers to correct them. (He'*s/is* good-looking.) For Answer Key see p. 70. For Audioscript see p. 72.

OPTIONAL ACTIVITIES

Guessing game Pupils work in groups of four. They don't tell anyone their hero's name. They write a description of him or her and read it to their friends, who guess. *(Is it ...?)*

Whispers Play *Whispers*. See p. 300.

Grammar Booklet p.1 See answer key p. 285.

Lesson 3

Lesson aims
To extend the vocabulary for describing personality from Lesson 1; to practise the unit vocabulary with a song

Target language
bossy, kind, sporty, lazy, clever, shy, talkative, helpful, friendly, hard-working

Receptive language
and, but, because

Materials
Audio CD; Flashcards and Wordcards (Personal descriptions)

Optional activity materials
Active Teach; Digital Activity Book; Photocopiable 1.2; Photocopiable 1.3; Reading and Writing Booklet

Starting the lesson

- Review appearance words. Describe three or four pupils to the class without saying their names. Pupils guess who they are.
- Ask pupils to think about what kind of a person they are.
- Ask volunteers for examples, e.g. *I'm funny!*

Presentation

Pupil's Book page 14

7  Listen and repeat.

- Give pupils time to look at the pictures.
- Play the recording. Pause for pupils to repeat each word.
- Play the recording again. Repeat each word, varying the volume of your voice, e.g. whispering, shouting. Pupils repeat in chorus, imitating you.

Song

  Listen and sing.

- Play the song. Pupils follow in their books.
- Play the song again. Encourage pupils to sing.
- Have a competition. Divide the class in two groups. Play the song twice more, each group singing in turn. Decide which group is best!
- You can now play the karaoke song (Active Teach).

Practice

9 Ask and answer.

- Read the question and talk about it.

Activity Book page 10

8 Match.

- Give pairs time to match. Then check answers.

9 Tick (✓). What makes a good friend?

- Ask *Is a good friend good-looking?* Ask two or three pupils for their opinions.
- Tell pupils there is no correct answer.
- After pupils have completed the questionnaire, check and compare their answers.

10 Describe five people. Use the words in the box.

- Give pupils time to write.

Ending the lesson

- Ask volunteers to read to the class what they wrote for AB Activity 10. For Answer Key see p. 70. For Audioscript see p. 72.

OPTIONAL ACTIVITIES

Writing
Pupils write three half sentences, e.g. *She's kind but … She's kind and … She's kind because ….* Swap their half sentences and finish the ones they are given.
Crazy guessing game! Put in a bag all the personal description wordcards. Ask one pupil to take four or five cards from the bag. Decide who is best described by those adjectives.
Photocopiable 1.2 See teacher's notes p. 287.
Photocopiable 1.3 See teacher's notes p. 287.
Reading and Writing Booklet pp. 1–2. See answer key p. 283.

Lesson 4

Lesson aims
To revise vocabulary; to learn and practise the use of conjunctions

Target language
and, but, because

Materials
Audio CD

Optional activity materials
Active Teach; Digital Activity Book; Grammar Booklet

Starting the lesson

- Revise character adjectives. Mime one for the class to guess. Volunteers continue.

Presentation

Pupil's Book page 15

Skills

- Ask the class to silently read the Look! box.
- Read it and pause after each line for pupils to repeat the sentences.
- Remind pupils we use *and*, *but* and *because* to join statements or words together.
- Remind pupils that these three conjunctions show a different relationship between the facts contained in the statements. Give them examples.

Practice

10 Listen and point. Then ask and answer.

- Give pupils time to look at the pictures and read the adjectives.
- Play the recording. Remind pupils to pay attention to the conjunctions and adjectives.
- Play the recording again. Then, for checking, choose four pairs to ask and answer about the four characters for the class.

11 Read and choose.

- Give pupils time to read the sentences and the possible relationship between the two words or sentences. Tell them they must look for the best conjunction to join the words or sentences.
- When checking answers, ask pupils to explain their answers.

KEY
1 because **2** and **3** but **4** because **5** but **6** because

12 Think about two people in your family. Then tell a partner.

- Give pupils time to think and choose the two people.
- Give pairs time to do the activity.
- Circulate, prompting and correcting.
- Ask volunteers to tell the class.

Activity Book page 11

11  Listen and match. Then write.

- Give pupils time to look at the pictures and read the captions and the text.
- Play the recording, without pausing.
- Give pupils time to write.
- Play the recording again, pausing for pupils to check and correct.

12 Read and circle.

- Give pupils time to read and think which is the best option and why.
- Ask pupils to read aloud to check the answers.

13  Listen and match.

- Ask pupils to predict the answers.
- Play the recording.
- Give pupils time to finish matching before checking answers.

14 Imagine you are staying with this family. Then write.

- Give pupils time to write.
- Ask volunteers to read their email to the class.

Ending the lesson

- Ask the class what they would find easy and difficult about going on an exchange visit. For Answer Key see p. 70. For Audioscript see p. 72.

OPTIONAL ACTIVITIES

Roleplay
Pairs imagine they are staying with the family in AB Activity 14, and roleplay a telephone conversation at home.

Bingo
Pupils play a game of *Bingo* using adjectives from the unit. See p. 300.

What's he/she like?	He's sporty and he's clever.
	She's bossy but hard-working.
I like him because he's kind.	

  **Listen and point. Then ask and answer.**

11 Read and choose.

1 I like my new teacher *because* / *but* she isn't bossy.

2 He's sporty *and* / *but* clever. A perfect combination!

3 My best friend is talkative *and* / *but* funny. She makes me laugh!

4 She gets good marks *because* / *but* she's very hard-working.

5 He's lazy at home *but* / *and* he's hard-working in class. Strange!

6 He hasn't got many friends *because* / *but* he's very shy. Let's talk to him!

12 Think about two people in your family. Then tell a partner.

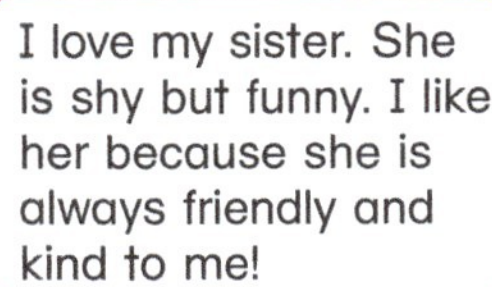

Team game
Put all the adjectives for physical appearance in one bag and the ones for personality in another bag. Write on the board *AND* / *BUT* / *BECAUSE*. Divide the class in two groups and ask one pupil from each group to take a pair of adjectives from each bag. They have to think of two sentences in one minute, joined with the best conjunctions. The pupil with the best sentences helps their team to win one point.
Grammar Booklet p. 2 See answer key p. 285.

Lesson 5

Lesson aims
To consolidate the unit language with a story

Values
Help your friends in class

Receptive language
Present continuous short answers

Materials
Audio CD

Optional activity materials
Active Teach; Digital Activity Book; Photocopiable 1.4

Starting the lesson

- Pupils close their books. Ask *What's the Islands story called? (Ice Island.) Who are the children in the story? (Finn, Dylan, Jenny.) Who are the adults in the story? (Dr Al, Captain Formosa, Rufus, Ivan.) Are Rufus and Ivan good? (No.) Where are the children and Dr Al? (At Dr Al's house.) Where is Captain Formosa? (On a submarine.) What do you think Rufus and Ivan want? Who or what helps Captain Formosa? (Two penguins, Penn and Gwyn.)*

Presentation

Pupil's Book page 16

- Ask the class questions about each picture. Pupils answer or guess, e.g.
  (Picture 1) *What are Jenny and Finn doing? (They're drinking.) What's Dylan got? (A telescope.)*
  (Picture 2) *What's Dylan wearing? (A scarf and a jacket.)*
  (Picture 3) *What's Captain Formosa doing?* (Pupils guess.) Elicit *message* and *emergency*. Write these words on the board.
  (Picture 5) *What are the children doing? (They're snowboarding.)*
  (Picture 6) *Is Captain Formosa happy? (No, he isn't.)*

13 Look at the pictures. Tell the story.

- Ask the class to look again at the pictures.
- Ask six volunteers to go in front of the class and tell the story just looking at the pictures without reading. Each pupil tells one picture.

Practice

  Listen and read. Then act out.

- Play the recording. Pupils listen and follow the story.
- Ask the class *Is Dylan drinking in picture 1? (No, he isn't.) Is Jenny snowboarding in picture 1? (No, she isn't.) Is Jenny drinking in picture 1? (Yes, she is.) Is Captain Formosa dancing in picture 3? (No, he isn't.) Is Captain Formosa snowboarding in picture 5? (No, he isn't.) Is Captain Formosa happy in picture 6? (No, he isn't.) Does Captain Formosa like penguins? (Yes, he does.) Is Captain Formosa kind? (Yes, he is.)*
- Play the recording again. Pause for the class to repeat each line in chorus.
- Divide the class into five, e.g. by rows/tables, and allocate these parts: Dr Al, Jenny, Finn, Dylan, Captain Formosa.
- Play the recording again. Pause for pupils to repeat their character's lines.
- Ask five volunteers to act out the story.
- Take a class vote for the best actor/actress!
- Pairs predict what happens next.
- Volunteers tell the class their ideas.
- Take a vote to find the most popular idea.

Values

- Ask the class why it's important to **help your friends in class**, e.g. We can't expect others to help us if we don't help our friends.
- Groups of four discuss what helping your friends in class means to them and present their ideas to the class.

Home-School Link

- Ask your pupils to go home and tell their family about their classmates. What are they like? What do they like about them?

Activity Book page 12

15 Match and write.

- Give pupils time to do the activity.
- Pointing to different pictures, pairs take it in turns to ask *What does he look like?* and to describe the character.
- Volunteers describe the characters to the class.

16 Tick (✓).

- Give pupils time to do the activity.
- Check the answers.

17 Find the words in the story and write.

- Give pupils time to do the activity.
- Check the answers.

18 What happens next? Imagine.

- Give pupils time to write.
- Ask volunteers to tell the class their ideas.
- Take a vote to find the most popular idea.

Ending the lesson

- Ask the class to imagine what Ice Island is like. For Answer Key see p. 70. For Audioscript see p. 72.

 Look at the pictures. Tell the story.

 Listen and read. Then act out.

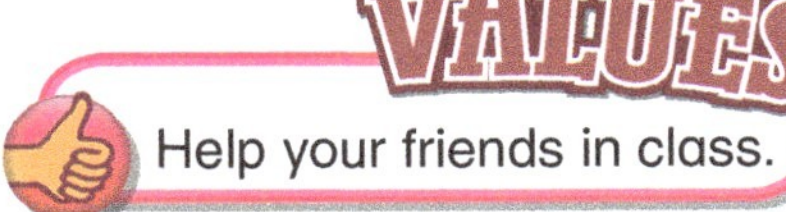

Help your friends in class.

HOME-SCHOOL LINK

Tell your family about your classmates. What are they like? What do you like about them?

OPTIONAL ACTIVITIES

Guessing game

Pairs take it in turns to ask and answer about a story character and to guess who he/she is, e.g. Pupil A: *What does he/she look like?* Pupil B: *He's got glasses. I think she's clever.* Pupil A: *Is it Jenny?* Pupil B: *Yes, that's right!*

Word game

Play *I spy* using words from the story so far. See p. 300. Ask the pupil whose turn it is to pretend he/she is Captain Formosa.

Photocopiable 1.4 See teacher's notes p. 287.

Lesson 6

Lesson aims
To pronounce *–er* and *–or* endings; to blend words with the final /ə/ sound

Materials
Audio CD; Phonics and spelling poster

Optional activity materials
Active Teach; Digital Activity Book; Photocopiable 1.5

Starting the lesson

- Show pupils the Phonics and spelling poster (see teacher's notes on p. 26).
- Read the words from the first picture aloud and ask pupils to find a common sound.

Presentation

- State the goal of the lesson.
- Tell pupils that the schwa /ə/ is a very common and important sound in the English language.
- Explain that in English different spelling combinations make the shwa sound. Specify that today they're going to learn the correspondence between that sound and *–er* and *–or* endings.
- Write the words *painter*, *actor* and *bigger* on the board. Explain that at times we add *–er* or *–or* to a verb to express the person who does something (*teach* → *teacher*).
- Encourage pupils to sound out each word.
- We also add *–er* to an adjective to compare two things, e.g. *big* → *bigger*.

Practice

Pupil's Book page 17

15  Listen and repeat.

- Give pupils time to read the words.
- Play the recording for pupils to repeat the words.

16   Listen and clap when you hear the sound at the end of the word.

- Play the recording. Pause after the first item for pupils to decide if they should clap or not. Play the rest of the sentences. Give pupils time to clap if/when they hear the schwa sound at the end of a word.

17 Look at Activity 15. Read and blend each word with a partner.

- Tell pupils that good readers are able to blend, that is to link sounds to produce a word. Model with the word *actor*: say /a/ /k/ /t/ /ə/. Explain that at times you can produce a completely different word by changing or adding just one sound. If you add /f/, you know how to pronounce the word *factor*.
- Give pairs time to do the activity.
- Ask fast finishers to think of other words with the same sound to blend. Ask the class to share.

18 Read and practise.

- Give pupils time to read and notice the connection between the spelling and the sounds.
- Ask pupils to cover the table. Say words at random from the table for pupils to listen and decide if it's a *–er* or *–or* word.

19  Listen and repeat.

- Give pupils time to look at the picture.
- Play the recording. Then ask pupils to find the words ending *–er* or *–or* in the rhyme.
- Play the recording again. Encourage the class to learn and repeat the rhyme.

Activity Book page 13

  Listen. Then circle the words with the same final sound.

- Read aloud the first pair (1. *worker, thirty*) to provide another opportunity to recognise the sound.
- Play the recording.
- Encourage the fast finishers to make up their own pairs.
- Use these words to practise with the whole class.
- Correct the activity as a whole-group discussion.

20 Read the sentences. Then underline the words with the final *–er* or *–or* sound.

- Read aloud the first sentence. Ask the class to find the word with the final /ə/ sound.
- Check the activity as a whole-group discussion.

21 Write four sentences. Use words with the final *–er* or *–or* sound. Then read.

- Encourage the class to make up their own sentences orally.
- Write some sentence prompts on the board to provide support for all learners. *I saw a ______ at the hospital.*
- Ask volunteers to read their sentences. Encourage pupils to point out the words with the final /ə/ sound.

22 Read. Then write the words again adding *–er* or *–or.*

- Write the first word *(calculate)* on the board. Ask the class if you need to add *–er* or *–or* to change the word.
- Give pupils time to complete the rest of the activity.
- Check the activity as a whole-group discussion.

Ending the lesson

- Revisit the goal of the lesson and ask pupils to evaluate their own progress. For Answer Key see p. 70. For Audioscript see p. 72.

1

–er/–or endings

When a word ends with –er/–or, the ending sounds the same.

15 

Listen and repeat.

1 
taller

2 
painter

3 
viewer

4 
paper

5 

poster

6 
collector

7 
actor

8 
director

9 
inventor

16 (1:23) **Listen and clap when you hear the sound at the end of the word.**

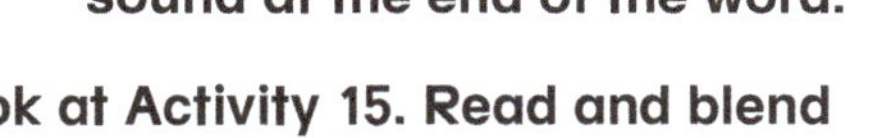

17 **Look at Activity 15. Read and blend each word with a partner.**

18 **Read and practise.**

–or	–er
calculate → calculator	teach → teacher
visit → visitor	sing → singer
project → projector	play → player

19 (1:24) **Listen and repeat.**

The swimmers can't dance and the dancers can't swim.

The singers can't act and the actors can't sing.

OPTIONAL ACTIVITIES

Poets' Workshop Start a class poetry book. You can start the book with a schwa page: pupils write a poem in which all the lines end in a word finishing in the schwa sound.

Schwa Bingo Ask pupils to make their own bingo cards with words from the lesson.

Sound and Word Wall Start a word wall with high-frequency words and sounds. Add a section for the taught sound and use it as a reference for the future.

Photocopiable 1.5 See teacher's notes p. 287.

Lesson 7

Lesson aims
To extend the vocabulary for describing appearance and personality; to learn and practise comparative forms

Cross-curricular focus
Art – describing the characters in a painting

Target language
intelligent, bored, excited, important, lovely, little

Materials
Audio CD; CLIL poster

Optional activity materials
Family pictures or photographs; Active Teach; Digital Activity Book; Photocopiable 1.6; Reading and Writing Booklet; Grammar Booklet

Starting the lesson

- Ask the class to tell you about the names of any famous painters. Model expectations for **student talking time** (STT) with a volunteer.
- Remind pupils that STT is a great opportunity to learn and practise English with their friends.
- During STT pupils talk in pairs or in small groups.
- We stay ON topic during STT.
- Agree upon a sign (clapping, counting down, etc.) so that everyone knows that STT is over.
- Give pupils time to talk about artists and practise the stop sign.
- Ask volunteers to share information about their family members with the class.

Presentation

Pupil's Book page 18

- Before reading, give pupils time to look at the pictures on page 18. Ask them *What can you see? Do the people in the painting look like your family? Why? What do you think this text is going to be about?*
- Use class volunteers to model how to compare. *Who is taller? Who is the tallest? Who is the oldest person in the classroom / in the painting?*
- Remind pupils that when we use one-syllable adjective to compare, we add *–er* and *–est* and for adjectives with two or more syllables, we use *more* and *most*. Draw a table on board for pupils' reference. Write *old* → *older* → *the oldest*; *beautiful* → *more beautiful* → *the most beautiful*.
- Give pupils time to look at the different pictures and the adjectives. Use the vocabulary routine: **mime and define**. Next, **use each adjective in a sentence**. Last, **ask questions** with each adjective.

Practice

20 Read and match.

- Read the title and the introduction to the text.
- Remind the pupils how to read years in English (1656 = sixteen fifty six).
- Review some royal family words like *queen, king, prince* and *princess*.
- Set purpose for reading: *Let's read to match Katy's notes with the characters in the painting.*
- Read the whole text: use expression and intonation to model proficient reading.
- Ask pupils to follow your reading.

21 Ask and answer.

- Complete the activity as a whole-group discussion.

KEY
1 Answers will vary (but not girl with red hair).
2 The boy on the far right. **3** Answers will vary (girl with red hair or boy on far left). **4** The character at the back with the dark hair **thinks** he is important.

22 Think about your family. Talk to your partner.

- Remind pupils about the STT practice at the beginning of the lesson. Pairs talk to each other.
- Ask one or two volunteers to share what they have discussed with the class.

Activity Book page 14

23 Read and complete.

- Model how to complete this type of activity. Discuss the different choices for the first sentence. Encourage children to ask themselves *Does it look right? Does it sound right? Does it make sense?*
- Check answers as a whole-group discussion.

24 Complete this table.

- Use the reference on the board to support all learners.
- Point out that the words ending with *–y* have differences in spelling when we add *–er* and *–est*.

25 Look at this family picture. Then complete the sentences using the words from your table.

- Give pupils time to complete the table.
- Encourage fast finishers to make up their own sentences. Read some of them aloud.

Ending the lesson

- Revisit the objective of the lesson. Ask what pupils found easy and more difficult.
- Ask pupils to draw two pictures with characters so that a partner has to describe the differences. For Answer Key see p. 70. For Audioscript see p. 72.

20 Read and match.

Katy is visiting a museum in Madrid. She is looking at a painting of the royal family in 1656. Have a look at her notebook. Can you match her notes with the characters in the painting?

1. He's the youngest and he's got short blond hair. He doesn't look excited, he looks bored.
2. He is older than the others. He looks intelligent and likes to think about things a lot.
3. She's got long blonde hair and looks bossy. She doesn't look very hard-working.
4. He's got brown hair and is the youngest. He gets very excited about things and is very talkative.
5. She's the smallest and has got red hair. She looks kind and helpful.
6. He's got dark hair. He doesn't look very friendly. He thinks that he is very important.

intelligent

bored

excited

important

lovely

little

Comparatives and Superlatives

She is taller than me	She is the tallest
He is lazier than his brother	He is the laziest
I am more talkative than my sister	I am the most talkative

I think that... I believe that...

21 Ask and Answer.

1 Who is taller than the boy?

2 Who is older than the other people?

3 Who is the friendliest character?

4 Who is the most important character?

22 Think about your family. Talk to your partner.

Who is taller and older than you in your family?

Who is the friendliest?

Who is the most interesting member of your family? Why?

OPTIONAL ACTIVITIES

Researcher's Workshop Make copies of a famous painting and ask pupils to compare the characters. Find out more about a famous artist.

Family Art Gallery Ask pupils to paint pictures or bring in photographs of their families and add captions with comparative adjectives.

Photocopiable 1.6 See teacher's notes p. 287.

Reading and Writing Booklet p. 3 See answer key p. 283.

Grammar Booklet p. 3 See answer key p. 285.

Lesson 8

Lesson aims
To learn about other cultures and respect cultural differences; to learn about families in other countries

Receptive language
quite big, argue, husband, help

Materials
Audio CD

Optional activity materials
World map/globe; Active Teach; Digital Activity Book; CLIL poster; Photocopiable 1.7

Starting the lesson

- Volunteers say who they live with, e.g. *I live with my mum, my dad and my brother.* Pre-teach *husband,* e.g. *(Name) lives with his mother and her husband.*
- Pointing to each photo in turn, ask the class *Is the family big or small?*
- Pre-teach *argue, help,* by miming or drawing.

Presentation

Pupil's Book page 19

23 Read these blogs. Then look and match.

- Ask the class *Have you got a blog? What do you write about?*
- If you have a world map, ask a volunteer to point out China and Britain.
- Give pupils time to read the blogs and match them with the correct photos.
- After checking the answers, ask pupils if they are surprised by any of the information. Ask which family is the most similar to theirs.

KEY **1** b **2** a

Practice

24 Read again and answer the questions.

- Give pupils time to answer.

KEY
1 Yes, she is.
2 granny
3 different (big and small)
4 his mum's new husband and his new brothers

Portfolio activity

- Develop the discussion. Ask how many brothers and sisters pupils think is normal in their country. Ask *Is it usual to live with your grandparents and aunts/uncles?*
- Ask pupils to tell you one or two things that are good/bad about having a big/small family.
- Pupils compare their ideas with a partner.
- Volunteers share their ideas with the class.

Mini project

- Arrange the class into four or five groups.
- Give each group a big board and ask them to write the title *Our families.*
- Each completes their poster, glueing on their photos and writing labels about their families.

Activity Book page 15

26 Read Activity 23, page 19, in the Pupil's Book again. Then complete.

- Give pupils time to read the blogs again and complete.
- Ask volunteers to read aloud and check.

27 Think and write.

- Ask pupils to write the good/bad things they talked about having a big/small family in the portfolio activity.
- Pupils read aloud their ideas and compare with others.

28 Answer the questions.

- Give pupils time to write.
- Ask volunteers to read their answers.

Wider world

Families of the world

23 Read these blogs. Then look and match.

1

2

a

Kyle's blog

In Britain, we've got a lot of different families – some are big and some are small. My family is quite big now. My mum has got a new husband and he's great. He's very clever and he helps me with my homework. He's got two sons so now I've got two brothers. We play football together every Saturday. We argue but, after five minutes, it's all OK! They're my brothers and my good friends.

Kyle, 12, Britain

b

Lang's blog

A lot of families here in China have got only one child. My friends and I haven't got brothers or sisters but we aren't sad. Brothers and sisters can be bossy! We can do what we want. We've got a good life and we've got very good friends. I live with my mum and dad and my granny and grandad. It's fun because my granny plays games with me. I love my small family.

Lang, 11, China

24 Read again and answer the questions.

1 Is Lang happy?

2 Who does Lang play with?

3 What are families like in Britain?

4 Who does Kyle like?

PORTFOLIO

Think and talk.

Have you got a big family or a small family?

Ending the lesson

- Display the posters; pupils talk about their families. For Answer Key see p. 70. For Audioscript see p. 72.

OPTIONAL ACTIVITIES

Dictionary work

Ask pupils to underline the new words in the blogs and check them in a dictionary. They can write them in their notebooks.

Photocopiable 1.7 See teacher's notes p. 287.

Lesson 9

Lesson aims
To review the unit language with a game, to use the Picture dictionary

Revision language
She's ... /She's got ..., What does he/do they look like? Comparatives, Adjectives (physical appearance) (personal description), *fat, thin, ugly, handsome*

Materials
Audio CD

Optional activity materials
Realia (wigs, glasses, clothes ...); Active Teach; Digital Activity Book; Reading and Writing Booklet

Starting the lesson

- Call two pupils with evidently different hair. Invite the class to spot the differences, e.g. X has got long dark hair and Y has got short blonde hair.

Pupil's Book page 20

25 Look at the characters. Then spot the differences.

- Give the class time to look at the pictures.
- Divide the class in two groups. Give them two minutes to note down the differences.
- Check the answers and count the number of pupils with the right differences in each group.

KEY Accept any sensible answer, e.g. fat–thin; straight hair–spiky hair; moustache–beard; braces–no braces, etc.

26 Draw. What does he/she look like? What is he/she like? Use your notebook.

- Give pupils time to read the words.
- Ask pupils to draw someone using some of these adjectives.
- Give pupils time to draw.
- Ask a pupil to read the speech bubble. Then invite the class to work in pairs. One describes and the other draws and vice versa.
- Give pupils time to compare and decide which pair has drawn the most similar pictures.
- Winners show their drawings to the class and explain the differences using the comparative structure, e.g. *In my picture the character is thinner than in his picture.*

Picture dictionary

- Pupils can do the picture dictionary of the unit on Activity Book page 104.
- Ask pupils to look at the pictures and try to write the vocabulary on their own in their notebooks. Then ask them to look for the words they don't remember in the Pupil's Book.
- As they finish, ask pupils to exchange notebooks to check answers. (Notebooks can be collected for checking.)

Activity Book page 16

29 Look and read. Write *Yes* or *No.*

- Give pupils time to look at the pictures and read the sentences.
- Invite the class to compare the two people.
- Give pupils time to do the activity.

30 Write in the correct column.

- Ask a volunteer to read the adjectives in the box.
- Invite the class to say sentences, e.g. *My father is bald! He has got blue eyes.*
- Give pupils time to do the activity.

31 Write. Then match.

- Give pupils time to look at the pictures and read the sentences.
- Give pupils time to do the activity.

32 Unscramble and write questions.

- Give pupils time to do the activity.
- To check answers, ask volunteers to write the sentences on the board.

Ending the lesson

- Invite your pupils to write three positive adjectives to describe their classmate on a piece of paper, e.g. *X is friendly, kind and clever!* Collect the papers and read them aloud. For Answer key see p. 70 for Audioscript see p. 72.

 Look at the characters. Then spot the differences.

a

b

26 **Draw. What does he/she look like? What is he/she like? Use your notebook.**

helpful	talkative	kind
sporty	clever	dark hair
funny	friendly	spiky hair
bossy	hard-working	cute
shy	lazy	

He is tall and handsome. He's got short dark hair and green eyes. He's shy but helpful.

AB p.104

OPTIONAL ACTIVITIES

Costume party!

Show the pupils the realia you brought. Ask volunteers to try on whatever they want. Then the class describes them!

If your pupils are good at acting, invite them to perform a strong type of personality, e.g. very bossy, very kind, very hardworking, etc. and the class guess the adjective.

Reading and Writing Booklet p. 4. See answer key p. 283.

Lesson 10

Lesson aims
To personalise and assess efforts

Materials
Audio CD

Optional activity materials
Online World; Active Teach; Digital Activity Book; Grammar Booklet; Test Booklet; Grammar reference (PB); Unit review (AB)

Starting the lesson

- Invite the class to think of these activities as a way to assess their work, in order to find out if they need extra work in any of the unit contents.

Pupil's Book page 21

27 Look and describe the pictures. How are a and b similar/different? Use your notebook.

- Give the class time to look at the pictures. Invite them to talk about the similarities and differences between the pictures.
- Give the class time to do the activity.
- Ask volunteers to read aloud their answers. (Notebooks can be collected for checking.)

28 Read and choose the right word.

- Give pupils time to read the words.
- Give pupils time to do the activity.
- Check the answers.

KEY **1** friendly **2** have **3** he **4** bald

29 Read and answer.

- Give pupils time to quickly scan the email. Set a time limit to focus your pupils' attention. Tell them the time we need to read depends on our purpose. Here they are just looking for the answer to three questions.
- After checking answers, ask pupils to explain why Seb is happy.

KEY
1 shy, kind and clever
2 Nerea – sporty, Lucia – funny, bossy
3 yes

30 Role play Seb's conversation with his mum.

- Complete the conversation with a confident pupil.
- Give pairs time to do the role play and swap roles.
- Circulate, prompting and correcting.

Activity Book page 17

33 Match.

- Give pupils time to do the activity.
- Divide the class in two groups and alternatively ask one group to read the definition and the other to say the correct word.

34 1:26 Read. Then listen and write.

- Give pupils time to read the word and the email before you play the recording. Explain that they are going to hear one boy talking about his friend Miki.
- Play the recording. Give pupils time to complete the text.
- Play the recording again, pausing to elicit answers.

35 Read Activity 29 on page 21 in the Pupil's Book again. Then write your own email about your family and friends.

- Give pupils time to write.
- Ask volunteers to read their emails.

Pupils can now go online to Ice Island and enjoy the fun and games.

Ending the lesson

- Give pupils time to read the sentences in the 'I can' section.
- Ask pupils to think carefully about whether they are able to do the 'I can' points. Ask them what they found easy or difficult in the unit and why.
- For Answer Key see p. 70. For Audioscript see p. 72.

27 **Look and describe the pictures. How are a and b similar/different? Use your notebook.**

1 a  b 

2 a  b 

3 a b 

4 a  b 

28 **Read and choose the right word.**

1 Harry always says 'Hi'. I think that he is *lazy / friendly / small.*
2 I *am / are / have* got long hair.
3 What is *he / we / you* like?
4 He hasn't got any hair. He's *young / clever / bald.*

29 **Read and answer.**

The Torres family

1 What's Carlos like?
2 What are his family like?
3 Is Seb happy?

From: seb@yoohoo.com
To: matt@gogomail.com
Subject: Spain!

Seb

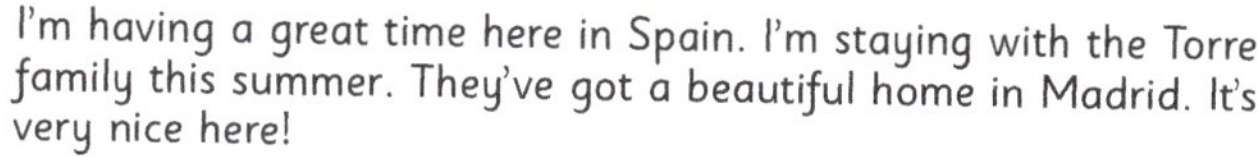

Hi Matt,

I'm having a great time here in Spain. I'm staying with the Torres family this summer. They've got a beautiful home in Madrid. It's very nice here!

Carlos is twelve. He's shy but he's very kind. He's clever, too. My Spanish isn't very good but he speaks great English! His granny lives in Los Angeles and she speaks English with Carlos.

He's got two sisters, Nerea and Lucia. Nerea is eighteen. She's got beautiful black har and she's very sporty. She isn't at home this week because she's playing in a big tennis competition. Lucia is nine. She's funny but she's very bossy. She wants to play games all the time!

See you soon,

Seb

30 **Role play Seb's conversation with his mum.**

Are you having a good time?

Yes, I am. I'm having a great time.

OPTIONAL ACTIVITIES

Quiz
Prepare a quiz in a PowerPoint presentation or on the board to assess the class as a group.

Grammar reference (PB p. 104) and Unit review (AB p. 96) You may want pupils to do the Grammar reference and Unit review activities for Unit 1.

Test Booklet You could give the Unit 1 test.
Grammar Booklet p. 4 See answer key p. 285.

Activity Book Answer Key

p. 8, Activity 1
blonde hair, bald, spiky hair, dark hair, cute, handsome, good-looking, beautiful

p. 8, Activity 2
1 long, curly, blonde **2** long, straight, dark **3** spiky **4** bald

p. 9, Activity 4
1 What does she look like?
She has curly brown hair.
2 What do they look like?
They have long straight hair.
3 What does he look like?
He has a long, thin face.

p. 9, Activity 5
a 1 is ✓, 2 has got; **b** 1 is ✓, 2 has got;
c 1 are, 2 have got ✓

p. 9, Activity 6
Dad (tall, bald, brown eyes)
Mum (curly hair, green eyes)
Grandad (blue eyes, grey hair, big moustache)

p. 9, Activity 7
1 big brown eyes
2 long curly hair, big green eyes
3 short grey hair, big grey moustache

p. 10, Activity 8
1 c **2** a **3** b **4** e **5** f **6** d

p. 11, Activity 11
1 sporty, talkative **2** Emma, friendly, shy **3** What's Maddy like? talkative, bossy **4** What's Robbie like? helpful, hardworking

p. 11, Activity 12
1 because **2** and **3** and **4** because **5** but

p. 11, Activity 13
1 short, funny, bossy **2** kind **3** nice **4** happy

p. 12, Activity 15
1 Rufus **2** Captain Formosa, **3** Ivan, **4** Dr Al

p. 12, Activity 16
1 b **2** c

p. 12, Activity 17
1 come on **2** map **3** penguins **4** eye
5 snowboard **6** dancing

p. 13, Activity 19
1 worker **2** father **3** actor **4** doctor

p. 13, Activity 20
visitor, player, better, calculator

p. 13, Activity 22
calculator, visitor, projector, teacher, singer, player

p. 14, Activity 23
1 important **2** little **3** excited **4** intelligent
5 lovely **6** bored

p. 14, Activity 24

friendly	friendlier	the friendliest
interesting	more interesting	the most interesting
happy	happier	the happiest
lovely	lovelier	the loveliest
important	more important	the most important
excited	more excited	the most excited

p. 15, Activity 26
Text 1: and, big, because, husband, new, his, but, and
Text 2: One, haven't got, but, bossy, and, play, small

p. 16, Activity 29
1 No **2** No **3** Yes **4** No **5** Yes **6** Yes

p. 16, Activity 30
am/is/are: bald, beautiful, tall, good-looking;
have got/has got: straight hair, long hair, spiky hair, blue eyes

p. 16, Activity 31
1 does, She's, a **2** does, He's, c **3** do, They're, b

p. 16, Activity 32
1 What are they like? b **2** What is she like? a
3 What is your uncle like? c

p. 17, Activity 33
1 i, **2** j, **3** f, **4** h, **5** c, **6** d, **7** g, **8** e, **9** a,**10** b

p. 17, Activity 34
1 got **2** got **3** talkative

Audioscript

PB Lesson 1 page 12

Lesson 1, Activity 1, p. 12 CD1:11

Emma = E Robbie = R Dan = D Maddy = M

E There's a new family at number twelve!
R What do they look like?
D The dad is tall and bald. There's a girl, too. She's got curly blonde hair.
E Hi, I'm Emma. Can I help?
M Thanks. I'm Maddy.
D Is that your cat?
M What does it look like?
R It's got spiky red hair.
M Spiky red hair? My cat, Kipper, is black and white.
R Oh, no! Red paint!

Lesson 1, Activity 2, p. 12 CD1:12

1 dark hair
2 spiky hair
3 handsome
4 good-looking
5 moustache
6 blonde hair
7 bald
8 beautiful
9 cute
10 beard
11 straight hair
12 curly hair

Lesson 1, Activity 3, p. 12 CD1:13

Girl 1 = G1 Girl 2 = G2

G1 This is my brother Joe.
G2 He has lovely dark hair and glasses. Cool!
G1 This is my friend Jack. He has spiky hair. Do you like it?
G2 Yes, I do.
G1 My aunt Sara is great. She's beautiful.
G1 This is my grandad. He's bald.
G1 This is my cousin Eric. He's really tall and good-looking
G1 The handsome man is my uncle.
G1 And this is my baby sister Rose. She´s cute.
G2 So cute!
G2 I know this one. She has blonde hair and is very good-looking!
G1 Yes! She's my best friend and I think she's very good-looking!

PB Lesson 2 page 13

Lesson 2, Activity 4, p. 13 CD1:14

1 What does she look like?
She's got blonde hair and blue eyes.
Maddy!
2 What does he look like?
He's got spiky hair and brown eyes.
3 What does she look like?
She's got straight hair and glasses.
4 What does he look like?
He's got brown hair and green eyes.
5 What do they look like?
They've got brown hair.

AB Lesson 2 page 9

Lesson 2, Activity 6, p. 9 (AB) CD1:15

Emma = E Maddy = M

E So, Maddy, who have you got in your family?
M There's me, my mum and dad, my grandad ... and Kipper the cat, of course. Dad is very tall and he's bald. He's got brown eyes.
E What about your mum? What does she look like?
M She's got curly hair and green eyes.
E And your grandad?
M Grandad's got blue eyes. He's got grey hair and a big moustache.

PB Lesson 3 page 14

Lesson 2, Activity 7, p. 14 CD1:16

1 bossy
2 kind
3 sporty
4 lazy
5 clever
6 shy
7 talkative
8 helpful
9 friendly
10 hard-working

Lesson 3, Activity 8, p. 14 CD1:17

You've got me
And I've got you.
You help, you listen
And I do, too.
We're friends. We're friends.
You're lazy at home.
You're shy at school.
But you're sporty and clever
And very cool.
We're friends. We're friends.
You're sometimes bossy
But I don't mind.
I like you
Because you're kind.
We're friends. We're friends.
We're friends. We're friends.

PB Lesson 4 page 15

Lesson 4, Activity 10, p. 15 CD1:18

1 Dan has got spiky hair and brown eyes. He's kind and funny.
2 Emma has got grey eyes and wears glasses. She's sporty and clever.
3 Maddy has got blonde hair and blue eyes. She is clever but lazy.
4 Robbie has got green eyes. He's sporty but sometimes bossy.

AB Lesson 4 page 11

Lesson 4, Activity 11, p. 11 (AB) CD1:19

1 Dan is sporty and talkative.
2 Emma is friendly but a little shy.
3 Maddy is talkative but she isn't bossy.
4 Robbie is helpful and hardworking.

Lesson 4, Activity 13, p. 11 (AB) CD1:20

Carlo = C Grandma = G

C Hi, Granny.
G Hi, Carlos. Are you having fun in England?
C Yes, I am! Seb's family are great. He's got a sister, Megan. She's five and she's very funny.
G What does she look like?
C She's short – well, she's only five, so of course she's short ... and she's got curly blonde hair. She's very bossy but she makes me laugh!
G And are you having a good time?
C Yes, it's fantastic! Seb's mum and dad are very kind. The food's nice. We do a lot of fun things. I´m very happy here!
G That's good, Carlos ...

PB Lesson 5 page 16

Lesson 5, Activity 14, p. 16 CD1:21

Dylan = D Finn = F Dr. Al = Dr Jenny = J Captain Formosa = C

D There's a man on the submarine!
F What does he look like, Dylan?
D He's old and he's got one eye.
Dr Oh, that's Captain Formosa. He's kind. He likes penguins.
F I can see him! What's he doing?
J Look! He's dancing!
D He isn't dancing. It's a message. E ... M ... E ... Emergency!
F Come on, Dylan!
C My map! Where is the map?

PB Lesson 6 page 17

Lesson 6, Activity 15, p. 17 CD1:22

1 taller
2 painter
3 viewer
4 paper
5 poster
6 collector
7 actor
8 director
9 inventor

Lesson 6, Activity 16, p. 17 CD1:23

taller
painter
viewer
paper
poster
collector
actor
director
inventor

Lesson 6, Activity 19, p. 17 CD1:24

The swimmers can't dance and the dancers can't swim. The singers can't act and the actors can't sing.

AB Lesson 6 page 13

Lesson 6, Activity 19, p. 13 (AB) CD1:25

1	worker	thirty
2	party	father
3	actor	pencil
4	shirt	doctor

AB Lesson 10 page 17

Lesson 10, Activity 34, p. 17 (AB) CD1:26

Boy = B Girl = G

B Tell us about your friend. What does she look like?
G My friend's name is Miki. She's tall and she has got dark straight hair. She has got brown eyes and she wears glasses. She likes skirts and colourful T-shirts.
B What's she like?
G She's clever and sporty. She's a bit bossy but it's OK. I like her because she's funny, talkative, and kind.

2 My life

Objectives

- talk about daily routines
- give orders and advice
- talk about frequency
- talk about food and digestion
- correctly pronounce the third person singular of present simple verbs

Language

Vocabulary

Daily routines: brush my teeth, make my bed, wash my face, tidy my room, do my homework, meet my friends, revise for a test, take notes in class, take out the rubbish, be on time

Adverbs of frequency: never, sometimes, usually, often, always

Structures

You must brush your teeth.
You should brush your teeth.
I never brush my teeth.
Infinitive of purpose

Revision

days of the week, food, first, then, next

Receptive language

You must brush your teeth. (Order)
You should brush your teeth. (Advice)
Present simple

CLIL and Wider world language

CIIL (Food): butter, chocolate, flour, sugar, salt, smell, taste, plate, snack, digestion
Wider world (Shopping)

Topics

- daily routines
- life at home and school
- frequency expressions
- food

Values

Giving is great!

Stories

- Who is hard-working? Who is lazy?
- Island mystery: chapter 2

Song

Matt's room.

Socio-cultural aspects

- finding out about other people's daily routines and frequency
- giving orders and advice to other people
- finding out about other people's shopping places
- working in pairs
- shopping for food around the world; giving is great!

Phonics

Present simple third person singular
/s/ /z/ /ɪz/
blending words

Learning strategies

- making use of prior knowledge
- following instructions
- recording new words
- using a survey to research information
- using a table to organise information
- critical thinking: discriminating and classifying
- collaborative learning
- integrating contents: discussing and approaching new cultures
- reflecting on learning and self assessment

Cross-curricular contents

Science: digestion
Music: song, pronunciation rhyme
Language skills: reading a story, acting out, telling a story

Basic competences

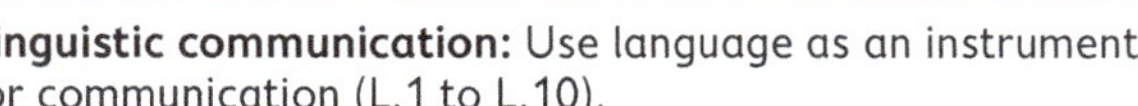

Linguistic communication: Use language as an instrument for communication (L.1 to L.10).
Knowledge and interaction with the physical world: Take responsibility for personal spaces and hygiene (L.1 to L.4). Talk about your body's digestive system (L.7).
Mathematical competence: Calculate a personal score, times of the day (L.4).
Processing information and digital competence: Use Active Teach, Digital Activity Book and Ice Island Online World

Social and civic competence: Fulfil obligations (L.1). Be generous(L.5).
Cultural and artistic competence: Show awareness of other culture's approach to food and shopping (L.8).
Learning to learn: Reflect on what has been learnt and self evaluate progress (L.10).
Autonomy and personal initiative: Use own judgement and ideas and further develop social skills (L.1 to L.10).

Skills

Listening
- can understand people talking about their daily routines and frequency
- can understand a dialogue about daily routines and frequency
- can understand questions about daily routines and frequency
- can understand a physical process (digestion)
- can understand a song about a boy's daily routines and frequency
- can understand a pronunciation rhyme

Speaking
- can give personal information about daily routine and frequency
- can sing the *Matt's room* song
- can talk about a physical process (digestion)
- can talk about a survey they carried out
- can say the pronunciation rhyme

Taking part in conversations
- can ask and respond to questions about daily routines and frequency
- can ask and respond to questions about other people's shopping routines and frequency
- can take part in a dialogue about daily routines and frequency
- can ask and respond to factual questions about a physical process (digestion)

Reading
- can read and understand personal information (about daily routines and frequency) in sentences, short paragraphs and texts
- can read and understand a cartoon strip story, captions and speech bubbles
- can read and understand factual information about shopping around the world
- can read and understand factual information about a physical process (digestion)

Writing
- can write daily routine and frequency words
- can use frequency adverbs correctly in sentences
- can complete sentences to write personal information about daily routines and frequency
- can write sentences about their own daily routines and frequency
- can write questions about daily routines and frequency
- can write a short text to describe someone's daily routines and frequency

Classroom ideas

- Use the CLIL poster of the unit to decorate the class.
- Use the family photos they brought for the previous unit and ask pupils to describe their family members' daily routines and frequency.
- If you have pupils from other countries in your class, ask them to compare their daily routines and frequency (meals, school timetable, etc.).
- You or your pupils could use websites below to access more information about daily routines in different countries around the world:
  http://www.oxfam.org.uk/coolplanet/kidsweb/wakeup/imdex.htm
  http://www.timeforkids.com/destination/egypt/day-in-life
- Play games from the Games Bank.
- Photocopiables 2.1–2.7

Take-home English

- Letters for parents. When you begin Unit 2, complete and give pupils a copy of the letter for the unit (Active Teach). This explains what pupils are going to learn in this unit.
- Home-School Link. Encourage pupils to talk to their families about what they usually do at school. (L.5)
- Grammar Booklet and Reading and Writing Booklets. Pupils take these home to show their parents.
- Pupils' Digital Activity Books.
- Portfolios. Encourage pupils to take their portfolio files home to show their parents when they finish Unit 2.

Evaluation

Self assessment
- Pupils can talk about daily routines
- Pupils can give orders and friendly advice
- Pupil's Book page 31
- Activity Book page 27
- Grammar reference (Pupil's Book page 105)

Resources
- Unit review (Activity Book page 97)
- Picture dictionary (Activity Book page 105)
- Test Booklet – Unit 2 (pages 10–13)
- Grammar Booklet (pages 5–8), Reading and Writing Booklet – Unit 2 (pages 5–8)

2 My life

Lesson 1

Lesson aims
To present and practise new vocabulary: daily routines

Target language
brush my teeth, make my bed, wash my face, tidy my room, do my homework, meet my friends, revise for a test, take notes in class, take out the rubbish, be on time

Receptive language
You must brush your teeth. (Order) / You should brush your teeth. (Advice)

Materials
Audio CD; Flashcards and Wordcards (Daily routines)

Optional activity materials
Active Teach; Digital Activity Book; Photocopiable 2.1

Starting the lesson

- Write *In the morning/In the afternoon/In the evening* on the board.
- See what daily routine vocabulary pupils can remember. Say *In the morning I get up, I …* . Invite volunteers to continue, e.g. *I have breakfast … , I go to school …* . Repeat with *In the afternoon …* , and *In the evening …* .

Presentation

- Present the vocabulary using the flashcards (daily routines). Hold up each flashcard in turn and say the word for pupils to repeat. Hold up the flashcards in a different order for pupils to repeat again.

Pupil's Book page 22

1  Listen and read. Who is hard-working? Who is lazy?

- Ask *Who can you see in the pictures? (Maddy, Robbie, Emma and Dan … and Kipper the cat!) Are they at school? (No.)*
- Play the recording. Pupils listen and follow the story. Elicit the answer.
- Play the recording again and ask pupils to join in and shout *Go away, Kipper!* (pictures 1, 2 and 3).

KEY hard-working (Emma and Dan), lazy (Maddy and Robbie)

2 Listen and repeat.

- Give pupils time to look at the pictures.
- Play the recording. Pause for pupils to find and point.
- Play the recording again, pausing after each word so that pupils can say and mime the actions.

3 Work in pairs. Play the memory game.

- Pupils look at the example dialogue while you read it with a volunteer. The game continues until one of you can't remember the other's sentence. You must both get the order right!
- Pupils play the game in pairs.

Practice

Activity Book page 18

1 Match. Then write sentences. Use your notebook.

- Give pupils time to match and write the sentences.
- To check answers, you could ask volunteers to read their sentences.

2 Write. Then listen and tick (✓) for Dan.

- Check pupils understand *before*, *after* and *every day*.
- Give pupils time to write and check answers.
- Ask the class to predict what is true for Dan.
- Play the recording and allow pupils do the activity.
- Play the recording again, pausing to elicit and check answers, e.g. pause after *get up* and elicit *in the morning*.

3 Tick (✓) or cross (✗) for you. What should you do? Write sentences.

- Make sure pupils understand the difference between *What should you do?* and *What do you do?* before they start.
- Give pupils time to do the activity.
- Volunteers read their writings.

Ending the lesson

- Volunteers use the new vocabulary to say what they like, and don't like doing, e.g. *I like brushing my teeth. I don't like tidying my room.* For Answer Key see p. 96. For Audioscript see p. 98.

2 My life

1 Listen and read. Who is hard-working? Who is lazy?

1 After school, Maddy meets her friends.

2 In the afternoon, Emma and Dan do their homework. Maddy and Robbie play computer games.

3 In the evening, Maddy brushes her teeth. Kipper wants to brush his teeth, too!

5 Before bed, Maddy does her homework.

2 Listen and repeat.

1  brush my teeth

2  make my bed

3  wash my face

4  tidy my room

5  do my homework

6 meet my friends

7  revise for a test

8  take notes in class

9  take out the rubbish

10 

be on time

3 Work in pairs. Play the memory game.

OPTIONAL ACTIVITIES

Writing
Pupils write about their school holiday routine, e.g. *I don't do my homework in the morning. I haven't got any!*

Pair work
In pairs, pupils guess what their partner does at different times of day in the holidays, e.g. *I think you brush your teeth in the afternoon!*
Photocopiable 2.1 See teacher's notes p. 288.

Lesson 2

Lesson aims
To revise the Lesson 1 vocabulary; to learn and practise structures with *must/should*

Target language
You must brush your teeth. (order) / You should brush your teeth. (advice)

Materials
Audio CD; Flashcards and Wordcards (Daily routines)

Optional activity materials
Active Teach; Digital Activity Book; Grammar Booklet

Starting the lesson

- Write on the board *You must brush your teeth every day. / You should brush your teeth every time you eat something*. Read aloud and talk about the difference in meaning. Repeat the sentence changing the action, e.g. *eat fruit in your diet/eat fruit every day*.
- Encourage pupils to give more examples.

Pupil's Book page 23

Presentation

- Display the flashcards (daily routines), learnt in Lesson 1, around the room and play *I Spy* (see p. 300). Ask individual pupils to come and write the words on the board.
- Ask the class to silently read the Look! box.
- Remind pupils we use *must* to give orders and *should* to give advice.

4 Listen and point, then say. What must Emma do before bed?

- Give the class time to look at the pictures.
- Play the recording, pausing for pupils to find the correct pictures.
- Play the recording again, pausing for pupils to say the full sentences, e.g. *She must take out the rubbish.*

KEY
1 She must take out the rubbish.
2 She should wash her face.
3 She must do her homework.
4 She should brush her teeth.

5 Look and say. What advice can you give Maddy?

- Give pupils time to look at the pictures and read.
- Read the first speech bubble and ask pupils to give advice, e.g. *You should be on time.*
- Give pupils time to do the activity in pairs.
- Check the answers. You can do the activity again using the third person singular, e.g. *Emma is late. She should be on time.*

KEY
1 You should be on time.
2 You should revise before a test.
3 You should meet your friends.
4 You should take notes in class.

Practice

6 Read Activity 5 again. Give advice to your classmates.

- Ask two confident pupils to read one example dialogue from Activity 5. The class looks at the pictures and identifies which picture they are talking about.
- Pairs continue, giving some advice to each other.

Activity Book page 19

4 What should they do before bed? Listen and match. Then write.

- Ask pupils to predict the answers.
- Play the recording. Pupils do the activity. Check answers.

5 What should your family do before bed? Write.

- Ask a confident pupil to talk about his/her family.
- Give pupils time to do the activity. Then read some examples.

6 What must they do on Saturday mornings? Listen and match. Then write.

- Give pupils time to read before you play the recording. Ask them what they think they are going to listen to.
- Play the recording. Give pupils time to match and write. Play the recording again to check answers.

Ending the lesson

- Write five class rules on the board. Ask pupils to make sentences giving advice or orders to their classmates.
For Answer Key see p. 96. For Audioscript see p. 98.

4 Listen and point, then say.
What must Emma do before bed?

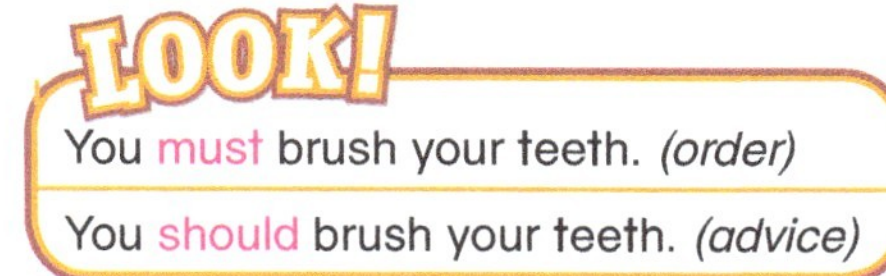

5 Look and say. What advice can you give Maddy?

take notes in class | meet her friends | be on time | revise before a test

6 Read Activity 5 again. Give advice to your classmates.

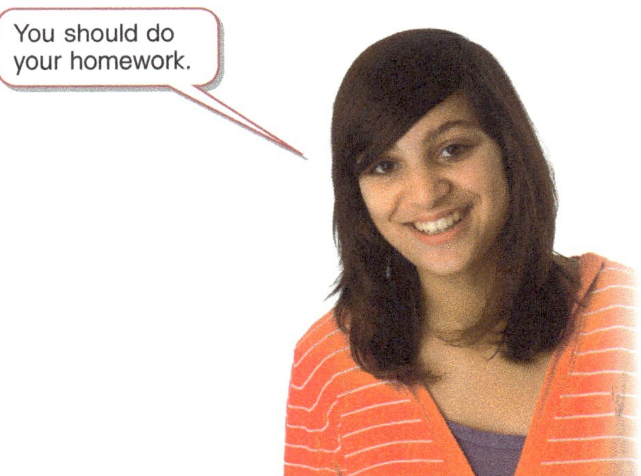

OPTIONAL ACTIVITIES

Group work
Groups of four tell each other about their families, e.g. *My sister and I must tidy our room on Sundays. How about you?*

Guessing game Pupils write a sentence about what they must/should do on Sundays on a slip of paper and give it to you. Read out the sentences one at a time. Pupils guess who wrote them.
Grammar Booklet p. 5 See answer key p. 285.

Lesson 3

Lesson aims
To extend the unit vocabulary; to practise the unit vocabulary with a song

Target language
never, sometimes, usually, often, always

Receptive language
Present simple, possessive 's

Materials
Audio CD; Flashcards and Wordcards (Adverbs of frequency)

Optional activity materials
Active Teach; Digital Activity Book; Photocopiable 2.2; Photocopiable 2.3; Reading and Writing Booklet

Starting the lesson

- Ask the class to visualise their bedrooms. Ask *What can you see? (I can see my bed and my clothes. My clothes are on a chair ….)*

Presentation

- Introduce the new words using the flashcards. Hold them up and say the words for pupils to repeat.
- Put the flashcards on the board. Point to the different flashcards and ask the class to say the words.

Pupil's Book page 24

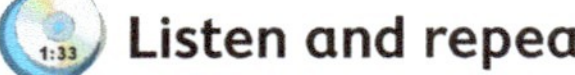

7 Listen and repeat.

- Give pupils time to look at the pictures.
- Play the recording. Pause for pupils to find and say each word.
- Play the recording again. Repeat each word. Pupils repeat in chorus.

Song

8 Listen to the song. Why is Matt's room a mess?

- Ask pupils *Does your bedroom look like Matt's bedroom?* Play the song. Pupils follow in their books.
- Play the song again. Encourage pupils to sing.
- Have a competition. Divide the class in two groups. Play the song twice more, each group singing in turn. Decide which group is best!
- Ask pupils why Matt's room is a mess.

KEY He never tidies his room.

- Ask the class to silently read the Look! box.
- Remind pupils we use **frequency adverbs** to talk about routines and habitual actions.
- Remind pupils that these adverbs indicate different frequency from 100% (*always*) to 0% (*never*). Give them examples.
- You can now play the karaoke song (Active Teach).

9 Sasha is Matt's sister. Look at the table and say.

- Give pupils time to look at the photo and table. Explain that the blue shading indicates what she does; the white what she doesn't do.
- Elicit the correct adverb for each task and write it on the board.
- Say *Sasha always brushes her teeth.* Encourage the class to say sentences about Sasha.

Practice

Activity Book page 20

7 Write.

- Look at the graph with the class. Elicit example sentences to check understanding. (See 'Ending the lesson', below, for practice of talking about where people do their homework.)
- Pupils do the activity. Then check answers.

8 Complete the chart for yourself. Then write a sentence for each room.

- Demonstrate how to add to the graph with a volunteer and elicit corresponding sentences. Circulate, monitor and help.

9 Find, unscramble and write.

- Give pupils time to do the activity.
- Volunteers read their sentences to the class.

Ending the lesson

- Ask the class where they usually do their English homework.
- Collect information by a quick show of hands and write it in a table on the board. For Answer Key see p. 96. For Audioscript see p. 98.

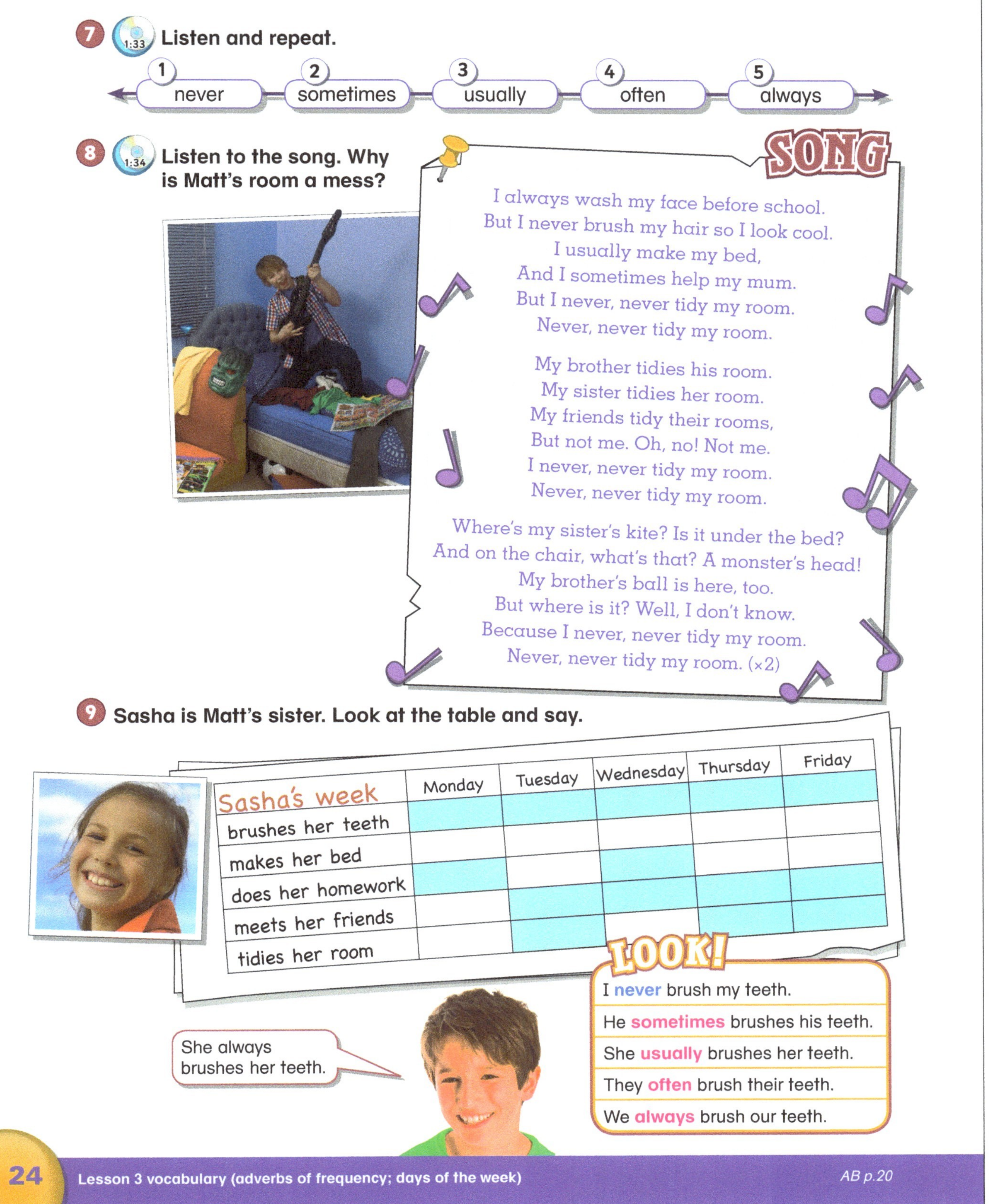

7 1:33 **Listen and repeat.**

1 never — 2 sometimes — 3 usually — 4 often — 5 always

8 1:34 **Listen to the song. Why is Matt's room a mess?**

SONG

I always wash my face before school.
But I never brush my hair so I look cool.
I usually make my bed,
And I sometimes help my mum.
But I never, never tidy my room.
Never, never tidy my room.

My brother tidies his room.
My sister tidies her room.
My friends tidy their rooms,
But not me. Oh, no! Not me.
I never, never tidy my room.
Never, never tidy my room.

Where's my sister's kite? Is it under the bed?
And on the chair, what's that? A monster's head!
My brother's ball is here, too.
But where is it? Well, I don't know.
Because I never, never tidy my room.
Never, never tidy my room. (×2)

9 **Sasha is Matt's sister. Look at the table and say.**

Sasha's week	Monday	Tuesday	Wednesday	Thursday	Friday
brushes her teeth					
makes her bed					
does her homework					
meets her friends					
tidies her room					

She always brushes her teeth.

LOOK!

I **never** brush my teeth.
He **sometimes** brushes his teeth.
She **usually** brushes her teeth.
They **often** brush their teeth.
We **always** brush our teeth.

24 Lesson 3 vocabulary (adverbs of frequency; days of the week)

AB p.20

OPTIONAL ACTIVITIES

Guessing game

Seven or eight pupils secretly put possessions in a bag. Invite different pupils to take an object and have one guess at whose they think it is, e.g. *I think it's (name)'s pencil-case.*

Photocopiable 2.2 See teacher's notes p. 288.
Photocopiable 2.3 See teacher's notes p. 288.
Reading and Writing Booklet pp. 5–6
See answer key p. 283.

Lesson 4

Lesson aims
To revise vocabulary; to practise using adverbs of frequency

Target language
Adverbs of frequency (position)

Receptive language
Present simple

Materials
Audio CD

Optional activity materials
Active Teach; Digital Activity Book; Grammar Booklet

Starting the lesson

- Write on the board *What time do you get up in the morning? What time do you go to bed?*
- Encourage pupils to use frequency adverbs in their sentences, e.g. *I usually get up at 8 o'clock and I never go to bed before 9.30.*

Presentation

Pupil's Book page 25

Skills

10 Read and choose. What's your score?

- Give pupils time to do the quiz and to work out their score.

11 Look at Activity 10 and talk about your day.

- Ask a confident pupil to talk about him/herself, using the information from the quiz.
- Give pupils time to work in pairs. Circulate, monitor and help.

12 1:35 Listen and say *True* or *False*.

- Give pupils time to read the sentences.
- Play the recording. Pupils do the activity. Play the recording again to check answers.

KEY **1** F **2** F **3** T **4** T **5** T **6** F

Practice

Activity Book page 21

10 1:36 Listen and tick (✓). Then write. What does she do each day?

- Give pupils time to look at the table.
- Play the recording, without pausing. Give pupils time to tick.
- Play the recording again, pausing for pupils to check and correct.
- Give pupils time to write the sentences and ask volunteers to read their work.

11 Complete. Use the words from the box.

- Give pupils time to read the words and think which is the best option and why.

Pupils can now, or at the end of this unit, go online to Ice Island and enjoy the fun and games.

Ending the lesson

- Volunteers read out what they have written for Activity Book Activity 11. For Answer Key see p. 96. For Audioscript see p. 98.

10 **Read and choose. What's your score?**

ARE YOU A MORNING PERSON?

Some people like mornings. What about you?

1 Do you get up on time in the morning?
1 No, never.
2 Yes, sometimes.
3 Yes, usually.
4 Yes, often.
5 Yes, always.

2 Do you have a big breakfast?
1 No, never.
2 Yes, sometimes.
3 Yes, usually.
4 Yes, often.
5 Yes, always.

3 Do you talk to your friends and family before school?
1 No, never.
2 Yes, sometimes.
3 Yes, usually.
4 Yes, often.
5 Yes, always.

4 Do you make your bed in the morning?
1 No, never.
2 Yes, sometimes.
3 Yes, usually.
4 Yes, often.
5 Yes, always.

5 Do you make your family's breakfast?
1 No, never.
2 Yes, sometimes.
3 Yes, usually.
4 Yes, often.
5 Yes, always.

6 Do you get to school on time?
1 No, never.
2 Yes, sometimes.
3 Yes, usually.
4 Yes, often.
5 Yes, always.

YOUR SCORE!

6–14 You're not a morning person. You shouldn't do important things before lunch!

15–22 You're OK in the morning but not great.

23–30 Wow, you're a morning person. You should do everything in the morning!

11 **Look at Activity 10 and talk about your day.**

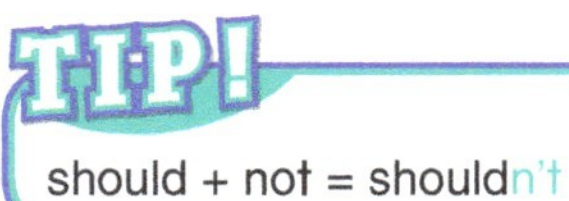

12 1:35 **Listen and say *True* or *False*.**

1 Emma loves getting up early.
2 Emma always makes her bed in the morning.
3 Emma never has a big breakfast.
4 Emma sometimes helps in the kitchen.
5 Emma usually doesn't like talking in the morning.
6 Emma often doesn't get to school on time.

OPTIONAL ACTIVITIES

Interview the teacher
Pupils ask you the quiz questions and decide if you are a morning person or not!

Noughts and crosses
Play this game with the class using adverbs of frequency and daily routine words. See p. 301.
Grammar Booklet p. 6 See answer key p. 285.

Lesson 5

Lesson aims
To consolidate the unit language with a story

Values
Giving is great.

Materials
Audio CD

Optional activity materials
The names of the story characters on separate slips of paper; Active Teach; Digital Activity Book; Photocopiable 2.4

Starting the lesson

- Pupils close their books. Ask *Who is good in the story? (Dr Al, Finn, Dylan, Jenny, Captain Formosa and the penguins.) Who is bad? (Rufus and Ivan.)*
- Ask *Is Captain Formosa happy in the story so far? (No.) Why not? (Because he hasn't got his map.)*

Presentation

Pupil's Book page 26

- Pre-teach any new language using the pictures *(escaping)* and a drawing or translation *(treasure)*. Ask the class questions about each picture. Pupils answer or guess, e.g.
  (Picture 1) *What's Captain Formosa eating? (A fish sandwich.)*
  (Picture 2) *Are the penguins hungry? (No, they aren't.)*
  (Picture 3) *What's Finn asking about? (Captain Formosa's map.)*
  (Picture 4) *Can you see a map? (No, I can't.)*
  (Picture 5) *Who can you see? (Captain Formosa, the penguins, Rufus and Ivan.)*
  (Picture 6) *Who is smiling? (Rufus and Ivan.) Why?* (Pupils guess.)

13 Look at the pictures. Tell the story.

- Ask the class to look again at the pictures.
- Ask six volunteers to go in front of the class and tell the story just based on looking at the pictures without reading. Each pupil tells the story of one picture.

14 1:37 Listen and read. Then act out.

- Play the recording. Pupils listen and follow the story.

Practice

- Ask the class true/false questions about the story. *Captain Formosa gets up at eight o'clock. True/False? (False. He gets up at six o'clock.) He goes swimming after breakfast. True/False? (False. He gives fish to the penguins and he reads his map.) His map is a treasure map of Ice Island. True/False? (True.) Captain Formosa has got the map. True/False? (False. Rufus and Ivan have got it.)*
- Play the recording again. Pause for the class to repeat each line in chorus.
- Ask eight volunteers to act out the story. Allocate these roles: Captain Formosa, Finn, Dylan, Jenny, Penn, Gwyn, Rufus and Ivan. (Remember only Captain Formosa and Finn speak!)
- Take a class vote for the best actor/actress.
- Pairs discuss what they think happens next.
- Volunteers tell the class their predictions.

Values

- Ask the class to talk about their routines at school, e.g. timetable, rules, games, etc.

Home-School Link

- Ask the class to tell their family what they usually do at school.

Activity Book page 22

12 Read and complete the sentences.

- Give pupils time to do the activity.

13 Write.

- Give pupils time to do the activity.
- If your class needs support, remind pupils the third person singular forms of *have* and *tidy* are *has* and *tidies*. If necessary, read the clocks as a class.
- Check the answers.

14 What happens next? Write and say.

- Give pupils time to write.
- Ask volunteers to tell the class their ideas and take a vote to find the most popular idea.

Ending the lesson

- Put slips of paper with the story characters' names on, into a bag or other container. Volunteers take a slip and, without saying the character's name, describe him/her. The class guesses which character it is. For Answer Key see p. 96. For Audioscript see p. 98.

STORY

13 Look at the pictures. Tell the story.

14 1:37 Listen and read. Then act out.

VALUES

Giving is great!

HOME-SCHOOL LINK

PARENT

Tell your family what you usually do at school.

OPTIONAL ACTIVITIES

Code game In pairs, pupils imagine they are Rufus and Ivan. They write their location in code. See Activity Book p. 66.

Roleplay Brainstorm questions to ask Penn and Gwyn about what they do in the mornings and at what time. Pupils role play in pairs.

Photocopiable 2.4 See teacher's notes p. 288.

Lesson 6

Lesson aims
To identify the /z/, /s/ and /ɪz/ sounds in the present simple third person singular

Materials
Audio CD; Phonics and spelling poster

Optional activity materials
Active Teach; Digital Activity Book; Photocopiable 2.5

Starting the lesson

- Show pupils the Phonics and spelling poster (see teacher's notes on p.26).
- Read the words from the second picture aloud and ask pupils to find a sound common to all the verbs.

Presentation

- State the goal of the lesson.
- Remind pupils that in the present simple third person singular, we add *–s* to the verb. Explain that this is pronounced in different ways if the previous sound is voiced or unvoiced. Write examples (e.g. *she finds, she eats*) on the board and underline the verbs.
- Tell pupils to put their hands on their throats to feel the difference between voiced and unvoiced sounds. Explain that voiced sounds use voice, so if you feel a vibration the consonant is voiced. Model /b/, /v/, /d/, /z/, /g/, /ð/ (as in 'the'). Now do the same for unvoiced sounds. Explain that those sounds do not use voice so they won't feel any vibration. Model /p/, /f/, /θ/ (as in 'theory'), /t/, /s/, /ʃ/, /tʃ/, /k/. Ask the pupils to determine if the last sound at the end of the verb that you underlined is voiced or unvoiced.
- Model the pronunciation of /s/, /z/ and /ɪz/. Describe the position of the tongue for each sound.
- Model how /s/ sounds like a snake and /z/ like a bee. Tell pupils that the *s* is pronounced /ɪz/ in verbs and nouns which end in these sounds tʃ, dʒ, ʃ, ʒ, s, z, e.g. nouns: oranges, churches; verbs: fixes, finishes, etc.

Practice

Pupil's Book page 27

15  Listen and repeat.

- Give pupils time to read the words.
- Play the recording for pupils to repeat the words chorally.
- Play the recording again, pausing after each word and asking volunteers to repeat it as accurately as possible. Encourage the class to repeat energetically.

16  Listen, point and say.

- Play the recording. Pause for pupils to point to each sound and say the verbs.
- Ask pupils to make up their own sentences with the words.
- Write a three-column table on the board, with the taught sounds as the three headings, /s/, /z/ /ɪz/. Volunteers tell you a verb (in the third person). Elicit from them in which column you should write it.

17 Read and blend each word with a partner.

- Read and model the first example.
- Give pupils time to do the activity in pairs. Ask fast finishers to think of other words with the same sound to blend.
- Ask the class to share.

  Listen and repeat.

- Give pupils time to look at the picture.
- Play the recording. Then ask pupils to find the words ending in *–s* sounds within the rhyme.
- Play the recording again. Encourage the class to learn and repeat the rhyme.

Activity Book page 23

  Listen and complete the sentences.

- Read aloud the first sentence in the box. Then play the recording. Ask the class *What does she do with her friend after school?*
- Play the recording again and give pupils time to complete the activity. Encourage the fast finishers to make up their own sentences.
- Point out the /s/, /z/ and /ɪz/ sound in these sentences.

16 Write the third person singular of the verbs in the correct phonetic group.

- Read aloud the words. Then ask pupils to read and colour code the final sound in each word. (Blue for voiced and red for unvoiced.)
- Say the third person of *smile* (/smaɪlz/). Elicit from pupils where this should go in the table (under /z/). Read the rest of the words in the third person.
- Give the class time to complete the activity.

17 Write four sentences. Use verbs in the third person singular. Then read.

- Encourage the class to make up their own sentences orally.
- Record some sentence starters on the board to provide support for all learners.
- Give pupils time to do the activity.
- Ask volunteers to read their sentences aloud. Encourage pupils to identify the final /s/, /z/ or /ɪz/ sound in the verbs.

18 Read and write the third person singular.

- Give pupils time to do the activity.
- Ask volunteers to complete the words on the board.

Present simple 3rd person singular final –s can be pronounced /s/ /z/ /ɪz/

After voiced sounds it is pronounced /z/
After unvoiced sounds it is pronounced /s/
After –s, –z, –ch, –sh, or –x we add –es and we pronounce /iz/

15 1:38 **Listen and repeat.**

1 works	2 watches	3 sits	4 brushes
5 stops	6 misses	7 plays	8 goes
9 studies	10 helps	11 buzzes	12 cooks
13 fixes	14 ends		

16 1:39 **Listen, point and say.**

/s/ /z/ /iz/

Irregular spelling! '–o' and 'consonant + y'

go → goes study → studies
do → does fly → flies
They are pronounced /z/.

17 **Read and blend each word with a partner.**

/s/	/z/	/iz/
help → he helps	play → he plays	mix → he mixes
eat → it eats	sing → she sings	kiss → she kisses
look → she looks	dream → it dreams	catch → it catches

18 1:40 **Listen and repeat.**

SOUNDS FUN!

She goes home and does her homework.

She washes her hair and nose.

But she never brushes her cats.

Ending the lesson

- Revisit the goal of the lesson and ask pupils to evaluate their own progress.
- Team game: write verbs (infinitives) on slips of paper and /s/, /z/ and /ɪz/ on the board. Ask pupils to stick the verbs in the correct position on the board and say the third person form as they do so. For Answer Key see p. 96. For Audioscript see p. 98.

OPTIONAL ACTIVITIES

Poets' Workshop
Write a poem in a shared writing experience. Encourage the pupils to write and illustrate their own poems and add them to their poem book.
Photocopiable 2.5 See teacher's notes p. 288.

Lesson 7

Lesson aims
To extend vocabulary in the context of food; to learn and practise the use of infinitives of purpose

Cross-curricular focus
Science – Your digestion

Target language
Infinitives of purpose
butter, flour, sugar salt, smell, taste, plate, snack

Materials
Audio CD; CLIL poster

Optional activity materials
Realia: chocolate biscuit, flour, sugar, salt, pepper, card or paper for posters; Active Teach; Digital Activity Book; Photocopiable 2.6; Reading and Writing Booklet; Grammar Booklet

Starting the lesson

- Our digestive system is made of different parts of our body that work together to turn food and liquids into the energy that our body needs.
- In addition to needing food to live and grow, our body uses food to repair itself. Sometimes, when we feel tired, it may mean that our body does not have enough nutrients like carbohydrates or iron.
- Food goes through a process of transformation in our body.

Presentation

Pupil's Book page 28

- Ask the class *What have you eaten today? Why did you eat those foods? What happened to the food after you ate it?*
- Allow some STT, then ask volunteers to share information about what they have eaten.
- Give pupils time to look at the first picture on page 28. Ask them *What can you see?*
- Use the vocabulary routine: **mime and define**. Next, **use each word in a sentence**. Last, **ask questions** with each word. Use realia if possible.
- Give pupils time to look at the second picture on page 28 (the digestive system).
- Ask pupils to point at the different body parts as you model their pronunciation.
- Use the illustrations and the vocabulary routine to preview these words: *swallow, enter, store, absorb.*
- Pre-teach the infinitive of purpose. Write two columns on the board. Write *pencil* and *book* on one side and draw a small picture. Write *to write* and *to read* on the other side of the board. Ask pupils *What do we use a pencil for?* Mime and model. Then connect the columns, e.g. *We use a pencil to write. We use a book to read.* Elicit other answers (to learn, to draw, etc.). Practise with other familiar objects and ideas.
- Encourage the class to describe what digestion is, using the connectors *first, then, next, finally* and the sentence bank.

Practice

19 Read and find these words in the text.

- Read the title and the introduction to the text.
- Set purposes for reading: *Let's read to find out what our body does when we eat.*
- Read the whole text as a shared reading experience: use expression and intonation to model proficient reading.
- Ask pupils to follow your reading. Then ask them to find the words in the text and explain their meaning.

20 Read and match.

- Complete the activity as a whole-group discussion.

KEY 1 b **2** a **3** d **4** c

21 Talk to your partner.

- Read the first question and ask volunteers to answer. Then allow some STT in pairs.
- Ask one or two volunteers to share what they have discussed with the class.

Activity Book page 24

19 Read and complete.

- Model how to complete this type of activity with the first item. Discuss the different choices for the sentence *When you eat some* _ _ _ _ *your body starts to work.*
- Give pupils time to do the activity.
- Check answers as a whole-group discussion.

20 Write. What is the job of these parts of your body? Write the parts of your body that help you to … .

- Encourage pupils to use the picture and text on Pupil's Book page 28.
- Point out that the job of the oesophagus is NOT in the book. Encourage them to write their own sentence.
- Correct the activity as a whole-group discussion.

21 Read and order.

- Give pupils time to do the activity.
- Check answers as a whole-group discussion.

Ending the lesson

- Make a poster of the digestive system. Then label the parts of the body and their job. For Answer Key see p. 96. For Audioscript see p. 98.

19 Read and find these words in the text.

CLIL

chocolate butter flour sugar salt
smell taste plate snack digestion

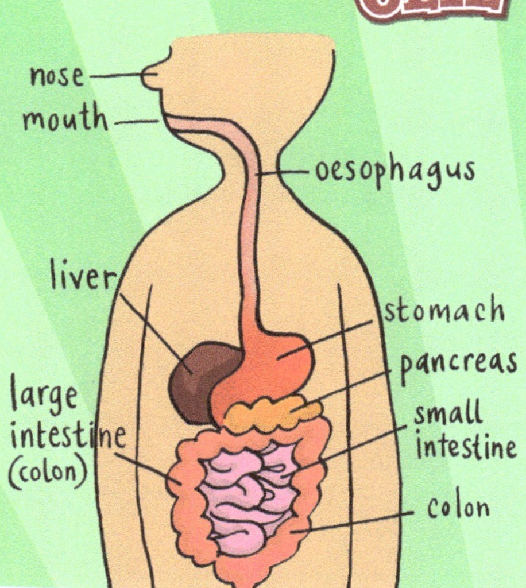

Your Digestion

When you eat a snack like a chocolate biscuit, your body starts a big science experiment. Your plate can be empty, but your stomach has some flour, salt, pepper, butter and other types of food in it. Many parts of your body start to work. This is called digestion.

First the saliva helps to make the food easy to swallow. Your tongue pushes the food to the oesophagus. Your tongue is also there for you to taste the food. Your saliva starts to work when you smell food in the fridge or on the cooker!

Next the food enters your stomach. The job of your stomach is to store and to break down the food into smaller pieces. There are also muscles and juices to help with this.

Then the food travels to the small intestine. Your intestine gets help from the pancreas and the liver to absorb all the vitamins, proteins and nutrients.

Finally, the food goes through the large intestine. Your colon can absorb some water and minerals. The waste is the food that your body can't use.

Don't forget to eat healthy food! Fruits, vegetables and water are helpful to digest food better!

20 Read and match.

1 Your tongue helps you
2 You produce saliva
3 Your stomach
4 The pancreas and the liver

a to make the food easy to swallow.
b to taste the food.
c absorb all the vitamins, proteins and nutrients.
d breaks down the food into smaller pieces.

21 Talk to your partner.

What is your favourite food?
What part of the body tastes it?
What should you eat to digest food better?

LOOK!

I've got a dog to protect my house.
I'm going to London to learn English.

OPTIONAL ACTIVITIES

Researcher's Workshop

- Find out more about the other systems in our body, e.g. the circulatory system.

Spelling Bee Ask pupils to learn the words related to the parts of the body. Then host a spelling bee.

Photocopiable 2.6 See teacher's notes p. 288.
Reading and Writing Booklet p. 7 See answer key p. 283.
Grammar Booklet p. 7 See answer key p. 285.

Lesson 8

Lesson aims
To learn about other cultures and respect cultural differences; to learn about shopping for food in other countries

Receptive language
bakery, coconut, float, grow, problem, seed

Materials
Audio CD

Optional activity materials
World map or globe; Active Teach; Digital Activity Book; CLIL poster; Photocopiable 2.7

Starting the lesson

- Ask if any pupils have been to a different country. What food did they eat? Did they like it?
- Discuss why people in different countries eat different foods, e.g. The food we eat depends on our climate.

Presentation

Pupil's Book page 29

22 Read these blogs. Then look and match.

- Ask pupils to guess which countries the photos show (tell them the names of the countries: Vietnam, Argentina and the United Kingdom). Volunteers point to them on the map/globe.
- Ask the class about the foods in each photo, e.g. (Photo a) *What food can you see?* (Photo b) *What do they sell in this type of shop?* (Photo c) *What do you think is growing in this garden?* Write pupils' ideas on the board.
- Teach *coconut, bakery, grow* and *floating market* using the photos and/or a quick translation. Remind pupils about the importance of using the context to work out the meaning of new words.
- Ask a different volunteer to read each text as you check the answers.

KEY **1** b **2** a **3** c

Practice

23 Read again and choose.

- Give pupils time to look at the photos and read the sentences.
- Give pupils time to read the blogs and choose the correct answer.

KEY
1 morning **2** snakes **3** often **4** vegetables **5** garden

- After checking the answers, ask pupils if they are surprised by any of the information. Ask which food is the most delicious and which the most healthy, in their opinion.

Portfolio activity

- Ask pupils where they usually do the shopping.
- Help them realise the different places where they can do the shopping for food in their country.
- Write the shopping places on the board. Ask pupils to put their hands up to see the number of pupils who usually do the shopping in the different places.

Activity Book page 25

22 Read Silvia's blog, page 29 of the PB again. Then write.

- Give pupils time to read the blog again and complete.
- Ask volunteers to read aloud and check.

Project template

- Give pupils time to ask each other questions and complete the survey table on Activity Book page 25. Allow them to walk around to do their research.
- Ask them to write in the Activity Book about the information they have put into the table.
- Pupils could write a report in a Word document or their notebooks, with the title *Class X Favourite Shopping Places*.

Ending the lesson

- Volunteers read aloud what they have written about the survey (Project, Activity Book p. 25) and compare. For Answer Key see p. 96. For Audioscript see p. 98.

Wider world

Shopping for food

22 Read these blogs. Then look and match.

1 **Bao's blog**

We buy our food at the floating market. It opens at four o'clock in the morning. There are a lot of boats and you can climb from one boat to another to buy things. You can buy fish, rice, coconuts, bananas… and snakes, too! Some of the snakes can dance. I love watching them. Some people buy snakes for their dinner but I don't eat snakes – they're too expensive.

Bao, 12, Vietnam

3 **Lily's blog**

We don't buy our fruit at the supermarket. We grow it in our garden. The UK is too cold for peaches and bananas but there's a big plum tree and two apple trees in the garden. In the spring and summer, we grow vegetables, too. There are some hens in the garden and we eat their eggs. There's only one problem – they love eating our vegetable seeds!

Lily, 12, United Kingdom

2 **Silvia's blog**

In my city, Buenos Aires, there are some amazing bakeries. You can buy a lot of different types of cakes there. There's a lot of *dulce de leche* in the cakes. I often go to a bakery after school with my friends. Cake is my favourite food.

Silvia, 11, Argentina

23 Read again and choose.

1 The floating market opens in the *morning / evening*.
2 You can buy *snakes / cakes* at the floating market.
3 Silvia *always / often* goes to a bakery after school.
4 In the summer, Lily's family grows *flowers / vegetables*.
5 Lily gets her fruit from the *garden / supermarket*.

PORTFOLIO

Think and talk.

Where do your classmates usually do the shopping? Do a survey.

OPTIONAL ACTIVITIES

Poster Groups research and find out more about the food people eat in Vietnam, the United Kingdom and Argentina. They write about what they learnt. They arrange their work in a poster.

Word game Play *Alphabet tennis*. See p. 300.
Photocopiable 2.7 See teacher's notes p. 289.

Lesson 9

Lesson aims
To review the unit language with a game
To use the Picture dictionary

Revision language
must/should
Adverbs of frequency

Materials
Audio CD

Optional activity materials
Dice; Wordcards (Adverbs of frequency); Active Teach; Digital Activity Book; Reading and Writing Booklet

Starting the lesson

- Choose two pupils with different personalities and ask them to talk about their routines and hobbies. Encourage the class to listen out for and compare the frequency words.

Pupil's Book page 30

24 Play the game.

- Give the class time to look at the pictures.
- Divide the class into groups of four and ask pupils to read the board game.
- Encourage the class to explain the rules to play the game.
- Give pupils time to play the game.
- Circulate, monitor and help.

Picture dictionary

- Pupils can do the picture dictionary of the unit on Activity Book page 105.
- Ask pupils to look at the pictures and try to write the vocabulary on their own in their notebooks. Then ask them to look for the words they don't remember in the Pupil's Book.
- As they finish, ask pupils to exchange notebooks to check answers. (Notebooks can be collected for checking.)

Activity Book page 26

23 Read and complete the conversations.

- Give pupils time to read the conversations and do the activity.
- Ask volunteers to read aloud for checking answers.

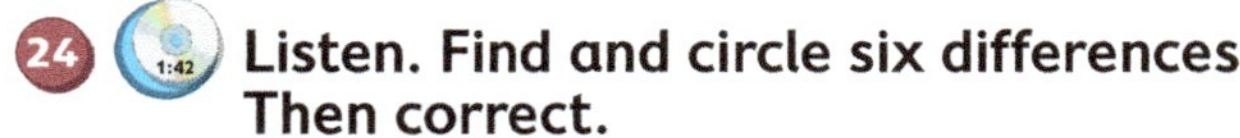

24 Listen. Find and circle six differences. Then correct.

- Give pupils time to read.
- Play the recording for pupils to listen.
- Give pupils time to read, circle and correct the differences.
- Play the recording again. Pause for pupils to say the six differences.

25 Write.

- Give pupils time to do the activity.
- Remind them about present simple third person singular.
- To check answers, you could ask volunteers to write the sentences on the board.

Ending the lesson

- Ask pupils to give their opinion about what the person in Actvity Book Activity 24 *should* write in his application form. For Answer Key see p. 96. For Audioscript see p. 98.

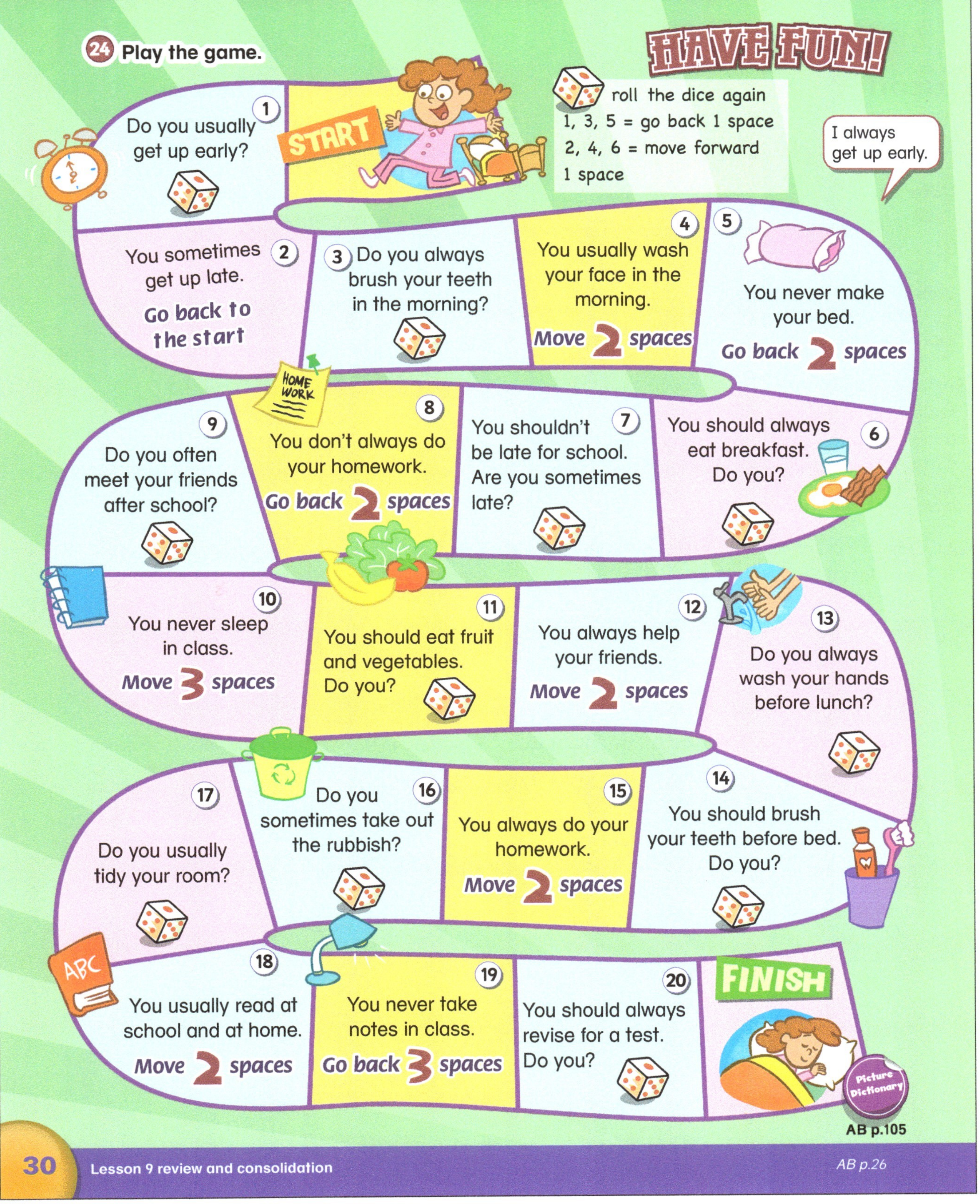

OPTIONAL ACTIVITIES

Frequency adverbs game Put all the frequency Wordcards in one bag. Ask a confident pupil to take one. They must make a sentence, e.g. *always/ I always come to school by car.*

Reading and Writing Booklet p. 8 See answer key p. 283.

Lesson 10

Lesson aims
To personalise and assess efforts

Materials
Audio CD

Optional activity materials
Online World; Active Teach; Digital Activity Book; Grammar Booklet; Test Booklet; Grammar reference (PB); Unit review (AB)

Starting the lesson

- Invite the class to think of these activities as a way to assess their work, in order to find out if they need extra work in any of the unit contents.

Pupil's Book page 31

25 Read and choose the right word.

- Give the class time to do the activity.
- Ask volunteers to read aloud their answers.

KEY
1 should, **2** always, **3** make, **4** on, **5** at

26 1:43 Look and say. Then listen and repeat.

- Ask one confident pupil to read the two first lines aloud.
- Give pupils time to do the activity in pairs.
- Play the recording for pupils to listen and repeat.

KEY
1 meet my friends **2** do their homework **3** tidies his room **4** washes her hair **5** make my bed **6** brush our teeth

27 Look and say six sentences.

- Give pupils time to read the activity.
- Encourage the class to give examples.
- Give pupils time to do the activity in pairs. Then ask volunteers to read their sentences.

Activity Book page 27

26 Read and match.

- Give pupils time to do the activity.
- Divide the class in two groups and alternately ask one group to read the definition and the other to say the correct word.

27 Unscramble and match.

- Give pupils time to write the sentences.
- Check the answers reading aloud. Then ask pupils to match.

28 Complete.

- Give pupils time to read and write.
- Read aloud and stop for the class to say the answers in chorus.

Ending the lesson

- Give pupils time to read the sentences in the 'I can' section in the Activity Book (p. 27).
- Ask pupils to think carefully about whether they are able to do the 'I can' points. Ask them what they found easy or difficult in the unit and why. For Answer Key see p. 96. For Audioscript see p. 98.

Online World Pupils can now go online to Ice Island and enjoy the fun and games.

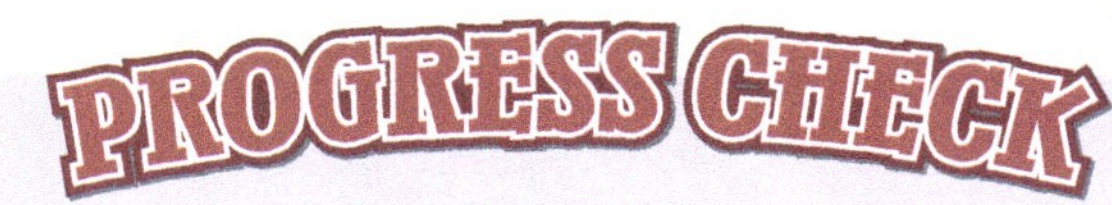

25 Read and choose the right word.

1 You (always / should) eat fruit and vegetables to help your body to digest your food better.
2 I (make / always) brush my teeth before going to bed.
3 She never has time to (should / make) her bed.
4 I've got my test (on / at) Monday.
5 I like helping (on / at) home.

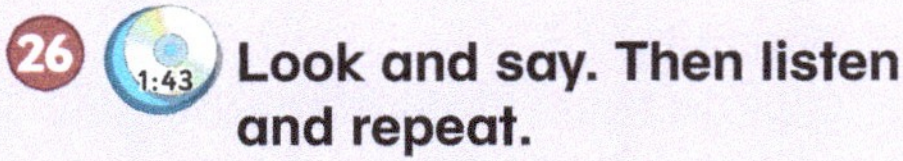

26 Look and say. Then listen and repeat.

my his her our their

In the evening, I sometimes meet my friends.

In the evening,…

1 I sometimes — *meet / friends*
2 Fergus and Ben always — *do / homework*
3 Fergus never — *tidy / room*
4 Mum often — *wash / hair*
5 I usually — *make / bed*
6 Ben and I always — *brush / teeth*

27 Look and say six sentences.

He
They

never

They never take out the rubbish but they often tidy the living room.

they often tidy the living room.
he's bald.
they never do their homework.
he never brushes his teeth.
he washes his face every morning.
they're lazy.

Ice Island

AB p.27

OPTIONAL ACTIVITIES

Quiz Prepare a quiz in a PowerPoint presentation or on the board to assess the class as a group.
Active Teach Pupils can watch the animated story Episode 1.

Grammar reference (PB p. 105) and Unit review (AB p. 97)
Test Booklet You may wish to give the Unit 2 test at this time.
Grammar Booklet p. 8 See answer key p. 285.

Activity Book Answer Key

p. 18, Activity 1
1 i **2** b **3** e **4** a **5** f **6** c **7** h **8** d **9** j **10** g

p. 18 Activity 2
1 brush my teeth **2** make my bed **3** take out the rubbish **4** on time **5** take notes **6** revise **7** meet my friends **8** tidy my room
KEY ✓ 1, 5, 6, 7

p. 19, Activity 4
1 Say good night to their parents. / Robbie and Emma
2 Wash her hair. / Emma
3 Brush his teeth. / Robbie
4 Walk the dog. / Dad
5 Turn off her mobile phone. / Mum

p. 19, Activity 6
1 Robbie and Emma must tidy their rooms.
2 Mum and Dad must take out the rubbish.
3 Maddy must practise the piano.
4 Dan must do his homework.

p. 20, Activity 7
2 always **3** sometimes **4** often/usually

p. 20, Activity 9
1 I go skateboarding on Tuesday.
2 I play football on Friday.
3 I ride my bicycle on Thursday.
4 I meet my friend on Monday.

p. 21, Activity 10
brush my teeth: every day **make my bed:** Tuesday and Thursday **do my homework:** Monday, Wednesday and Friday **set the table:** Monday, Wednesday, Thursday and Friday **take out the rubbish:** none of the days/never

p. 21, Activity 11
1 usually **2** often **3** sometimes **4** never **5** always

p. 22, Activity 12
1 six **2** breakfast **3** fish **4** reads **5** treasure **6** there

p. 22, Activity 13
2 He tidies his room at quarter past one.
3 He meets his friends at two o'clock.
4 He goes swimming at half past three.
5 He has dinner at quarter to eight.
6 He goes to bed at ten o'clock.

p. 23, Activity 15
a meets **b** reads **c** teaches **d** studies **e** writes **f** fetches

p. 23, Activity 16
/**s**/ picks, hops, waits /**z**/ smiles, rains, understands /**ɪz**/ crosses, fishes, washes

p. 23, Activity 18
1 goes **2** does **3** flies **4** studies

p. 24, Activity 19
1 chocolate **2** tastes **3** butter **4** salt **5** sugar **6** smells **7** stomach **8** pieces **9** to

p. 24, Activity 20
1 tongue **2** saliva **3** pancreas and liver **4** stomach

p. 24, Activity 21
1 a **2** d **3** c **4** e **5** b

p. 25, Activity 22
Buenos Aires/Argentina, (amazing) bakeries, cakes, lots of, often, bakery, cake

p. 26, Activity 23
1 a **2** a **3** c **4** a

p. 26, Activity 24
~~seven~~/ten, ~~eggs and toasts~~/chocolate and lemonade, ~~never~~/always, ~~football~~/computer games, ~~watch a film~~/have a shower, ~~nine~~/twelve. No, (not a healthy person).

p. 26, Activity 25
1 must go
2 watches/shouldn't watch
3 makes/should make

p. 27, Activity 26
1 c **2** e **3** a **4** b **5** d

p. 27 Activity 27
1 You must make your bed every day.
2 They should brush their teeth after breakfast.
3 We should help our parents tidy the house.
4 I must finish this homework before 10 p.m.
1 d, **2** b, **3** c, **4** a

p. 27, Activity 28
1 must **2** sometimes/always/often **3** dinner **4** help **5** do **6** always/often **7** often/sometimes **8** should

Audioscript

PB Lesson 1 page 22

Lesson 1, Activity 1, p. 22 CD1:27

Maddy = M Dan = D Mum = Mu

After school, Maddy meets her friends.

M Go away, Kipper!

In the afternoon, Emma and Dan do their homework. Maddy and Robbie play computer games.

D Oh no! Our homework.

M Go away, Kipper!

In the evening, Maddy brushes her teeth. Kipper wants to brush his teeth too.

M Go away, Kipper!

Before bed, Maddy does her homework.

M Oh, no. My homework is about Kipper! Kipper, where are you?

Lesson 1, Activity 2, p. 22 CD1:28

1 Brush my teeth.
2 Make my bed.
3 Wash my face.
4 Tidy my room.
5 Do my homework.
6 Meet my friends.
7 Revise for a test.
8 Take notes in class.
9 Take out the rubbish.
10 Be on time.

AB Lesson 1 page 18

Lesson 1, Activity 2, p. 18 (AB) CD1:29

I get up in the morning and I brush my teeth every day – in the morning and in the evening, too. I wash my face before school. I don't make my bed every day. I haven't got time! I don't go to bed in the afternoon. I meet my friends after school and then I do my homework before bed. I don't do my homework at breakfast! And I'm sorry but I don't tidy my room every day. No way!

PB Lesson 2 page 23

Lesson 2, Activity 4, p. 23 CD1:30

1 She must take out the rubbish.
2 She should wash her face.
3 She must do her homework.
4 She should brush her teeth.

AB Lesson 2 page 19

Lesson 2, Activity 4, p. 19 (AB) CD1:31

1 Robbie and Emma should say goodnight to their parents.
2 Emma should wash her hair.
3 Robbie should brush his teeth.
4 Dad should walk the dog.
5 Mum should turn off her mobile.

Lesson 2, Activity 6, p. 19 (AB) CD1:32

1 Robbie and Emma must tidy their rooms.
2 Mum and Dad must take out the rubbish.
3 Maddy must practise the piano.
4 Dan must do his homework.

PB Lesson 3 page 24

Lesson 3, Activity 7, p. 24 CD1:33

1 never
2 sometimes
3 usually
4 often
5 always

Lesson 3, Activity 8, p. 24 CD1:34

I always wash my face before school.
But I never brush my hair so I look cool.
I usually make my bed,
And I sometimes help my mum.
But I never, never tidy my room.
Never, never tidy my room.

My brother tidies his room.
My sister tidies her room.
My friends tidy their rooms,
But not me. Oh, no! Not me.
I never, never tidy my room.
Never, never tidy my room.

Where's my sister's kite? Is it under the bed?
And on the chair, what's that? A monster's head!
My brother's ball is here, too.
But where is it? Well, I don't know.
Because I never, never tidy my room.
Never, never tidy my room.
Never, never tidy my room.

PB Lesson 4 page 25

Lesson 4, Activity 12, p. 25 CD1:35

Woman = W Emma = E

W Do you get up on time in the morning?
E No, never. I love my bed!
W Do you make your bed in the morning?
E Yes, sometimes. But I haven't always got time to make my bed.
W Do you have a big breakfast?
E No, never. I drink juice and I sometimes eat an apple but I don't like big breakfasts.
W Do you make your family's breakfast?
E No, never. I sometimes help in the kitchen in the evening but never in the morning.
W Do you talk to your friends and family before school?
E Yes, sometimes but not usually. I don't like talking in the morning.
W Do you get to school on time?
E I often get to school on time but not always!

AB Lesson 4 page 21

Lesson 4, Activity 10, p. 21 (AB) CD1:36

I always brush my teeth before going to school and at night. Of course I do this every day. I should make my bed every day but I only do it on Tuesday and Thursday. I do my homework after dinner on Monday, Wednesday and Friday. My brother sets the table on Tuesday but I set it on Monday, Wednesday, Thursday and Friday. Sometimes I tidy my room, but I never take out the rubbish – that's Dad's job!

PB Lesson 5 page 26

Lesson 5, Activity 14, p. 26 CD1:37

Captain Formosa = C Finn = F

C I always get up at six and I have my breakfast.
C I give some fish to the penguins and I read my map.
F Your map?
C It's a treasure map of Ice Island!
C But it isn't here. Look!
C What do you want, Penn?
F I can see them! They're escaping! And they've got the Captain's map!

PB Lesson 6 page 27

Lesson 6, Activity 15, p. 27 CD1:38

1 works
2 watches
3 sits
4 brushes
5 stops
6 misses
7 plays
8 goes
9 studies
10 helps
11 buzzes
12 cooks
13 fixes
14 ends

Lesson 6, Activity 16, p. 27 CD1:39

/s/ /z/ /ɪz/

Lesson 6, Activity 18, p. 27 CD1:40

She goes home and does her homework.
She washes her hair and nose.
But she never brushes her cats.

AB Lesson 6 page 23

Lesson 6, Activity 15, p. 23 (AB) CD1:41

1 She often meets her friend after school.
2 He reads about Poland in the school library.
3 She teaches Maths to my sister.
4 Emma studies her notes for the test.
5 He always writes emails to me.
6 The dog fetches the ball.

AB Lesson 9 page 26

Lesson 9, Activity 24, p. 26 (AB) CD1:42

I get up at ten o'clock.
I have chocolate and lemonade for breakfast.
I never brush my teeth after breakfast.
I often play computer games in the afternoon.
After that, I watch a film, eat dinner, and I go to bed at twelve o'clock.

PB Lesson 10 page 31

Lesson 10, Activity 26, p. 31 CD1:43

1 In the evening, I sometimes meet my friends.
2 In the evening, Fergus and Ben always do their homework.
3 In the evening, Fergus never tidies his room.
4 In the evening, Mum often washes her hair.
5 In the evening, I usually make my bed.
6 In the evening, Ben and I always brush our teeth.

3 Free time

Objectives

- talk about free time activities and hobbies
- describe abilities and say how well you can do things
- talk about what people were doing in the past
- use an accurate intonation for questions and answers
- talk about your preferences

Language

Vocabulary

Hobbies: hitting, kicking, throwing, catching, diving, going shopping, telling jokes, reading poetry, playing video games, trampolining, playing chess, acting, playing the drums, running races, singing karaoke, rollerblading, reading magazines, drawing, skateboarding

Free time activities and sports: ski, score, team, player, bicycle, go out, programme, swing, sledge, snowball, snowman

Structures

What is she good at? She is good at ...+*ing*

What were you doing yesterday at 7.00? I was going to school.

Were you going to school? Yes, I was. / No, I wasn't.

Do you prefer acting or singing in the play? I prefer dancing to singing./ I'd rather dance, but not sing.

Revision

climbing. What does she like/love/hate doing? She likes/loves going shopping

Receptive language

be good/not good at ..., time expressions, *Wh*- question words, polar bear, be careful, dangerous, thieves

CLIL and Wider world language

CLIL (Graphing favourite hobbies): score, team, graph, calculate, range, highest, lowest

Wider world (Funny sports in other countries)

Phonics

Questions and answers intonation blending words

Topics

- hobbies and abilities
- actions in the past
- funny sports

Values

Try new things. Have a hobby.

Stories

- Is Robbie good at throwing?
- Island mystery: chapter 3

Song

Fun club.

Socio-cultural aspects

- finding out about other people's hobbies
- finding out about funny sports around the world
- working in pairs

Learning strategies

- making use of prior knowledge
- following instructions
- recording new words
- using a graph to organise information
- critical thinking: discriminating and classifying
- critical thinking: making personal decisions
- collaborative learning
- integrating contents: discussing and approaching new cultures
- reflecting on learning and self assessment

Cross-curricular contents

Maths: graphing hobbies

Music: song, pronunciation rhyme

Language skills: reading a story, acting out, telling a story

Basic competences

Linguistic communication: Use language as an instrument for communication (L.1 to L.10).
Knowledge and interaction with the physical world: Talk about funny sports and unusual forms of exercise (L.8).
Mathematical competence: Tell the time (L.4) Draw and interpret graphs (L.7).
Processing information and digital competence: Use Active Teach, Digital Activity Book and Ice Island Online World
Social and civic competence: Conduct a survey. Be aware of other people's preferences (L.7).
Cultural and artistic competence: Talk about physical activities in other countries (L.8) Talk about the importance of hobbies (L.5).
Learning to learn: Reflect on what has been learnt and self evaluate progress (L.10).
Autonomy and personal initiative: Use own judgement and ideas and further develop social skills (L.1 to L.10).

Skills

Listening
- can understand people talking about hobbies, abilities and preferences
- can understand a dialogue about hobbies and abilities
- can understand questions about hobbies, abilities and preferences
- can understand people talking about what they were doing in the past at a particular time
- can understand a graph
- can understand a song about abilities
- can understand a pronunciation rhyme

Reading
- can read and understand personal information (about hobbies, abilities and preferences) in sentences, short paragraphs and texts
- can read and understand what people were doing in the past at a particular time in sentences, short paragraphs and texts
- can read and understand a cartoon strip story, captions and speech bubbles
- can read and understand factual information about funny sports around the world
- can read and understand factual information from a graph on hobbies

Speaking
- can give personal information about hobbies, abilities and preferences
- can talk about what people were doing in the past at a time
- can sing the *Fun Club* song
- can talk about a graph
- can talk about a personal decision
- can say the pronunciation rhyme

Taking part in conversations
- can ask and respond to questions about hobbies, abilities and preferences
- can ask and respond to questions about other people's hobbies, abilities and preferences
- can take part in a dialogue about hobbies, abilities and preferences
- can ask and respond to questions about what people were doing in the past at a particular time
- can ask and respond to factual questions about a graph on hobbies

Writing
- can write hobby, ability and preference words
- can complete sentences to write personal information about hobbies, abilities and preferences
- can write sentences about their own hobbies, abilities and preferences
- can write questions about daily hobbies, abilities and preferences
- can write sentences using the past continuous tense to talk about what someone was doing in the past at a particular time
- can create a graph about hobbies
- can write a short text to describe someone's hobbies, abilities and preferences

Classroom ideas

- Use the CLIL poster of the unit to decorate the class.
- Use posters of famous people who are good at certain activities and have certain hobbies to decorate the class.
- You or your pupils could use the websites below to access more information about funny sports in different countries around the world: http://pbskids.org/kws/sports/ http://questgarden.com/105/01/5/100616061732/index.htm
- Play games from the Games Bank.
- Photocopiables 3.1–3.7.

Take-home English

- Letters for parents. When you begin Unit 3, complete and give pupils a copy of the letter for the unit (Active Teach). This explains what pupils are going to learn in this unit.
- Home-School Link. Encourage pupils to talk to their families about what they did the previous evening. (L.5)
- Grammar Booklet and Reading and Writing Booklet. Pupils take these home to show their parents
- Pupils' Digital Activity Books.
- Portfolios. Encourage pupils to take their portfolio files home to show their parents when they finish Unit 3.

Evaluation

Self assessment
- Pupils can talk about hobbies and abilities
- Pupils can talk about what they were doing in the past
- Pupils can express their preferences
- Pupil's Book page 41
- Activity Book page 37
- Grammar reference (Pupil's Book page 106)

Resources
- Unit review (Activity Book page 98)
- Picture dictionary (Activity Book page 106)
- Test Booklet – Unit 3 (pages 14 –17)
- Grammar Booklet (pages 9–12) and Reading and Writing Booklet – Unit 3 (pages 9–12)

3 Free time

Lesson 1

Lesson aims
To learn and practise new vocabulary about hobbies

Target language
hitting, kicking, throwing, catching, diving, going shopping, telling jokes, reading poetry, playing video games, playing golf, playing volleyball

Receptive language
be good/not good at ...

Materials
Audio CD; Flashcards and Wordcards (Hobbies and activities)

Optional activity material
Internet/magazine photos of known sports and free time activities; a simple drawing of each of the new action words (one picture per A4 page); Active Teach; Digital Activity Book; Photocopiable 3.1

Starting the lesson

- Using photos, revise the names of known sports and free time activities, e.g. *fishing, snorkelling, sailing.*
- Ask what pupils do in their free time. Encourage them to use the language they have learnt in Units 1 and 2, e.g. *I usually go swimming after school.*

Presentation

- Present the vocabulary using the flashcards (hobbies and activities). Hold up each flashcard in turn and say the word for pupils to repeat. Hold up the flashcards in a different order for pupils to repeat again.

Pupil's Book page 32

1  Listen and read. Is Robbie good at throwing?

- Ask *Who can you see in the pictures? (Robbie, Emma, Kipper and a bird.) Where are they? (At home in the garden.)*
- Play the recording. Pupils listen, follow the story and find the answer to the question.
- Divide the class into two. Tell half the class they are Emma and the others that they are Robbie. Play the recording again, pausing for pupils to repeat their lines. Swap roles.

KEY No, he isn't.

2 Listen and repeat.

- Give pupils time to look at the pictures.
- Play the recording. Pause for pupils to repeat.
- Play the recording again, pausing after each word so that pupils can say the words and mime the actions.

3   Listen and point to the words in Activity 2.

- Play the recording. Pause for pupils to find and point.
- Play the recording again, pausing after each word so that pupils can say the actions.

KEY
1 reading poetry **2** diving **3** hitting **4** going shopping
5 throwing **6** catching **7** playing video games
8 kicking a ball **9** telling jokes

Practice

Activity Book page 28

1 Match. Then draw the missing picture.

- Give pupils time to match.
- To check answers, you could ask volunteers to read their sentences.

2 Write.

- Give pupils time to do the activity.
- Volunteers read their writings.

3  Look at Activity 2. Listen and circle. Who is talking?

- Explain that pupils must identify Robbie or Dan from the recording.
- Play the recording and allow pupils to circulate. Count 1, 2, 3 and ask the class to say the right name in chorus.
- After you've checked the answer, pupils close their Activity Books. Play the recording again. Pause after *good at/not good at* and try to elicit the action words.

Ending the lesson

- Stick the action word pictures you've prepared on the board.
- Divide the class into three or four teams. Each team chooses one runner.
- Say an action word. The first runner to run to and touch the correct picture wins a point. Teams change runners after each go. For Answer Key see p. 122. For Audioscript see p. 124.

3 Free time

1 1:44 **Listen and read. Is Robbie good at throwing?**

2 1:45 **Listen and repeat.**

3 1:46 **Listen and point to the words in Activity 2.**

OPTIONAL ACTIVITIES

Caption competition Pairs draw a fifth cartoon picture to continue the story in Pupil's Book Activity 1 and write a caption. Tell pupils they must include at least two of the new action words they have learnt this lesson. Pairs show their work to the class and read out the captions. Take a class vote to decide on the best caption.

Writing Write on the board *I'm Maddy. I'm good at … /I'm not good at … . I'm Emma. I'm good at … /I'm not good at … .* Pairs finish the sentences using the action words from this lesson or other vocabulary they know. Volunteers read their sentences to the class.

Photocopiable 3.1 See teacher's notes p. 289.

Lesson 2

Lesson aims
To revise the Lesson 1 vocabulary; to use +*ing* to say what you are good at

Target language
Be good at +*ing*

Materials
Audio CD; Flashcards and Wordcards (Hobbies and activities)

Optional activity material
Active Teach; Digital Activity Book; Grammar Booklet

Starting the lesson

- Ask pupils if they have ever been to a circus. If this is unlikely in your country, ask if they have seen one on TV. Ask *What can you see at the circus?* Encourage them to use any English words they know, e.g. the names of animals.

Presentation

- Display the flashcards (hobbies and activities), learnt in Lesson 1, around the room and play *I spy* (see p. 300). Ask individual pupils to come and write the words on the board.
- Ask the class to silently read the Look! box.
- Read the Look! Box out loud. Pause for pupils to repeat.
- Remind pupils we use +*ing* form of verbs after the expression *be good at*.

Pupil's Book page 33

4  Listen and read. Then look and match.

- Give the class time to look at the pictures.
- Play the recording, pausing for pupils to find the correct picture.
- Play the recording again; pausing for pupils to say the full sentence, e.g. *She's good at diving.*

KEY **1** a **2** d **3** e **4** c **5** f **6** b

5 Look at the picture in Activity 4. Ask and answer.

- Perform the example with a confident pupil.
- Give pupils time to do the activity in pairs.
- Ask pupils to close their books and divide the class into two groups. Read aloud the beginning of the sentences in Activity 4. Ask one pupil in each group to finish them, e.g. *'A' is good at ... / ... diving.* The faster pupil wins the point.

Practice

6 What are you good at? Answer using words from Activity 4.

- Ask two confident pupils to read the example dialogue.
- Give pupils time to do the activity in pairs. Then ask a few pairs to do it aloud.

Activity Book page 29

4 Look and write.

- Give pupils time to look at the cartoon and to complete the gaps.
- Pupils compare answers.

5 Write questions. Then circle for yourself.

- Elicit the action words before you give pupils time to write the questions, e.g. *What's number 2? (Climbing) What's number 4? (Diving)*
- Check pupils' work before you give pairs time to ask, answer and circle.

6 Write about your friends. What do they like doing?

- Give pupils time to do the activity.
- Ask fast finishers to write about another partner. They ask each other two or three questions from Activity 5 and write the answers in their notebooks.
- Encourage pupils to ask their partners to check and comment (constructively!) on their work.

Ending the lesson

- Ask confident pupils to talk about what they are/are not good at doing, and what they like/don't like doing. Then ask the others about what their classmates are saying, which of the actions they think are easy and which are difficult for them, e.g. *Is dancing easy for you? Is riding difficult for you?* For Answer Key see p. 122. For Audioscript see p. 124.

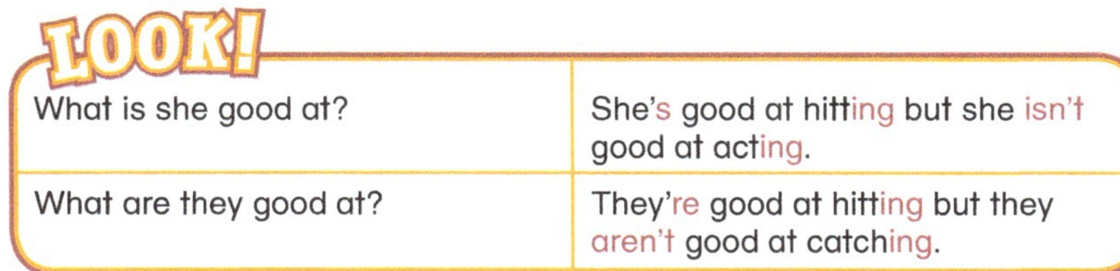

LOOK!

What is she good at?	She's good at hitting but she isn't good at acting.
What are they good at?	They're good at hitting but they aren't good at catching.

4 Listen and read. Then look and match.

1:48

1 She's good at diving.
2 He's good at throwing.
3 She isn't good at dancing.
4 They aren't good at climbing.
5 He isn't good at hitting.
6 They're good at riding.

5 Look at the picture in Activity 4. Ask and answer.

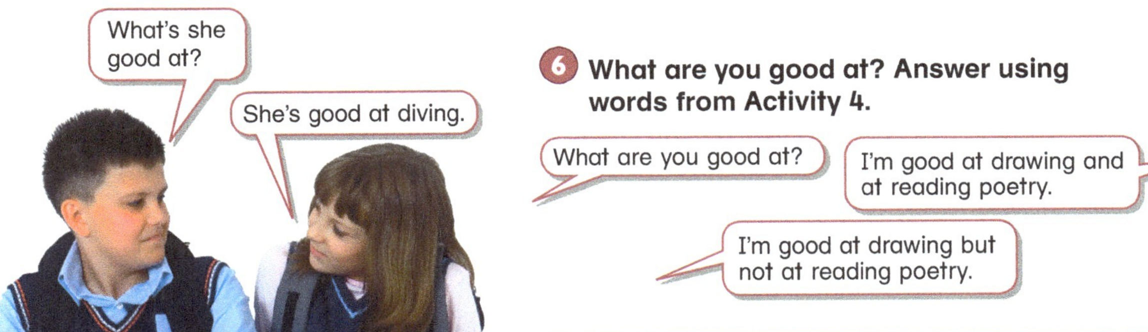

6 What are you good at? Answer using words from Activity 4.

What are you good at?

I'm good at drawing and at reading poetry.

I'm good at drawing but not at reading poetry.

OPTIONAL ACTIVITIES

Guessing game
Write on the board *nationality/sport/description/good at?* Give pupils time to choose a favourite sports star. Invite volunteers to tell the class about their star, using the prompts on the board. Help with vocabulary where necessary. The class guess who it is, e.g. *He's from Switzerland. He plays tennis. He's tall and good-looking. He's very good at hitting. I think he's good at running, too. Who is he? (Roger Federer.)*

Whispers Play *Whispers* see p. 300.

Grammar Booklet p. 9 See answer key p. 285.

Lesson 3

Lesson aims
To extend the vocabulary of action words; to practise the unit vocabulary with a song

Target language
trampolining, playing chess, playing the drums, acting, rollerblading, running races, singing karaoke, skateboarding, reading magazines, drawing

Materials
Audio CD; Flashcards and Wordcards (Hobbies and activities; Graphing hobbies)

Optional activity materials
Active Teach; Digital Activity Book; Photocopiable 3.2; Photocopiable 3.3; Reading and Writing Booklet

Starting the lesson

- Ask *Are you good at throwing?* Pupils who are good at throwing stand up. Continue with other action words.

Presentation

- Introduce the new words using the flashcards. Hold them up and say the words for pupils to repeat.
- Put the flashcards on the board. Point to the different flashcards and ask the class to say the words.

Pupil's Book page 34

  **Listen and repeat.**

- Give pupils time to look at the pictures.
- Play the recording. Pause for pupils to find and say each word.
- Play the recording again. Repeat each word. Pupils repeat in chorus miming the hobbies.

Song

  **Listen and sing.**

- Play the song. Pupils follow in their books.
- Play the song again. Encourage pupils to sing.
- Have a competition. Divide the class into two groups. Play the song twice more, each group singing in turn. Decide which group is best!
- You can now play the karaoke song (Active Teach).

Practice

9 Ask and answer. Play a memory game.

- Pupils look at the example dialogue while you read it with a volunteer. The game continues until one of you can't remember the other's sentence. You must both get the order right!
- Pupils play the game in pairs, two groups or whole group.

Activity Book page 30

7 Make a wordsearch using the words in the box. Then swap it with a classmate.

- Read the words in the box before pupils do the activity.
- Give pupils time to swap and complete their classmate's wordsearch.

8 Write. Are you good at …?

- Draw pupils' attention to the key on the right (to be good at/not to be good at).
- Ask a volunteer to do one example.
- Give pupils time to do the activity.
- Volunteers read their sentences to the class.

Ending the lesson

- Ask the class *Are you good at kicking a ball? Yes, I'm good at kicking the ball because I love football. / No, I'm not good at kicking a ball and I hate football!* For Answer Key see p. 122. For Audioscript see p. 124.

7 1:49 **Listen and repeat.**

1 trampolining
2 playing chess
3 playing the drums
4 acting
5 rollerblading
6 running races
7 singing karaoke
8 skateboarding
9 reading magazines
10 drawing

8 1:50 **Listen and sing.** SONG

Chorus:
Come and have fun at the Fun Club. Come here and meet new friends.
Drawing, trampolining, rollerblading, At the Fun Club, the fun never ends.
What do you like doing?
Do you like playing the drums? Or skateboarding or acting?
There's fun for everyone.
What are you good at? Are you good at playing chess?
We love Fun Club! It's fun here. Yes! Yes! Yes!
Chorus

9 **Ask and answer. Play a memory game.**

I'm good at trampolining. What are you good at?

She is good at trampolining and I'm good at acting. What are you good at?

They are good at trampolining and acting. I'm good at…

34 Lesson 3 vocabulary (hobbies) AB p.30

OPTIONAL ACTIVITIES

Pair work In pairs, pupils tell each other which activities from the lesson they like, love or hate. Volunteers tell the class about their partner.
Class survey Organise a class survey to find out which activities are the most popular. Help groups of four draw a pie chart showing the results.

Photocopiable 3.2 See teacher's notes p. 289.
Photocopiable 3.3 See teacher's notes p. 289.
Reading and Writing Booklet pp. 9–10
See answer key p. 283.

Lesson 4

Lesson aims
To revise vocabulary; to learn and practise the use of the past continuous

Target language
Past continuous questions and answers

Receptive language
Time expressions; *Wh-* words

Materials
Audio CD

Optional activity materials
Active Teach; Digital Activity Book; Grammar Booklet

Starting the lesson

- Write on the board ... *yesterday at 18.00* ...
- Ask the class to think about it. Then encourage them to say *I was watching TV yesterday at six* or *Yesterday at six I was doing my homework.*
- Now write on the board *What were you doing yesterday at ...?* Encourage the class to make questions changing the time.

Presentation

Skills

- Ask the class to silently read the Look! box.
- Then read it out loud. Pause after each line for pupils to repeat the sentences.
- Remind pupils we use **past continuous** to talk about actions that were in progress in the past.
- Remind pupils that we answer open questions (*Wh-* words) with specific information and we answer closed questions with *yes* or *no*. Give them examples.

Pupil's Book page 35

10 Listen and point. Then ask and answer.

- Give pairs time to read the table.
- Play the recording. Give pupils time to point.

KEY
1 2.45 Robbie was studying English; Emma was playing volleyball; Maddy and Dan were drawing pictures
2 5.00 Robbie was reading comic books; Emma was shopping; Maddy and Dan were acting

- Pupils look at the example dialogue while you read it with a volunteer.
- Give pupils time to do the activity in pairs.

Practice

11 Listen and match. Then ask and answer.

- Give pupils time to read before they listen.
- Play the recording. Pupils work in pairs to ask and answer questions about what the characters were doing when.
- Play the recording again to check answers.

KEY
Dan and Maddie 7.00 walking to school, 10.00 swimming, 11.00 reading, 12.00 having lunch
Robbie 7.00 sleeping, 10.00 rollerblading, 11.00 doing a project, 12.00 having lunch
Emma 7.00 having breakfast, 10.00 writing a story, 11.00 playing chess, 12.00 having lunch

- Pupils look at the example dialogue while you read it with a volunteer.
- Give pupils time to do the activity in pairs.

Activity Book page 31

9 Write.

- Ask pupils to look at the table and read.
- Give pupils time to do the activity.
- Pupils check and correct in pairs. At the end, ask a pair to read the answers aloud.

10 Write. Then look at the table in Activity 9 and circle the correct answer.

- Ask pupils closed questions about Robbie, Emma, Maddy and Dan. Remind them how to form short answers with the simple past of *to be* (*Yes, I was / No, I wasn't. Yes, you were / No, you weren't.* etc).
- Give pupils time to do the activity.
- Pupils check and correct in pairs.

Ending the lesson

- Volunteers ask their classmates what they were doing yesterday at a specific time. For Answer Key see p. 122. For Audioscript see p. 124.

Pupils can now, or at the end of this unit, go online to Ice Island and find the ski poles that Penn and Gwyn are holding. They are outside the observatory, the set to the right of the entrance. Once pupils click on the ski poles they are taken to a supplementary language game based on the vocabulary in this unit.

LOOK!

What were you doing yesterday at 7:00?	I was going to school.
What was he/she doing yesterday at 7:00?	He/She was going to school.
What were they doing yesterday at 7:00?	They were going to school.
Were you going to school?	Yes, I was. / No, I wasn't.
Was he/she going to school?	Yes, he/she was. / No, he/she wasn't.
Were they going to school?	Yes, they were. / No, they weren't.

10 1:51 **Listen and point. Then ask and answer.**

P.M.	Robbie	Emma	Maddy and Dan
2:45	studying English	playing volleyball	reading in the classroom
	singing in music class	trampolining	drawing pictures
5:00	playing chess at school	shopping	doing their homework
	reading comic books	playing video games	acting

What was Robbie doing yesterday at 2:45?

He was studying English.

11 1:52 **Listen and match. Then ask and answer.**

What was Robbie doing yesterday at 7:00?

He was ….

3

1	2	3
7:00 sleeping	10:00 rollerblading	12:00 having lunch
11:00 doing a project	7:00 walking to school	10:00 swimming
12:00 having lunch	11:00 playing chess	11:00 reading in class
7:00 having breakfast	10:00 writing a story	12:00 having lunch

OPTIONAL ACTIVITIES

Guessing game Pupils draw themselves doing an action they were doing at nine o'clock yesterday: *I was having dinner; I was having a shower*, etc. Collect all the drawings and put them in a bag. Take one and show it to the class. *Who was having a shower yesterday at nine?* The one who guesses first takes another card and continues the game. Alternatively, take two drawings so that pupils can practise the plural form *were +ing*. Then encourage your pupils to ask closed questions *Were you having a shower yesterday at nine?* The pupil answers and shows his/her drawing.

Grammar Booklet p. 10 See answer key p. 285.

Lesson 5

Lesson aims
To consolidate the unit language with a story

Values
Try new things. Have a hobby.

Receptive language
polar bear, be careful, dangerous, thieves

Materials
Audio CD

Optional activity materials
Realia associated with the sports and activities in the unit; a large non-transparent bag; Active Teach; Digital Activity Book; Photocopiable 3.4

Starting the lesson

- Ask the class what happened in the last episode.
- Divide pupils into teams.
- Write on the board *are/aren't good at climbing, at fishing, at reading, at running, at singing.*
- Teams take it in turns to ask, e.g. *Are polar bears good at fishing?* Pass incorrect statements to the next team to win a bonus point. *Yes, they are. They like fishing in the ice. Are polar bears good at singing? No, they aren't. They can't sing!*

Presentation

Pupil's Book page 36

- Ask the class questions about each picture and teach some of the new language using the pictures. Pupils answer or guess, e.g.
  (Picture 1) *What can you see? (The children, Dr Al, a telescope.)*
  (Picture 2) *Who can you see? (Finn.) What's he doing?* (Pupils look and guess.)
  (Picture 3) *What can you see? (Polar bears.)*
  (Pictures 4 and 5) *What are the polar bears doing? (Climbing, reading.)*
  (Picture 6) *Who's running? (The polar bears/Ivan and Rufus.)*
  (Picture 7) *What's Finn doing? (He's snowboarding.)*
  (Picture 8) *Who is under the snow? (Finn)*

12 Look at the pictures. Tell the story.

- Ask the class to look again at the pictures.
- Ask seven volunteers to go in front of the class and tell the story based on just looking at the pictures, without reading. Each pupil tells the story of one picture.

13 1:53 Listen and read. Then act out.

- Play the recording. Pupils listen and follow the story.

Practice

- Ask the class about the story, e.g. *Who's watching polar bears? (Finn.) Are polar bears dangerous? (They can be.) Can they stand up? (Yes, they can.) Are the polar bears in the story reading? (Yes, they are.) Who says 'Finn! They aren't polar bears!' (Dylan.) The polar bears are ...* (elicit) *(Rufus and Ivan.) Who can't stop? (Finn.)*
- Play the recording again. Pause for the class to repeat each line in chorus.
- Divide the class into three and allocate these roles: Finn, Dylan and Jenny. Play the recording again. Pause for pupils to repeat their character's lines.
- Ask eight volunteers to act out the story (Dr Al, Finn, Dylan, Jenny, two polar bears/Rufus and Ivan, Penn and Gwyn).
- Take a class vote for the best actor/actress.
- Pairs predict what happens next then tell the class their ideas. Take a vote to find the most popular idea.

Values

- Ask the class to talk about their hobbies.
- Help them realise that it is important to try new things to know if they like them or not and if they are good at them or not.
- Ask the class what they are not good at but would like to be good at. *What do they need to do to achieve your goal?* e.g. *It's important to practise a lot.*

Home-School Link

- Ask pupils to tell their family what they were doing yesterday evening.

Activity Book page 32

11 Look. Then write. Are they good at ...?

- Give pupils time to do the activity. Remind them to write *+ing* form of verbs after the expressions *be good at* and *like, love, hate.*
- If your class needs support, remind pupils of the present simple third person singular *is/isn't*. If necessary, ask them closed questions, e.g. *Is the bear good at diving? Yes, he is! Is the bear good at riding the bike? No, he isn't.*

12 What happens next? Imagine.

- Give pupils time to think and write.
- Ask volunteers to tell the class their ideas and take a vote to find the most popular idea.

13 Read and complete the conversation.

- Give pupils time to do the activity.
- Ask fast finishers to practise the dialogue.
- Check the answers asking different pairs to read aloud.

Ending the lesson

- Ask *Are Rufus and Ivan clever? Why (not)?* For Answer Key see p. 122. For Audioscript see p. 124.

12 Look at the pictures. Tell the story.

13 Listen and read. Then act out.

VALUES

Try new things. Have a hobby.

HOME-SCHOOL LINK PARENT

Tell your family what you were doing yesterday evening.

OPTIONAL ACTIVITIES

Touch and guess game Play *Touch and guess* with the class using realia from home. See p. 301. Instead of naming the objects, pupils have to name the activity/sport each is associated with.

Drawing game Play *Pictionary* using the activity words from the unit. See p. 300.

Photocopiable 3.4 See teacher's notes p. 289.

Lesson 6

Lesson aims
To identify and practise rising intonation in questions and falling intonation in answers

Materials
Audio CD; Phonics and spelling poster

Optional activity materials
Sentence strips, a ball of wool/string; Active Teach; Digital Activity Book; Photocopiable 3.5

Starting the lesson

- Write questions and answers on the board.
- Read the sentences from the third picture aloud and ask pupils to find a common pattern.

Presentation

- Show the Phonics and spelling poster (see teacher's notes on p. 26).
- State the goal of the lesson.
- Explain that intonation is the rising or falling pitch in the speaker's voice as he/she says words or phrases. In English we change intonation to differentiate questions and answers or express how we feel.
- Model intonation with a piece of yarn. Then pass a piece to each pupil. Ask them to stretch it out horizontally on their tables as you reread the sentences. Point out if the intonation is going up, their string should go up as well. The same, going down, for falling intonation.

Pupil's Book page 37

14  Listen and repeat.

- Invite pupils to show the right intonation by pointing up or down.
- Play the recording for pupils to repeat the words chorally, pointing up or down to show the intonation.

15 Listen and read. Then repeat.

- Give pupils time to look at the speech bubbles.
- Play the recording. Pause for pupils to listen and read.
- Encourage volunteers to repeat the question and answers. Ask the pupils to point up or down, according to their intonation. Also, point out the stressed words by clapping.

16 Read and practise with a partner. Point up or down.

- Model the first question and answer. Invite pupils to clap when they hear the stress in the highlighted words in the sentence and point up or down depending on the intonation.
- Give pupils time to do the activity in pairs.
- Ask fast finishers to practise this skill with their own questions and answers.
- Encourage pupils to read aloud. Point out that all the practised questions are *Yes/No* questions.

KEY All questions with raised intonation – all answers with falling intonation.

  Listen and repeat.

- Give pupils time to look at the pictures.
- Play the recording. Then ask pupils to repeat with the correct intonation.
- Play the recording again. Encourage the class to learn and repeat the rhyme.

Practice

Activity Book page 33

  Listen and circle.

- Read the first sentence aloud and ask pupils to point up or down.
- Play the recording. Then give pupils time to complete the activity.
- Read each sentence chorally to correct the activity.

15 Complete the sentences. Then circle.

- Read aloud the first sentence. Ask the class to find the word with the final /ə/ sound.
- Give pupils time to complete the activity.
- Check the activity as a whole-group discussion. Ask the class to make up a sentence with the remaining word from the word bank: *loves*.

16 Write four sentences and four answers. Then circle.

- Encourage the class to make up their own sentences orally.
- Write some sentence starters on the board to provide support for all learners. Point out the punctuation of question and statements.
- Give pupils time to do the activity.
- Ask volunteers to read their sentences.

Ending the lesson

- Review the lesson objectives and ask pupils to evaluate their own progress. For Answer Key see p. 122. For Audioscript see p. 124.

Intonation: Questions and answers.

Questions have rising intonation ↗
Answers have neutral or falling intonation. ↘

14  **Listen and repeat.**

Question ↗ Answer ↘

15  **Listen and read. Then repeat.**

1
Do you like music?
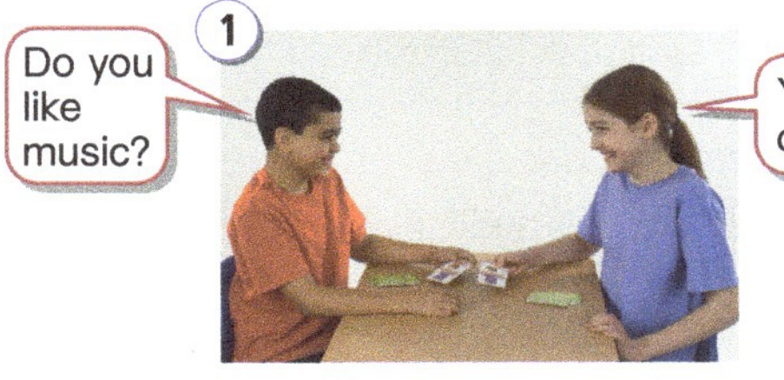
Yes, I do. I love classical music.

2
Yes, she is.

Is she coming to the picnic?

3
Can she dance?
Yes, she can. She practises every day.

4
Can they play golf today?

No, they can't. They are busy at school.

16 **Read and practise with a partner. Point up or down.**

Questions	Answers
Are you good at playing catch?	Yes, I am. I'm good at playing catch.
Do you play any other sports?	Yes, I do.
Is she going fishing?	No, she isn't. She doesn't like it.
Can I see your video games?	I'm sorry. They're at home.
Did he go to the cinema yesterday?	Yes, I think so.

17 **Listen and repeat.**

SOUNDS FUN!

Where's the bear with the spiky hair?
It's there, under your chair!

OPTIONAL ACTIVITIES

Art Gallery Use sentence strips and the wool/string to record the sentences that pupils wrote on AB page 33, Activity 16. Glue the wool/string on top to show the right intonation of each sentence. Display the sentences to share the learning.

Photocopiable 3.5 See teacher's notes p. 289.

Lesson 7

Lesson aims
To extend the vocabulary on activities; to learn and practise the use of *rather, prefer*

Cross-curricular focus
Maths – Creating a graph of our favourite hobbies

Materials
Audio CD; CLIL poster

Optional activity materials
Family pictures or photographs; Active Teach; Digital Activity Book; Photocopiable 3.6; Reading and Writing Booklet; Grammar Booklet

Starting the lesson

- People use graphs to display information visually. Graphs can show information very quickly.
- Graphs take many forms. There are bar graphs, pie charts and line graphs.
- Graphs are used to show the results of data collection (surveys).

Presentation

- Ask the class what their favourite hobbies are. Allow some STT in pairs.
- Ask every pupil to share and tally their answers on the board. Use their results to introduce the new structure.
- Explain the use of *to* in the sentences using *prefer. The class prefers X to Y.*
- Explain the use of *would* with *rather. Three students would rather read ….*
- Before reading, give pupils time to look at the pictures on page 38. Ask them *What can you see? What do you think this text is going to be about?*
- Share the background information from the Starting the lesson section.
- Use the vocabulary routine to present the new vocabulary: **mime and define**. Next, **use each adjective in a sentence**. Last, **ask questions** with each word.

Pupil's Book page 38

18 Read and find the correct graphs. Then find these words in the texts.

- Read the title and the introduction to the text.
- Set purpose for reading: *Let's read and find the graph that has the same information.*
- Read the whole text as a shared reading experience.
- Give pupils time to complete the activity.

KEY **1** Graph a **2** Graph c **3** Graph b

Practice

19 Look at Activity 18. Ask and answer.

- Complete the activity as a whole-group discussion.

KEY
1 volleyball, going out/meeting friends, skiing; **2** following football scores on TV, playing on the swings, hockey **3** Skiing **4** following football scores on TV **5** Graph a 9, Graph b 9, Graph c 8

- Make connections between the results on the board and the graphs in the book. *Can any of the graphs show the favourite hobbies of your class? Why? (not?)*

20 Talk to your partner.

- Allow some STT so that pupils can work in pairs.
- Encourage one or two volunteers to share what they have discussed with the class.
- Ask pupils to think about the following question about Graph c: *Why would the pupils in that class rather do snow activities?* Discuss how our hobbies are often related to our climate and our environment.

Activity Book page 34

17 Read and complete.

- Remind pupils that we use the *+ing* form of the verb after *prefer* and infinitive without *to* with *would rather.*
- Explain that in the activity they can make their own choices about their preferences and whether to use *prefer +ing* or *would + rather +* infinitive.
- Check answers as a whole-group discussion.

18 Record the results of your class. Then fill in the graph.

- Use the results of the class survey (see the Presentation section) on the board to support all learners.
- Help pupils determine the maximum, minimum and range of your class results.
- Allow time so that the pupils record the class results in the graph.
- Encourage pupils to ask questions about the graph using *prefer +ing* and *would rather +* infinitive.

19 Write *snowy, sunny* or *any time*. When would you rather do these activities?

- Reconnect with the previous idea of hobbies in different places. Pupils complete the table.
- Encourage fast finishers to add extra hobbies and activities in the table.

Ending the lesson

- Volunteers read aloud some of the graph results (Activity Book p. 34). For Answer Key see p. 122. For Audioscript see p. 124.

18 Read and find the correct graphs. Then find these words in the texts.

score team graph calculate range highest lowest

Our Favourite Hobbies

What is the most popular hobby in your class? A graph is a great way to find this out. You can collect and see lots of information. These students wanted to find out the favourite hobbies of the students in their classes. They can get to know what most people like and what people like the least. They can also calculate the range: the difference between the highest and the lowest scores.

1 Volleyball has the highest number. My class prefers playing volleyball to playing golf. Three students would rather read a magazine during their free time. The least popular hobby is following the football scores of your favourite team on T.V. There is only one student who enjoys this!

2 Ten students in my class prefer going out to playing sports. Meeting friends has the highest number. Six students would rather watch their favourite TV programme. Only two students prefer playing on swings and that is the least favourite hobby in our class.

3 It's usually cold in our city and we enjoy snow activities. My class prefers skiing to sledging. There are twelve students who like this. Five students would rather make a snowman or play with snowballs. Three students are hockey players and that sport is the least favourite.

a

b

c

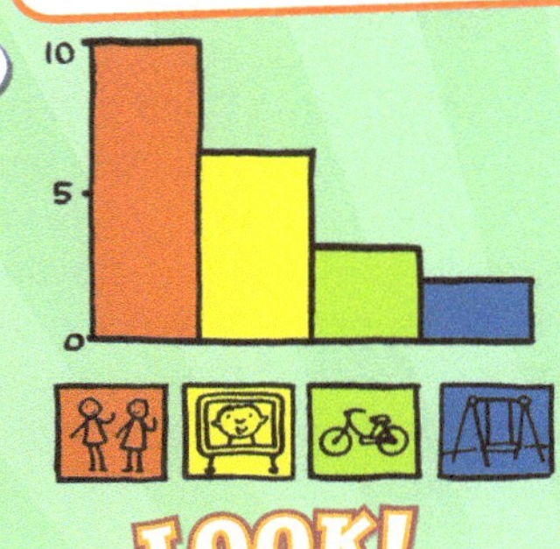

19 Look at Activity 18. Ask and answer.

1 What hobbies do the students prefer?
2 What hobbies would the students rather not do?
3 What hobby has the highest number of votes in all the classes?
4 What hobby has the lowest number of votes in all the classes?
5 What is the range in each graph?

LOOK!

I'd rather sing than dance.

I prefer singing to dancing.

20 Talk to your partner.

What hobbies do you prefer?
What hobbies does your class prefer?
What hobbies can you do where you live?
What hobbies are hard to do where you live?

OPTIONAL ACTIVITIES

School survey What is your school's favourite hobby? Organise a visit to different classes so that pupils can interview other pupils in English. Then share the results of each class.

Photocopiable 3.6 See teacher's notes p. 290.
Reading and Writing Booklet p.11 See answer key p. 283.
Grammar Booklet p. 11 See answer key p. 285.

Lesson 8

Lesson aims
To learn about other cultures and respecting cultural differences; to learn about unusual sports in other countries

Receptive language
mud racing, cheese rolling, reindeer racing, elephant polo

Materials
Audio CD

Optional activity materials
World map or globe; realia and bag as in Lesson 5; pupils bring internet/magazine photos of hobbies or sports that people love in your country; Active Teach; Digital Activity Book; CLIL posters; Photocopiable 3.7

Starting the lesson

- Ask different volunteers to find and to point to Britain and India on your map if you have one.
- Ask, e.g. *What sports do people like in Britain?* Encourage pupils to share any knowledge or ideas they have about sports which are popular in that and other countries, e.g. the USA – baseball, Britain – cricket, India – field hockey, Norway – cross-country skiing, Japan – judo.

Pupil's Book page 39

Presentation

21  Look. What are the people doing? Then listen.

- Give pupils time to look at the photos.
- Ask the class questions about each photo in turn. Pupils speculate. Encourage them to use English by teaching them the vocabulary they need to express their ideas, e.g. ask *What are the people doing in picture 2? (Six people are riding three elephants. The elephants are wearing some decorations.)*
- Play the recording. Pupils listen and imagine what the people are doing. Pause after each description to check understanding.
- Play the recording again. Ask pupils to close their eyes while they listen and to imagine the scene.

KEY **1** cheese rolling **2** elephant polo

22 Read and answer.

- Ask pupils to read the sentences.
- Give pupils time to do the activity.

KEY **1, 3** elephant polo **2, 4** cheese rolling

Practice

23 Read again and choose. Tell a friend.

- Ask pupils to read the statements in Activity 22 again before they silently read the texts. In pairs, pupils identify the correct sport.
- Alternatively, if your class likes reading aloud, ask volunteers to read the texts. Then elicit the answers from the class.
- Give pupils time to practise the dialogue.

Portfolio activity

- As a portfolio activity, ask pupils to read the example dialogue about hobbies.
- Encourage them to talk about themselves.

Activity Book page 35

20 Read and write. Who? What sport? Where?

- Give pupils time to read the blogs and complete.
- Ask volunteers to read aloud and check.
- After reading, ask pupils if they are surprised by any of these sports. Ask which sport is the one they would rather try and why.

21 Is there any special sport or physical activity in your country? Write about it.

- Give pupils time to write.
- Ask volunteers to read aloud their works.
- For the Project, give pupils time to look at the pictures and read.
- Ask them to write what they are good at and what they want to try.
- Pupils can write a description of their hobbies and favourite activities in a Word document or their notebooks, with the title *My hobbies*.

Ending the lesson

- Volunteers read aloud their descriptions of what they are good at and what they want to try (Activity Book, Project, p. 35). For Answer Key see p. 122. For Audioscript see p. 124.

Wider world

Funny sports

21 1:58 **Look. What are the people doing? Then listen.**

1

Cheese rolling

Every May, people roll a big cheese down Cooper's Hill here in England. Then everyone runs down the hill. They want to catch the cheese. The winner can eat the cheese. My dad likes doing the race but he never wins. He isn't very good at running!

Freddy, 11, United Kingdom

2

Elephant polo

People usually play polo on horses but, here in India, people sometimes play polo on elephants. They sit on elephants and hit the ball with very long sticks. I don't play because I'm not good at hitting the ball. But I like watching.

Rajeev, 12, India

22 **Read and answer.**

1 This is a ball sport.
2 This is a sport with food.
3 People ride in this sport.
4 People run in this sport.

23 **Read again and choose. Tell a friend.**

A: I want to do cheese rolling.
B: Why?
A: Because I'm good at running and I love eating cheese!

PORTFOLIO

Think and write.

What do you want to try?
Tell your friends!

I'm good at sports, I should…

OPTIONAL ACTIVITIES

Poster Groups research and find out more about the funny sports they have learnt. They write about what they learnt. They arrange their work in a poster.
Crazy sports Reuse the realia used in Lesson 5 and, in turns, ask your pupils to take one object from the bag, invent a crazy sport you can do with it and explain it to the class! The craziest wins.
Photocopiable 3.7 See teacher's notes p. 290.

Lesson 9

Lesson aims
To review the unit language with a game
To use the Picture dictionary

Revision language
Be good at *+ing*; Past continuous questions and answers

Materials
Audio CD

Optional activity materials
Active Teach; Digital Activity Book; Reading and Writing Booklet

Starting the lesson

- Choose two pupils with different personalities and ask them to talk about their hobbies and favourite activities.
- Encourage the class to compare what they were doing yesterday at the same time.

Pupil's Book page 40

24 Follow the lines. Find and unscramble the letters. Then complete the sentences.

- Give the class time to look at the pictures.
- Ask a confident pupil to explain the activity.
- Give pupils time to do the activity. Circulate, monitor and help. Fast finishers read the solutions.

KEY
Robbie is good at acting. He likes poetry, too.
Maddie loves dancing. She likes playing the drums, too.
Dan is good at Maths. He likes chess, too.
Emma loves shopping. She likes diving, too.

Picture dictionary

- Pupils can do the picture dictionary of the unit on AB page 106.
- Ask pupils to look at the pictures and try to write the vocabulary on their own in their notebooks. Then ask them to look for the words they don't remember in the Pupil's Book.
- As they finish, ask pupils to exchange notebooks to check answers. (Notebooks can be collected for checking.)

Activity Book page 36

22 Read and find four mistakes. Then correct

- Give pupils time to read and do the activity.
- Ask volunteers to read aloud.

23 Read again and write the answers.

- Give pupils time to read and do the activity.
- Divide the class into two groups. Alternatively ask the groups to ask/answer to check.

24 Read and match.

- Give pupils time to do the activity.
- To check answers, ask volunteers or fast finishers to read their answers to the class.

25 Think of three friends or family members. Suggest hobbies and explain why.

- Give pupils time to do the activity.
- To check answers ask volunteers or fast finishers to read their writings to the class. (Notebooks can be collected for checking.)

Ending the lesson

- Ask your pupils to give their opinion about activity holidays. For Answer Key see p. 122. For Audioscript see p. 124.

OPTIONAL ACTIVITIES
Test your memory! Draw clock faces on the board. Ask one pupil to write the time on the clocks and another to say what they were doing yesterday at that time. Give a few seconds thinking time. If he/she can't remember, choose another pair to continue.

24 Follow the lines. Find and unscramble the letters. Then complete the sentences.

HAVE FUN!

Robbie is good at acting. He …, too.

Maddy … . She … playing …, too.

Dan … . He …, too.

Emma … . She …, too.

AB p.106

 AB p.36

A new personality! Ask pupils to think of a famous person whose identity they would like to take. Ask a volunteer to tell the class who he/she is, why is he/she is famous, what is he/she good at, etc. e.g. *Hello, I'm Shakira, I'm a Colombian singer and I'm very good at dancing.*

Reading and Writing Booklet p.12 See answer key p. 283.

Lesson 10

Lesson aims
To personalise and assess efforts

Target language
Be good at; Past continuous questions and answers; prefer/rather

Materials
Audio CD

Optional activity materials
Online World; Active Teach; Digital Activity Book; Grammar Booklet; Test Booklet; Grammar reference (PB); Unit review (AB)

Starting the lesson

- Invite the class to think of these activities as a way to assess their work, in order to find out if they need extra work in any of the unit contents.

Pupil's Book page 41

  **Listen and choose.**

- Give the class time to look at the pictures and read the question and the names.
- Ask volunteers to explain what they are going to do. Tell the class they will have to choose more than one action.
- Play the recording for pupils to listen and choose.
- Play the recording again for pupils to check their answers.

KEY **1** a and c **2** a and c **3** c and b **4** a and c

  **Listen and answer.**

- Ask one confident pupil to read the three questions.
- Give pupils time to read.
- Play the recording for pupils to listen.
- Play the recording again. Pause after each description to check answers.

KEY
1 She was playing tennis. / She isn't good at tennis. / She likes playing tennis.
2 He was watching TV and playing computer games. / He likes playing computer games. / He is good at playing computer games.
3 He was playing basketball. / He doesn't like playing basketball. / He isn't very good at playing basketball, he is not very tall.

Activity Book page 37

26 Match.

- Give pupils time to do the activity.
- Divide the class into two groups and alternatively ask one group to read the definition and the other to say the correct word.

  **Write. Then listen and circle T = *True* or F = *False*.**

- Ask one confident pupil to explain the code.
- Give pupils time to look at the pictures and write.
- Play the recording for pupils to circle.
- Play the recording again. Pause after each description to check answers.

28 Read and complete.

- Give pupils time to read and write.
- Read aloud and stop for the class to say the answers in chorus.

29 Write about your abilities, likes and dislikes. Use your notebook.

- Give pupils time to write. Pupils can write in their notebooks.
- Ask volunteers to read their writings. (Notebooks can be collected for checking.)

Ending the lesson

- Give pupils time to read the sentences in the 'I can' section in the Activity Book p. 37.
- Ask pupils to think carefully about whether they are able to do the 'I can' points. Ask them what they found easy or difficult in the unit and why. For Answer Key see p. 122. For Audioscript see p. 124.

Online World Pupils can now go online to Ice Island and enjoy the fun and games.

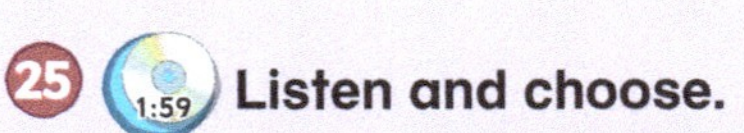

25 Listen and choose.

What were they doing yesterday?

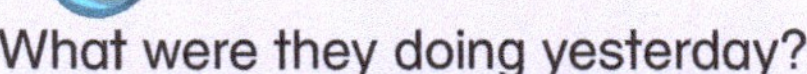

1 Emma	2 Dan	3 Maddy	4 Mum and Dad

26 Listen and answer.

1 What was Amy's mum doing?

Is she good at it?

Does she like it?

2

What was Amy's brother doing?

What does he like doing?

Is he good at it?

3 What was Amy's friend doing?

Does he love doing it?

Is he good at it?

OPTIONAL ACTIVITIES

Quiz Prepare a quiz in a PowerPoint presentation or on the board to assess the class as a group.

Grammar reference (PB p. 106) and Unit review (AB p. 98) You may wish to refer pupils to the Grammar reference and Unit review activities for Unit 3 at this point.

Test Booklet You could give the Unit 3 test.

Grammar Booklet p. 12 See answer key p. 285.

Activity Book Answer Key

p. 28, Activity 1
1 e **2** a **3** c **4** b **5** d **6** h **7** f **8** i **9** g

p. 28, Activity 2
2 hitting
3 diving
4 I'm good at catching.
5 I'm not good at playing video games.
6 I'm good at telling jokes.

p. 28, Activity 3
Robbie

p. 29, Activity 4
1 What **2** I'm **3** at **4** isn't **5** you **6** Are **7** good
8 am **9** they're

p. 29, Activity 5
1 Are you good at playing football?
2 Are you good at (rock-)climbing?
3 Are you good at fishing?
4 Are you good at diving?

p. 31, Activity 9
1 sleeping
2 were, swimming
3 was, was eating
4 were, were reading
5 was, doing, 5.00, He was playing
6 was, doing, She was meeting friends

p. 31, Activity 10
1 was
2 Were, eating, were, weren't
3 Was, working, he wasn't
4 Were, watching, they were, they weren't

1 Yes, she was.
2 No, they weren't.
3 No, he wasn't.
4 Yes, they were.

p. 32, Activity 11
1 running
2 Is he good at diving? Yes, he is.
3 Is he good at riding?, No, he isn't.
4 Are they good at skiing? No, they're not.

p. 32, Activity 13
1 b **2** a **3** b **4** c

p. 33, Activity 14
1 up **2** down **3** down **4** down **5** up **6** up

p. 33, Activity 15
like, up; at, down; computer, up; throwing, down

p. 35, Activity 20
1 Rajeev, elephant polo, India
2 Freddy, cheese rolling, United Kingdom
3 Bianca, mud racing, United States

p. 36, Activity 22
1 swim – swimming
2 good – well
3 feeling – feel
4 run – running

p. 36, Activity 23
1 swimming **2** Yes, he can. **3** No, he isn't. **4** Yes, she is. **5** trampolining **6** Yes, they like playing tennis./Yes, they do.

p. 36, Activity 24
1 c **2** a **3** b

p. 37, Activity 26
1 g **2** e **3** f **4** d **5** a **6** b **7** c **8** h

p. 37, Activity 27
1 T **2** F **3** F **4** T

p. 37, Activity 28
1 playing **2** was **3** go **4** went **5** last

Audioscript

PB Lesson 1 page 32

Lesson 1, Activity 1, p. 32 CD1:44

Robbie = R Emma = E

R Hey, Emma. Let's play football!
E I don't like playing football, Robbie.
R Emma! Catch!
E You're good at kicking balls, Robbie, but you aren't good at throwing balls.
R I am good at throwing! Look!
R Oh, no!
E Are you good at climbing trees, Robbie?

Lesson 1, Activity 2, p. 32 CD1:45

1 hitting **2** kicking **3** throwing **4** catching **5** diving **6** going shopping **7** telling jokes **8** reading poetry **9** playing video games

Lesson 1, Activity 3, p. 32 CD1:46

a She loves reading poetry. She has a lot of poetry books.
b He's good at diving. He loves the sea and is good at swimming, too.
c He's good at tennis. He's fast and is good at hitting the ball.
d They like going shopping. They usually go shopping on Saturday afternoon.
e He's really good at throwing because he practises throwing every week.
f He's good at catching. He often plays baseball after school.
g He's good at playing video games. He always wins.
h She's good at kicking a ball. She likes playing outside every day.
i He's really good at telling jokes. He always makes his friends laugh!

AB Lesson 1 page 28

Lesson 1, Activity 3, p. 28 (AB) CD1:47

I'm good at diving and I'm good at throwing but I'm not good at hitting.

PB Lesson 2 page 33

Lesson 2, Activity 4, p. 33 CD1:48

1 She's good at diving. **2** He's good at throwing. **3** She isn't good at dancing. **4** They aren't good at climbing. **5** He isn't good at hitting. **6** They're good at riding.

PB Lesson 3 page 34

Lesson 3, Activity 7, p. 34 CD1:49

1 trampolining **2** playing chess **3** playing the drums **4** acting **5** rollerblading **6** running races **7** singing karaoke **8** skateboarding **9** reading magazines **10** drawing

Lesson 3, Activity 8, p. 34 CD1:50

Chorus:
Come and have fun at the Fun Club.
Come here and meet new friends.
Drawing, trampolining, rollerblading,
At the Fun Club, the fun never ends.

What do you like doing?
Do you like playing the drums?
Or skateboarding or acting?
There's fun for everyone.
What are you good at?
Are you good at playing chess?
We love Fun Club!
It's fun here. Yes! Yes! Yes!
Chorus

PB Lesson 4 page 35

Lesson 4, Activity 10, p. 35 CD1:51

Woman = W Girl = G

W What were they doing yesterday in the afternoon?
G At two forty five Robbie was studying English. Emma was playing volleyball. And Maddy and Dan were drawing pictures in art class.
At 5 o'clock Robbie was reading comic books. Emma was shopping with her mum. And Maddy and Dan were acting in a play.

Lesson 4, Activity 11, p. 35 CD1:52

Woman = W Boy = B Girl = G

W What were they doing yesterday morning?
B At seven o'clock Robbie was sleeping. Emma was having breakfast. And Maddy and Dan were walking to school.
G At ten o'clock Emma was writing a story. Robbie was rollerblading. And Maddy and Dan were swimming.
B At eleven o'clock Maddy and Dan were reading in class. Robbie was doing a project. And Emma was playing chess.
G At twelve o'clock Maddy and Dan were having lunch. Robbie and Emma were having lunch, too.

PB Lesson 5 page 36

Lesson 5, Activity 13, p. 36 CD1:53

Jenny = J Dylan = D Finn = F Gwyn = G Penn = P

J Where's Finn?
D He's watching polar bears!
J Polar bears?!
D Be careful! Polar bears can be dangerous.
F Hey, Dylan. Can polar bears stand up?
D Yes, they can and they can run!
F Are they good at climbing?
F And do they like reading?
D Reading?
F Hey! They've got the map!
D Finn! They aren't polar bears!
F I know! It's the thieves!
D Wait!
F I can't stop!
G 8.5?
P 9!

PB Lesson 6 page 37

Lesson 6, Activity 14, p. 37 CD1:54

Reader 1 = R1 Reader 2 = R2

R1 Do you like music?
R2 Yes, I do. I love classical music.
R1 Is she coming to the picnic?
R2 Yes, she is.
R1 Can she dance?
R2 Yes, she can. She practices every day.
R1 Can you play golf today?
R2 No, they can't. They are busy at school.

Lesson 6, Activity 15, p. 37 CD1:55

Do you like music? Yes, I do. I love classical music. Is she coming to the picnic? Yes, she is. Can she dance? Yes, she can. She practises every day. Can they play golf today? No, they can't. They are busy at school.

Lesson 6, Activity 17, p. 37 CD1:56

Where's the bear with the spiky hair?
It's there, under your chair!

AB Lesson 6 page 33

Lesson 6, Activity 14, p. 33 (AB) CD1:57

a Is it fun to climb a mountain?
b She plays volleyball.
c They won the match.
d I played golf with my sister.
e Are they having a picnic?
f Is he good at video games?

PB Lesson 8 page 39

Lesson 8, Activity 21, p. 39 CD1:58

1 Every May, people roll a big cheese down Cooper's Hill here in England. Then everyone runs down the hill. They want to catch the cheese. The winner can eat the cheese. My dad likes doing the race but he never wins. He isn't very good at running!
2 People usually play polo on horses but, here in India, people sometimes play polo on elephants. They sit on elephants and hit the ball with very long sticks. I don't play because I'm not good at hitting the ball. But I like watching.

PB Lesson 10 page 41

Lesson 10, Activity 25, p. 41 CD1:59

Yesterday was Saturday. Emma was acting in the morning and playing video games in the afternoon.
Dan is good at football. Yesterday he was practising kicking and throwing with friends.
In the evening he was reading his favourite comic book.
Maddy was dancing in the morning then she was trampolining with friends in the afternoon.
Mum and Dad had a relaxed day yesterday. In the morning they were reading in the garden. Then in the evening they were watching TV.

Lesson 10, Activity 26, p. 41 CD1:60

1 Last weekend I was playing tennis. I usually play on Saturday. I'm not good at playing but I like playing tennis. It's fun.
2 Last weekend I was watching TV and playing computer games with friends. I like computer games because I'm good at playing them.
3 Hi. I'm Fergus. Last weekend I was playing basketball at the school open day. I don't really like basketball because I'm not good at it. I'm too short but the teacher asked me to play.

AB Lesson 10 page 37

Lesson 10, Activity 27, p. 37 (AB) CD1:61

1 I love playing my guitar.
2 I win!! I can play chess!
3 Oh, they aren't very good at singing.
4 Do you want to come skateboarding, Rick?
Uh, no! I don't like skateboarding.

4 Around the world

Objectives

- talk about countries and places
- describe countries and places
- ask and answer questions about what there is/are in countries and places
- pronounce negative contractions properly
- ask and answer questions about quantity

Language

Vocabulary

Countries: the United States, Mexico, Brazil, Argentina, the United Kingdom, Spain, Italy, Egypt, China, Australia, Poland, Turkey, Korea, Japan

Places: forest, desert, pyramid, statue, city, cave, volcano, lake

Structures

There is/isn' t ... / There are/aren't ...

Is there ...? Yes, there is. / No, there isn't. /Are there ...? Yes, there are some. No, there aren't any.

Plural nouns

How much/many ...? Not much, a little, a lot. / Not many, a few, a lot.

Revision

beautiful, crocodile, beach, mountain, river, rainforest, this, that, these, those

Receptive language

There are some/aren't any .../There's/There isn't a ..., round-the-world holiday, competition

CLIL and Wider world language

CLIL (Solar system): air, future, hill, planet, sky, space

Wider world (Weather around the world)

Topics

- countries and places
- there is/there are
- quantity
- weather conditions around the world

Values

Teamwork is important.

Stories

- Does Dan like crocodiles?
- Island mystery: chapter 4

Song

- Mexico.

Socio-cultural aspects

- finding out about other countries and places
- team work
- weather conditions around the world

Learning strategies

- making use of prior knowledge
- following instructions
- recording new words
- critical thinking: observing, describing and classifying
- logical thinking: deductive reasoning
- creative thinking: imagining
- using a diagram to organise information
- collaborative learning
- integrating contents: discussing and approaching new cultures
- reflecting on learning and self assessment

Phonics

- negative contractions

Cross-curricular contents

- Geography: countries and landforms, weather
- Science: describing planets
- Social Sciences: living in different weather conditions around the world; working in teams is important
- Music: song, pronunciation rhyme
- Language skills: reading a story, acting out, telling a story

Basic competences

Linguistic communication: Use language as an instrument for communication (L.1 to L.10).
Knowledge and interaction with the physical world: Learn about countries and world maps (L.1). Learn about natural and man-made environments (L.3 to L.4), space and planets (L.7) and the weather and seasons (L.8).
Mathematical competence: Learn singular and plural forms (L.2). Give numeric details (L.7).
Processing information and digital competence: Use Active Teach, Digital Activity Book and Ice Island Online World

Social and civic competence: Take an interest in the daily life and environmental challenges of others (L.8). Learn about the importance of teamwork (L.5).
Cultural and artistic competence: Learn about architecture and past civilizations (L.3, L.4 and L.10). Learn about physical environments in other countries (L.8).
Learning to learn: Reflect on what has been learnt and self evaluate progress (L.10).
Autonomy and personal initiative: Use own judgement and ideas and further develop social skills (L.1 to L.10).

Skills

Listening
- can understand people talking about countries, places and weather conditions
- can understand a dialogue about countries, places and weather conditions
- can understand questions about countries, places and weather conditions
- can understand a description about a country, a place or a weather condition
- can understand a song about a country
- can understand a pronunciation rhyme

Reading
- can read and understand information (about countries, places and weather conditions) in sentences, short paragraphs and texts
- can read and understand a cartoon strip story, captions and speech bubbles
- can read and understand factual information about weather conditions around the world
- can read and understand a paragraph length description of a country, place or weather condition

Speaking
- can give information about a country, a place or weather conditions
- can sing the *Mexico* song
- can describe a country, a place and weather conditions
- can say the pronunciation rhyme

Taking part in conversations
- can ask and respond to questions about countries, places and weather conditions
- can ask and respond to questions about weather conditions in other places
- can take part in a dialogue about countries, places and weather conditions
- can ask and respond to factual questions about the Solar System and different weather conditions in different countries

Writing
- can write the name of countries and places and weather words correctly
- can use quantifiers correctly in sentences
- can complete sentences to write information about countries, places and weather conditions
- can write sentences about their own country and weather conditions
- can write questions about countries, places and weather conditions
- can write a short text to describe an imaginary planet

Classroom ideas

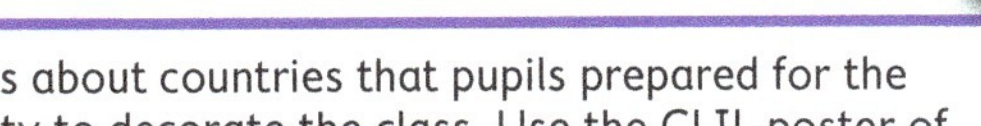

- Use the posters about countries that pupils prepared for the portfolio activity to decorate the class. Use the CLIL poster of the unit.
- Ask pupils to bring photos of countries they have visited to class and to present them to the class.
- If you have pupils from other countries in your class, ask them to make flags to decorate the classroom.
- You or your pupils could use the websites below to access more information about the lives and families of children who live in different countries around the world:
  http://www.exploreandmore.org/world/default.htm
  http://www.familiesoftheworld.com
- Play games from the Games Bank.
- Photocopiables 4.1–4.7.

Take-home English

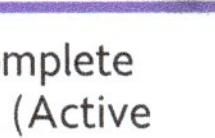

- Letters for parents. When you begin Unit 4, complete and give pupils a copy of the letter for the unit (Active Teach). This explains what pupils are going to learn in this unit.
- Home-School Link. Encourage pupils to talk to their families about a place they would like to visit for a holiday and why. (L.5)
- Grammar Booklet and Reading and Writing Booklet. Pupils take these home to show their parents.
- Pupils' Digital Activity Books.
- Portfolios. Encourage pupils to take their portfolio files home to show their parents when they finish Unit 4.

Evaluation

Self assessment
- Pupils can talk about countries or places
- Pupils can say what there is or there isn't in a place
- Pupil's Book page 51
- Activity Book page 47
- Grammar reference (Pupil's Book page 107)

Resources
- Unit review (Activity Book page 99)
- Picture dictionary (Activity Book page 107)
- Test Booklet – Unit 4 (pages 18–21)
- Grammar Booklet (page 13–16), Reading and Writing Booklet – Unit 4 (pages 13–16)

4 Around the world

Lesson 1

Lesson aims
To present and practise new vocabulary: countries

Target language
the United States, Mexico, Colombia, Brazil, Argentina, the United Kingdom, Spain, Italy, Egypt, China, Australia, Canada, Greece, Ireland, Poland, Thailand, Turkey

Receptive language
There are some/aren't any…, There's/There isn't a …, round-the-world holiday, competition

Materials
Audio CD; Flashcards and Wordcards (Countries)

Optional activity materials
Active Teach; Digital Activity Book; Photocopiable 4.1; a world map or globe

Starting the lesson

- Teach *holiday*. Ask *Where do you usually go for your holidays?* If any pupils mention a foreign country, ask them to point to it on your map.

Presentation

- Present the vocabulary using the flashcards (countries). Hold up each flashcard in turn and say the word for pupils to repeat. Hold up the flashcards in a different order for pupils to repeat again.

Pupil's Book page 42

1 Listen and read. Does Dan like crocodiles?

- Ask the class *Who can you see in the picture? (Dan and Maddy.) What do you think they are talking about?* (e.g. *holidays/crocodiles.*) Using gesture and pointing to the map, say *A round-the-world holiday competition*. Ask pupils what they think *competition* means.
- Play the recording. Pupils listen, follow the text and find the answer to the question.

KEY No. Dan doesn't like crocodiles.

2 Listen and repeat. Then find on the map.

- Give pupils time to look at the pictures.
- Play the recording. Pause for pupils to repeat.
- Play the recording again, pausing after each word so that pupils can say and point to the country on the map.

3 Find your country on the map and say where it is.

- Ask pupils to find their country on the map.
- Then ask a pupil to say and point to another country; see who is the fastest to find the next country.

Practice

Activity Book page 38

1 Listen and number.

- Give pupils time to look at the picture and read.
- Play the recording. Pause for pupils to number.
- Play the recording again, pausing after each word so that pupils can say the answer.

2 Complete the crossword. Use words from Activity 1.

- Give pupils time to do the activity.
- Faster finishers can do their own crossword.

Ending the lesson

- Divide the class into two teams. Play Noughts and crosses. See p. 301. Point to a country on your map for each square. Pupils have to say and spell the name correctly to be allowed to write their nought or cross.

For Answer Key see p. 148. For Audioscript see p. 150.

OPTIONAL ACTIVITIES

Pairwork
Pairs take it in turns to point to a country on the map and to ask their partner, e.g. *Is this Australia? (Yes, it is. / No, it isn't.)*

4 Around the world

1 2.01 **Listen and read. Does Dan like crocodiles?**

Dan: Look! There's a competition for a round-the-world holiday. The winner goes to Egypt and China, then Australia and Brazil.

Maddy: There are some beautiful beaches in Australia.

Dan: Cool!

Maddy: But, erm, Dan … there are a lot of crocodiles in Australia, too.

Dan: WHAT?!

Maddy: Poor Dan. Maybe you can have a holiday in Britain. There aren't any crocodiles here.

2 2.02 **Listen and repeat. Then find on the map.**

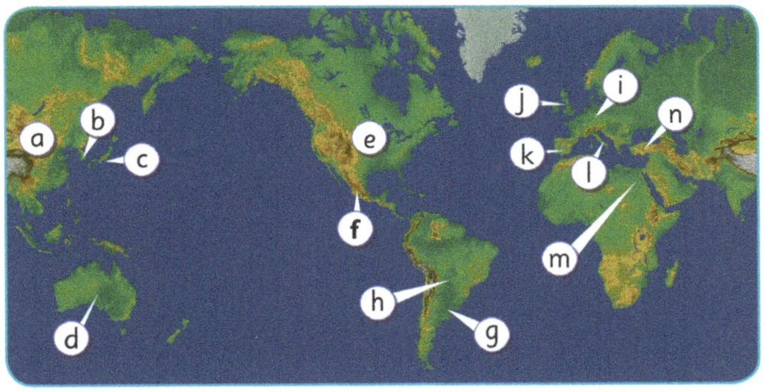

1 China

2 Korea

3 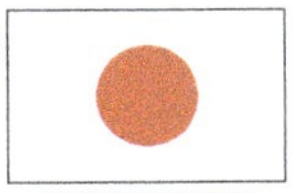 Japan

5 the United States

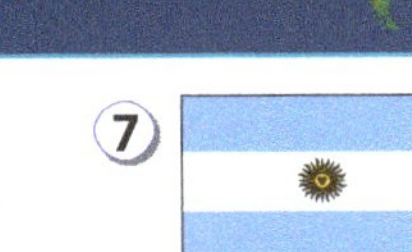

7 Argentina

9 Poland

13 Egypt

11  Spain

12  Italy

4 Australia

6 Mexico

8 Brazil

10 the United Kingdom

14 Turkey

Map labels: a, b, c, d, e, f, g, h, i, j, k, l, m, n

3 **Find your country on the map and say where it is.**

It's near China.

 AB p.38

Action game

Give each pupil a country name on a piece of paper. Make sure at least two pupils have the same country. Pupils mingle, repeating the name on their piece of paper. When they find someone with the same country, they check its location on the map and sit down. Set a time limit, e.g. three or four minutes. You could ask fast finishers to sit together and tell each other what they know about their country.

Photocopiable 4.1 See teacher's notes p. 290.

Lesson 2

Lesson aims
To revise the Lesson 1 vocabulary; to learn and practise using *There is(n't)/are(n't) (any)*

Target language
There are some/aren't any ..., There's/There isn't a ...

Materials
Audio CD; Flashcards and Wordcards (Countries)

Optional activity material
Active Teach; Digital Activity Book; Grammar Booklet

Starting the lesson

- Draw a line down the middle of the board. Ask the class to tell you the names of animals they know. On the left, write any common pets they say, and on the right, the wild animals. Ask a volunteer to explain what the two categories are.

Presentation

- Display the flashcards (countries), learnt in Lesson 1, around the room and play *I spy* (see p. 300). Ask individual pupils to come and write the words on the board.

Pupil's Book page 43

- Ask the class to silently read the Look! box.
- Remind pupils that the contractions *there's/isn't* mean *there is/is not*. Explain that we use *there is* with singular nouns and *there are* with plural nouns to express quantity.
- Elicit or explain that we use *some* with *there are* + a plural noun and *any* with *there aren't* + a plural noun.

4 2:04 Listen and look. Then say.

- Give the class time to look at the pictures. Point out the ticks and crosses on the table.
- Play the recording. Pause after each description to let pupils find the information on the table.
- Play the recording again, pausing for pupils to say the correct sentence.

5 Play the game.

- Pupils look at the example dialogue while you read it. The pupil who says the right answer takes the turn and continues the game.
- Pupils play the game in pairs, two groups or whole group.

6 Look and say.

- Give pupils time to read and look at the picture.
- Divide the class into two groups. In turns, one pupil from each group says one singular and one plural description of the picture using the words from the box. Correct sentences earn points.
- Remind pupils about the importance of the agreement *there is/are* with *singular/plural nouns*.
- Pupils can write the sentences in their notebooks. (Notebooks can be collected for checking.)

Practice

3 2:05 Listen and draw.

- Play the recording. Explain that they are going to hear a description of the scene and they have to draw it.
- Play the recording. Give pupils time to draw.
- Play the recording again for pupils to check their drawings.

4 Read and write *a*, *some* or *any*.

- Elicit when we use *some/any*.
- Give pupils time to do the activity.
- Check answers.

5 Read and write.

- Give pupils time to write.
- Check answers by inviting volunteers to write the sentences on the board.

6 Write three things about your country.

- Brainstorm ideas with the class before giving pupils time to write. Note any common mistakes with agreement.
- Write the sentences on the board to check agreement.

Ending the lesson

- Ask volunteers to read out their answers to Activity Book Activity 6. For Answer Key see p. 148. For Audioscript see p. 150.

4 Listen and look. Then say.

LOOK!

There's a rainforest in Brazil.
There isn't a rainforest in Spain.
There are some penguins in Argentina.
There aren't any penguins in Italy.

	penguins	monkeys	snakes
Argentina	✓		
Italy	✗		
China			

5 Play the game.

6 Look and say.

monkey dog people boat rocks shark
in the sea in the tree on the beach

OPTIONAL ACTIVITIES

Pair work
Pupils draw three more animals/people/objects on the picture in Activity Book Activity 3. They tell a partner about their picture, using forms of *there is/are*.

Guessing game
Pairs choose a country and find out about it using the internet (at home or at school). Without naming it, they write three or four sentences about it. They swap with another pair and guess the country.
Grammar Booklet p. 13 See answer key p. 285.

Lesson 3

Lesson aims
To extend the vocabulary on places to see from Lesson 1; to practise the unit vocabulary with a song

Target language
forest, desert, pyramid, statue, city, cave, volcano, lake

Receptive language
Is there a …? Yes/No, there is/isn't. Are there any …? Yes/No, there are/aren't.

Materials
Audio CD; Flashcards and Wordcards (Countries; Places)

Optional activity materials
World map or globe; Active Teach; Digital Activity Book; Photocopiable 4.2; Photocopiable 4.3; Reading and Writing Booklet

Starting the lesson

- Ask a volunteer to find and point to Mexico on your map/globe.
- Ask pupils what they know about Mexico, e.g. *Some people wear a big hat, a 'sombrero'. The capital city is Mexico City. Most people speak Spanish.*

Presentation

- Introduce the new words using the flashcards. Hold them up and say the words for pupils to repeat.
- Put the flashcards on the board. Point to the different flashcards and ask the class to say the words.

Pupil's Book page 44

  **Listen and repeat.**

- Give pupils time to look at the pictures.
- Play the recording. Pause for pupils to find and repeat each word.
- Play the recording again. Pause after each word. Pupils give an example of each feature from their country or other countries, e.g. *forest* (the Amazon rainforest), *desert* (the Sahara), *pyramid* (the Great Pyramid of Giza, Egypt), *statue* (the Statue of Liberty, New York), *city* (London), *cave* (the Mammoth Cave, Kentucky, USA), *volcano* (Vesuvius, Italy), *lake* (Lake Garda, Italy).

Song

  **Listen and sing. Does the singer like Mexico?**

- Play the recording. Pupils follow in their books and answer the question.
- Play the song again. Encourage pupils to sing.
- Divide the class into two groups. Play the song again. One group sings the chorus, the other group sings the verses.
- You can now play the karaoke song (Active Teach).

KEY Yes, the singer likes Mexico.

9 Look at these words and say the plurals.

- Ask pupils to read the Tip! box. Explain that some words change their spelling when they are plural. Elicit the irregular plurals and write examples on the board.
- Give pupils time to do the activity. Circulate, monitor and help.

Practice

Activity Book page 40

7 Look and complete.

- Give pupils time to look at the pictures and write the missing singular or plural nouns.
- Read aloud the answers and say long sentences according to the ticks and crosses. When pupils hear a mistake, they put their hands up and correct it. If they are right, they take the turn and continue with the next sentence.

8 Look at Activity 7 and write.

- Give pupils time to write.
- Ask pupils to ask each other questions *Is there/Are there …?* to check the written answers.

Ending the lesson

- Ask the class if they would like to go to Mexico. *Why/(not)?* For Answer Key see p. 148. For Audioscript see p. 150.

7 Listen and repeat.

8 Listen and sing. Does the singer like Mexico?

Chorus:
The drums are calling. My home is calling.
I want to be there – in Mexico.

Tell me about your country.
I can tell you a lot.
Is there a desert?
Yes, there is. It's hot, hot, hot!

Chorus

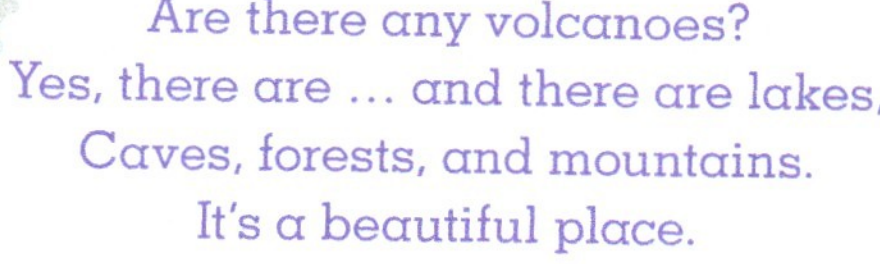

Are there any volcanoes?
Yes, there are … and there are lakes,
Caves, forests, and mountains.
It's a beautiful place.

Chorus

Are there any old cities?
Yes, there are. It's true.
With wonderful big pyramids
And statues, too.

Chorus

desert – deserts
lake – lakes
volcano – volcanoes
beach – beaches
city – cities
beach – beaches

9 Look at these words and say the plurals.

1 pyramid – pyramids
2 statue – statues
3 cave – caves
4 child – children
5 forest – forests
6 beach – beaches

OPTIONAL ACTIVITIES

Guessing game One pupil chooses a flashcard of a country. The class ask questions to guess the country.

Pair work Pupils draw an imaginary country using some of the new vocabulary from this lesson and name it. Pairs ask and answer about their partner's country, e.g. *Is there a volcano in Snakelandia?*

Photocopiable 4.2 See teacher's notes p. 290.

Photocopiable 4.3 See teacher's notes p. 290.

Reading and Writing Booklet pp. 13–14 See answer key p. 283.

Lesson 4

Lesson aims
To revise the Lesson 3 vocabulary and plural nouns; to practise asking and answering questions with *there is/are*

Target language
Is there a ...? Yes/No, there is/isn't. Are there any ...? Yes/No, there are/aren't.
Plural nouns

Materials
Audio CD

Optional activity materials
Magazines about travelling; Active Teach; Digital Activity Book; Grammar Booklet

Starting the lesson

- Revise places from Lesson 3. Mime or sketch one for the class to guess. Volunteers continue.

Presentation

Pupil's Book page 45

Skills

- Ask the class to silently read the Look! box.
- Remind pupils that we change the word order to make a question with the expressions *there is* and *there are*.

Practice

10 2:08 **Listen and point. Then ask and answer.**

- Give pupils time to look at the pictures and read the speech bubbles.
- Play the recording. Remind pupils to pay attention to the word order for questions.
- Play the recording again. Pause after each line for pupils to ask and answer.

11 Look at the pictures in Activity 10. Ask and answer.

- Give pupils time to look at the pictures. Check that they remember the name of the places. Tell them they must pay attention to the plural or singular and the word order.
- In pairs, ask pupils to ask and answer looking at the pictures.

12 Ask and answer about your country.

- Read the example dialogue with a confident pupil.
- Give pairs time to do the activity.

Activity Book page 41

9 Look at Activity 7 again. Then write.

- Ask pupils to look at the pictures in Activity 7 again.
- Give pupils time to write.
- Pupils read aloud to check answers.

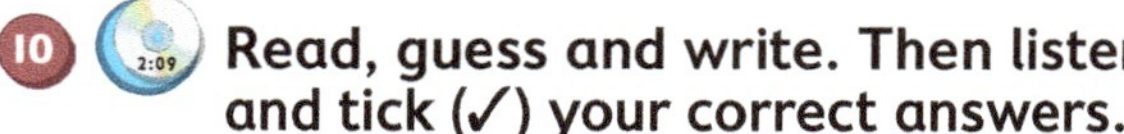

10 2:09 **Read, guess and write. Then listen and tick (✓) your correct answers.**

- Give pupils time to read, think and write.
- Play the recording, pausing for pupils to tick.
- Play the recording again. Pupils check their answers.

11 Make your own quiz.

- Give pupils time to write.
- You can ask pupils to look for information about countries on the internet or reading the magazines.

Ending the lesson

- Ask the class what they would find interesting, dangerous, amazing about travelling. For Answer Key see p. 148. For Audioscript see p. 150.

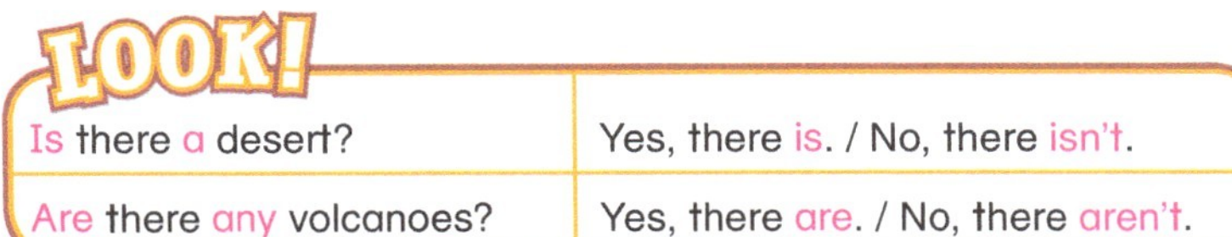

LOOK!

Is there a desert?	Yes, there is. / No, there isn't.
Are there any volcanoes?	Yes, there are. / No, there aren't.

10  **Listen and point. Then ask and answer.**

11 **Look at the pictures in Activity 10. Ask and answer.**

- animals / in the desert
- island / in the lake
- statues / on the pyramid
- trees / in the forest
- volcano / in the city

12 **Ask and answer about your country.**

Are there any deserts?

No, there aren't.

OPTIONAL ACTIVITIES

Writing pair work Pupils work in pairs. One pupil writes questions and answers about Britain, the other about Spain. They ask their partner about his/her country.
Roleplay Pairs imagine they are on a trip with their family, and role play a telephone conversation, e.g. Where are you? Are there ...? Is there ...?
Team game Divide the class into two groups and use a quiz written by a fast finisher in Activity 11.
Grammar Booklet p. 14 See answer key p. 285.

Lesson 5

Lesson aims
To consolidate the unit language with a story

Values
Teamwork is important.

Receptive language
There's a ..., There aren't any ..., Are there any ...?

Materials
Audio CD

Optional activity materials
Active Teach; Digital Activity Book; Photocopiable 4.4

Starting the lesson

- Pupils look at the pictures. Ask *Where is the Captain? (At the pub.) What is he doing? (Trying to remember the map.) What are the penguins doing in picture 2? (They are pretending to be a forest.) And in picture 3? (A statue.) In picture 4? (A pyramid.) Is there a cave in Snow Mountain? (Yes, there is.)*

Presentation

Pupil's Book page 46

13 Look at the pictures. Tell the story.

- Ask the class to look again at the pictures.
- Ask six volunteers to go in front of the class and tell the story just based on looking at the pictures, without reading. Each pupil tells the story of one picture.

14 2:10 Listen and read. Then act out.

- Play the recording. Pupils listen and follow the story.
- Ask the class *Can Captain Formosa remember the map? (Yes, he can.) Is there a forest on the map? (Yes, there is.) Is there a statue? (Yes, there is.) Is there a pyramid? (No, there isn't.) Where is the treasure? (In a cave.) Are there any caves on Ice Island? (Yes, there's a cave on Snow Mountain.)*
- Play the recording again. Pause for the class to repeat each line in chorus.
- Divide the class into three and allocate these parts: Captain Formosa, Dylan and Jenny.
- Play the recording again. Pause for pupils to repeat their character's lines.
- Ask ten volunteers to act out the story (Captain Formosa, Dylan, Jenny, Finn, four–six penguins).
- Take a class vote for the best actor/actress!

Values

- Ask the class why teamwork is important, e.g. Sharing ideas we have got more ideas.
- Groups of four discuss what teamwork means to them and present their ideas to the class.

Home-School Link

- Ask the pupils to tell their family about a place they would like to visit for a holiday and why.

Practice

Activity Book page 42

12 Read and correct.

- Give pupils time to do the activity.
- Pointing to the pictures of the story, pairs take it in turns to ask questions for these sentences, e.g. *Has Captain Formosa got the map?*
- Volunteers ask and answer to check.

13 What happens next? Imagine.

- Pairs predict what happens next.
- Volunteers tell the class their ideas.

14 Read and complete the conversations.

- Give pupils time to do the activity.
- Ask fast finishers to practise the dialogue.
- Check the answers asking different pairs to read aloud.

Ending the lesson

- Ask pupils if they would like to live on Ice Island. *Why (not)?* For Answer Key see p. 148. For Audioscript see p. 150.

13 Look at the pictures. Tell the story.

14 2.10 Listen and read. Then act out.

VALUES

Teamwork is important.

HOME-SCHOOL LINK PARENT

Tell your family about a place you would like to visit for a holiday and why.

 AB p.42

OPTIONAL ACTIVITIES

Practice
Pupils tell you where the other penguin is in each picture in Activity 14. Picture 1: Penn is next to the fish and chip shop. Picture 2: Gwyn isn't near the forest. Picture 3: Gwyn is/isn't in front of the statue.

Code game Pairs write two or three affirmative or negative sentences about Ice Island in code using *There is/are.* They swap sentences with another pair and decipher the code.
Photocopiable 4.4 See teacher's notes p. 290.

Lesson 6

Lesson aims
To form and identify negative contractions

Materials
Audio CD; Phonics and spelling poster

Optional activity materials
gloves, masks, glue, scissors and sentence strips; Active Teach; Digital Activity Book; Photocopiable 4.5

Starting the lesson

- Show pupils the Phonics and spelling poster (see teacher's notes on p. 26).
- Read the words from the fourth picture aloud and ask pupils to find a pattern.

Presentation

- State the goal of the lesson.
- Tell pupils that contractions are very common when we speak and write informal English. Write the same sentence twice with and without contraction. Explain that the sentences sound different but the meaning is the same.
- Point out the apostrophe and explain its use. Sing the following rhyme: *If you don't want to say 'not', drop the 'o' and fill in the spot.*

Pupil's Book page 47

 15  Listen and repeat.

- Give pupils time to read the words in the box.
- Play the recording for pupils to repeat the words chorally. Stop after each word and ask volunteers to repeat it as accurately as possible. Encourage the class to repeat energetically.

16  Listen and read. Then repeat.

- Play the recording. Pause for pupils to find the correct picture.
- Play the recording again and walk around the class to make sure that pupils find the matching picture.
- Play the recording again, pausing between sentences for pupils to repeat chorally.
- Divide the class into two groups. Assign sentences to each group. Encourage one group to read the full sentence and the other group to echo with the contraction.

Practice

17 Read and practise the sentences in Activity 16 with your partner.

- Tell pupils to practise the last activity in pairs.
- Give pairs time to do the activity.

 18  Listen and repeat.

- Give pupils time to look at the text and the picture.
- Play the recording. Then ask pupils to say aloud the contractions in the rhyme.
- Play the recording again. Encourage the class to learn and repeat the rhyme.

Activity Book page 43

 15  Listen and complete.

- Read aloud the first sentence.
- Play the recording.
- Point out the adverb *today*. Explain that this word tells you that 1 has to be in the present tense.
- Play the recording and allow time for the pupils to complete the activity.
- Correct the activity as a whole-group discussion.

16 Read and circle the contraction.

- Read aloud the first sentence. Ask the class to find the word with the contraction.
- Give pupils time to complete the activity.
- Check the activity as a whole-group discussion.

17 Write the contractions.

- Read aloud the two words. Ask the class to say the contraction.
- Give pupils time to complete the activity.
- Check the activity as a whole-group discussion.

18 Write six sentences of your own. Use the contractions from Activity 15.

- Encourage the class to make up their own sentences orally.
- Record some sentence starters on the board to provide support for all learners.
- Give pupils time to do the activity.
- Ask volunteers to read their sentences.

Ending the lesson

- Revisit the goal of the lesson and ask pupils to evaluate their own progress. For Answer Key see p. 148. For Audioscript see p. 150.

Negative contractions

isn't, aren't, wasn't, weren't, hasn't, haven't, don't, doesn't, didn't
Contractions have the same meaning as long forms but are used more when speaking and in informal writing.

Listen and repeat.

isn't, aren't, wasn't, weren't, hasn't, haven't, don't, doesn't, didn't

Listen and read. Then repeat.

1 She is not on holiday  She isn't on holiday.

2 They are not travelling in Italy. 

They aren't travelling in Italy.

3 I was not there.  I wasn't there.

4 They were not going to the beach.  They weren't going to the beach.

5 You do not need a passport. 

You don't need a passport.

6 She has not arrived yet.  She hasn't arrived yet.

7 He does not like going on boats.  He doesn't like going on boats.

8 He did not see the pyramid.  He didn't see the pyramid.

17 Read and practise the sentences in Activity 16 with your partner.

Listen and repeat.

She can't sing but she doesn't care.
It wasn't a problem. We weren't there!

OPTIONAL ACTIVITIES

Poets' Workshop
Invite pupils to add a new poem with contractions to their poetry books.

Contraction Surgery
Use gloves and masks to invite pupils to perform some contraction surgeries. Divide the words into different groups, so that pupils cut out the words and glue them to form the contraction. Display all the contracted words in the word wall.
Photocopiable 4.5 See teacher's notes p. 290.

Lesson 7

Lesson aims
To extend the vocabulary about the environment; to learn and practise the use of *How much/many?*

Cross-curricular focus
Science – The Solar System

Target language
air, environment, future, hill, planet, sky, space;
How much water is there in the lake? Not much, a little, a lot
How many lakes are there in that country? Not many, a few, a lot

Materials
Audio CD; CLIL poster

Optional activity materials
Earth model; Active Teach; Digital Activity Book; Photocopiable 4.6; Reading and Writing Booklet; Grammar Booklet

Starting the lesson

- The Solar System is made up of all the planets that orbit around the Sun. Each of them is very different and fascinating. In addition to planets the Solar System also contains moons, comets, asteroids, dust and gas.
- The creation of the Solar System took place billions of years ago. The evolution of the Solar System is closely related to the evolution of mankind.

Presentation

- Use a Solar System poster to introduce the topic. Name each planet and encourage pupils to repeat after you.
- Ask pupils to tell you what the planets look like. After allowing STT in pairs, record their answers in a web of ideas on the board.
- Before reading, give pupils time to look at the headings of the table on page 48. Ask pupils to make predictions about the text.
- Use the vocabulary routine: **mime and define**. Next, **use each adjective in a sentence**. Last, **ask questions** with each new vocabulary word.
- Point out the facts in the table. Explain the difference between countable and uncountable nouns. Tell the pupils that countable and uncountable things may be different in English and in your language.
- Share the background information from the *Starting the lesson* section.

Pupil's Book page 48

19 Read and compare. How is the Earth similar and different to these planets?

- Read the title and the introduction to the text.
- Review some words related to the things we find on Earth: *trees*, *water*, *fields*, *forests*, *grass*, *lakes*, *mountains*, etc. Sort the words into uncountable and countable nouns on the board.
- Set purpose for reading: *Let's read to see how Earth is different from other planets.*
- Read the whole text as a shared reading experience: use expression and intonation to model proficient reading.
- Ask pupils to follow your reading.
- Give pupils time to complete Activity 19.

Practice

20 Ask and answer.

- Remind pupils that we use *much/How much?* with uncountable nouns and *many/How many?* with countable nouns. Give pupils time to read the Look! box.
- Complete the activity as a whole-group discussion.

KEY
1 one large cloud **2** 63 **3** a lot of land **4** no air
5 planet Earth, because it has air, land and water and is not too hot or too cold

- Discuss the idea in the opening paragraph *What do you think that they will discover in the future?* and the question *Can living things survive on the planets we've learnt about?*

21 Talk to your partner.

- Read aloud the first question and model expectations for STT.
- Give pairs time to talk to each other.
- Ask one or two volunteers to share what they have discussed with the whole class.

Activity Book page 44

19 Read and complete.

- Complete the first gap together.
- Give pupils time to do the activity.
- Check answers as a whole-group discussion.

20 Write about an imaginary planet. Use these questions.

- Ask pupils to visualise and draw an imaginary planet.
- Read aloud the questions and invite them to share in pairs.
- Model how to use the questions to organise a narrative piece of writing.

Ending the lesson

- Pupils read aloud what they have written for Activity Book Activity 20. For Answer Key see p. 148. For Audioscript see p. 150.

19 **Read and compare. How is the Earth similar and different to these planets?**

THE SOLAR SYSTEM

We live on a wonderful planet called planet Earth. Beyond the sky, there are many other planets in space. Our planet is part of a Solar System with a lot of planets and stars that move around the Sun in space. Space is a fascinating place where there's lots to discover.

air future hill planet sky space

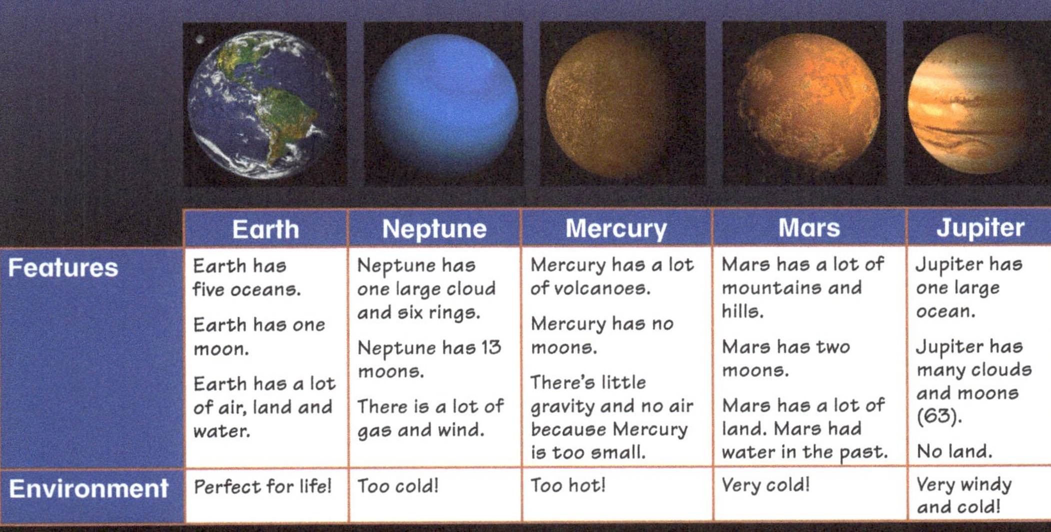

	Earth	Neptune	Mercury	Mars	Jupiter
Features	Earth has five oceans. Earth has one moon. Earth has a lot of air, land and water.	Neptune has one large cloud and six rings. Neptune has 13 moons. There is a lot of gas and wind.	Mercury has a lot of volcanoes. Mercury has no moons. There's little gravity and no air because Mercury is too small.	Mars has a lot of mountains and hills. Mars has two moons. Mars has a lot of land. Mars had water in the past.	Jupiter has one large ocean. Jupiter has many clouds and moons (63). No land.
Environment	Perfect for life!	Too cold!	Too hot!	Very cold!	Very windy and cold!

20 **Ask and answer.**

1 How many clouds are there on Neptune?
2 How many moons has Jupiter got?
3 How much land is there on Mars?
4 How much air is there on Mercury?
5 Which planet has the best environment for life? Why?

LOOK!

How much water is there?
Not much / a little / a lot

How many lakes are there?
Not many / a few / a lot

21 **Talk to your partner.**

How much water is there where you live? Is there an ocean or a river?
Are there any mountains or hills where you live?
How many volcanoes are there where you live?
Which planet do you think is the most interesting? Why?

OPTIONAL ACTIVITIES

Planet models Create a model of the Solar System with recycled materials. Write labels to explain the features of each planet.

Researcher's Workshop Find out more about other planets and galaxies.

Photocopiable 4.6 See teacher's notes p. 290.

Reading and Writing Booklet p. 15 See answer key p. 283.

Grammar Booklet p. 15 See answer key p. 285.

Lesson 8

Lesson aims
To learn about other cultures and respect cultural differences; to learn about the weather in other countries and places

Materials
Audio CD

Optional activity materials
World map or globe; internet/magazine photos of Greenland; pupils' magazines, internet or own photos of summer/winter; Active Teach; Digital Activity Book; CLIL Poster; Photocopiable 4.7

Starting the lesson

- Ask pupils if they know any countries similar to Ice Island.
- Greenland is the world's largest island that isn't also a continent. It has a population of about 57,000 people, most of whom live in one of the 18 towns. It has an arctic climate, a famous ice-sheet, glaciers, hot springs, underground volcanic activity and the world's biggest national park.
- Point to Greenland on your map/globe. Ask what pupils know about it or imagine it is like.

Presentation

Pupil's Book page 49

22 Listen and read. Does Inuk like summer or winter?

- Ask the class to predict the answer.
- Play the recording. Pupils listen and follow Inuk's blog in their books.

KEY She likes summer.

23 Read again and say. *Summer* or *winter*?

- Give pairs time to do the activity.

KEY
1 summer **2** winter **3** summer **4** winter

Practice

24 Look at the pictures. Talk about the weather in these countries.

- Give pupils time to look at the pictures. Ask them what they know about Egypt and Brazil.
- In pairs, ask pupils to ask and answer, looking at the pictures about places in these countries, e.g. *Are there any deserts in Egypt?*
- Ask two confident pupils to read the captions. Elicit vocabulary to talk about weather (*hot*, *cold*, *rainy*, *sunny*, *snowy*, etc.).
- Pairs continue, using the photos to talk about the weather in both countries.

Portfolio

- For the portfolio activity, help pupils plan their speech. Write *Summer* on the left and *Winter* on the right of the board. Write *Weather? Months? Clothes? Short/long nights? Free time?* under each heading. Pupils read.
- Ask volunteers to talk about winter and summer in their country.

Mini-project

- For the Project activity, divide the class into four or five groups.
- Give each group a big board and ask them to write the title *Our favourite country*.
- Pupils complete the poster following the instructions in their Activity Book.

Activity Book page 45

21 Listen and write.

- Ask *What can you see in the photos? (A polar bear and a reindeer.)*
- Play the recording. Pupils listen and write.
- Give them time to finish writing, then play the recording again. Pause before each space to elicit and check the answers.

22 Read and tick (✓). Is a holiday in Greenland right for you?

- Give pupils time to read and tick. Explain that they tick according to their own personal answers.
- Ask volunteers to read aloud their result.

Ending the lesson

- Display the posters pupils worked on in the project activity (Activity Book p. 45). For Answer Key see p. 148. For Audioscript see p. 150.

Wider world
The weather

Hi. I'm Inuk. I live in Greenland. Winter and summer are very different here.

22 

Listen and read. Does Inuk like summer or winter?

i-Blog   Home | My favourites | Pictures | Log out

My recent blogs

Winter

In the winter, we don't see the sun very much. There's one long night for four weeks in December and January. There are some big snowstorms and it is very, very cold. We go to school by snowmobile because we can't use a car.

Summer

In the summer, there aren't any snowstorms. There are often long sunny days. For a month, it is never night-time! I go kayaking and fishing every day. The summer is great but it's very short. In September, it's time for my winter clothes again.

23 Read again and say. *Summer* or *winter*?

1. People use kayaks.
2. People use snowmobiles.
3. There are some very long days.
4. There are some big snowstorms.

24 Look at the pictures. Talk about the weather in these countries.

a 

There are deserts in Egypt.

b 

There are rainforests in Brazil.

PORTFOLIO

Think and talk.

	Good	Bad
Summer	swim	hot
Winter		

Talk about summer and winter in your country.

OPTIONAL ACTIVITIES

Roleplay
Pupils write questions about Greenland. They swap questions with a partner and research answers.

Quiz Groups of four write a quiz similar to that in Activity Book Activity 22, about another country. They swap with another group and do the quiz.
Photocopiable 4.7 See teacher's notes p. 290.

Lesson 9

Lesson aims
To review all the unit language with a game
To use the Picture dictionary

Revision language
There are some/aren't any..., There's/There isn't a ...; Is there a ...? Yes/No, there is/isn't. Are there any ...? Yes/No, there are/aren't. Countries, places, be good at +*ing*, like/love/hate +*ing*, hobbies and action words

Materials
Audio CD

Optional activity material
Active Teach; Digital Activity Book; Reading and Writing Booklet

Starting the lesson

- Ask pupils to tell you three places where it is very hot, three things they like doing, three things they are good at and three countries.

Pupil's Book page 50

25 Play the game.

- Ask pupils to look at How to play on p. 50 to see the points system. Tell pupils:
  – each group can start on any square;
  – each group member must start on the same square;
  – they must move clockwise around the board;
  – the winner in each group is the pupil with the most points when the teacher ends the activity;
  – they must follow the instructions exactly;
  – they can have only one attempt at each question;
  – they mustn't look at their books or notebooks for help!
- In classes needing more support, you may choose to allow two or three attempts per question. You may also choose to allow pupils to refer to their books.

Playing the game

- Set a time limit, e.g. 20 minutes.
- Circulate, helping and encouraging pupils as they play. Note anything they have particular difficulty with and do some remedial work as a class at a later date.
- Give pupils time to play. Circulate, monitor and help.

Picture dictionary

- Pupils can do the picture dictionary of the unit on Activity Book page 107.
- Ask pupils to look at the pictures and try to write the vocabulary on their own in their notebooks. Then ask them to look for the words they don't remember in the Pupil's Book.
- As they finish, ask pupils to exchange notebooks to check answers. (Notebooks can be collected for checking.)

Activity Book page 46

23 Listen and circle.

- Ask *What can you see in the picture? (Carnival)*
- Give pupils time to read the sentences. Play the recording. Pupils listen and circle.
- Give them time to review, then play the recording again. Pause before each space to elicit and check the answers.

24 Write.

- Ask a volunteer to read the words in the box.
- Give pupils time to do the activity.

25 Match.

- Give pupils time to do the activity.
- Divide the class into two groups and alternatively ask one group to read the definition and the other to say the correct word.

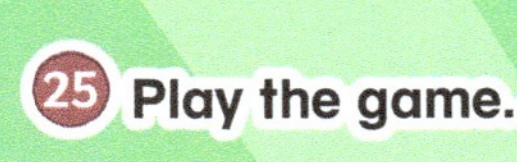

25 Play the game.

HAVE FUN!

How to play

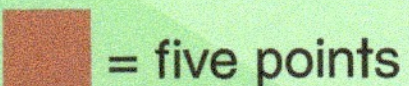

= five points

He missed the bus.

= three points

Where's the cinema?

It's next to the clothes shop.

= two points

Name a famous Italian food.

Spaghetti.

= one point

What's behind the swimming pool?

The supermarket is behind the swimming pool.

Sylvia	José
5	3
1	5

AB p.107

Ending the lesson

- Invite your pupils to describe their favourite place. For Answer Key see p. 148. For Audioscript see p. 150.

OPTIONAL ACTIVITIES

Wordsearch

Pupils create their own wordsearch using the place words or countries from the unit. They swap with a partner.

Reading and Writing Booklet p. 16

See answer key p. 283.

Lesson 10

Lesson aims
To personalise and assess efforts

Target language
There are some/aren't any ..., There's/There isn't a ...; Is there a ...? Yes/No, there is/isn't. Are there any ...? Yes/No, there are/aren't.

Materials
Audio CD

Optional activity materials
Online World; Active Teach; Digital Activity Book; Grammar Booklet; Test Booklet; Grammar reference (PB); Unit review (AB)

Starting the lesson

- Invite the class to think of these activities as a way to assess their work, in order to find out if they need extra work in any of the unit contents.

Pupil's Book page 51

26 Read. What is the name of the statue?

- Give the class time to read the postcard. Invite them to talk about it.
- Ask volunteers to read aloud.

KEY the Sphinx

27 Read again and say *True* or *False*.

- Give pupils time to read the sentences.
- Give pupils time to do the activity.
- Check the answers.

KEY **1** T **2** T **3** F **4** T **5** F

28 Talk about places to visit in your country.

- Divide the class into groups. Each group must agree on a place to visit. Set a time limit for them to prepare a presentation. Tell them they have to talk about what they find interesting about the place.
- The groups talk about their favourite place. All members of the group must say something.

Activity Book page 47

26 Imagine you are on holiday. Write a postcard to a friend.

- Give pupils time to do the activity.
- Ask pupils to address the postcard to the classmate next to them. Pupils give their postcards (Activity Books) to the classmate.
- Ask volunteers to read aloud the postcards they have received.

27 Unscramble and write the questions. Then write the answers.

- Give pupils time to unscramble and write.
- In pairs, pupils take turns to ask and answer.

Ending the lesson

- Give pupils time to read the sentences in the *I can* section in the Activity Book (p. 47).
- Ask pupils to think carefully about whether they are able to do the *I can* points. Ask them what they found easy or difficult in the unit and why. For Answer Key see p. 148. For Audioscript see p. 150.

Online World Pupils can now go online to Ice Island and enjoy the fun and games.

Pupils can now, or at the end of this unit, go online to Ice Island and find the globe that Penn and Gwyn are holding. It is inside the headquarters of the Satellite Monitoring Station, on the desk at the top of the stairs. Once pupils click on the globe they are taken to a supplementary language game based on the vocabulary in this unit.

26 **Read. What is the name of the statue?**

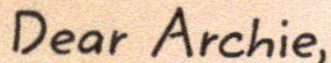

Dear Archie,
Hello from Egypt! It's very hot here but it's fun. This postcard is from Giza. In the desert at Giza, there are some big pyramids and there's a big statue, too. It's called the Sphinx. It's got a man's head and a lion's body. It's very, very old. From Giza, you can see the city of Cairo.
Our hotel is on an island in the River Nile. There aren't any cars on the island. Everyone goes by boat. I can see some big white birds on the river. This round-the-world trip is fantastic! Are there any fun lessons at school this week?
See you soon!
Mia

Archie Joseph
103 Park Street
London W6
United Kingdom

27 **Read again and say *True* or *False*.**

1 There are some big pyramids in the desert.
2 The Sphinx is a very old statue.
3 The Sphinx has got a lion's head.
4 Mia's hotel is on an island.
5 There are some hippos in the river.

28 **Talk about places to visit in your country.**

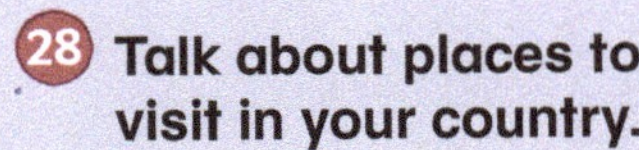

OPTIONAL ACTIVITIES

Quiz Prepare a quiz in a PowerPoint presentation or on the board to assess the class as a group.
Active Teach Pupils can watch the animated story Episode 2.

Grammar reference (PB p. 107) and Unit review (AB p. 99) You may wish to refer pupils to the Grammar reference and Unit review activities for Unit 4.
Test Booklet You may wish to give the Unit 4 test.
Grammar Booklet p. 16 See answer key p. 285.

Activity Book Answer Key

p. 38, Activity 1

a 8 (Spain) **b** 1 (UK) **c** 2 (Argentina) **d** 9 (Italy)
e 6 (US) **f** 10 (Brazil) **g** 4 (Mexico) **h** 7 (Egypt)
i 5 (Australia) **j** 13 (Poland) **k** 3 (China)
l 11 (Japan) **m** 12 (Korea) **n** 4 (Turkey)

p. 38, Activity 2

4	Mexico	**5**	Australia
7	Egypt	**8**	Spain
9	Italy	**11**	Japan
12	Korea	**13**	Poland

p. 39, Activity 3

To be added to drawing: a lion running on the beach near the boys, bananas being eaten by the monkeys in the tree, a dog swimming in the sea

p. 39, Activity 4

1 some **2** a **3** any **4** some **5** some

p. 39, Activity 5

2 There's a rainforest in Australia.
3 There isn't a snowy mountain in Egypt.
4 There aren't any elephants in Mexico.
5 There are some beautiful beaches in Spain.

p. 40, Activity 7

1 volcanoes **2** city **3** statues **4** pyramids **5** caves
6 forest **7** deserts **8** lake

p. 40, Activity 8

1 (some) statues/caves
2 (some) volcanoes/deserts, any (volcanoes/deserts)
3 city/forest/lake
4 Answers may vary
5 Answers may vary

p. 41, Activity 9

1 Are there any, in
2 Are there any, in, Yes, there are.
3 Are there any, in, No, there aren't.
4 Are there any, in, Yes, there are.

p. 41, Activity 10

2 Yes, there is.
3 Yes, there are.
4 Yes, there are.
5 No, there isn't.
6 No, there isn't.

p. 42, Activity 12

1 Captain Formosa **hasn't got** the map
2 The Captain **hasn't got** a good memory.
3 There **aren't any** pyramids on Ice Island.
4 The treasure is **in a cave**.
5 There is a cave **on Snow Mountain**.

p. 42, Activity 14
1 a **2** b **3** c **4** b

p. 43, Activity 15
1 isn't **2** don't **3** wasn't **4** doesn't **5** haven't **6** didn't

p. 43, Activity 16
1 don't **2** didn't **3** doesn't **4** haven't

p. 43, Activity 17
1 haven't **2** wasn't **3** don't **4** isn't **5** didn't **6** doesn't

p. 44, Activity 19
1 is **2** of **3** are **4** planets **5** environment **6** lot **7** to **8** has **9** one **10** interesting **11** a lot of **12** two **13** it **14** had

p. 45, Activity 21
1 Ride **2** mountains **3** caves **4** any **5** some **6** bears **7** day

p. 46, Activity 23
1 Grandma **2** Brazil **3** city **4** beaches **5** statue **6** dancing

p. 46, Activity 24
1 Grandma **2** rainforest **3** trees **4** animals **5** lake **6** beautiful

p. 46, Activity 25
1 h **2** d **3** c **4** a **5** f **6** e **7** g **8** b

p. 47, Activity 27
1 Is there a desert in Asia? Yes, there is.
2 Is there a rainforest in Italy? No, there isn't.
3 Are there any pyramids in Brazil? Yes, there are.
4 Are there any volcanoes in Egypt? No, there aren't.
5 Are there any castles in China? Yes, there are.

Audioscript

PB Lesson 1 page 42

Lesson 1, Activity 1, p. 42 CD2:01

Dan = D Maddy = M

D Look! There's a competition for a round-the-world holiday. The winner goes to Egypt and China, then Australia and Brazil.
M There are some beautiful beaches in Australia.
D Cool!
M But, erm, Dan ... there are a lot of crocodiles in Australia, too.
D What?!
M Poor Dan. Maybe you can have a holiday in Britain. There aren't any crocodiles here.

Lesson 1, Activity 2, p. 42 CD2:02

1 China
2 Korea
3 Japan
4 Australia
5 the United States
6 Mexico
7 Argentina
8 Brazil
9 Poland
10 the United Kingdom
11 Spain
12 Italy
13 Egypt
14 Turkey

AB Lesson 1 page 38

Lesson 1, Activity 1, p. 38 (AB) CD2:03

1 the United Kingdom
2 Argentina
3 China
4 Mexico
5 Australia
6 the United States
7 Egypt
8 Spain
9 Italy
10 Brazil
11 Japan
12 Korea
13 Poland
14 Turkey

PB Lesson 2 page 43

Lesson 2, Activity 4, p. 43 CD2:04

1 There are some monkeys in Argentina.
2 There are some penguins in China.
3 There are some snakes in Italy.
4 There aren't any penguins in Italy.
5 There are some snakes in Argentina.
6 There aren't any monkeys in China.

AB Lesson 2 page 39

Lesson 2, Activity 3, p. 39 (AB) CD2:05

There's a lion on the beach.
It is with the two boys.
It's running.
There's a tree.
There are some monkeys in the tree.
They're eating bananas.
In the sea, there's a dog swimming.

PB Lesson 3 page 44

Lesson 3, Activity 7, p. 44 CD2:06

1 forest
2 desert
3 pyramid
4 statue
5 city
6 cave
7 volcano
8 lake

Lesson 3, Activity 8, p. 44 CD2:07

Chorus:
The drums are calling. My home is calling.
I want to be there – in Mexico.
Tell me about your country.
I can tell you a lot.
Is there a desert?
Yes, there is. It's hot, hot, hot!
Chorus
Are there any volcanoes?
Yes, there are ... and there are lakes,
Caves, forests and mountains.
It's a beautiful place.
Chorus
Are there any old cities?
Yes, there are. It's true.
With wonderful big pyramids
And statues, too.
Chorus

PB Lesson 4 page 45

Lesson 4, Activity 10, p. 45 CD2:08

Woman = W Boy = B Girl = G

1 W Are there any factories in the forest?
B No, there aren't.
2 W Are there any camels in the desert?
G Yes, there are some camels in the desert.
3 W Are there any pyramids in Egypt?
B Yes, there are some pyramids in Egypt. They're beautiful.
4 W Is there an island in the lake?
G Yes, there is.
5 W Is there a volcano in the city?
G No, there isn't.

AB Lesson 4 page 41

Lesson 4, Activity 4, p. 41 (AB) CD2:09

Woman = W Man = M

1 W Are there any beaches in Australia?
M Yes, there are. In Australia there are a lot of great beaches.
2 W Is there a rainforest in Brazil?
M Yes, there is.
3 W Are there any volcanoes in Italy?
M Yes, there are.
4 W Are there any volcanoes in Mexico?
M Yes, there are.

5 W Is there a mountain taller than 5000 metres in Spain?
M No, there isn't.
6 W Is there a river longer than the Amazon in China?
M No, there isn't.

PB Lesson 5 page 46

Lesson 5, Activity 14, p. 46 CD2:10
Dylan = D Captain = C Jenny = J
D Captain, the thieves have got the map but can you remember it?
C Yes! There's a forest ...
And there's a statue.
And there's a pyramid.
D A pyramid? There aren't any pyramids on Ice Island.
C Oh, yes. Sorry. That's a different map.
C Wait! I remember! The treasure's in a cave!
D A cave? Are there any caves on the island?
D Oh, no! Snow again!
J Hey, snow ... Snow Mountain! There's a cave on Snow Mountain.

PB Lesson 6 page 47

Lesson 6, Activity 15, p. 47 CD2:11

isn't	weren't	don't
aren't	hasn't	doesn't
wasn't	haven't	didn't

Lesson 6, Activity 16, p. 47 CD2:12
1 She is not on holiday. She isn't on holiday.
2 They are not travelling in Italy. They aren't travelling in Italy.
3 I was not there. I wasn't there.
4 They were not going to the beach. They weren't going to the beach.
5 You do not need a passport. You don't need a passport.
6 She has not arrived yet. She hasn't arrived yet.
7 He does not like going on boats. He doesn't like going on boats.
8 He did not see the pyramid. He didn't see the pyramid.

Lesson 6, Activity 18, p. 47 CD2:13
She can't sing but she doesn't care.
It wasn't a problem. We weren't there!

AB Lesson 6 page 43

Lesson 6, Activity 15, p. 43 (AB) CD2:14
1 She isn't working today.
2 Please don't wait for me.
3 He wasn't shopping in the market.
4 She doesn't want tea.
5 We haven't helped them.
6 I didn't enjoy the trip.

PB Lesson 8 page 49

Lesson 8, Activity 22, p. 49 CD2:15
Hi, I'm Inuk. I live in Greenland. Winter and summer are very different here.
In the winter, we don't see the sun very much. There's one long night for four weeks in December and January. There are some big snowstorms and it is very, very cold. We go to school by snowmobile because we can't use a car.
In the summer, there aren't any snowstorms. There are often long sunny days. For a month, it is never night-time. I go kayaking and fishing every day. The summer is great but it's very short. In September, it's time for my winter clothes again.

AB Lesson 8 page 45

Lesson 8, Activity 21, p. 45 (AB) CD2:16
Come to Greenland!
Ride on snowmobiles! Climb snowy mountains! See caves and waterfalls of ice! There aren't any big cities here but there are some beautiful polar bears and reindeer in this cold place. Every day in Greenland is an adventure!

AB Lesson 9 page 46

Lesson 9, Activity 23, p. 46 (AB) CD2:17
Mia = M Grandma = G
M Hi, Grandma.
G Hello, Mia. Where are you?
M I'm in Brazil.
G Are you in the rainforest?
M No, I'm not. I'm in a fantastic city – Rio de Janeiro. There are some nice places here.
G Are there any pyramids in Rio de Janeiro?
M No, there aren't. There are some beautiful beaches though. There's a big statue, too – on a mountain next to the city.
G What's that music?
M It's the samba music of Brazil. I'm watching some people dancing. A lot of people here are very good at dancing!

5 Shopping

Objectives

- talk about clothing and accessories
- ask and answer about prices using the UK's official currency
- learn cardinal numbers from 100 to 1000
- talk about possessions
- use exclamations using appropriate intonation

Topics
- clothing and accessories
- shopping
- dressing correctly

Values
Dress correctly for each occasion.

Language
Vocabulary

Clothing and accessories: swimsuit, watch, bracelet, wallet, umbrella, gloves, belt, pocket, tracksuit, label
Adjectives: tight, baggy, (a) cheap, expensive, old-fashioned, modern
Numbers: 101, 102 ... 999 and 1000

Structures

How much is/are ...? It's/They're ...
It is/They are too expensive.
Whose ... is this/are these? It's/They're William's/Louis'/mine/yours/his/hers/its/ours/theirs
Future tenses

Revision

jacket, scarf, sunglasses, sandals, colours, demonstratives, backpack, hiking boots, tights, uniform, trainers, shorts, cardinal numbers 1–100

Receptive language

pound, charity shop, second-hand, low prices, donate, bargain

CLIL and Wider world language

CLIL (Shopping): shop assistant, receipt, advertisement, change, money, customer, department store
Wider world (Charity shops)

Stories
Does Emma buy the jacket?
Island mystery: chapter 5

Song
Baggy trousers.

Socio-cultural aspects
- finding out about prices
- talking about likes and dislikes related to clothing and accessories
- finding out about other people's shopping likes and dislikes
- working in pairs
- showing responsible habits when shopping
- shopping in charity shops

Phonics
Intonation – exclamations

Cross-curricular contents
- Social Sciences: clever customers; charity shops
- Music: song, pronunciation rhyme
- Language skills: reading a story, acting out, telling a story

Learning strategies
- making use of prior knowledge
- following instructions
- recording new words
- reflecting on habits for responsible consumption
- using ICT resources to research, obtain, process and communicate information
- individual autonomous learning
- using a table to organise personal information
- critical thinking: discriminating and classifying
- logical thinking: calculating, deductive reasoning and problem solving
- integrating contents: discussing and approaching new cultures
- reflecting on learning and self assessment

Basic competences

Linguistic communication: Use language as an instrument for communication (L.1 to L.10).
Knowledge and interaction with the physical world: Make responsible consumer choices (L.7).
Mathematical competence: Say and understand prices (L.2 to L.3).
Processing information and digital competence: Use Active Teach, Digital Activity Book and Ice Island Online World

Social and civic competence: Talk about appropriate language and behaviour when shopping (L.1 to L.3 and L.6). Be a responsible consumer (L.7). Make alternative shopping choices and talk about socially-responsible shopping (L.8).
Cultural and artistic competence: Talk about colours and styles of clothes and accessories (L.1 to L.4 and L.6).
Learning to learn: Reflect on what has been learnt and self-evaluate progress (L.10).
Autonomy and personal initiative: Use own judgement and ideas and further develop social skills (L.1 to L.10).

Skills

Listening
- can understand people talking about shopping
- can understand a dialogue about shopping
- can understand a dialogue about who things belong to
- can understand questions about shopping
- can understand responsible shopping habits
- can understand a song about clothing and accessories
- can understand a pronunciation rhyme

Reading
- can read and understand information (about shopping and prices) in sentences, short paragraphs and texts
- can read and understand a text about who things belong to
- can read and understand a cartoon strip story, captions and speech bubbles
- can read and understand factual information about shopping in charities
- can read and understand a text about responsible consumption

Speaking
- can give information about shopping
- can sing the *Baggy trousers* song
- can talk about prices
- can talk about who things belong to
- can talk about responsible shopping habits
- can talk about future plans and promises
- can say the pronunciation rhyme

Taking part in conversations
- can ask and respond to questions about shopping and prices, and about possession
- can ask and respond to questions about other people's shopping habits
- can take part in a dialogue about shopping
- can give their opinion about shopping
- can ask and respond to factual questions about shopping

Writing
- can write clothing and accessories words
- can write cardinal numbers 100–1000
- can use possessive pronouns in sentences
- can write about future plans and promises
- can complete written sentences about shopping
- can write sentences about their own clothing and shopping likes and dislikes
- can write questions and answers about prices using UK's official currency
- can write a short text about a charity shop

Classroom ideas

- Use the CLIL poster of the unit to decorate the class.
- Use photos or realia (if possible) of clothing and accessories to decorate the class.
- Show pupils real pound notes and pence coins.
- If you have pupils from other countries in your class, ask them to compare shopping in their countries (types of shops, opening hours, etc.).
- You or your pupils could use the websites below to access more information about shopping in different countries around the world: http://www.maths-aids.com/money/ http://www.globalclassroom.org/money2.html
- Play games from the Games Bank.
- Photocopiables 5.1–5.7.

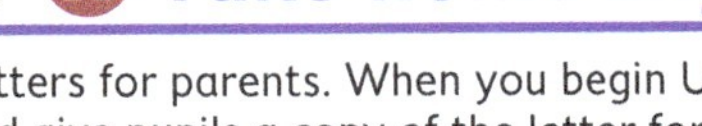

Take-home English

- Letters for parents. When you begin Unit 5, complete and give pupils a copy of the letter for the unit (Active Teach). This explains what pupils are going to learn in this unit.
- Home-School Link. Encourage pupils to talk to their families about the clothes they wear and why. (L.5)
- Grammar Booklet and Reading and Writing Booklet. Pupils take these home to show their parents.
- Pupils' Digital Activity Books.
- Portfolios. Encourage pupils to take their portfolio files home to show their parents when they finish Unit 5.

Evaluation

Self assessment
- Pupils can buy things and talk about how much things cost
- Pupils can talk about who things belong to
- Pupil's Book page 61
- Activity Book page 57
- Grammar reference (Pupil's Book page 108)

Resources
- Unit review (Activity Book page 100)
- Picture dictionary (Activity Book page 108)
- Test Booklet – Unit 5 (pages 22–25)
- Grammar Booklet (pages 17–20), Reading and Writing Booklet – Unit 5 (pages 17–20)

5 Shopping

Lesson 1

Lesson aims
To learn and practise new vocabulary: clothes, accessories

Target language
tracksuit, swimsuit, bracelet, watch, wallet, pocket, belt, umbrella, gloves, label

Receptive language
How much is/are ... ? It's/They're ..., Can I buy ..., please? pound

Materials
Audio CD; Flashcards and Wordcards (Clothing and accessories), magazine/internet photos of clothes pupils know; English currency, or internet/magazine photos of English notes and coins

Optional activity material
Drawings/tracings of twelve items of clothing from this lesson, copies for each group
Active Teach; Digital Activity Book; Photocopiable 5.1

Starting the lesson

- Stick the photos on the board. Ask the class *Do you like this dress/that hat/those boots?* Elicit the difference between *that* and *those*.
- Say *In our country we buy things with (your currency). In Britain people buy things with* (elicit or say) *pounds.* (Show pupils any coins/notes/photos you have.)

Presentation

- Present the vocabulary using the flashcards (clothing and accessories). Hold up each flashcard in turn and say the word for pupils to repeat. Hold up the flashcards again in a different order for pupils to repeat again.

Pupil's Book page 52

1 Listen and read. Does Emma buy the jacket?

- Ask the class *Who can you see in the pictures? (Emma, Robbie, a woman.) Where are they? (In a shop.) What are Emma and Robbie doing? (They're buying clothes.)*
- Play the recording. Pupils listen, follow the text and find the answer to the question.
- Play the recording again, pausing for pupils to repeat each price in chorus.

KEY No, she doesn't.

2 Listen and repeat.

- Give pupils time to look at the pictures.
- Play the recording. Pause for pupils to repeat.
- Play the recording again, pausing after each word so that pupils can repeat.

Practice

3 Look and say. Use words from Activity 2.

- Pupils look at the example dialogue while you read it.
- Point out or elicit *that* and *this* are used with singular nouns and *those* is used with plural nouns.
- Remind pupils *that* and *those* are used to refer to things at a distance from the speaker. Elicit one or two examples. Encourage a confident pupil to continue.
- Pupils do the activity in pairs.

Activity Book page 48

1 Find and circle.

- If your pupils need support, check the clothes words first. Ask *What's number (1)?* etc.
- Give pupils time to do the activity in pairs.

2 Write. Use *is* or *are* and words from Activity 1.

- Give pupils time to write and check answers.
- Volunteers read the sentences aloud.

3 Unscramble.

- Give pupils time to do the activity.
- Volunteers read the words aloud.

Ending the lesson

- Volunteers use the new vocabulary to say what they like and don't like wearing, e.g. *I like wearing a jacket but I don't like wearing gloves.* For Answer Key see p. 174. For Audioscript see p. 176.

OPTIONAL ACTIVITIES

Game
Ask pupils to close their eyes and stand back-to-back with a friend. Without looking, they describe what he/she is wearing.

Find the pairs Play *Pelmanism* in groups of three or four using the clothes words. See p. 301. Each group of pupils prepares the Pelmanism cards by colouring in two sets of clothes outlines that you've prepared.
Photocopiables 5.1 See teacher's notes p. 291.

Lesson 2

Lesson aims
To revise the Lesson 1 vocabulary; to learn and practise questions with *How much?*

Target language
How much is/are ... ? It's/They're ...

Receptive language
Can I buy ..., please? It's/They're too ...

Materials
Audio CD; Flashcards and Wordcards (Clothing and accessories)

Optional activity materials
Active Teach; Digital Activity Book; Grammar Booklet

Starting the lesson

- Play *Bingo* using numbers 1–99.

Presentation

- Display the flashcards (clothing and accessories), learnt in Lesson 1, around the room and play I Spy (see p. 300). Ask individual pupils to come and write the words on the board.
- Ask the class to silently read the Look! box.
- Read the first part of the Look! box.
- Tell pupils we use *How much ...?* to ask for the price, then *is/are* must agree with the noun. Write £ on the board and tell pupils it stands for *pound*.

Practice

Pupil's Book page 53

4 

Listen and point. Then ask and answer.

- Give the class time to look at the pictures.
- Play the recording, pausing for pupils to repeat.
- Play the recording again, pausing for pupils to ask and answer. Give pupils time to do the activity in pairs.

5 Read and say the prices.

- Give pupils time to look at the prices on the labels.
- Read number one and ask pupils to repeat. Ask confident pupils to read the rest.
- Give pupils time to do the activity in pairs. One points and asks *How much is this?* And the other answers *It's seventy-nine pounds fifty.*

6 What are you wearing? How much is it? Invent prices. Then do a roleplay.

- Ask two confident pupils to read the example dialogue.
- Pairs continue, asking each other and inventing the prices.

Activity Book page 49

4 

Listen and circle the correct price.

- Play the recording. Pupils do the activity.
- Play the recording again to check answers.

5 Write the correct prices in Activity 4 in words.

- Ask a confident pupil to write the first one on the board.
- Give pupils time to do the activity. Then write the numbers on the board to check spelling.

6 Write.

- Give pupils time to read and do the activity. Ask pupils to complete the dialogue in pairs and read it.
- Ask a pair to read the dialogue to check answers.

For the next lesson

Ask pupils to bring in magazine/internet photos of clothes that they like.

Ending the lesson

- Ask the class if anyone has ever been to a country with a different currency. Was it easy to get used to or not? For Answer Key see p. 174. For Audioscript see p. 176.

Pupils can now, or at the end of this unit, go online to Ice Island and find the skis that Penn and Gwyn are holding. They are inside the tent, leaning against the four-drawer tower on the left. Once pupils click on the skis they are taken to a supplementary language game based on the vocabulary in this unit.

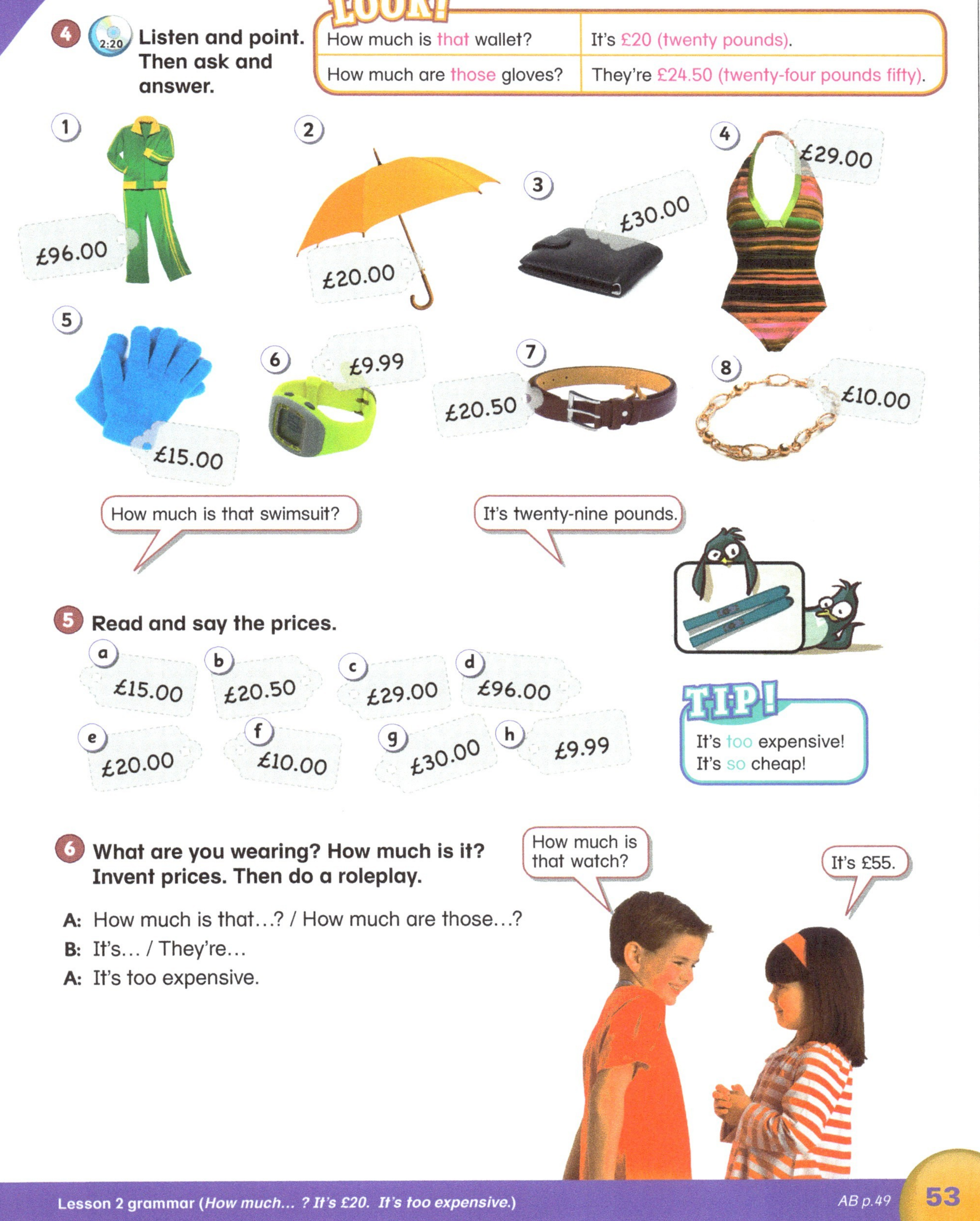

4 2:20 **Listen and point. Then ask and answer.**

LOOK!

How much is that wallet?	It's £20 (twenty pounds).
How much are those gloves?	They're £24.50 (twenty-four pounds fifty).

5 **Read and say the prices.**

a £15.00 b £20.50 c £29.00 d £96.00
e £20.00 f £10.00 g £30.00 h £9.99

TIP!
It's too expensive!
It's so cheap!

6 **What are you wearing? How much is it? Invent prices. Then do a roleplay.**

A: How much is that…? / How much are those…?
B: It's… / They're…
A: It's too expensive.

Lesson 2 grammar (*How much… ? It's £20. It's too expensive.*) *AB p.49* **53**

OPTIONAL ACTIVITIES

Number dictation
Pupils write five prices in their notebooks, e.g. £2.50. They say the prices to their partner, who writes them.

Bingo
Play *Bingo* with prices. Write twenty different prices on the board. Pupils choose and copy down nine of them. See p. 301.
Grammar Booklet p. 17 See answer key p. 286.

Lesson 3

Lesson aims
To extend the vocabulary, adding adjectives to clothes and accessories; to practise the vocabulary with a song

Target language
tight, baggy, cheap, expensive, old-fashioned, modern
Cardinal numbers 100–1000)
It's/They're too ...
It's/They're so ...

Materials
Audio CD; Flashcards and Wordcards (Clothing and accessories; Adjectives for clothes)

Optional activity materials
Photos of clothes and accessories (as for Lesson 1); Active Teach; Digital Activity Book; Photocopiable 5.2; Photocopiable 5.3; Reading and Writing Booklet

Starting the lesson

- Say *jeans*. A pupil repeats this and adds another clothes word. Pupils continue round the class. If a pupil says the words in the wrong order or hesitates, they are out.

Presentation

- Introduce the new words using the flashcards. Hold them up and say the words for pupils to repeat.
- Put the flashcards on the board. Point to the different flashcards and ask the class to say the words.

Pupil's Book page 54

  Listen and repeat.

- Give pupils time to look at the pictures.
- Play the recording. Pause for pupils to repeat each word.
- Play the recording again. Repeat each word. Pupils repeat in chorus.

Song

  Listen and sing.

- Play the song. Pupils follow in their books. Ask them *What does the singer like wearing? (Baggy trousers)*
- Play the song again. Encourage pupils to sing.
- Have a competition. Divide the class into two groups. Play the song twice more, each group singing in turn, or the two groups singing alternate lines. Decide which group is best!
- Ask the class to silently read the Tip! box. Ask them for examples from the pictures in Activity 7.
- You can now play the karaoke song (Active Teach).

Practice

- Ask the class to silently read the second Tip! box. Ask them for examples from the pictures in activity 7.

9 Invent prices from £1 to £1000. Then do a roleplay.

- Give pupils time to read the Tip! box at the bottom. Explain that we use *and* after the word hundred.
- Write some numbers 100–1000 on the board and ask pupils to read them.
- Then ask a pair to read the example dialogue.
- Give pupils time to invent the prices of the items in the box. Encourage them to work in pairs and role play the dialogue changing the items and prices.

Activity Book page 50

7 Number.

- Give pupils time to look at the pictures.
- Pupils do the activity. Then check answers.

8 Write.

- Give pupils time to look at the pictures and write the sentences. Circulate, monitor and help.
- Ask pupils to read the sentences for checking.

9 Match the opposites.

- Give pupils time to do the activity.
- Divide the class into two groups and alternately ask the opposites.

10 Write the prices in words.

- Give pupils time to do the activity.
- Divide the class into two groups and alternately ask the prices.

Ending the lesson

- Stick the photos you've brought labelled A, B, C, etc. round the room so they are easily visible. Pupils walk round the room, look carefully at each and secretly choose one to describe. They write four or five sentences in their notebooks. Tell them others will have to guess which picture it is. Encourage them to use *too* + different adjectives. Groups of four read their descriptions to each other. The listeners guess the picture.
- For the next lesson, ask pupils to bring in their favourite magazine adverts. For Answer Key see p. 174. For Audioscript see p. 176.

7 2:22 **Listen and repeat.**

1 tight
2 baggy
3 cheap £9.99
4 expensive £96.00
5 old-fashioned
6 modern

8 2:23 **Listen and sing.**

SONG

That jacket's too short
And the colour's too light.
That hat's too expensive
And the size isn't right.

Chorus:

I only like wearing…
Baggy trousers, baggy trousers,
baggy trousers, baggy trousers.
Baggy trousers are cheap,
baggy trousers are cool.
Baggy trousers rule!

That jumper's too tight.
Those shorts are too long.
Those shoes are too dark.
And the size isn't right.

Chorus

TIP!
too tight
too expensive

9 **Invent prices from £1 to £1,000. Then do a roleplay.**

How much is that old-fashioned watch?
It's…
It's too cheap. / It's too expensive!

TIP!
100 one hundred
101 one hundred and one – 102 one hundred and two
110 one hundred and ten – 111 one hundred and eleven
120 one hundred and twenty – 121 one hundred...
200 two hundred – 300 three hundred …
999 nine hundred and ninety-nine
1,000 one thousand

54 Lesson 3 vocabulary (adjectives for clothing and accessories numbers to 1000) AB p.50

OPTIONAL ACTIVITIES

Favourite clothes Ask volunteers to tell the class about their favourite summer and winter clothes.

Make a poster: Cool clothes! Groups of four cut out cool clothes from the photos they've brought, stick them on card and label them, e.g. *baggy trousers, a light-green T-shirt, expensive trainers, etc.*

Photocopiable 5.2 See teacher's notes p. 291.

Photocopiable 5.3 See teacher's notes p. 291.

Reading and Writing Booklet p. 19 See answer key p. 284.

Lesson 4

Lesson aims
To revise the Lesson 3 vocabulary; to learn and practise the use of *Whose* and possessives

Target language
Whose ... is/are this/those? Possessive Pronouns; They are Harry's.

Materials
Audio CD

Optional activity materials
Active Teach; Digital Activity Book; Grammar Booklet

Starting the lesson

- Write on the board *Whose bag is this?* Show the pupils your bag. Elicit the possessive pronoun *yours* by asking them *Is it yours? Or yours?* Answer *This bag is mine!* Repeat with your sunglasses or pen.

Presentation

Pupil's Book page 55

- Ask the class to silently read the Look! box.
- Tell pupils we use the pronoun *Whose?* to ask for possession. Explain the difference between the possessive adjectives and possessive pronouns. Write on the board: *This is my bag. / This is mine*. Encourage them to give more examples.
- Remind pupils that *is/are* must agree with the noun. Give them examples. Point out the expression *a friend of _____ 's/a friend of mine.*

Skills

10 Listen and point. Then ask and answer.

2:24

- Give pupils time to look at the pictures and predict whose the objects are.
- Play the recording. Give pupils time to find and point. Play the recording again pausing for pupils to say the answers.
- Ask a pair to read the dialogue. Give pairs time to do the dialogue four times.

11 Look above and say.

- Read the example (Question 1) slowly. Then ask a confident pupil to read aloud the completed version of Question 2.
- Give pupils time to work in pairs. Circulate, monitor and help.
- Divide the class in two groups and ask three pupils from each group to read sentences 3 and 4 respectively. The team with no mistakes wins!

KEY
2 The gloves are Robbie's. They're Robbie's gloves. They're his.
3 The bracelet is Emma's. It's Emma's. It's hers.
4 The swimsuit is Maddy's. It's Maddy's. It's hers.

Practice

12 Play the memory game.

- Pupils look at the example dialogue while you read it with a volunteer. The game continues until one of you can't remember the other's sentence or makes a mistake with the possessive pronouns. You must be accurate!
- Pupils play the game in pairs, two groups or whole group.

Activity Book page 51

11 Write.

- Give pupils time to look at the pictures and to write the sentences. Make sure they understand they must follow the model in question 1.
- Ask volunteers to read the answers.

12 Complete. Whose is this?

- Give pupils time to read and write. Check answers reading aloud.

13 Look at Activity 11 and write.

- Give pupils time to read the sentences they wrote in activity 11.
- Ask them *Whose is the jacket?* Model number 1 or encourage a confident pupil to do so.
- Give pupils time to do the activity. Check answers by pupils reading aloud.

14 What can you remember from the memory game in Pupil's Book page 55 Activity 12? Write.

- Give pupils time to remember and write what they practised.

Ending the lesson

- Volunteers read out what they have written for Activity Book Activity 14. For Answer Key see p. 174. For Audioscript see p. 176.

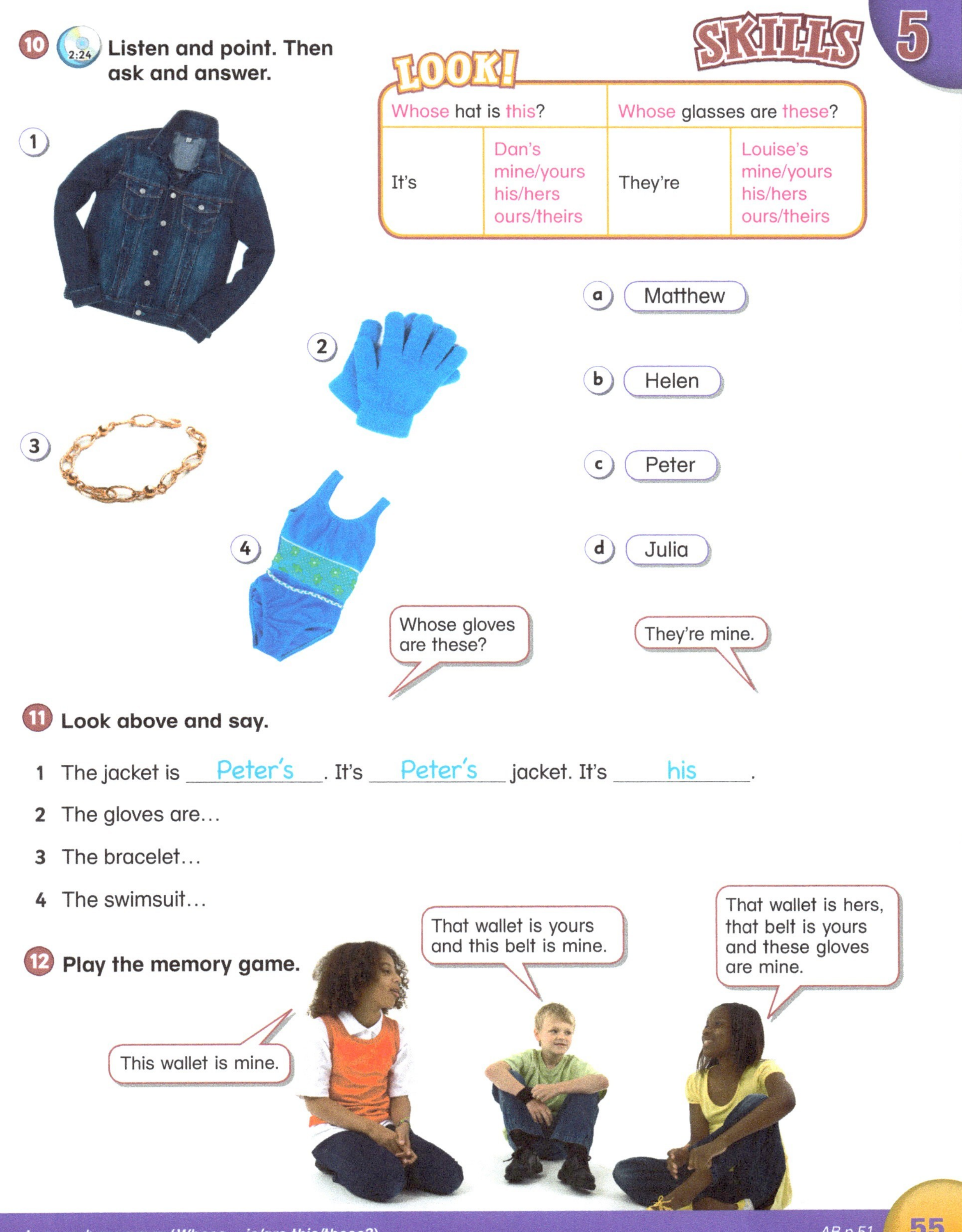

SKILLS 5

10 2:24 **Listen and point. Then ask and answer.**

LOOK!

Whose hat is this?		Whose glasses are these?	
It's	Dan's mine/yours his/hers ours/theirs	They're	Louise's mine/yours his/hers ours/theirs

1 2 3 4

a Matthew

b Helen

c Peter

d Julia

Whose gloves are these?

They're mine.

11 **Look above and say.**

1 The jacket is Peter's. It's Peter's jacket. It's his.

2 The gloves are…

3 The bracelet…

4 The swimsuit…

12 **Play the memory game.**

This wallet is mine.

That wallet is yours and this belt is mine.

That wallet is hers, that belt is yours and these gloves are mine.

Lesson 4 grammar (*Whose… is/are this/these?*)

AB p.51

55

OPTIONAL ACTIVITIES

Guessing game Collect personal belongings from everybody in the class and put them in a bag. Take them one by one asking *Whose ... is/are this/these ...?* The one who guesses correctly, using *It's/they're* _____ *'s* takes the next object from the bag.

Grammar Booklet p. 18 See answer key p. 286.

Lesson 5

Lesson aims
To consolidate the unit language with a story

Values
Dress correctly for each occasion.

Materials
Audio CD

Optional activity materials
The names of the story characters on separate slips of paper; Active Teach; Digital Activity Book; Photocopiable 5.4

Starting the lesson

- Ask *Where's the treasure? (In a cave on Snow Mountain.) Where are Rufus and Ivan?* (Pupils guess.)

Presentation

- Ask questions about each picture and teach *changing room*. Pupils answer or guess. e.g. (Picture 1) *Where are the children? (In a shop.) What clothes can you see? (Gloves, wetsuits, goggles, jackets and a bag.)* (Pictures 2 and 3) *Who is in the changing room?* (Picture 6) *Who's running? (Finn, Jenny and Ivan.) Where's Rufus? (In a boat.)*

Pupil's Book page 56

13 Look at the pictures. Tell the story.

- Ask the class to look again at the pictures.
- Ask six volunteers to go in front of the class and tell the story just based on looking at the pictures, without reading. Each pupil tells the story of one picture.

14 2:25 Listen and read. Then act out.

- Play the recording. Pupils listen and follow the story.
- Ask true/false questions about the story, e.g. *Jenny wants to buy a wetsuit. True or false? (False. She wants to buy gloves.) Dylan and Finn are in the changing room. (False. They're sitting in the shop.) Rufus is too thin. (True.) The thieves have got a boat. (True.)*
- Play the recording again. Pause for the class to repeat each line in chorus.
- Allocate these five parts to individuals or groups: Jenny, Dylan, Finn, Rufus and Ivan.
- Play the recording again. Pause for individuals or groups to repeat their character's lines.
- Ask seven volunteers to act out the story (Jenny, Dylan, Finn, Rufus, Ivan, the shop assistant, Penn.)
- Pairs predict what happens next.
- Volunteers tell the class their ideas.

Values

- Write on the board: PARK/PARTY/SCHOOL. Ask the class to talk about the different types of clothes you need to wear for each occasion. Ask them *Is it important to dress correctly for each occasion? Why?*

Home-School Link

- Ask the class to talk at home about the different kinds of clothes each member in their family wears and then think why.

Practice

Activity Book page 52

15 Write.

- Give pupils time to do the activity.
- Ask pupils to ask and answer for checking.

16 Look at the prices. Jenny has got £105. What can she buy?

- Give pupils time to look and calculate. Tell them there are several possible answers.
- If necessary, do the maths on the board.
- Check the different answers together.

17 What happens next? Imagine.

- Give pupils time to write what they think happens next in the story.
- Ask volunteers to tell the class their ideas and take a vote to find the most popular idea.

18 Write a dialogue between Jenny and the shop assistant.

- Give pupils time to write the dialogue in pairs.
- Ask volunteers to role play their dialogues.

Ending the lesson

- Show a flashcard of a scarf and ask the class *Whose scarf is this? Dylan's or Jenny's? (Dylan's)* Continue with the following flashcards: sunglasses (Jenny's), skateboard (Finn's), glasses (Dr Al's), patch (Captain Formosa's), goggles (Rufus's and Ivan's). For Answer Key see p. 174. For Audioscript see p. 176.

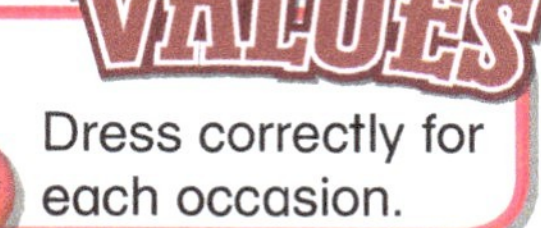

Dress correctly for each occasion.

HOME-SCHOOL LINK

Talk about the different kinds of clothes each member of your family wears. Then think why.

PARENT

OPTIONAL ACTIVITIES

Word game Play *Touch and guess*. See p. 301.
How much is it? Make enough clothes wordcards for half the class and enough matching clothes wordcards with prices for the other half. Pupils mingle, asking for and giving price information until they find the matching clothes/clothes + price card.
Photocopiable 5.4 See teacher's notes p. 291.

Lesson 6

Lesson aims
To form and identify exclamations

Materials
Audio CD; Phonics and spelling poster

Optional activity materials
Active Teach; Digital Activity Book; Photocopiable 5.5

Starting the lesson

- Show pupils the Phonics and spelling poster (see teacher's notes on p. 26).
- Read the sentences for this unit aloud and ask pupils to find a common pattern.

Presentation

- State the goal of the lesson.
- Explain that exclamations are used to express surprise, agreement, disagreement, greeting, attracting attention, etc. and so we use different intonation.
- Write the same sentence with and without an exclamation mark and model the intonation.
- Point out the exclamation mark and compare how it is used in your language.

Pupil's Book page 57

15 Listen and repeat.

- Give pupils time to read the expressions.
- Play the recording for pupils to repeat the phrases chorally. Stop after each phrase and ask volunteers to repeat it as accurately as possible. Encourage the class to repeat energetically.

16 Listen and read. Then repeat.

- Give pupils time to look at the pictures without reading the dialogue and make predictions about the dialogue.
- Set purpose for listening: *Let's listen to find out what happened at the hat shop*. Agree upon a sign to show when pupils identify the exclamations while listening.
- Play the recording.
- Check comprehension. Then encourage pupils to read and act out the dialogue in pairs.

17 Listen, point and say.

- Encourage pupils to read the pairs of sentences.
- Play the recording. Pupils listen and decide whether it is the exclamation or the non-exclamation sentence that they hear.
- Ask the class to read the exclamations aloud.

Practice

18 Read and practise with your partner.

- Explain the structure *how* + adjective.
- Model the first sentences in each column. Encourage the class to repeat. They can exaggerate the intonation for fun.
- Ask the class to work in pairs.

19 Listen and repeat.

- Give pupils time to look at the pictures.
- Play the recording. Then ask pupils to identify the exclamations.
- Play the recording again. Encourage the class to learn and repeat the rhyme.

Activity Book page 53

19 Read and sort.

- Read all the sentences aloud. Ask volunteers to imitate you and act out a couple of sentences.
- Give pupils time to read the sentences.
- Encourage the fast finishers to add new sentences to each column.
- Correct the activity as a whole-group discussion.

20 Read and complete.

- Read aloud the first sentence. Ask the pupils to look for an adjective that looks right, sounds right and makes sense. Complete the first sentence as a whole group.
- Give pupils time to complete the activity.
- Check the activity as a whole-group discussion.

21 Read and match.

- Tell pupils to draw lines linking the pairs of phrases.
- Pupils practise the three mini-dialogues in pairs.

22 Write four sentences. Use exclamations.

- Encourage the class to make up their own sentences orally.
- Record some sentence starters on the board to provide support for all learners.
- Give pupils time to do the activity.

Ending the lesson

- Ask volunteers to read the sentences they wrote for Activity Book Activity 22, using their best intonation. Take a vote on who had the best sentence with the best intonation.
- Revisit the goal of the lesson and ask pupils to evaluate their own progress. For Answer Key see p. 174. For Audioscript see p. 176.

Intonation: Exclamations!

Exclamations are used to express surprise, agreement, disagreement, greeting, for attracting attention, etc.

15 2:26 **Listen and repeat.**

1 Good luck!
2 It's not too expensive!
3 Good morning!
4 Thank you!
5 Oh dear!

16 2:27 **Listen and read. Then repeat.**

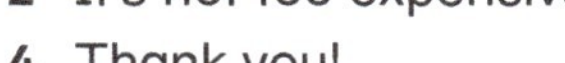

Shopping for hats

A: Good morning, Sir!
B: Good morning, Madam!
A: Can I help you?
B: Yes, please. I need a new hat.
A: Of course! We have brown, blue and black hats, Sir.
B: Oh, excellent!
Can I try the blue one, please?
A: Indeed! Here you are!
B: Oh, I think this one is too tight.
A: What about this one, Sir?
B: I'm afraid it is too bright.
A: Let's see… what about this dark blue hat, Sir?
B: It doesn't look too silly. How nice!
A: It looks perfect, Sir.
B: Thank you! I'll take the dark blue one then.
A: Great choice! Your total is 20 pounds, Sir.
B: Excellent! It's not too expensive. Oh dear!
A: Yes, Sir?
B: I left my wallet in the taxi!
A: Oh, I'm sorry to hear that! Look! The taxi is still there!
B: Thank you!
A: Good luck!

17 2:28 **Listen, point and say.**

1 I like it very much. / I like it very much!
2 You are very intelligent! / You are very intelligent.
3 They are tired. / They are tired!
4 I hate vegetables. / I hate vegetables!

18 **Read and practise with your partner.**

How expensive!	It's so cheap!
How beautiful!	It's so ugly!
How funny!	It's so silly!
How interesting!	It's so boring!

19 2:29 **Listen and repeat.**

I like this wallet.
And I love that bracelet!
And that jacket!
But they're too expensive for me.

OPTIONAL ACTIVITIES

Poets' Workshop Add a new poem with exclamation to the class poetry book.

Drama Ask pupils to perform the dialogue on Pupil's Book page 57, Activity 16.

Write a script as a whole class using the sentences from Activity Book page 53, Activity 21.

Photocopiable 5.5 See teacher's notes p. 291.

Lesson 7

Lesson aims
To extend the unit vocabulary on shopping; to learn and practise the use of future forms

Cross-curricular focus
Social Science – Clever consumers

Target language
I'll buy this belt
I am going to save money this year
shop assistant, advertisement, receipt, change, cash, customer, department store

Materials
Audio CD; CLIL poster

Optional activity materials
Realia: money (euros, cents, pounds, pence, receipt); Active Teach; Digital Activity Book; Photocopiable 5.6; Reading and Writing Booklet; Grammar Booklet

Starting the lesson

- A consumer is a person who buys goods or services for personal use, or their own consumption.
- Being a clever consumer means being able to save money. Saving for the future requires patience and giving up some things you may want today. But it can be worth it when you get what you want the most.

Presentation

- Ask the class to tell you about what they like shopping for and how much things cost.
- Allow some STT and discuss, as a closure, if they know how to make the best of their money.
- Before reading give pupils time to look at the pictures on page 58. Ask them *What can you see? Where are Helen and David?*
- Use the vocabulary routine: **mime and define**. Next, **use each adjective in a sentence**. Last, **ask questions** with each adjective. You may also use realia to show different currencies and shopping vocabulary.
- Use *will* sentences to model predictions.
- Explain that the characters want to solve a problem. David has a plan, therefore, he uses *going to*. However, Helen is making promises and she uses *will*.
- Share the background information from the Starting the lesson section.

Pupil's Book page 58

20 Read and find these words in the text. What are Helen and David going to do?

- Read the title and the introduction to the text.
- Set purpose for reading: *Let's read to see what the characters are going to do to be clever consumers.*
- Read the whole text as a shared-reading experience: use expression and intonation to model proficient reading.
- Ask pupils to follow your reading.
- Read the text again.
- Ask pupils to find the words from the wordbank in the text and then explain their meaning.
- Ask the class to silently read the Look! box.
- Read the Look! box and pause for pupils to repeat.
- Explain the difference between the use of *will* and *going to*.

Practice

21 Ask and answer.

- Complete the activity as a whole-group discussion.

KEY
1 ask the shop assistant **2** do some planning
3 during the sales **4** check her receipts and change

22 Talk to your partner.

- Pairs talk to each other.
- Ask one or two volunteers to share with the class what they have discussed.

Activity Book page 54

23 Read and complete.

- Read aloud the first sentence and discuss the choices as a whole group.
- Give pupils time to do the activity.
- Check answers as a whole-group discussion.

24 Read and answer the questions. Then write.

- Read the questions aloud and encourage the pupils to answer them orally.
- Revise the structures *will* and *going to*.

Ending the lesson

- Review the different places where we can shop. Make a web of ideas on the board
- Allow time for pupils to complete the idea web.
- Encourage fast finishers to add extra products to each shop. For Answer Key see p. 174. For Audioscript see p. 176.

20 Read and find these words in the text. What are Helen and David going to do?

shop assistant advertisement receipt change money customer department store

Clever consumers

a

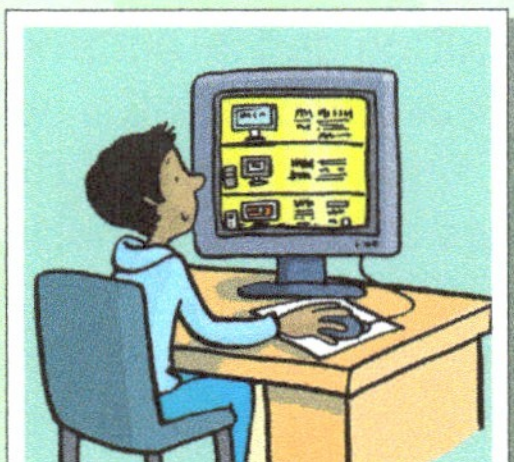

I want to save money to buy a new computer. It costs 500 euros. This is my plan.

I'm going to do some research before buying. I'm going to read the advertisements and I'm going to check the prices online. Some department stores are cheaper than others.

I'm also going to write a list before going shopping. I'm going to save some extra cash by doing some planning.

I'm going to use customer vouchers. I'm a student and sometimes you can also get a discount if you ask the shop assistant.

David, Spain

b

Last year I didn't have enough money for my sister's birthday. Sometimes I spend too much. This is my promise to be a responsible consumer.

I'll wait for the sales. Everything is a lot cheaper. You can see many great things on the shelves.

I'll do my maths, too. Last week I overspent by 20 pounds and 50 pence because I didn't check the receipt and the change.

I'll ask myself: Do I really need it?

Helen, United Kingdom

I will buy this belt.

I'm going to save some money this year.

21 Ask and answer.

1 What is David going to do to get a student discount?
2 What is he going to do to save some extra cash?
3 When will Helen go shopping?
4 What will she do with her receipt and change?

22 Talk to your partner.

OPTIONAL ACTIVITIES

A money box Make a money box using recycled materials.

Posters Make posters to teach friends at school how to be clever consumers.

Dialogues Use realia to write and act out a dialogue at a department store.

Photocopiable 5.6 See teacher's notes p. 292

Reading and Writing Booklet p. 19 See answer key p. 284

Grammar Booklet p. 19 See answer key p. 286

Lesson 8

Lesson aims
To learn about other cultures and respect cultural differences; to learn about shopping for clothes in other countries.

Receptive language
charity shop, second-hand, low prices, donate, bargain

Materials
Audio CD

Optional activity materials
World map or globe; Active Teach; Digital Activity Book; CLIL poster; Photocopiable 5.7

Starting the lesson

- Say *Look at your clothes!* Ask *What are you wearing?* Ask pupils to explain where they bought their clothes, e.g. ask *Where did you buy that jacket? (In a department store/shop/open market.)*
- Discuss the different places that your clothes come from, e.g. *The clothes we wear can be made in China, designed in Italy,* etc.

Presentation

Pupil's Book page 59

23 Look and read. Are there any charity shops in your country?

- Write *Charity Shops* on the board. Ask pupils to guess which kind of shops they are. Tell them the names of any famous charities in your country.
- Give the class time to read silently. Ask *What is a charity shop? (A shop where the money they receive helps the charity.) What do they sell in this type of shop? (Second-hand clothes and other things.) What is different in these shops? (Low prices) Why can these shops offer low prices? (Things are obtained for free – donations.)* Write pupils' answers on the board around the title you wrote.
- Teach *safe* and *bargain* using miming and/or a quick translation from a confident pupil. Remind pupils about the importance of using the context to work out the meaning of new words.
- Ask the class about the three opinions given in the Pupil's Book, e.g. *What is good about reusing clothes? What does 'safe' mean in this context? Who do you think usually buys in these shops and why?* Write the three opinions on the board (*recycling/safe/bargain*).

Practice

24 Read again and discuss buying in charity shops.

- Ask a different volunteer to read each text as the class check pronunciation and intonation.
- Give pupils time to look at the photos again. Divide the class into four groups. Ask two of them to think about the advantages of buying in charity shops and the other two about the disadvantages. Write on the board *Advantages/Disadvantages*. Encourage the groups to discuss and give their opinions. Ask pupils from the different groups to write on the board each new idea that comes up.

Portfolio activity

- Ask pupils to read the activity. If possible, ask them to look for a charity shop on the Internet. Remind pupils they have to collect the information in a Word document following the steps in the Pupil's Book. Depending on the number of pupils, ask them to do this activity individually, in small groups or larger groups.

Activity Book page 55

25 Read and complete the sentences.

- Give pupils time to read the word bank and complete the activity.
- Fast finishers could make up additional sentences.

26 Read these adverts. Then write your opinion.

- Give pupils time to read the ads silently.
- Ask volunteers to read aloud. Ask *What are these ads asking for? (People to donate used clothes.) Do they focus on the same reasons to persuade people to donate? (No)*
- Write on the board *Reasons for donating clothes and things* and below *Text 1/Text 2/Text 3.* Ask three pupils to write their answers on the board. Then check and discuss.
- Ask *In your opinion, which is the best reason for donating clothes?*
- For the Project activity, give pupils time to display the printed Word documents on charity shops from the Portfolio activity.
- Invite another class to visit yours and ask pupils to explain their pieces of work to the other class.

Ending the lesson

- Find out the names of the charity shops pupils have researched in the Project activity (Activity Book p. 55) and write them on the board. Group together all pupils with similar shops. Ask pupils to tell the class the most important information about these shops that they can remember. For Answer Key see p. 174. For Audioscript see p. 176.

Wider world

Charity shops

23 **Look and read. Are there any charity shops in your country?**

Charity shops!

Charity shops are a type of social shop that sells second-hand clothes and things donated by people. The people who work in these shops are volunteers. Everything in these shops is obtained for free. For this reason they can sell at very low prices. Charity shops sell a lot of things: clothes, books, music, shoes and many other things too.

In my opinion the things sold in charity shops are safe… and less expensive!

A British charity shop

I think reusing second-hand clothes is a form of recycling. It can help protect our environment!

An American thrift store

I believe it is an excellent way to buy shoes, clothes and anything at a bargain price!

An Australian OpShop

24 **Read again and discuss buying in charity shops.**

PORTFOLIO

Think and write.

ICT Project
Look for a charity shop on the Internet and collect the following information in a Word document:
– Name of the charity shop (TITLE)
– Cut and paste a photograph
– Where the charity shop is
– Whose responsibility it is
– What the charity shop sells
– Why they can offer low prices
Save the document.
Print your document!

OPTIONAL ACTIVITIES

Our charity shop Let's pretend! Divide the class into three groups: Group 1 (donate clothes and other things), Group 2 (shop assistants), Group 3 (customers). Ask the groups, in turns, to role play the situation:

1. Someone goes to a charity shop to donate used clothes and gives reasons for this.
2. The shop assistant looks carefully all the items and checks. He/she gives reasons for accepting the item or not.
3. The customer enters to buy something and gives reasons why.

Photocopiable 5.7 See teacher's notes p. 291.

Lesson 9

Lesson aims
To review the unit language with a game
To use the Picture dictionary

Revision language
clothes, cardinal numbers 100–1000; How much ...? This ... is too ... . / These ... are too ... . Future tenses
Clothes

Materials
Audio CD

Optional activity materials
Active Teach; Digital Activity Book; Reading and Writing Booklet

Starting the lesson

- Choose two pupils wearing different clothes and ask the class to talk about their clothes. Encourage the class to ask them where they bought them, how much they were, etc.

Pupil's Book page 60

25 Play noughts (0) and crosses (✗).

- Give the class time to look at the pictures.
- Divide the class into groups of four and ask pupils to read the game.
- Encourage the class to explain the rules of the game.
- Give pupils time to play. Circulate, monitor and help.

Picture dictionary

- Pupils can do the picture dictionary of the unit on Activity Book page 108.
- Ask pupils to look at the pictures and try to write the vocabulary on their own in their notebooks. Then ask them to look for the words they don't remember in the Pupil's Book.
- As they finish, ask pupils to exchange notebooks to check answers. (Notebooks can be collected for checking.)

Activity Book page 56

27 Number to make a conversation.

- Give pupils time to read the conversation and do the activity.
- Ask volunteers to read aloud for checking answers.
- If you want to use this dialogue for a roleplay (see Optional Activities), write the correctly ordered sentences on the board or ask pupils to write them in their notebooks.

28 What should they wear? Write ✓ or ✗ .

- Give pupils time to read and do the activity. Remind them of the importance of dressing correctly for each occasion.
- Ask volunteers to read their choices.

Ending the lesson

- Ask pupils if they usually shop on their own and if not, with whom. Encourage them to explain why. For Answer Key see p. 174. For Audioscript see p. 176.

25 Play noughts (0) and crosses (X).

Name 4 things that you're wearing today.	Count from 500 to 1,000 in tens.	Name these things 
Read and say the opposite. 1 These trousers are too cheap! 2 That shirt is too baggy! 3 This hat is too old-fashioned!	**Say 3 things that you're going to do tomorrow.** I'm going to …	Name these things 
Name these things. 	**Name 4 things that your teacher is wearing today.**	**Count from 500 to 600 in ones.**

AB p.108

AB p.56

OPTIONAL ACTIVITIES

Memory game Ask pupils to add vocabulary from the Picture dictionary (Activity Book p. 108) to the sentence *I went to a shop and bought a belt, I went to a shop and bought a belt and a wallet*, etc.

Roleplay Role play the re-ordered dialogue in Activity Book Activity 27.

Reading and Writing Booklet p. 20
See answer key p. 284.

Lesson 10

Lesson aims
To personalise and assess efforts

Target language
clothes; cardinal numbers 100–1000; How much ...? This ... is too ... . / These ... are too ... . Possessives; Future tenses

Materials
Audio CD

Optional activity materials
Online World, Active Teach; Digital Activity Book; Grammar Booklet; Test Booklet; Grammar reference (PB); Unit review (AB)

Starting the lesson

- Invite the class to think of these activities as a way to assess their work, in order to find out if they need extra work in any of the unit contents.

Pupil's Book page 61

26 Read, look and choose a present for each person.

- Give the class time to do the activity.
- Ask volunteers to read aloud their answers and give reasons.

KEY **1** d **2** b **3** e **4** c **5** a

27 Order the sentences to make a dialogue.

- Give pupils time to do the activity in pairs.
- Ask two confident pupils to read the dialogue for checking.

KEY
1 Dan: How much are those baggy trousers?
2 Shop assistant: They're eighteen pounds fifty.
3 Dan: May I buy the trousers, please?
4 Shop assistant: Yes, of course. Eighteen pounds fifty, please.

28 Role play the dialogue for the other objects in Activity 26.

- Give pupils time to do the activity in pairs. Circulate, monitor and help.

Activity Book page 57

29 Match.

- Give pupils time to do the activity.
- Divide the class into two groups and alternately ask one group to read the definition and the other to say the correct word.

30 Read and complete the sentences.

- Give pupils time to read and complete the sentences.
- Check the answers reading aloud.

31 Write about your favourite clothes.

- Give pupils time to write about their favourite clothes: colour, size, style, price, place to sell/buy, occasions to wear it, etc.
- Read aloud some of them.

Ending the lesson

- Give pupils time to read the sentences in the 'I can' section.
- Ask pupils to think carefully if they are able to do the 'I can' sentences. Ask them what they found easy or difficult through the unit and why. For Answer Key see p. 174. For Audioscript see p. 176.

Online World Pupils can now go online to Ice Island and enjoy the fun and games.

27 **Order the sentences to make a dialogue.**

1 Shop assistant: Yes, of course. Eighteen pounds fifty, please.

2 Shop assistant: They're eighteen pounds fifty.

3 Dan: May I buy the trousers, please?

4 Dan: How much are those baggy trousers?

28 **Roleplay the dialogue for the other objects in Activity 26.**

Ice Island

OPTIONAL ACTIVITIES

Quiz Prepare a quiz in a PowerPoint presentation or on the board to assess the class as a group.

Grammar reference (PB p. 108) and Unit review (AB p. 100) You may want pupils to do the Grammar reference and Unit review activities for Unit 5.

Test Booklet You could give the Unit 5 test at this time.

Grammar Booklet p. 20 See also answer key p. 286.

Activity Book Answer Key

p. 48, Activity 1
1 belt **2** swimsuit **3** watch **4** bracelet **5** wallet **6** tracksuit **7** umbrella **8** gloves **9** pocket

p. 48, Activity 2
1 is swimsuit **2** are belts **3** is wallet **4** are gloves

p. 48, Activity 3
label, tracksuit, pocket, watch, umbrella, wallet, bracelet, belt

p. 49, Activity 4
1 c, £29 **2** a, £12.50 **3** b, £19 **4** a, £212 **5** c, £42 **6** b, £25.50

p. 49, Activity 5
1 twenty-nine pounds **2** twelve pounds fifty **3** nineteen pounds **4** two hundred and twelve pounds **5** forty-two pounds **6** twenty-five pounds fifty five

p. 49, Activity 6
1 much **2** pounds **3** how **4** hundred **5** please **6** course

p. 50, Activity 7
a 2 **b** 3 **c** 6 **d** 4 **e** 5 **f** 1

p. 50, Activity 8
1 These trousers are too tight. **2** That robot is too expensive. **3** This sweater is too baggy. **4** These hats are too old-fashioned.

p. 50, Activity 9
1 expensive/cheap **2** modern/old fashioned **3** tight/baggy **4** big/small **5** short/long

p. 50, Activity 10
1 seven hundred and ninety pounds fifty
2 two hundred and thirty pounds
3 five hundred and fifty pounds
4 three hundred and fifteen pounds
5 one hundred and five pounds.
6 one hundred and eighty-two pounds
7 one hundred pounds
8 one thousand pounds

p. 51, Activity 11
1 She's wearing a short jacket.
2 She's wearing baggy trousers.
3 He's wearing a tight sweater.
4 He's wearing shorts.

p. 51, Activity 12
2 Harry's, his
3 Michael's and Louis', theirs

p. 51, Activity 13
1 It's, Sky's.
2 They're Lee's. / his.
3 Whose sweater is this? / his.
4 Whose shorts are these? / They're his.

p. 52, Activity 14
1 mine **2** yours, mine **3** hers, yours, mine

p. 52, Activity 15
1 In a shop **2** They are bored **3** Rufus and Ivan **4** swimsuits **5** No they don't **6** In a boat

p. 53, Activity 19
Surprise Oh dear!
Greeting Good morning, Sir!
Agreement How nice!
Disagreement It's too silly, It's too bright!
Attracting attention Look!

p. 53, Activity 20
beautiful, expensive, lazy, rude, boring

p. 53, Activity 21
Thank you! / You're welcome! Good bye! / See you later! I'm sorry, we haven't got it! / Oh, no problem!

p. 54, Activity 23
customers, department store, price, money, receipt, assistant, change.

p. 55, Activity 25
1 raincoat **2** vegetables **3** game / doll **4** computer DVD **5** T-shirt

p. 56, Activity 27
a 3 **b** 8 **c** 7 **d** 4 **e** 5 **f** 2 **g** 1 **h** 6

p. 57, Activity 29
1 f **2** j **3** h **4** b **5** c **6** i **7** d **8** g **9** e **10** a

p. 57, Activity 30
3 Emma's/hers, your **4** mine **6** his

Audioscript

PB Lesson 1 page 52

Lesson 1, Activity 1, p. 52 CD2:18

Emma = E Shop Assistant = SA Robbie = R

E How much is that scarf?
SA It's six pounds fifty.
R And how much are those sunglasses?
SA They're fifteen pounds.
E Wow! I love that jacket and it's only twelve pounds.
E Can I buy this jacket, please?
SA Yes, of course. A hundred and twenty-four pounds, please.
E/R What?!

Lesson 1, Activity 2, p. 52 CD2:19

1 tracksuit
2 swimsuit
3 watch
4 bracelet
5 wallet
6 pocket
7 belt
8 umbrella
9 gloves
10 label

PB Lesson 2 page 53

Lesson 2, Activity 4, p. 53 CD2:20

Assistant = A Customer = C

1 **C** How much are those gloves?
A They're fifteen pounds.
2 **C** How much is that swimsuit?
A It's twenty-nine pounds.
3 **C** How much is that belt?
A It's twenty pounds fifty.
4 **C** How much is that umbrella?
A It's twenty pounds.
5 **C** How much is that tracksuit?
A It's ninety-six pounds.
6 **C** How much is that bracelet?
A It's ten pounds.
7 **C** How much is that wallet?
A It's thirty pounds.
8 **C** How much is that watch?
A It's nine pounds ninety-nine.

AB lesson 2 page 49

Lesson 2, Activity 4, p. 49 (AB) CD2:21

Assistant = A Customer = C

1 **C** How much is that wallet?
A It's twenty-nine pounds.
2 **C** How much is that bracelet?
A It's twelve pounds fifty.
3 **C** How much is that swimsuit?
A It's nineteen pounds.
4 **C** How much is that tracksuit?
A It's two hundred and twelve pounds.
5 **C** How much are those gloves?
A They're forty-two pounds.
6 **C** How much is that umbrella?
A It's twenty-five pounds fifty.

PB Lesson 3 page 54

Lesson 3, Activity 7, p. 54 CD2:22

1 tight
2 baggy
3 cheap
4 expensive
5 old-fashioned
6 modern

Lesson 3, Activity 8, p. 54 CD2:23

That jacket's too short
And the colour's too light.
That hat's too expensive
And the size isn't right.

Chorus:
I only like wearing …
Baggy trousers, baggy trousers,
Baggy trousers, baggy trousers.
Baggy trousers are cheap,
Baggy trousers are cool.
Baggy trousers rule!

That jumper's too tight.
Those shorts are too long.
The shoes are too dark
And the size isn't right.

Chorus

PB Lesson 4 page 55

Lesson 4, Activity 10, p. 55 CD2:24

NARRATOR: 1
MATTHEW: Helen, whose jacket is this?
HELEN: It's not mine and it's not Julia's. It's too big for her. Maybe it's Peter's?
MATTHEW: Yes, it's his because his name is on the inside.

NARRATOR: 2
HELEN: Matthew, whose gloves are these?
MATTHEW: They're mine.
HELEN: Aren't they Peter's?
MATTHEW: They were his. But now they're mine because they were too small for him.

NARRATOR: 3
PETER: Julia, is this yours?
JULIA: No, I don't wear expensive bracelets like that.
PETER: Well, whose is it?
JULIA: It's Helen's. It was a birthday present from her mum and mad.

NARRATOR: 4
PETER: Matthew, whose swimsuit is this?
MATTHEW: Well, it's not mine. Ha-ha-ha! Helen, is it yours?
HELEN: No, it's Julia's. It's her new swimsuit. Last year's was too tight.

PB Lesson 5 page 56

Lesson 5, Activity 14, p. 56 CD2:25

Jenny = J Ivan = I Rufus = R Finn = F
J Ooh! Can I buy those gloves, please?
I Argh! Ow! It's too tight!
R You're too fat!
I No! You're too thin!
F Hey! The thieves!
J Where's the map?
R Quick! Run!
J Stop!
J Hey! Come back!

PB Lesson 6 page 57

Lesson 6, Activity 15, p. 57 CD2:26

1 Good luck!
2 It's not too expensive!
3 Good morning!
4 Thank you!
5 Oh dear!

Lesson 6, Activity 16, p. 57 CD2:27

Woman = W, man = M
W Good morning, Sir!
M Good morning, Madam!
W Can I help you?
M Yes, please. I need a need new hat.
W Of course! We have brown, blue and black hats, Sir.
M Oh, excellent!
M Can I try the blue one, please?
W Indeed! Here you are!
M Oh, I think this one is too tight.
W What about this one, Sir?
M I'm afraid it is too bright.
W Let's see ... what about this dark-blue hat, Sir?
M It doesn't look too silly! How nice!
W It looks perfect, Sir.
M Thank you! I'll take the dark-blue one then.
W Great choice! Your total is twenty pounds, Sir.
M Excellent! It's not too expensive. Oh dear!
W Yes, Sir?
M I left my wallet in the taxi!
W Oh, I'm sorry to hear that! Look! The taxi is still there!
M Thank you!
W Good luck!

Lesson 6, Activity 17, p. 57 CD2:28

1 I like it very much!
2 You are very intelligent.
3 They are tired.
4 I hate vegetables!

Lesson 6, Activity 19, p. 57 CD2:29

I like this wallet.
And I love that bracelet!
And that jacket!
But they're too expensive for me!

6 Party time

Objectives

- talk about the past
- ask and answer questions about the past
- describe what people were like in the past
- learn ordinal numbers from 21st to 31st
- talk about possibility in the past
- talk about obligation
- ask questions using appropriate intonation

Language

Vocabulary

Ordinal numbers: twenty-second, twenty-third, twenty-fourth, twenty-fifth, twenty-sixth, twenty-seventh, twenty-eighth, twenty-ninth, thirtieth, thirty-first

Structures

Irregular past tense verbs: make/made, have/had, come/came, give/gave, see/saw, sing/sang, bring/brought, meet/met, eat/ate, get/got
They brought a present.
They didn't bring any presents.
They could come to the party.
They couldn't eat everything.
Where/When/What/Who did you ...?
I must ... / I have to ...

Revision

uncle, aunt, cousins, parents, grandparents, ordinal numbers (first–twentieth), winter, autumn, spring, summer

Receptive

balloon, piece of cake, candle, card
was/were

CLIL and Wider world language

CLIL (The First Thanksgiving): month, diary, settler, voyage, Native American
Wider world: New Year's Eve around the world

Topics

- party time
- Thanksgiving day
- New Year's Eve
- solving problems

Values

Be a creative problem solver.

Stories

Why is there a cake?
Island mystery: chapter 6

Song

Happy New Year!

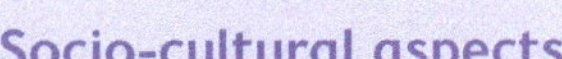

Socio-cultural aspects

- finding out about our family members past life
- talking about the origin of worldwide celebrations
- celebrating together
- working in pairs and groups

Phonics

Intonation – asking questions

Cross-curricular contents

History: Thanksgiving Day origin
Social Sciences: traditional celebrations in the world
Music: song, pronunciation rhyme
Language skills: reading a story, acting out, telling a story

Learning strategies

- making use of prior knowledge
- following instructions
- recording new words
- researching information about the past
- reflecting on how people and things change with the passing of time
- creative thinking: inventing
- using a table to organise information
- critical thinking: discriminating and classifying
- logical thinking: deductive reasoning and problem solving
- collaborative learning
- integrating contents: discussing and approaching new cultures
- reflecting on learning and self assessment

Basic competences

Linguistic communication: Use language as an instrument for communication (L.1 to L.10).
Knowledge and interaction with the physical world: Discuss travelling abroad and experiencing a foreign physical environment (L.4).
Mathematical competence: Learn ordinal numbers (L.3) and dates (L.4 and L.9).
Processing information and digital competence: Use Active Teach, Digital Activity Book and Ice Island Online World

Social and civic competence: Compare social celebrations (L.1 and L.3). Talk about other people's abilities and actions (L.2). Make arrangements (L.6). Dress appropriately (L.5).
Cultural and artistic competence: Learn about the past: The Thanksgiving story: Native Americans and settlers (L.7). Talk about New Year's Eve around the world (L.8).
Learning to learn: Reflect on what has been learnt and self-evaluate progress (L.10).
Autonomy and personal initiative: Use own judgement and ideas and further develop social skills (L.1 to L.10).

Skills

Listening
- can understand people talking about the past
- can understand a dialogue about the past
- can understand questions about the past
- can understand a song about a traditional celebration
- can understand a pronunciation rhyme

Reading
- can read and understand information (about the past) in sentences, short paragraphs and texts
- can read and understand a text about traditional celebrations
- can read dates
- can read and understand a cartoon strip story, captions and speech bubbles
- can read and understand factual information about traditional celebrations

Speaking
- can give information about the past
- can use dates when talking about the past
- can sing the *Happy New Year* song
- can talk about the past
- can talk about what people were like in the past
- can talk about the origin of traditional celebrations
- can talk about obligation
- can say the pronunciation rhyme

Taking part in conversations
- can ask and respond to questions about the past
- can ask and respond to questions about the origin of traditional celebrations
- can take part in a dialogue about traditional celebrations
- can ask and respond to factual questions about traditional celebrations

Writing
- can write simple past forms of irregular verbs
- can write ordinal numbers 21st to 31st
- can write dates
- can complete sentences to write about the past
- can write questions and answers about the past
- can use simple past tense in sentences, paragraphs and short texts
- can write about past events
- can write a short text about a traditional celebration

Classroom ideas

- Use the CLIL poster of the unit to decorate the class.
- Decorate the class for a party. Pupils can make their own garlands.
- If you have pupils from other countries in your class, ask them to compare traditional celebrations in their countries.
- You or your pupils could use the websites below to access more information about worldwide celebrations: http://kids.nationalgeographic.com/kids/stories/peopleplaces/winter-celebrations http://www.kidsturncentral.com/holidays/glossary/holidaysgloss.htm
- Play games from the Games Bank.
- Photocopiables 6.1–6.7.

Take-home English

- Letters for parents. When you begin Unit 6, complete and give pupils a copy of the letter for the unit (Active Teach). This explains what pupils are going to learn in this unit.
- Home-School Link. Encourage pupils to talk to their families about a problem they have solved at school. (L.5)
- Grammar Booklet and Reading and Writing Booklet. Pupils take these home to show their parents.
- Pupils' Digital Activity Books
- Portfolios. Encourage pupils to take their portfolio files home to show their parents when they finish Unit 6.

Evaluation

Self assessment
- Pupils can talk about events that happened in the past
- Pupils can say the date using ordinal numbers up to 31st
- Pupil's Book page 71
- Activity Book page 67
- Grammar reference (Pupil's Book page 109)

Resources
- Unit review (Activity Book page 101)
- Picture dictionary (Activity Book page 109)
- Test Booklet – Unit 6 (pages 26–29)
- Grammar Booklet (pages 21–24), Reading and Writing Booklet – Unit 6 (pages 21–24)

6 Party time

Lesson 1

Lesson aims
To learn and practise new vocabulary

Target language
make/made, have/had, come/came, give/gave, get/got, sing/sang, bring/brought, meet/met, eat/ate, see/saw

Receptive language
was/were

Materials
Audio CD; Flashcards and Wordcards (Regular and irregular past tense verbs)

Optional activity materials
Active Teach; Digital Activity Book; Photocopiable 6.1

Starting the lesson

- Write or draw a balloon, a cake and a present on the board. Ask *Where/When do you see these things? (At a party!)* Ask *Do you like parties? Why (not)?*

Presentation

- Present the vocabulary using the flashcards (regular and irregular past tense verbs). Hold up each flashcard in turn and say the word for pupils to repeat. Hold up the flashcards in a different order for pupils to repeat again.

Pupil's Book page 62

1 2:30 Listen and read. Why is there a cake?

- Ask *Who can you see in Picture 1? (Maddy, her family and Kipper.) Where are they?* (Pupils guess, e.g. *At Maddy's house.*) *Who do you think Maddy is speaking to in Picture 2? (Her mum.) Is her mum happy? (No, she isn't.) What's Maddy got in Picture 3? (A big cake.) Is Maddy happy in Picture 4? (No, she isn't!)*
- Play the recording. Pupils listen, follow the text and find the answer to the question.
- Play the recording again. Pause for pupils to hum each sentence, to practise sentence stress. Use gesture to indicate the main sentence stress, too. Tell pupils it's very important to use appropriate intonation when they speak.

KEY Because it's Grandad's birthday.

2 2:31 Listen and repeat.

- Give pupils time to look at the pictures.
- Play the recording. Pause for pupils to find and point.
- Play the recording again, pausing after each one. Tell them that in English language there is a group of verbs called **irregular verbs.** Explain that these verbs have a special verb form for the past tense which is not the *-ed* ending. These verbs are used very frequently so they will have to make an effort and learn them by heart.

Practice

3 Read and say. Use words from Activity 2.

- Give pupils time to read the words and the example.
- Ask pupils to say similar sentences looking at the story.

Activity Book page 58

1 Complete the table.

- Give pupils time to do the activity.
- To check answers, you could ask volunteers to write the present/past pairs on the board.

2 Write.

- Give pupils time to do the activity.
- If your class needs support, elicit the answers before pupils write.

3 2:32 Listen and tick (✓) the true sentences in Activity 2.

- Give pupils time to do the activity.
- Volunteers read aloud the sentences they have ticked.

Ending the lesson

- Ask a confident pupil to tell the class about his/her last birthday party. For Answer Key see p. 200. For Audioscript see p. 202.

OPTIONAL ACTIVITIES

Matching pairs
Take the wordcards and flashcards for irregular verbs. Stick the flashcards in one area and the wordcards in another area of the board, all face down.
Divide the class into two teams. Teams take it in turns to turn over a flashcard and wordcard to find matching pairs. If the pair doesn't match, the pupil puts the cards back in the same place.

6 Party time

Family tree
Pupils draw and label a family tree. You may want to brainstorm family vocabulary: elicit what pupils remember of these from Activity Book Activity 1. They draw a picture of each family member next to his/her name, or use a photo they've brought. They present their family to the class, e.g. *This is Jack. He's my cousin.* Display their work.
Photocopiable 6.1 See teacher's notes p. 292.

Lesson 2

Lesson aims
To revise the Lesson 1 vocabulary; to learn and practise irregular simple past forms

Target language
They brought ... / They didn't bring ...; could/couldn't

Receptive language
balloon, piece of cake, candle, card

Materials
Audio CD; Flashcards and Wordcards (Regular and irregular past tense verbs)

Optional activity materials
Active Teach; Digital Activity Book; Grammar Booklet

Starting the lesson

- Ask volunteers to tell you what they know about their parents' and grandparents' childhoods.

Presentation

- Display the flashcards (regular and irregular past tense verbs), learnt in Lesson 1, around the room and play *I Spy* (see p. 300). Ask individual pupils to come and write the words on the board.

Pupil's Book page 63

- Ask the class to silently read the Look! box.
- Remind pupils we use *didn't* to make the negative form of simple past. Remark that the past form of the verb is not used. Give examples, e.g. *I made a cake. / I didn't make a cake.* Remind pupils that the contraction *didn't* is *did not*.
- Tell pupils that the simple past of *can/can't* is *could/couldn't*.

4 Listen and read.

- Give the class time to look at the picture.
- Play the recording and ask pupils to look at the picture.
- Play the recording again and ask pupils to read as they listen.

Practice

5 Look and say.

- Give pupils time to read the words. Then ask a volunteer to read the examples.
- Give pupils time to do the activity in pairs. Circulate, monitor and help.
- Ask fast finishers to write the sentences in their notebooks.

6 Look at the picture in Activity 4. Play *True* or *False*.

- Pairs take it in turns to use the words in the word bank to make *true/false* sentences about the picture in Activity 4.

Activity Book page 59

4 Write.

- Give pupils time to do the activity. Then read for checking.

5 Look at the two pictures. Read and write *R* (Robbie) or *E* (Emma).

- Ask *When was Robbie's party? (February.) When was Emma's party? (July.)*
- Give pupils time to do the activity.

6 Complete the sentences. Use words from the box.

- Give pupils time to write. Note common mistakes with *was/were.*
- Write the sentences on the board to check.

Ending the lesson

- Divide the class into pairs or small groups. Give each group or pair a card with the word *was* and a card with the word *were*. Say sentences with *was/were* missing. Groups/pairs have five seconds to hold up the correct card. For Answer Key see p. 200. For Audioscript see p. 202.

Pupils can now, or at the end of this unit, go online to Ice Island and find the birthday cake that Penn and Gwyn are holding. It's inside the Science Lab, on top of one of the kitchen surfaces. The kitchen is on your right as you enter. Once pupils click on the birthday cake they are taken to a supplementary language game based on the vocabulary in this unit.

4 Listen and read.

LOOK!

I brought a present.	They didn't bring any presents.
They could come to the party.	They couldn't eat everything.

This is a photo of your Aunt Susan's birthday forty years ago. She was eleven and we had a small party at home. Those are her friends, Robert and Tracey. They brought her a great present and we gave her a bicycle – she really got a lot of presents! The girl with me is your mum. She was only five then. Those good-looking young people are your granny and me. Yes, we were only thirty-five! Your grandma made a big chocolate cake. And that baby in her arms is your Uncle David. He ate a lot of cake that day. What a mess!

5 Look and say.

1 Susan's family … (have)
2 Aunt Susan … (get)
3 Robert and Tracey … (bring)
4 Maddy's grandparents … (give)
5 Maddy's grandma … (make)
6 Uncle David … (eat)
7 Aunt Susan … (could/blow out)
8 Uncle David … (couldn't/walk)

Susan's family had a party.

6 Look at the picture in Activity 4. Play *True* or *False*.

the family Susan Susan's friends Maddy's mum balloon piece of cake the baby a doll pizza chocolate cake card

A: Uncle David could walk when he was one.
B: False! Uncle David couldn't walk when he was one.

OPTIONAL ACTIVITIES

True/False game Make up *true* and *false* sentences about the cartoon in Lesson 1.
Guessing game One pupil mimes what he did on his last birthday party. The class guesses.
Whispers Play *Whispers*. See p. 300.
Grammar Booklet p. 21 See answer key p. 286.

Lesson 3

Lesson aims
To extend the unit vocabulary on dates; to practise the vocabulary with a song

Target language
Ordinal numbers 21st to 31st; dates

Materials
Audio CD; Flashcards and Wordcards (Ordinal numbers)

Optional activity materials
Active Teach; Digital Activity Book; Photocopiable 6.2; Photocopiable 6.3; Reading and Writing Booklet

Starting the lesson

- Write the first letter of each month on the board in a column. Start with *J(anuary).*
- Volunteers complete the words.

Presentation

- Introduce the new words using the flashcards. Hold them up and say the words for pupils to repeat.
- Put the flashcards on the board. Point to the different flashcards and ask the class to say the words.

Pupil's Book page 64

  **Listen and repeat.**

- Give pupils time to look at the picture. Ask them to start counting from 1st, 2nd, etc. up to 31st.
- Play the recording. Pause for pupils to find and say each number.
- Play the recording again. Repeat each word. Pupils repeat in chorus.

Song

  **Listen and sing.**

- Play the song. Pupils follow in their books.
- Play the song again. Encourage pupils to sing.
- Have a competition. Divide the class into two groups. Play the song twice more, each group singing in turn. Decide which group is best!
- You can now play the karaoke song (Active Teach).

Practice

  **Listen, repeat and say the next date. Then continue with a partner.**

- Play the recording twice for pupils to listen and repeat.
- Point out we don't need to write *the* and *of.*
- Pairs continue, e.g. Pupil A: *the 7th of March.* Pupil B: *the 8th of March.*

Activity Book page 60

  **Listen and match.**

- Give pupils time to look at the calendar and pictures.
- Play the recording. Pupils listen and do the matching activity.

8 Write the date from Activity 7.

- Remind pupils that it isn't necessary to write *the* or *of.*
- After pupils have completed the questionnaire, check and compare their answers.

9 Write about something you did last month. What did you do? When did you do it?

- Give pupils time to write. Write some examples on the board.

10 Write the dates. Then read.

- Give pupils time to write. Write some examples on the board.

Ending the lesson

- Volunteers give you what they wrote for Activity Book Activity 10. Read out different events. The class guesses who wrote what. For Answer Key see p. 200. For Audioscript see p. 202.

7 2:34 **Listen and repeat.**

8 2:35 **Listen and sing.**

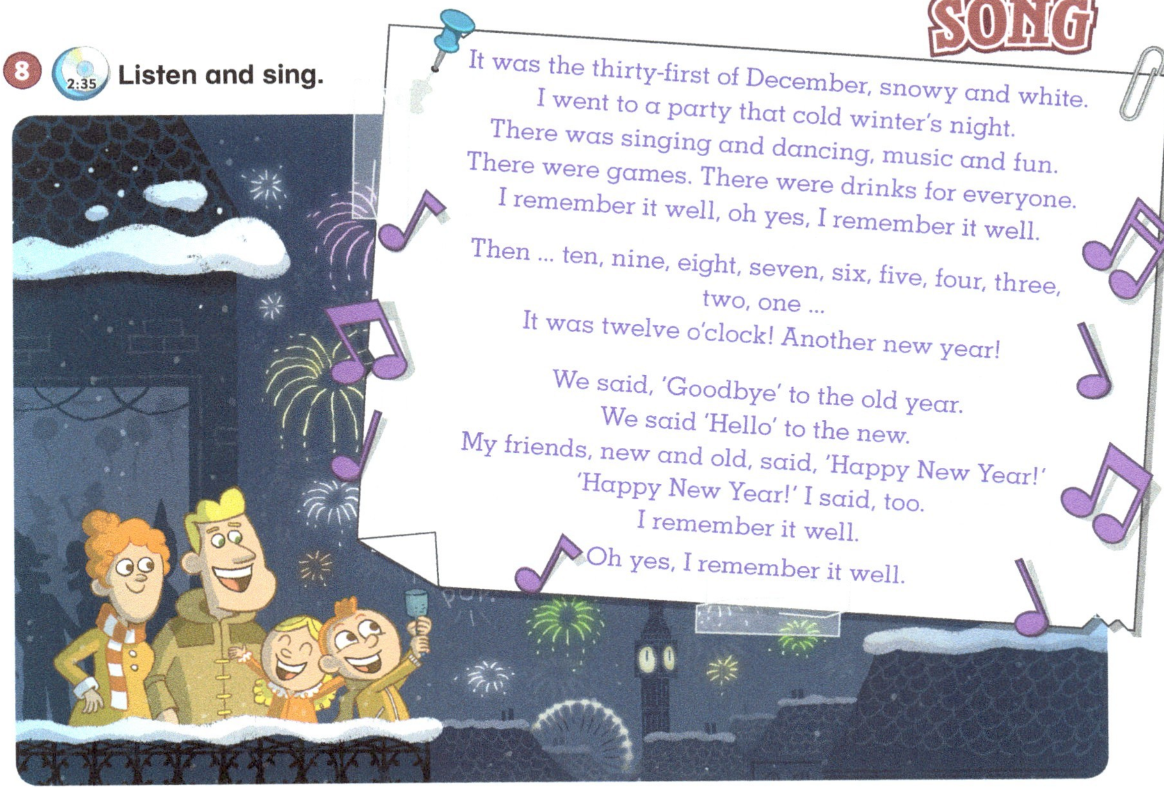

9 2:36 **Listen, repeat and say the next date. Then continue with a partner.**

22nd February 14th April 1st November
31st July 19th September

the twenty-second of February, the twenty-third of February

OPTIONAL ACTIVITIES

Pair work Pupils write three dates which are important to them. They tell a friend and explain, e.g. *The first of April is important because it's my mother's birthday*. Volunteers tell the class.

Birthday game Groups of four tell each other when their last birthday was and what they did.

Photocopiable 6.2 See teacher's notes p. 292.

Photocopiable 6.3 See teacher's notes p. 292.

Reading and Writing Booklet pp. 21–22 See answer key p. 284.

Lesson 4

Lesson aims
To revise the Lesson 3 vocabulary; to present the new structure

Target language
Simple past closed questions and answers
Where/When did you go? What/Who did you see?

Materials
Audio CD

Optional activity materials
Active Teach; Digital Activity Book; Grammar Booklet

Starting the lesson

- Ask a few pupils when their birthday is. Then ask them about the date of their last trip.

Presentation

Pupil's Book page 65

Skills

- Ask the class to silently read the Look! box.
- Remind pupils we use *did* to make the question form of simple past tense. Point out that we don't write the past form when *did* appears in the sentence.

10 (2:38) Listen and read. Point to the dates.

- Give pupils time to look at the pictures and read the text and the dates.
- Play the recording. Remind pupils to pay attention to the dates they hear.
- Play the recording again for children to point to the dates and repeat.

Practice

11 Ask and answer.

- Give pupils time in pairs to ask and answer questions about the dates. Circulate, monitor and help.

Activity Book page 61

11 Look and write.

- Give pupils time to look at the table and read the sentences.
- Ask pupils to fill in the gaps.
- Ask volunteers to read for checking.

12 Look at Activity 11. Then write questions.

- Give pupils time to write the questions. Remind pupils we don't write the past form of the verb when we use *did*.
- Ask pairs to ask and answer questions.

13 Unscramble and write the questions.

- Give pupils time to write.
- Ask volunteers to read the sentences.

Ending the lesson

- Ask pupils to ask and answer the questions they wrote in AB Activity 12. For Answer Key see p. 200. For Audioscript see p. 202.

10 2:38 **Listen and read. Point to the dates.**

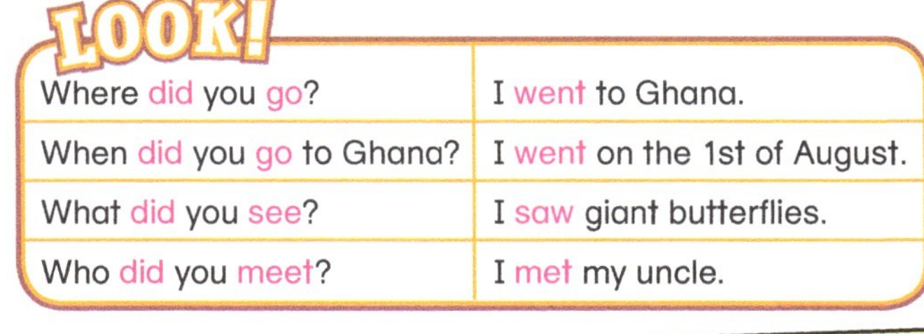

LOOK!

Where did you go?	I went to Ghana.
When did you go to Ghana?	I went on the 1st of August.
What did you see?	I saw giant butterflies.
Who did you meet?	I met my uncle.

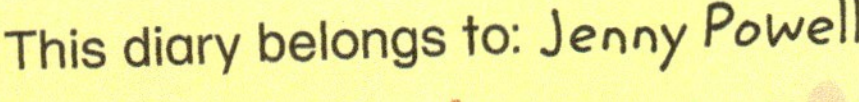

This diary belongs to: Jenny Powell

August

1st August I went to Ghana and met my relatives from Africa for the first time.

3rd August I went to Kakum National Park and saw beautiful giant butterflies.

5th August I went to a football game in Accra. Ghanaians love football! I danced and sang football songs with my new friends.

10th August I went to the north of Ghana. I saw the giant baobab trees and ate some baobab fruit, but I didn't like it!

22nd August I went to Lake Volta and sailed in a pirogue, a type of boat. It was cool!

28th August We had a party. My African friends gave me a lot of presents. 'Come back soon!' they said. I cried at the airport. ☹

30th August I came back home! I brought lots of presents for my mum, dad and brother. It was a great experience!

11 **Ask and answer.**

1 She … (go)
2 She … (see)
3 She … (dance)
4 She … (sing)
5 She … (eat)
6 She … (have)
7 She … (come)
8 She … (bring)

When did she go to Ghana?

She went on the 1st of August.

OPTIONAL ACTIVITIES

Writing contest

Pupils imagine they went on a long trip with their family last summer, and write a diary about the trip. The best one wins a prize.

Grammar Booklet p. 22 See answer key p. 286.

Lesson 5

Lesson aims
To consolidate the unit language with a story

Values
Be a creative problem solver

Materials
Audio CD

Optional activity materials
Active Teach; Digital Activity Book; Photocopiable 6.4

Starting the lesson

- Give the class two minutes to look at and read Episode 6 of Ice Island.
- Divide pupils into two teams. Ask each team questions about Episode 6, e.g. *Where did the thieves go first? (Into a shop)*

Presentation

Pupil's Book page 66

- Ask the class questions about each picture. Use the pictures and context to teach *snowmobile* and *need.* Pupils answer or guess, e.g.
  (Picture 1) *What are Jenny and Finn doing? (They're running.) Why? (Because they want to talk to Captain Formosa quickly.)*
  (Picture 2) *Who are they talking about? (Rufus and Ivan.)*
  (Pictures 4 and 5) *Is it a boring day? (No, it's exciting!)*
  (Pictures 5 and 6) *Where are they going? (To Snow Mountain.)*

12 Look at the pictures. Tell the story.

- Ask the class to look again at the pictures.
- Ask six volunteers to go in front of the class and tell the story just based on looking at the pictures, without reading. Each pupil tells the story of one picture.

Practice

  Listen and read. Then act out.

- Play the recording. Pupils listen and follow the story.
- The class finish sentences about the story, e.g. Say *Finn says the thieves went into a …* (shop). *Dylan says, 'Get in the …'* (snowmobile).
- Play the recording again. Pause for the class to repeat each line.
- Divide the class into five and allocate these parts: Jenny, Dylan, Finn, Captain Formosa, Dr Al.
- Play the recording again. Pause for pupils to repeat their character's lines.
- Ask seven volunteers to act out the story (Jenny, Dylan, Finn, Captain Formosa, Dr Al, Penn and Gwyn).
- Pairs predict what happens next.
- Volunteers tell the class their ideas.
- Take a vote to find the most popular idea.

Home-School Link

- Ask your pupils to go home and tell their family about a problem they solved at school – what happened, when it happened, where it happened, who was involved, etc.

Values

- Ask the class why it's important to **solve problems in a creative way**, e.g. *We can't expect our parents, teachers, etc. to solve all our problems.*
- Groups of four discuss what being a creative problem solver means to them and present their ideas to the class.

Activity Book page 62

14 Number the sentences in order.

- Give pupils time to do the activity.
- Pointing to different pictures, pairs take it in turns to ask *What does he look like?* and to describe the character.
- Volunteers describe the characters to the class.
- Pairs predict answers without looking at their Pupil's Books.
- Give pupils time to read the story again and do the activity.

15 Read and draw.

- Give pupils time to do the activity.
- If your pupils need support, work with the whole class. Volunteers read out one or two sentences at a time, pausing for the class to draw.

16 What happens next in the story? Imagine.

- Give pupils time to write.
- Ask volunteers to tell the class their ideas.
- Take a vote to find the most popular idea.

17 Write about your last holiday.

- Give pupils time to do the activity.
- Read some writing aloud.

Ending the lesson

- Play 'Spot the differences' with pupils' drawings from Activity Book Activity 15. For Answer Key see p. 200. For Audioscript see p. 202.

12 Look at the pictures. Tell the story.

13  Listen and read. Then act out.

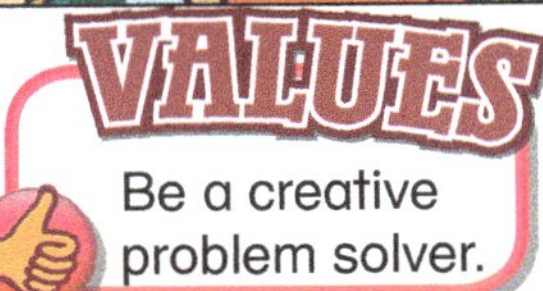

Be a creative problem solver.

HOME-SCHOOL LINK PARENT

Tell a family member about a problem you solved at school.

OPTIONAL ACTIVITIES

Pair work Pupils secretly draw three more things in their picture in Activity Book Activity 15. They take it in turns to tell a friend what they are, what colour they are and where they are. The friend adds them to his/her picture, e.g. *There was a big shark in the sea, too. It was grey. It was very near the boat.*

Writing Pairs imagine they are visiting Ice Island for the day. They write about their visit, using the words *went*, *said* and *was/were*, e.g. *We went to the submarine. Captain Formosa was there. We said hello.* Volunteers read their work to the class.

Photocopiable 6.4 See teacher's notes p. 292.

Lesson 6

Lesson aims
To identify raising intonation in *yes/no* questions; to identify falling intonation in *Wh-* questions

Materials
Audio CD; Phonics and spelling poster

Optional materials
Active Teach; Digital Activity Book; Photocopiable 6.5

Starting the lesson

- Ask pupils some social questions, e.g. *Are you having a good day? What did you eat for lunch/breakfast? Did you get a haircut?*
- Model intonation and point up and down depending on the intonation. Encourage pupils to ask you some questions.

Presentation

- Show pupils the Phonics and spelling poster (see teacher's notes on p. 26).
- State the goal of the lesson.
- Write a *yes/no* and a *Wh-* question on the board. Explain the difference.
- Make a T-chart with frequent sentence starters for each type of question so that pupils can use it as a reference. (A T-chart is an organiser that is used to list two different things. Make a T on the board and write the ideas on each upper line. The line in the middle separates the ideas.)
- Model the intonation in each example. Ask the pupils to point up or down depending on the intonation.
- Encourage pupils to ask questions so that the rest of the class can identify the intonation.

Pupil's Book page 67

14  Listen and repeat.

- Practise the first questions before listening. *Do you have any new CDs?*
- Play the recording for pupils to repeat the questions chorally. Stop after the first sentence and ask volunteers to repeat it as accurately as possible. Encourage the class to repeat energetically.

15 Listen and read. Then repeat.

- Give pupils time to look at the pictures and make predictions about the dialogue.
- Set purpose for listening: *Let's listen to find out what happened at the birthday party.* Ask pupils to point up or down as they listen to the questions.
- Play the recording.
- Check comprehension. Then encourage pupils to read and act out the dialogue in pairs.

16 Read and practise with a partner. Point up or down .

- Model the first questions in each column. Encourage the class to repeat.
- Ask the class to work in pairs.

17 Ask and answer.

- Give pupils time to read the dialogues.
- Then ask pupils to identify the rising and falling intonation in each sentence.
- Give pupils time to read the questions. They then answer the questions.
- Ask pupils to say similar questions and answers.

Practice

Activity Book page 63

18 Read and match.

- Read aloud all the sentences. Ask volunteers to follow and act out a couple of questions.
- Give pupils time to read the questions and the answers.
- Encourage the fast finishers to add new sentences to each column.
- Correct the activity as a whole-group discussion.

19 Read Activity 18 again and complete.

- Ask the class to reread the first column with the question in the previous activity.
- Give pupils time to complete the activity.
- Check the activity as a whole-group discussion.

20 Write questions.

- Ask pupils to read the answers. Brainstorm possible questions for number 1.
- Give pupils time to complete the activity.
- Check the activity as a whole-group discussion.

21 Write four questions. Then read and answer.

- Encourage the class to make up their own questions orally.
- Point out the T-chart on the board as a reference to provide support.
- Give pupils time to do the activity.

Ending the lesson

- Ask volunteers to read the questions they wrote for Activity Book Activity 21, while the class points up or down, depending on the intonation.
- Revisit the goal of the lesson and ask pupils to evaluate their own progress. For Answer Key see p. 200. For Audioscript see p. 202.

PHONICS & SPELLING

Intonation: Closed (or Yes/No) questions and information (or Wh-) questions

Yes / No questions have a rising intonation at the end of the sentence.
Wh- questions have a falling intonation at the end of the sentence.

14 2:40 **Listen and repeat.**

Yes/No QUESTION

1 Do you have any new CDs? ↗
3 Is there anything I can bring? ↗

Wh- QUESTION

2 Why don't you come to my place? ↘
4 When is your birthday? ↘

15 2:41 **Listen and read. Then repeat.**

William: Hello?
Sarah: Hi! It's Sarah.
William: Oh, Hi Sarah! How are you?
Sarah: Very well, thank you! How are you, William?
William: I'm fine, thank you.
Sarah: Can I ask you a question?
William: Yes, you can!
Sarah: When is your birthday?
William: Actually it's today! The twenty seventh of March!
Sarah: I wasn't too sure! Happy Birthday! Are you having a party?
William: Thank you! Yes, I am! Have you got any plans today?
Sarah: No, I haven't
William: Why don't you come to my place? I'm having a party at 6 o'clock
Sarah: Oh great! Thank you!
Sarah: Do you know who is coming to the party? I'd rather catch the bus with someone else.
William: Yes, Henry, Anna and Carlos will be there, too. You met them last time.
Sarah: Perfect, is there anything that I can bring?
William: Let me think… Have you got any new cds?
Sarah: No, I haven't. I need to buy new ones.
William: What about games? Didn't you buy one last week?
Sarah: Yes, I did! I will bring it tonight!
William: Perfect!
Sarah: See you later!
William: Bye!

16 Read and practise with a partner. Point up or down .

When is your birthday?	Have you got any plans today?
What can you bring?	Can I ask you something?
Where do you live?	Does she like music?
Who is coming to the party?	Are you having a good time?
What time is the party?	Do you know the address?

17 Ask and answer.

Are you having a birthday party?
Who is coming to the party?

AB p.63

OPTIONAL ACTIVITIES

Poets' Workshop Add a new poem with questions to the class poetry book.
Writer's Workshop Ask pupils to write an interview to find out more about a classmate.
Invite pupils to carry out their interviews using the right intonation.
Word Wall Add the *Wh-* questions to your word wall.
Photocopiable 6.5 See also teacher's notes p. 292

Lesson 7

Lesson aims
To extend the vocabulary; to learn and practise the use of *must* and *have to*

Cross-curricular focus
History – The First Thanksgiving

Target language
month, diary, settler, voyage, Native American
I must ...; I have to ...

Materials
Audio CD; CLIL poster

Optional activity materials
World map or globe; Active Teach; Digital Activity Book; Photocopiable 6.6; Reading and Writing Booklet; Grammar Booklet

Starting the lesson

- European settlers arrived in North America in the late fifteenth and early sixteenth centuries. The first two successful English colonies were the Virginia colony in Jamestown in 1607 and the Pilgrims' Plymouth Colony in 1620.
- Today, turkey with stuffing, mashed potatoes, cranberry sauce, gravy and pumpkin pie are essential in any Thanksgiving menu.

Presentation

- Write *the USA* on the board. Volunteers tell the class what they associate with it, e.g. *Hollywood, McDonald's, Disneyland*, etc. Allow some STT.
- Explain the journey that the Pilgrims embarked upon is very important in American history and its culture.
- Before reading, give pupils time to look at the pictures in the time line on page 68. Ask them *What can you see in this timeline?* Make sure pupils remember how to read a timeline.
- Use the vocabulary routine: **mime and define**. Next, **use each word in a sentence**. Last, **ask questions** with each new vocabulary word.
- Present the new structure. You can use a globe or a map to show that the settlers have to leave England to start a new life. In the new land they must learn many new things to survive.

Pupil's Book page 68

18 Read and find these words.

- Read the title and the introduction to the text.
- Remind the pupils how to read years in English (1620 = sixteen twenty).
- Explain that you know that this text is a diary because there are dates and the author is describing what happens each day.
- Revise words related to days, months and seasons.
- Read the whole text as a shared reading experience: use expression and intonation to model proficient reading.
- Ask pupils to follow your reading.
- Give pupils time to find the words in the texts.

Practice

19 Read again and answer.

- Complete the activity as a whole-group discussion.

KEY **1** In September 1620 **2** They must build new homes because winter is coming **3** The settlers must learn to farm because they need food **4** They have a Thanksgiving party to thank the Native Americans

20 Talk to your partner.

- Allow STT so that pairs can talk to each other.
- Ask one or two volunteers to share with the class what they have discussed.

Activity Book page 64

22 Read. Then write.

- Model how to complete this type of activity.
- Give pupils time to do the activity. Then correct it as a whole group.

23 Read and write *must* or *have to*. Then circle each sentence (summer = yellow circle, autumn = brown circle, winter = blue circle, spring = green circle).

- Use the reference on the board to support all learners.

24 Complete the table. Then write about a special celebration in your country.

- Create a web of ideas on the board as a reference.
- Model an expository piece of writing.
- Encourage fast finishers to include additional details.
- Invite pupils to share their writing through class presentations.

Ending the lesson

- Invite pupils to share the writing they did for Activity Book Activity 25 through class presentations. For Answer Key see p. 200. For Audioscript see p. 202.

18 Read and find these words.

month settler voyage Native American diary

The First Thanksgiving

On the last Thursday of November, Americans celebrate Thanksgiving. People meet with their families to eat turkey and to give thanks. How did the first Thanksgiving start? Read this diary of one of the settlers to find out.

September 1620

We are a total of 102 settlers. We have to leave Europe to start a new life somewhere else. After the summer, we are ready for the voyage. We have to cross the ocean to get to North America. We are leaving England on a ship called the Mayflower.

March 1621

Some Native Americans are here to help us. We must learn how to fish and farm during the spring to have food. They are teaching us many things.

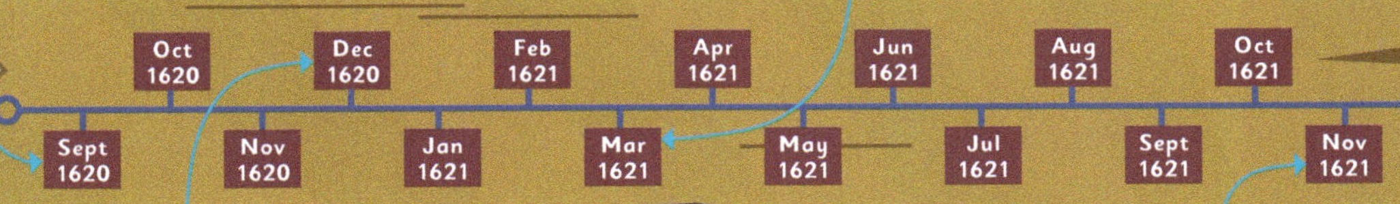

December 1620

Land! Finally we can leave the Mayflower after more than two months at sea. The voyage was horrible and dangerous. We must build some homes because winter is coming. It is very cold and foggy here in the new world and some settlers are getting ill.

November 1621

It is autumn and we have so much food now! We have to celebrate a Thanksgiving party with turkey and special food. We must say thank you to the Native Americans for all their help.

a

b

c

d

19 Read again and answer.

1 When did the settlers leave Europe?
2 Why did they have to build homes?
3 Why did they have to learn to farm during the spring?
4 Why did they have a Thanksgiving party?

20 Talk to your partner.

When do you have special celebrations in your country?

In July.

What do you celebrate?
How do you celebrate it?
Why do you celebrate it?

OPTIONAL ACTIVITIES

Pair work Pupils imagine they have just arrived on the *Mayflower*. They tell a partner what was and what wasn't on the boat.
Photocopiable 6.6 See teacher's notes p. 292.

Reading and Writing Booklet p. 23 See answer key p. 284.
Grammar Booklet p. 23 See answer key p. 286.

Lesson 8

Lesson aims
To learn about other cultures and respect cultural differences; to learn about different celebrations on New Year's Eve around the world

Receptive language
bell tolls, dummy, broadcast, bad luck

Materials
Audio CD

Optional activity materials
World map or globe; Active Teach; Digital Activity Book; CLIL poster; Photocopiable 6.7

Starting the lesson

- Write on the board New Year's Eve! Ask pupils if they know when this date is. Ask them what they usually do to celebrate New Year's Eve.

Pupil's Book page 69

Presentation

21 Look and read. Then find.

- If you have a world map, ask a volunteer to point out Spain, Australia, Colombia and Japan. Ask pupils what they know about these countries.
- Give pupils time to read the blogs silently.
- Ask pupils if they are surprised by any of the information. Ask which celebration is the most similar to theirs and why. And which one they like the most.
- Give pupils time to find the words in the blogs.

Practice

22 Read again and discuss. Where would you like to celebrate your next New Year's Eve?

- Ask a different volunteer to read each text as the class check pronunciation and intonation.
- Give pupils time to look at the blogs again. Divide the class into four groups and assign one country to each group. Ask them to discuss what is special in their country and why.
- Encourage the groups to discuss and give their opinions. Ask pupils from the different groups to tell the class the different opinions in their group.
- As a portfolio activity, develop the discussion. Ask how many different ways of celebrating New Year there are in the class. Ask *Is it usual to celebrate New Year's Eve in your house? How do you celebrate it?*
- Ask pupils to tell you one or two things that they usually do with their families on that date.
- Do the portfolio activity. Divide the class into groups of children who have similar ways of celebrating New Year. Ask pupils to make a poster in their group to explain the celebration.
- Finally, display the posters and invite the groups to talk about them, their similarities and differences. Remind them not to read their notes word for word as this doesn't help them improve their speaking.

Activity Book page 65

25 Read and complete.

- Give pupils time to read the blogs again and complete.
- Ask volunteers to read aloud and check.

26 Invent a new way of celebrating New Year's Eve!

- Ask pupils to write about the things they talked about in the Portfolio activity about celebrating New Year.
- Pupils read aloud their ideas and compare with others.
- Ask pupils to look again at the posters they made and choose one. They must invent a story that happened last year celebrating New Year's Eve in that way. Encourage pupils to use the irregular verbs they learnt in this unit.
- Have a vote for the most popular way of celebrating New Year's Eve in your class and pretend it's New Year!

Ending the lesson

- End the lesson with a smart dress prize after the 'party' (Activity Book p. 65)! For Answer Key see p. 200. For Audioscript see p. 202.

Wider world

New Year's Eve around the world

21 **Look and read. Then find.**

bell tolls | good luck | broadcast | bad luck

Hola! My name is Pedro. The New Year's tradition in Spain consists of having dinner with family and friends. When we finish dinner, we prepare the dessert... 12 grapes! And wait to eat them just before 12 o'clock. Then we eat one grape with each toll of the midnight bells, 12 in total! This is broadcast on all Spanish TV channels. This old tradition is thought to bring good luck if you are able to eat the 12 grapes with the 12 tolls. It isn't that easy and everybody usually ends up with their mouths full of grapes and laughing.

G'day! I'm Jamie. I am from Australia. Sydney's celebration of the New Year is often broadcast around the world. It's also one of the world's largest New Year's Eve celebrations. More than one million people meet around Sydney Harbour to watch the firework display!

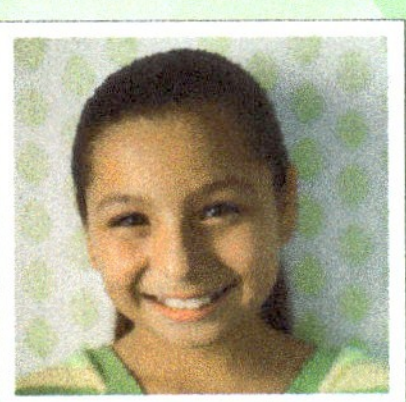

Hola! I'm Maria. I'm Colombian. In my country we build a dummy with bits of clothing representing the old year. It is stuffed with straw and firecrackers. Every family member writes a fault or a bit of bad luck on a piece of paper. The old year's bad luck and faults disappear when we burn the dummy at midnight!

Konnichiwa! My name is Kenta. Before midnight on New Year's Eve, temple bells across Japan slowly begin to toll 108 times. People welcome the New Year by listening to the sound of temple bells and eating long noodles called soba. It is said that the temple bell tolls purify us and the noodles will help us have a long life. At many temples, visitors can strike the bells. People wait in very long queues to participate in the ringing of the bells!

22 **Read again and discuss. Where would you like to celebrate your next New Year's Eve?**

PORTFOLIO

Think and write.

How many different ways of celebrating New Year's Eve are there? Make a poster of each one and display them along the corridors of your school.

OPTIONAL ACTIVITIES

Dictionary work

Ask pupils to underline the new words in the blogs and check them in a dictionary. They can write them in their notebooks.

Photocopiable 6.7 See teacher's notes p. 293.

Lesson 9

Lesson aims
To review the unit language with a game
To use the Picture dictionary

Revision language
Simple past tense of irregular verbs (+/–/?), Ordinal numbers 21st to 31st, must/have to

Materials
Audio CD

Optional activity materials
Active Teach; Digital Activity Book; CLIL poster; Reading and Writing Booklet

Starting the lesson

- Ask two pupils to tell the class what they did to celebrate their birthday last year. Encourage the class to ask questions and talk about the differences between them.

Pupil's Book page 70

23 Play the game.

- Give the class time to look at the pictures.
- Ask pupils to read the game.
- Encourage the class to explain the rules for playing the game.
- Give pupils time to play. Circulate, monitor and help.
- Fast finishers continue with sentence pairs of their own; they could keep score and play a 'set'.

KEY
1 I went to Ghana.
I saw giant butterflies.
2 She didn't sing a song.
She met her uncle.
3 They brought a present.
They didn't get a present.
4 They could eat everything.
He was five years old.
5 What did you see?
He could play the piano.

Picture dictionary

- Pupils can do the picture dictionary of the unit on Activity Book page 109.
- Ask pupils to look at the pictures and try to write the vocabulary on their own in their notebooks. Then ask them to look for the words they don't remember in the Pupil's Book.
- As they finish, ask pupils to exchange notebooks to check answers. (Notebooks can be collected for checking.)

Activity Book page 66

27 Can you read the messages? Write the answers.

- Give pupils time to look at the activity.
- Invite the class to explain what they have to do.
- Give pupils time to do the activity.
- Fast finishers can start doing Activity 28.

28 Make your own code. Write a message to a friend.

- Give pupils time to do the activity.
- Ask pupils to give the message to a friend.

Ending the lesson

- Invite pupils to write on a piece of paper two sentences, one using *must* and the other using *have to*, to describe their school life. Collect the papers and use the sentences to compile a set of rules. For Answer Key see p. 200. For Audioscript see p. 202.

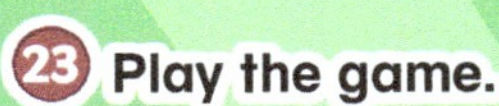

HAVE FUN!

Time Tennis!

I can play the piano.

I could play the piano.

Game 1

1 Choose a player.
2 Read the sentence and then say it in the past.
3 Keep track of your score (15, 30, 40, deuce, game). If there is a tie, you can make your own sentence.

PLAYER 1	PLAYER 2
1 I go to Ghana. I went to Ghana.	1 I see giant butterflies. I saw giant butterflies.
2 She doesn't sing a song.	2 She meets her uncle.
3 They bring a present.	3 They don't get a present.
4 They can eat everything.	4 He is five years old.
5 What do you see?	5 He can play the piano.

Game 2

1 Choose a player.
2 Read the number date and say it in its full form. Do your best!
3 Keep track of your score (15, 30, 40, deuce, game). If there is a tie, you can make up your own date.

PLAYER 1	PLAYER 2
1 01/01 The first of January	1 03/10 The third of October
2 25/07	2 14/04
3 05/12	3 21/08
4 01/11	4 31/07
5 22/03	5 07/05

AB p.109

 AB p.66

OPTIONAL ACTIVITIES

Calendar Show the pupils a calendar of last year. Ask volunteers to say what they did on a particular date or when they celebrated a particular occasion. If your pupils are good at acting, invite them to perform the actions and the class guesses, e.g. went to the beach, got a lot of presents, etc.

Reading and Writing Booklet p. 24 See answer key p. 284.

Lesson 10

Lesson aims
To personalise and assess efforts

Target language
Simple past tense of irregular verbs (+/–/?); Ordinal numbers 21st to 31st, must/have to

Materials
Audio CD

Optional activity materials
Online world; Active Teach; Digital Activity Book; Grammar Booklet; Test Booklet; Grammar reference (PB); Unit review (AB)

Starting the lesson

- Invite the class to think of these activities as a way to assess their work, in order to find out if they need extra work in any of the unit contents.

Practice

Pupil's Book page 71

  Listen and point.

- Give the class time to look at the pictures. Invite them to predict what might happen in a story based on them.
- Tell the class that the pictures are not in order. Ask them to listen and point to the correct picture.
- Play the recording twice. The second time, pause it for pupils to check the picture they are pointing to.

KEY **1** d **2** a **3** c **4** e **5** b

- Invite them to retell the story they heard.

25 Read. Was yesterday fun for Harry?

- Ask what text type they think the text is. (A diary entry.) Point out the date at the top.
- Give pupils time to read and find the answer to the question.

KEY Yes, yesterday was fun for Harry.

26 Read again. Then say *True* or *False*.

- Give pupils time to read the sentences. Set a time limit to focus your pupils' attention. Tell them the time we need to read depends on our purpose. Here they are looking for specific information.
- After checking answers, ask pupils to explain why yesterday was fun for Harry.

KEY **1** T **2** F **3** F **4** F **5** T **6** T

Activity Book page 67

29 Write the missing words.

- Give pupils time to do the activity.
- Ask pupils to write the numbers on the board for checking spelling. Their classmates dictate the answers.

30 Read and complete.

- Give pupils time to do the activity. Tell them to read the whole text before they start.
- Ask pupils to read for checking answers.

31 Look and write the story. Use your notebook

- Give pupils time to look at the pictures and think about what they are going to write. Set a time to do the activity.
- Ask volunteers to read out their writing for checking.

Ending the lesson

- Give pupils time to read the sentences in the 'I can' section.
- Ask pupils to think carefully if they are able to do the 'I can' sentences. Ask them what they found easy or difficult through the unit and why. For Answer Key see p. 200. For Audioscript see p. 202.

Online World Pupils can now go online to Ice Island and enjoy the fun and games.

24 Listen and point.

a

b

c

d

e

25 **Read. Was yesterday fun for Harry?**

Harry's blog

Sunday, April 19th

Yesterday, we had a welcome party for Sally, a new pupil at school. Before the party, I went to my friend Mark's house for pizza. Then we went to school together in his dad's car. We saw all our friends there. Sally's parents were there, too. There was cool music but the room was too hot. We talked and played games. Then there was a dancing competition. A lot of the girls were good at dancing and Mark was good, too. He and Sally got a prize! We had a lot of fun!

26 **Read again. Then say *True* or *False*.**

1 The party was at school.
2 Harry met Mark after the party.
3 The party was on Sunday.
4 There was good music at the party but the room was too cold.
5 The children ate, played and danced.
6 Mark and Sally got a prize.

OPTIONAL ACTIVITIES

Quiz Prepare a quiz in a PowerPoint presentation or on the board to assess the class as a group.

Active Teach Pupils can watch the animated story Episode 3.

Grammar reference (PB p. 109) and Unit review (AB p. 101) You may want pupils to do the Grammar reference and Unit review activities for Unit 6.

Test Booklet You give the Unit 6 test.

Grammar Booklet p. 24 See answer key p. 286.

Activity Book Answer Key

p. 58, Activity 1
1 made **2** had **3** came **4** gave **5** saw
6 brought **7** met **8** ate **9** got **10** sang

p. 58, Activity 2
1 was **2** was **3** came **4** were **5** ate **6** was

p. 58, Activity 3
True sentences: **1**, **2**, **4**, **5**

p. 59, Activity 4
A **1** had **2** came **3** brought **4** gave **5** made
B **1** come **2** make **3** sing **4** drink

p. 59, Activity 5
1 E **2** R **3** E **4** E **5** E **6** R

p. 59, Activity 6
1 could blow out **2** was **3** couldn't walk **4** was
5 could read **6** was **7** were **8** couldn't speak

p. 60, Activity 7
a 25th **b** 2nd **c** 11th **d** 20th **e** 17th **f** 13th

p. 60, Activity 8
2 25th December/December 25th
3 11th December/December 11th
4 2nd December/December 2nd
5 17th December/December 17th
6 13th December/December 13th

p. 61, Activity 11
1 5th/China/went/saw **2** 9th/walked **3** 14th/Korea/met/had **4** 19th/played **5** 23rd/Japan/saw
6 25th/climbed

p. 61, Activity 12
1 Where did you go on 5th July?
2 Who did you meet on 14th July?
3 What did you see on 23rd July?

p. 61, Activity 13
1 Could you write when you were five?
2 Could she talk when she was one?

p. 62, Activity 14
1 e **2** a **3** c **4** d **5** b **6** f

p. 63, Activity 18
Where did you go? I went to my uncle's wedding.
Who did she see? She saw her friends.
Could they go to the party? No, they couldn't.
Are they staying late? Yes, they are.
How do you get there? I get there by bus.
Did she bring any presents? Yes, she did.

p. 63, Activity 19
Yes/No questions: Could they go to the party? Are they staying late? Did she bring any presents?
***Wh*- Questions**: Where did you go? Who did she see? How do you get there?

p. 64, Activity 22
1 diary **2** dangerous **3** months **4** December **5** Thanksgiving

p. 64, Activity 23
1 must (blue)
2 have to (yellow)
3 must (green)
4 must (yellow)
5 have to (brown)

p. 65, Activity 25
Text 1: Spain, dinner, dessert, grapes, bells, luck, grapes
Text 2: New Year, world, largest, million, fireworks
Text 3: dummy, old year, fault, luck, paper, midnight
Text 4: midnight, begin, 108, temple bells, noodles

p. 66, Activity 27
Message 1 We had a big party.
Message 2 We ate a lot of cake.

p. 67, Activity 29
1 fourth, sixth
2 twelfth, thirteenth
3 twenty-first, twenty-third, twenty-fourth
4 twenty-eight, twenty-ninth, thirty-first

p. 67, Activity 30
1 went **2** came **3** were **4** ate **5** sang **6** played **7** danced **8** made **9** gave **10** was

Audioscript

PB Lesson 1 page 62

Lesson 1, Activity 1, p. 62 **CD2:30**

Maddy = M

M Yesterday was Grandad's birthday. All my aunts, uncles and cousins were at our house.
M There was a problem with the cooker.
MUM Oh, no! We can't cook the food.
M It's OK. We can eat Grandad's birthday cake.
M The cake was big but my baby cousin's cars were small.
M Aarrgh!
M I was very hungry yesterday.

Lesson 1, Activity 2, p. 62 **CD2:31**

1 make, made
2 have, had
3 come, came
4 give, gave
5 get, got
6 sing, sang
7 bring, brought
8 meet, met
9 eat, ate
10 see, saw

AB Lesson 1 page 58

Lesson 1, Activity 3, p. 58 (AB) **CD2:32**

Dan = D Mrs Baker (teacher) = MB

MB Hello, Dan. How was your weekend?
D Hi, Mrs Baker. It was great, thanks! Yesterday was my birthday. I was twelve.
MB Really? Happy Birthday!
D Thanks. My birthday party was fun. All my friends were there.
MB What about your cousins, Saskia and Ollie?
D My cousins were on holiday in Spain with my aunt and uncle. But my grandparents were at the party. There were some games in the garden.
MB But it was rainy yesterday!
D Yes. I was very wet after the games. Then there was food ... pizza and cake.
MB What colour was the cake?
D Brown. It was a chocolate cake.

PB Lesson 2 page 63

Lesson 2, Activity 4, p. 63 **CD2:33**

This is a photo of your Aunt Susan's birthday forty years ago. She was eleven and we had a small party at home. Those are her friends, Robert and Tracey. They brought her a great present and we gave her a bicycle – she really got a lot of presents! The girl with me is your mum. She was only five then. Those good-looking young people are your granny and me. Yes, we were only thirty-five! Your grandma made a big chocolate cake. And that baby in her arms is your Uncle David. He ate a lot of cake that day. What a mess!

PB Lesson 3 page 64

Lesson 3, Activity 7, p. 64 **CD2:34**

first, second, third, fourth, fifth, sixth, seventh, eighth, ninth, tenth, eleventh, twelfth, thirteenth, fourteenth, fifteenth, sixteenth, seventeenth, eighteenth, nineteenth, twentieth, twenty-first, twenty-second, twenty-third, twenty-fourth, twenty-fifth, twenty-sixth, twenty-seventh, twenty-eighth, twenty-ninth, thirtieth, thirty-first

Lesson 3, Activity 8, p. 64 **CD2:35**

It was the thirty-first of December, snowy and white.
I went to a party that cold winter's night.
There was singing and dancing, music and fun.
There were games. There were drinks for everyone.
I remember it well, oh yes, I remember it well.
Then ... ten, nine, eight, seven, six, five, four, three, two, one.
It was twelve o'clock! Another new year!
We said, 'Goodbye' to the old year.
We said, 'Hello' to the new.
My friends, new and old, said, 'Happy New Year!'
'Happy New Year!' I said, too.
Oh yes, I remember it well.

Lesson 3, Activity 9, p. 64 **CD2:36**

the twenty-second of February
the twenty-second of February
the twenty-third of February
the fourteenth of April
the first of November
the thirty-first of July
the nineteenth of September

AB Lesson 3 page 60

Lesson 3, Activity 7, p. 60 (AB) **CD2:37**

Hi, I'm Annabel. December was a really fun month – there were lots of parties! My cousin Taylor's birthday was on the 2nd December and I went to her party. Then, on the 11th December, it was my mum's birthday. The dance show was on the 13th December. That was a lot of fun! Then I went to my football club party on the 17th December, and there was a party at school on the 20th December. And, of course, on the 25th December it was Christmas Day and there was a big meal with all my grandparents, uncles, aunts, and cousins

PB Lesson 4 page 65

Lesson 4, Activity 10, p. 65 **CD2:38**

Woman = W Girl = G

W When did you go to Ghana?
G Well, I went in August. I arrived on the 1st of August. It was very exciting. I met my relatives from Africa.
W Where did you go in Ghana?
G Well, on the 3rd of August I went to Kakum National Park.
W What did you see there?
G I saw some amazing animals. The giant butterflies were beautiful. Very, very big butterflies. Then on the 5th of August we went to a football game in Accra. Ghanaians love football and they are very good at it. I danced and sang football songs with my new friends. Then on the 10th of August, I went to the north of Ghana to see the giant baobab trees and ate some baobab fruit, but I didn't like it! On the 22nd of August I went to Lake Volta and sailed in a pirogue, a type of boat. It was cool!
W What did you do before you came home?
G On the 28th of August we had a party. My African friends gave me a lot of presents. 'Come back soon!' they said. I cried at the airport.
W When did you come back?
G I came back home on the 30th of August. I brought lots of presents for my mum, dad and brother. It was a great experience!

PB Lesson 5 page 66

Lesson 5, Activity 13, p. 66 **CD2:39**

Finn = F Captain = C Jenny = J Dr Al = Dr Dylan = D

F Captain! Captain! The thieves!
C What? Where?
F They went into a shop.
J Then the tall thief was in a boat and ...
Dr Finn! Jenny! Get in the snowmobile!
F Why?
D The thieves were in their boat!
J Where?
D They were in the sea near Snow Mountain. They went into a cave.
F A cave? In the sea? We need a boat!
D It's OK, Finn. There's an entrance on Snow Mountain near the statue!
J We can catch them! Hurry!

PB Lesson 6 page 67

Lesson 6, Activity 14, p. 67 **CD2:40**

Do you have any new CDs?
Why don't you come to my place?
Is there anything that I can bring?
When is your birthday?

Lesson 6, Activity 15, p. 67 **CD2:41**

William = W Sarah = S

W Hello?
S Hi! It's Sarah
W Oh, hi Sarah! How are you?
S Very well, thank you! How are you, William?
W I'm fine, thank you.
S Can I ask you a question?
W Yes, you can!
S When is your birthday?
W Actually it's today! The twenty-seventh of March!
S I wasn't too sure! Happy Birthday! Are you having a party?
W Thank you! Yes, I am! Have you got any plans today?
S No, I haven't.
W Why don't you come to my place? I'm having a party at six o'clock
S Oh, great! Thank you!
S Do you know who's coming to the party? I'd rather catch the bus with someone else.
W Yes, Henry, Anna and Carlos will be there, too. You met them last time.
S Perfect. Is there anything that I can bring?
W Let me think ... Have you got any new CDs?
S No, I haven't. I need to buy new ones.
W What about games? Didn't you buy one last week?
S Yes, I did! I'll bring it tonight!
W Perfect!
S See you later!
W Bye!

PB Lesson 10 page 71

Lesson 10, Activity 24, p. 71 **CD2:42**

1 On Saturday I went to watch the last game of the season of my favourite baseball team. There were lots of people there.
2 My team won! My dad said, 'Yes, yes, yes!' We were very happy.
3 Our friends brought a lot of food and drinks.
4 We sang and danced.
5 We went home at ten in the evening. It was a great night.

7 School

Objectives

- give personal opinion
- describe books, films, etc.
- ask and answer questions about the past
- pronounce long and short vowels

Topics
- school
- family members' youth
- comparisons
- unusual schools around the world

Language
Vocabulary
Adjectives: interesting, boring, exciting, scary, funny, difficult, easy, romantic
School subjects: Computer Studies, Maths, Geography, Science, History, Art, Music, Sport (P.E.), Design, Drama
Structures
Was it interesting?
Yes, it was. / No, it wasn't.
Was there an alien in it?
Yes, there was. / No, there wasn't.
Were there any exciting stories?
Yes, there were. / No, there weren't.
Did you have Maths on Tuesday?
Yes, I did. / No, I didn't.
Present perfect (just, yet, already)
Revision
school objects, family members (grandparent, granddaughter, grandson, parent, aunt, uncle)
Receptive
Talking with friends is ... Was it .../ Were they ...
CLIL and Wider world language
CLIL: (Creating a storyboard): glue, scissors, characters, scene, storyboard, Wider world

Values
Learn about your older family members' youth.

Stories
Why are Emma and Robbie scared?
Island mystery: chapter 7

Song
School subjects

Socio-cultural aspects
- respecting other's opinions
- finding out about other people's past
- working in pairs and groups
- unusual schools around the world

Phonics
- long and short vowels
- blending words

Learning strategies
- making use of prior knowledge
- following instructions
- recording new words
- using tables to organise information
- creative thinking: creating and inventing
- critical thinking: observing, describing, giving opinion
- critical thinking: comparing and contrasting, classifying
- integrating contents: discussing and approaching new cultures
- reflecting on learning and self assessment

Cross-curricular contents
- Art: creating a storyboard
- Social Sciences: schooling around the world and learning about older family member's youth
- Music: song, pronunciation rhyme
- Language skills: reading a story, acting out, telling a story

Basic competences

Linguistic communication: Use language as an instrument for communication (L.1 to L.10).
Knowledge and interaction with the physical world: Talk about school experiences (L.3).
Mathematical competence: Talk about and understand timetables (L.3 to L.4).
Processing information and digital competence: Use Active Teach, Digital Activity Book and Ice Island Online World

Social and civic competence: Be a creative problem solver (L.5 and L.7).
Cultural and artistic competence: Talk about types of films (L.1). Create a storyboard (L.7). Talk about schools in other countries (L.8).
Learning to learn: Reflect on what has been learnt and self evaluate progress (L.10).
Autonomy and personal initiative: Use own judgement and ideas and further develop social skills (L.1 to L.10).

Skills

Listening

- can understand people talking about school
- can understand a dialogue about school
- can understand questions about school
- can understand questions about past events
- can understand a description of a book, film, etc.
- can understand a song about school
- can understand a pronunciation rhyme

Speaking

- can give opinion about school, books, films, etc.
- can sing the *School subjects* song
- can ask and answer questions about past events
- can ask and answer questions about past events connected to the present
- can say the pronunciation rhyme

Taking part in conversations

- can ask and respond to questions about school
- can ask and respond to questions about other people's youth
- can ask and respond to questions about past events
- can ask and respond to questions about past events connected to present time
- can take part in a dialogue about school

Reading

- can read and understand information (about school) in sentences, short paragraphs and texts
- can read and understand information (about past events) in sentences, short paragraphs and texts
- can read and understand a cartoon strip story, captions and speech bubbles
- can read and understand factual information about unusual schools around the world

Writing

- can write opinion and school words correctly
- can use simple past tense correctly in interrogative sentences
- can complete sentences to write about past events connected to the present
- can write sentences giving their own opinion
- can write questions about past events
- can create a storyboard
- can write a short text to describe their ideal school

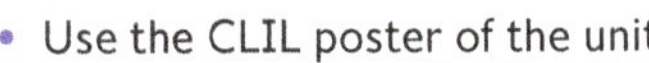

Classroom ideas

- Use the CLIL poster of the unit.
- Ask pupils to bring family photos to class and ask them to talk about their family members' youth. They can describe their physical appearance and personality.
- You or your pupils could use the websites below to access more information about schools around the world: http://ethemes.missouri.edu/themes/1809 http://www.woodlands-junior.kent.sch.uk/schday/start.html
- Play games from the Games Bank.
- Photocopiables 7.1–7.7.

Take-home English

- Letters for parents. When you begin Unit 7, complete and give pupils a copy of the letter for the unit (Active Teach). This explains what pupils are going to learn in this unit.
- Home-School Link. Encourage pupils to tell their family about their favourite subjects at school. (L.5)
- Grammar Booklet and Reading and Writing Booklet. Pupils take these home to show their parents.
- Pupils' Digital Activity Books.
- Portfolios. Encourage pupils to take their portfolio files home to show their parents when they finish Unit 7.

Evaluation

Self assessment

- Pupils can ask and answer about events that happaned in the past
- Pupils can talk about school in the past and now
- Pupil's Book page 81
- Activity Book page 77
- Grammar reference (Pupil's Book page 110)

Resources

- Unit review (Activity Book page 102)
- Picture dictionary (Activity Book page 110)
- Test Booklet – Unit 7 (pages 30–33)
- Grammar Booklet (pages 25–28), Reading and Writing Booklet – Unit 7 (pages 25–28)

7 School

Lesson 1

Lesson aims
To learn and practise new vocabulary (adjectives)

Target language
interesting, boring, exciting, scary, funny, difficult, easy, romantic

Receptive language
Talking with friends is ...

Materials
Audio CD; Flashcards and Wordcards (Adjectives)

Optional activity materials
Active Teach; Digital Activity Book; Photocopiable 7.1

Starting the lesson

- Ask the class if they like writing. *Why (not)?* Ask pupils what they write on a normal day, e.g. emails to friends, a note to their parents, 'chat' on the computer, homework.
- Ask if they think story-writing is easy or difficult. *Why?* Ask *Are you good at writing stories?*

Presentation

- Present the vocabulary using the flashcards (adjectives). Hold up each flashcard in turn and say the word for pupils to repeat. Hold up the flashcards in a different order for pupils to repeat again.

Pupil's Book page 72

1 Listen and read. Why are Emma and Robin scared?

- Ask *Who can you see in picture 1? (Emma and Robbie.) What do you think they're talking about?* (Pupils guess.) *Who is on the bus with them? (Dan.) What's he got? (A green hand!)*
- Play the recording while pupils listen, follow the text and find the answer to the question.

KEY They are scared because they think they can see the green hand from Dan's story.

2 Listen and repeat.

- Give pupils time to look at the pictures.
- Play the recording. Pause for pupils to find and point.
- Play the recording again, pausing after each word so that pupils can say and mime the actions.

Practice

3 Talk about these things. Use words from Activity 2.

- Pupils look at the example dialogue while you read it. Encourage some pupils to give their opinions.
- Give pupils time to do the activity in pairs.

Activity Book page 68

1 Listen and write.

- Give pupils time to read the adjectives. Start a sentence with each one, e.g. *a scary* .... Encourage pupils to finish the sentence.
- Give pupils time to do the activity.
- Ask volunteers to read the text for checking.

2 Listen and write for Maddy. Use words from Activity 1.

- Play the recording and allow pupils do the activity.
- Play the recording again, pausing to elicit and check answers.
- Ask the class to say what they think would be true for themselves.

3 Write a word under each book in Activity 2 for yourself.

- Give pupils time to do the activity.
- Volunteers read their opinions.

Ending the lesson

- Play *Hangman* using the adjectives from this lesson.
For Answer Key see p. 226. For Audioscript see p. 228.

7 School

1 3:01 **Listen and read. Why are Emma and Robbie scared?**

2 3:02 **Listen and repeat.**

1 interesting

2 boring

3 exciting

4 scary

5 funny

6 difficult

7 easy

8 romantic

3 **Talk about these things. Use words from Activity 2.**

Talking with friends is interesting.

OPTIONAL ACTIVITIES

Spelling game Divide the class into two teams. Ask a volunteer from each team in turn *How do you spell …* (adjective from this lesson)*?* Teams get a point for a correct answer and a bonus point for miming the word.

Pair work Pupils write three sentences about three different TV programmes they watched last week, using adjectives from this lesson, e.g. *Dr Who was exciting.* They read their sentences to a partner, but omit the adjective. The partner guesses.

Photocopiable 7.1 See teacher's notes p. 293.

Lesson 2

Lesson aims
To revise the Lesson 1 vocabulary; to learn and practise +/- short answer contractions

Target language
Was it ...? Yes/No, it was/wasn't.
Was there a/an ...? Yes/No, there was/wasn't
Were there any ...? Yes/No, there were/weren't

Materials
Audio CD; Flashcards and Wordcards (Adjectives)

Optional activity materials
Active Teach; Digital Activity Book; Grammar Booklet

Starting the lesson

- Write the adjectives from Lesson 1 on the board, jumbled up, e.g. *tegcxiin* (exciting), *aysrc* (scary), *fficdiult* (difficult). Pupils work in pairs: see which pair can unscramble them first.

Presentation

- Display the flashcards (adjectives), learnt in Lesson 1, around the room and play *I spy* (see p. 300). Ask individual pupils to come and write the words on the board.
- Ask the class to silently read the Look! box.
- Draw their attention to the contractions *wasn't* and *weren't*. Say *was* (hold up one finger), *not* (hold up a second finger) and *wasn't* (move your fingers together).
- If your class needs support, ask pupils to underline the examples of *was/were* in Lesson 1 Activity 1.
- Remind pupils we change word order to make questions with *was/were*.

Pupil's Book page 73

4 (3:05) Listen and read. Then look and say.

- Give pupils time to look at the table. Read the story titles together.
- Play the recording while pupils follow 1–4 in their books. Pause after each question and answer to give pupils time to find and say the correct story.
- Play the recording again. Pause for the class to repeat each question and answer in chorus.

KEY
2 Story b **3** Story c **4** Story b

5 Look at Activity 4. Ask and answer.

- In pairs, pupils take turns to ask each other questions based on the information given in Activity 4.
- Partners reply with a correct answer.

Practice

6 Play the guessing game.

- In pairs, pupils take it in turns to ask questions about the books in Activity 4 to guess which one their partner has chosen.

AB page 69

4 Read. Then match.

- Ask *What is Emma thinking about?* (Pupils guess.)
- Give them time to read the text and do the matching activity.

5 Unscramble and write questions about your first day at school. Then write the answers.

- Give pupils time to reorder the words and write the questions.
- Give pupils time to write the answers.

6 Write about the first time you did your favourite sport.

- Give pupils time to read and write. If you have pupils who aren't sporty, ask them to write about the first time they did a new sport at school.
- Pupils can write a longer text in their notebooks. (Notebooks can be collected for checking progress in writing skills.)

Ending the lesson

- Volunteers swap notebooks in pairs. Volunteers tell the class what their partner wrote for Activity Book Activity 6. For Answer Key see p. 226. For Audioscript see p. 228.

Pupils can now, or at the end of this unit, go online to Ice Island and find the backpacks that Penn and Gwyn are holding. They are above ground, to the right of the entrance to the caves. Once pupils click on the backpacks they are taken to a supplementary language game based on the vocabulary in this unit.

LOOK!

Was it interesting?	Yes, it was. / No, it wasn't.
Was there an alien in it?	Yes, there was. / No, there wasn't.
Were there any exciting stories?	Yes, there were. / No, there weren't.

4 3:05 **Listen and read. Then look and say.**

1 Were they exciting? Yes, they were.
2 Was it exciting? No, it wasn't.
3 Were there any children in it? No, there weren't.
4 Was there an alien in it? Yes, there was.

Story a and Story c.

	Story a	Story b	Story c
exciting	✓	✗	✓
scary	✓	✗	✗
funny	✗	✓	✗
children	✓	✓	✗
an alien	✗	✓	✗

5 **Look at Activity 4. Ask and answer.**

Was *Mike goes to Mars* exciting?

No, it wasn't.

6 **Play the guessing game.**

Was it exciting?

Yes, it was.

A: Was it exciting?
B: Yes, it was.
A: Were there any children in it?
B: Yes, there were.
A: It was *Island Adventure*.

OPTIONAL ACTIVITIES

Pair work Pupils choose three books they've read and liked. They draw and complete a table similar to that in PB Activity 4. Stretch pupils by suggesting they vary the words in the left-hand column. They ask a friend about their books.

Group work Pupils think about a memorable first-time experience. Groups of four take it in turns to ask one group member about their experience. Brainstorm ideas if necessary, e.g. *The first time I went on a plane/to an English class/to a zoo.*
Grammar Booklet p. 25 See answer key p. 286.

Lesson 3

Lesson aims
To extend the unit vocabulary on school subjects; to practise the vocabulary with a song

Target language
Computer Studies, Maths, Geography, Science, History, Art, Music, Sports (P.E.), Design, Drama

Receptive language
Was it ...? Were they ...?

Materials
Audio CD; Flashcards and Wordcards (Adjectives; School subjects)

Optional activity materials
Active Teach; Digital Activity Book; Photocopiable 7.2; Photocopiable 7.3; Reading and Writing Booklet

Starting the lesson

- Ask *What is your favourite day of the week? Why?*

Presentation

- Introduce the new words using the flashcards. Hold them up and say the words for pupils to repeat.
- Put the flashcards on the board. Point to the different flashcards and ask the class to say the words.

Pupil's Book page 74

7 Listen and repeat.

- Give pupils time to look at the pictures.
- Play the recording. Pause for pupils to say each word.
- Play the recording again. Repeat each word. Pupils repeat in chorus. Then ask, e.g. *Who likes Geography? Hands up!*

Song

8 Listen and sing.

- Ask pupils *What's your favourite subject at school?* Explain that P.E. stands for 'Physical Education'. Play the song. Pupils follow in their books.
- Play the song again. Encourage pupils to sing.
- Groups of four make up alternative verses to the song by changing the school subjects.
- Groups sing their new verses for the class.
- You can now play the karaoke song (Active Teach).

9 Look at Jill's classes below. Then say the school subjects.

- Give pupils time to look at the school timetable.
- Pupils do the activity.

KEY
1 Art **2** History and English **3** Geography
4 Science and Sport

Practice

Activity Book page 70

7 Read and write sentences for you.

- Look at the tables with the class. Elicit example sentences to check understanding.
- Pupils do the activity.
- Check answers by asking pupils to ask and answer in pairs, e.g. *Was Maths difficult for you last year? And this year?*

8 Write. Then listen and circle T = *True* or F = *False*.

- Give pupils time to write.
- Check answers, then play the recording while pupils listen and circle.
- Play the recording again, pausing to elicit and check answers.

9 Write three sentences about your lessons last week.

- Give pupils time to do the activity.
- Volunteers read their sentences to the class.

Ending the lesson

- Volunteers read out what they have written for Activity Book Activity 9. They pause before the adjectives for the class to guess! For Answer Key see p. 226. For Audioscript see p. 228.

7 Listen and repeat.

8 Listen and sing.

SONG

sport = P.E. (physical education)

Chorus:
Maths, Science, History, P.E., Art, Geography.
A lot of subjects every day. Is school boring? No way!

Last year, Maths wasn't easy. The lessons weren't always fun.
But now I can do all my homework. Maths is for everyone!

Chorus

Last year, P.E. was boring. P.E. lessons weren't my thing.
But now it's my favourite subject. I can play football and swim.

Chorus

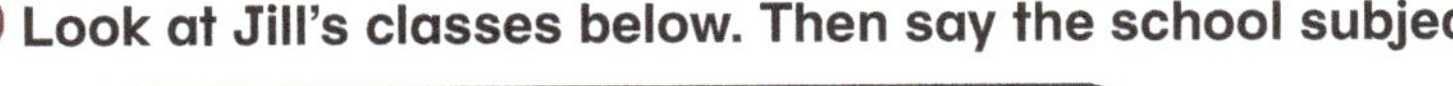

9 Look at Jill's classes below. Then say the school subjects.

Monday	Tuesday	Wednesday	Thursday	Friday
Maths Art Geography	English Science Maths	Geography History Maths	English Science Sport	History English Maths

1 It was on Monday but it wasn't on Wednesday.

2 They were on Friday but they weren't on Monday.

3 It was on Wednesday but it wasn't on Friday.

4 They were on Thursday but they weren't on Friday.

OPTIONAL ACTIVITIES

Card game Groups of four place the subject and verb cards you've prepared face down. They take it in turns to take a subject card, a verb card and to make true sentences about last week with an appropriate adjective, e.g. *History was easy.*

Photocopiable 7.2 See teacher's notes p. 293.
Photocopiable 7.3 See teacher's notes p. 293.
Reading and Writing Booklet pp. 25–26
See answer key p. 284.

Lesson 4

Lesson aims
To revise vocabulary; to learn and practise simple past short answer contractions

Target language
Did you have Maths on Tuesday? Yes, I did. / No, I didn't.
Did she have History on Friday? Yes, she did. / No, she didn't.

Materials
Audio CD

Optional activity materials
Active Teach; Digital Activity Book; Grammar Booklet

Starting the lesson

- Write on the board *Did you have Maths yesterday? What time did you have Maths yesterday?*
- Encourage pupils to make similar questions.

Presentation

Skills

- Ask the class to silently read the Look! box.
- Remind pupils we use short forms of *did/didn't* to answer *yes* or *no*.
- Remind pupils that the simple past is used to talk about past events. Point out that we usually use time expressions such as *yesterday*, *last week*, *last year*, *in 2009*. Give them examples.

Pupil's Book page 75

Practice

10 Listen and choose. Then ask and answer.

- Give pairs time to look at the table. Tell them that Robbie is going to talk about his last week at school.
- Play the recording, without pausing.
- Play the recording again, pausing for pupils to choose.
- Ask a pair of pupils to read the example dialogue. Give the class time to practise the dialogue in pairs. Circulate, monitor and help.

11 Listen and answer.

- Give pupils time to read the questions.
- Play the recording. Pupils do the activity. Play the recording again, pausing to check answers.

KEY
1 Yes, she did. / No, it wasn't.
2 Yes, she did. / No, it wasn't.
3 It was music homework. / It wasn't difficult.

Activity Book page 71

10 Listen and circle. Then write.

- Give pupils time to look at the table. Tell them that the listening is about Dan's homework last week.
- Play the recording, without pausing.
- Play the recording again, pausing for pupils to circle.
- Give pupils time to answer the questions. Then play the recording again, pausing for children to check their answers.

11 Read and write questions. Then write the answers.

- Give pupils time to look at the table. Ask *Did Maddy have Music on Monday? Was it easy?*
- Ask pupils to write questions about Maddy.
- Ask pupils to check in pairs: one asks and the other answers.

12 Write.

- Give pupils time to do the activity.

Ending the lesson

- Volunteers read out what they have written for Activity Book Activity 12. For Answer Key see p. 226. For Audioscript see p. 228.

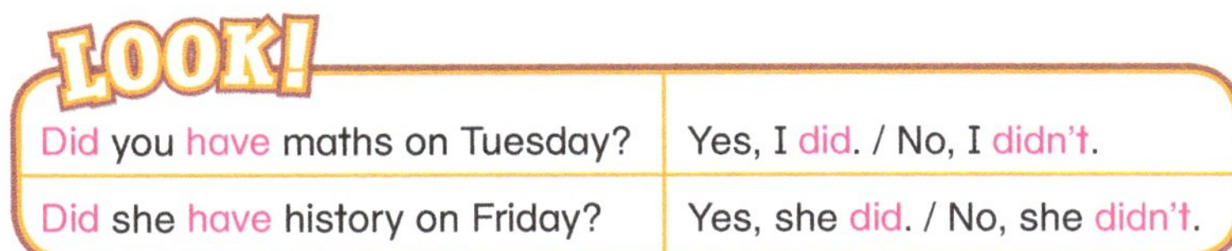

LOOK!

Did you have maths on Tuesday?	Yes, I did. / No, I didn't.
Did she have history on Friday?	Yes, she did. / No, she didn't.

Listen and choose. Then ask and answer.

	Monday	Tuesday	Wednesday	Thursday	Friday
Robbie	Maths	Music	Geography	English	History and Art
	easy / difficult	*easy / difficult*	*interesting / boring*	*easy / difficult*	*easy / difficult*

Listen and answer.

1 Did Maddy have Maths homework on Monday?
Was it easy?

2 Did she have Art homework on Wednesday this week?
Was it boring?

3 What was her homework on Friday?
Was it difficult?

OPTIONAL ACTIVITIES

Interview the teacher
Pupils ask you about your last week, e.g. *Did you teach English on Sunday?*

Did you know …?
Pupils invent a *Did you Know …?* about their favourite subject. Encourage them to write interesting or amazing things. Collect all of them and read them out.
Grammar Booklet p. 26 See answer key p. 286.

Lesson 5

Lesson aims
To consolidate the unit language with a story

Values
Learn about your older family members' youth

Materials
Audio CD

Optional activity materials
Active Teach; Digital Activity Book; Photocopiable 7.4

Starting the lesson

- Ask *Where are Rufus and Ivan? (In a boat.)* Pupils work in pairs and tell each other, from memory, what they know about Rufus and Ivan. Support your pupils by writing the first part of sentences on the board for them to finish, e.g. *Rufus is (tall/bad/thin). Ivan is (short/bad/fat). They are both (bad/thieves). They want (the treasure).*
- Pairs predict what they think will happen in Episode 7. Volunteers tell the class.

Presentation

Pupil's Book page 76

- Ask the class questions about each picture and teach *Be careful!* Pupils answer or guess, e.g.
  (Picture 1) *What can you see? (The children, Dr Al, a statue.)*
  (Picture 2) (L1) *What are they looking for? What are Penn and Gwyn looking at?*
  (Picture 3) (L1) *What's happening?*
  (Picture 5) *Where are the children? (In a cave.)*
  (Picture 7) *What has Rufus got? (The treasure)*

12 Look at the pictures. Tell the story.

- Ask the class to look again at the pictures.
- Ask seven volunteers to go in front of the class and tell the story just based on looking at the pictures, without reading. Each pupil tells the story of one picture.

13 (3:12) Listen and read. Then act out.

- Play the recording. Pupils listen and follow the story.

Practice

- Ask the class true/false questions about the story, e.g. *The children can see the cave in pictures 1 and 2.* (False.) *Dylan is good at Geography.* (True.) *Dylan finds the cave.* (False. Finn does.) *Finn thinks it was exciting.* (True.) *The children are too late.* (True.)
- Play the recording again. Pause for the class to repeat each line in chorus.
- Divide the class into six and allocate these parts: Jenny, Dylan, Finn, Dr Al, Rufus, Ivan.
- Play the recording again. Pause for pupils to repeat their character's lines.
- Ask eight volunteers to act out the story (Jenny, Dylan, Finn, Dr Al, Rufus, Ivan, Penn and Gwyn).
- Take a class vote for the best actor/actress.
- Pairs predict what happens next.
- Volunteers tell the class their ideas.

Home-School Link

- Ask the class to tell their family what their favourite subjects at school are. Tell pupils they have to explain why.
  Ask the class to find out information about their older family members' youth *(What was school like? What subjects did you study?)*

Values

- Write on the board: *YOUTH*. Ask the class to talk about their older family members' youth. Ask them *Do you think it is important to know about your granny's or grandad's youth? Why?*
- Encourage the class to talk about what they think their parents' and grandparents' lives were like when they were children, what they did at school and at home, what they did for fun, etc.

Activity Book page 72

13 Read and complete.

- Give pupils time to do the activity.
- Pairs compare answers before you check.

14 Tick (✓).

- Give pupils time to do the activity.
- Check the answers.

15 What happens next? Imagine.

- Give pupils time to write.
- Ask volunteers to tell the class their ideas and take a vote to find the most popular idea.

16 Read and circle.

- Give pupils time to do the activity.
- Ask volunteers to read the sentences.

Ending the lesson

- Ask pupils what they think the treasure is, e.g. gold bars, diamonds, jewellery, or something different. What? You could take a class vote! For Answer Key see p. 226. For Audioscript see p. 228.

12 Look at the pictures. Tell the story.

13 Listen and read. Then act out.

VALUES

Learn about your older family members' youth.

HOME-SCHOOL LINK

Tell your family about your favourite subjects at school. Explain why.

PARENT

OPTIONAL ACTIVITIES

Code game
In pairs, pupils imagine they are Rufus and Ivan. They write their location in code. See AB p. 66.

Roleplay
Brainstorm questions to ask Penn and Gwyn about what they do in the mornings. Pupils role play in pairs. **Photocopiable 7.4** See teacher's notes p. 293.

Lesson 6

Lesson aims
To identify long and short vowels; to blend words with long and short vowels

Receptive language
Words with long and short vowels

Materials
Audio CD; Phonics and spelling poster; Flashcards (Short and long vowels)

Optional activity materials
Active Teach; Digital Activity Book; Photocopiable 7.5, red crayons or colouring pencils

Starting the lesson

- Give pupils time to look at the Phonics and spelling poster. Read aloud some examples of short and long vowels.

Presentation

- State the goal of the lesson.
- Explain that vowels have two sounds in English.
- Demonstrate short vowels by making a web with different words (/a/ *cat, rat, map,* /e/ *egg, bell, elephant;* /ɪ/ *kitten, fish, pig;* /o/ *frog, dog;* /ʊ/ *sun, cub, duck*). Use a class sign such as clapping to show that it's a short vowel.
- Demonstrate long vowels by making a web with different words. (*cake, snake* for long A; *bee, feet* for long E; *note, bow* for long O; *tube, cube* for long U). Focus on the duration of the sounds. Use a class sign, like pretending that you're stretching a rubber band, to designate long vowels.
- Use flashcards to model more short and long vowels. Point out how the –*e* at the end changes the sound.
- Encourage pupils to sound out each word.

Practice

Pupil's Book page 77

14  Listen and repeat.

- Give pupils time to read the words.
- Play the recording for pupils to repeat the words chorally. Stop after each word and ask volunteers to repeat it as accurately as possible.
- Point out how the vowel change makes a completely different word with a different meaning.

15   Listen, point and say *long* or *short*.

- Play the recording. Pupils listen, point and say.
- Use the words from this activity to play *'The wheel of wisdom'*. Write a sentence with vowels missing so that pupils guess the words. Identify short and long vowels.

16  Listen and read. Then repeat.

- Allow time for pupils to check the pictures.
- Play the recording for pupils to listen and read.
- Encourage pupils to repeat the sentences.
- Use class signs to elicit if it is a short/long vowel.

17 Read and blend the words in Activity 14 with a partner.

- Remind pupils that we can make a completely different word by changing or adding just one sound. Blend *Tim/time.*
- Encourage pupils to identify long or short vowels in each word.
- Ask fast finishers to think of other pairs of words with the same sounds to blend. Share these with the class.

18   Listen and repeat.

- Play the recording. Then ask pupils to find the short and long vowels in the sentences.
- Play the recording again. Encourage the class to learn and repeat the sentences.

Practice

Activity Book page 73

17   Listen and colour the short vowels in red.

- Read aloud the first set *(pen, leg, web, free)* to provide another opportunity to distinguish short and long vowels. Play the recording.
- Encourage the fast finishers to make up their own 'odd one out' sets. Share these with the class.

18 Read and circle the long vowels.

- Read aloud the first sentence. Ask the class to find the words with the long vowels (focus on *same* and *tale*, though some may also spot the long *o* in *told*.
- Check the activity as a whole-group discussion.

19 Write words in the table. Then read.

- Give pupils time to do the activity.
- Use these words to practise with the whole class.

20 Write four sentences. Use the short and long sound of the vowel in the same sentence.

- Write a model sentence on the board to provide support for all learners.

Ending the lesson

- Revisit the goal of the lesson and ask pupils to evaluate their own progress. For Answer Key see p. 226. For Audioscript see p. 228.

Long and short vowels

Vowels have got short or long sounds depending on their position, the sound of the consonant next to them and the other vowels in the word.

  **Listen and repeat.**

	SHORT vowel	LONG vowel		SHORT vowel	LONG vowel
1	hat	hate	2	not	note
3	Tim	time	4	pet	Pete
5	kit	kite	6	Sam	same

15 **Listen, point and say *long* or *short*.**

1 a name flat
2 e meet bed
3 i five six
4 o open top
5 u music cup

 **16** **Listen and read. Then repeat.**

1 
Thats the hat that I hate!

2 
Please do not write me a note

3 
Tim is on time.

4 
Pete has a pet.

5 

This is a kit for a kite.

6 
Sam has the same number.

17 **Read and blend the words in Activity 14 with a partner.**

  **Listen and repeat.**

OPTIONAL ACTIVITIES

Poets' Workshop
Provide a short poem to the class where the vowels are missing. Complete the poem together and add it to the class poetry book.

Long and Short Vowel songs
Create a song based on rhyming short with short and long with long vowel sounds: can be done with any melody or as a rap chant. e.g. 'Let's make the sound of 'hat', /a/, /a/, /a/, Let's make the sound of 'cat', /a/, /a/, /a/'.
Photocopiable 7.5 See teacher's notes p. 294.

Lesson 7

Lesson aims
To extend the unit vocabulary; to learn and practise the present perfect

Cross-curricular focus
Art – Creating a storyboard

Target language
glue, scissors, storyboard, scene, characters
I have just finished. / I haven't finished.
She has arrived. / She hasn't arrived.

Materials
Audio CD; CLIL poster

Optional activity materials
Short clip from a cartoon film; Active Teach; Digital Activity Book; Photocopiable 7.6; Reading and Writing Booklet; Grammar Booklet

Starting the lesson

- Stories, like films or books, contain many different elements that all work together to help the audience understand what is happening. These elements include the images, the dialogue and in some cases, the music and sound effects. Images show us what is happening and the mood of the characters. The same happens with what the characters say and whether what they say helps further in the story.

Presentation

- Ask the class to tell you about the films and books that they like.
- Allow some STT for discussion about books and films.
- Before reading, give pupils time to look at the pictures on page 78. Ask *What can you see? Who are the characters? What is the problem/solution in the story?*
- Use the vocabulary routine: **mime and define**. Next, **use each new word in a sentence**. Last, **ask questions** with each new word.
- Demonstrate the new structure by retelling the story. Write some sentence starters for pupils to use as a reference. Review connectors *First*, *Then*, *Next*, *Finally*.
- Share some background information from the Starting the lesson section.

Pupil's Book page 78

19 Read and find these words in the text. How has Michael created a storyboard?

- Read the title and the introduction to the text.
- Set purpose for reading: *Let's read to find out how Michael has created his story.*
- Read the whole text as a shared reading experience: use expression and intonation to model proficient reading.
- Ask pupils to follow your reading and then find the words from the word bank in the text.
- Ask volunteers to explain their meaning.

Practice

20 Ask and answer.

- Discuss the question in Activity 19. *How has he created a storyboard?*
- Complete the activity as a whole-group discussion.

KEY
1 He's learnt how to make a storyboard.
2 He's used a pencil, paper, glue and scissors.
3 'The Competition'.
4 They have put them on the wall.

21 Look at the pictures. Then retell Michael's story.

- Point out the sentence starters on the board.
- In pairs, pupils discuss and then retell the story in a shared writing experience.

Activity Book page 74

21 Read and write *have* or *has*.

- Review the new structure and explain the difference between *have* and *has*.
- Check answers as a whole-group discussion.

22 Fill in the gaps.

- Read aloud the first sentence. Brainstorm possible answers. Then complete it together.
- Give pupils time to do the activity.

23 Look and match. Then number the words in alphabetical order.

- Review the vocabulary items.
- Give pupils time to look, match and sort into alphabetical order.

24 Create your own storyboard. Use your notebook.

- Ask pupils to visualise a story with a problem and a solution. Model a story using the new structure.
- Encourage pupils to think and pair-share their stories before they complete their storyboards.
- Give pupils time to complete the storyboards. Point out the sentence starters on the board.
- Invite pupils to share their stories.

Ending the lesson

- Revisit the objective of the lesson.
- Volunteers describe the storyboards they created for Activity Book Activity 24. For Answer Key see p. 226. For Audioscript see p. 228.

19 **Read and find these words in the text. How has Michael created a storyboard?**

glue scissors characters scene storyboard

Creating a storyboard

Michael's teacher taught his class how to create a storyboard for a writer's club. Michael has already finished his work. He has followed all the instructions so well that he could take a storyboard exam tomorrow!

1 I have used a pencil, paper, glue and scissors. I have drawn pictures to show each scene.
2 My story has the title 'The Competition'. I have written a story with some different characters.
3 I have made up a problem and a solution.
4 I have chosen a happy ending. The boy is very excited to see the flag at the end.
5 We have proof-read our stories in a small group. Our teacher has helped us with some words. We have shared our stories.
6 We have put all of the stories on the wall. Now everyone can read them.

20 **Ask and answer.**

1 What has Michael learned today?
2 What materials has he used?
3 What is the title of his story?
4 Where have they put the stories?

LOOK!

I have finished.
I haven't finished.

He has drawn the pictures.
He hasn't drawn the pictures.

21 **Look at the pictures. Then retell Michael's story.**

OPTIONAL ACTIVITIES

Author's Chair Author's chair is some pupil-led classroom time where pupils share and read aloud their own pieces of writing. Author's chair aims to culminate the writing process after drafting, editing and publishing. Pupils share out loud with the rest of the class, developing speech skills. The rest of the pupils practice how to be an audience. Questions and comments to the authors are allowed after the presentation.

Photocopiable 7.6 See teacher's notes p. 294.

Reading and Writing Booklet p. 27 See answer key p. 284.

Grammar Booklet p. 27 See answer key p. 286.

Lesson 8

Lesson aims
To learn about other cultures and respect cultural differences; to learn about unusual schools in other countries

Target language
Adjectives; School subjects; was/were

Receptive language
boarding school, international school, special school

Materials
Audio CD

Optional activity materials
World map or globe; Active Teach; Digital Activity Book; CLIL poster; Photocopiable 7.7

Starting the lesson

- Ask *Do you know any different schools?*
- Teach *boarding/international school.* Say *Children study and sleep at a boarding school. International schools are for children from different countries.*
- Discuss why people in different countries go to different kind of schools, e.g. *The school we go to depends on our climate, family context*, etc.

Presentation

Pupil's Book page 79

22 Look and read. What schools do they go to?

- Pointing to the photos, ask *What country is he/she/are they in?* (Pupils guess.)
- Ask the class about the photos, e.g. (Photo a) *What's the boy doing? (He's snowboarding.) What is there in the photo? (There's a mountain and there are some trees.)* Mime *skier* and explain *Olympic Games* in L1. (Photo b) *What can you see? (Six boys and a bedroom.) Where are they? (At school. They're wearing school clothes.)*
- Pupils identify which schools Kai, Abi and Matu go to.

KEY
1 **Kai** international school
2 **Abi** special school for winter sports
3 **Matu** boarding school

Practice

23 Read again and say.

- Remind pupils to read the questions first.
- Give pupils time to read the blogs and to underline relevant information.
- Pairs say the answers.
- Ask if anyone correctly guessed the countries. Volunteers point out Canada, Japan and Kenya on your map/globe.

KEY **1** Matu **2** Kai **3** Abi **4** Kai

- After checking the answers, ask pupils if they are surprised by any of the information. Ask which school is the most interesting in their opinion.
- Volunteers tell the class. Encourage them to explain, e.g. ask *Why do you want to go to Abi's school?*

Portfolio activity

- For the Portfolio activity, ask pupils *What kind of school is our school? Are all the schools the same in our country?*
- Help pupils to realise what different kinds of schools there are in their country.
- Ask them *What is important about school for you? Friends, sports, teachers, excursions*, etc.
- Give pupils time to read. Then ask pupils to talk and write about their ideal school.

Activity Book page 75

25 Read and complete.

- Give pupils time to read the blogs and complete.
- Ask volunteers to read aloud and check.

26 Which school in Activity 25 do you want to go to? Why?

- Give pupils time to read the blogs again and write.
- Ask volunteers to read aloud and check different opinions.
- Give pupils time to read the Project. Remind them that it is very important to organise our writing in advance. In this case the *I like* ideas can be one paragraph and the *I don't like* ideas can be another paragraph. Adding an introduction and a conclusion to their writings would be great!
- Ask them to write about 'My Ideal School'. If they don't finish on time, they can finish it at home.
- Collect the written work and give pupils specific feedback on paragraphs, introduction and conclusion.

Ending the lesson

- Volunteers present their ideal school (Activity Book Activity 26) to the class. For Answer Key see p. 226. For Audioscript see p. 228.

Wider world

Unusual schools

22 **Look and read. What schools do they go to?**

1

My new school in Tokyo is great. It's international so I have friends from forty different countries! They always speak to me in English— their English is great. I'm learning Japanese. It was difficult at first but my friends were kind when I said the wrong words. Now it's easy.

Kai, 12, Japan

2

I love my school! I go to a special school in the mountains. Students go there to study winter sports. Every day, after studying geography, maths and other subjects, we do sports for three hours. We go skiing and snowboarding. Some students from our school went to the Olympics. I want to be a famous skier, too.

Abi, 14, Canada

3

I live in my school because it's a boarding school. My friends and I all live in rooms next to the school. I love living with my friends and the teachers are all very nice. In the evening, there are a lot of activities. We can watch films or go swimming but usually we have homework.

Matu, 12, Kenya

23 **Read again and say.**

1 Who lives in a school?
2 Who is learning Japanese?
3 Who does sport for three hours a day?
4 Who has got friends from forty countries?

PORTFOLIO

Find out about another unusual school. Would you like to go there? Why? Why not? Write about it.

OPTIONAL ACTIVITIES

Word game Say a word connected to the topic 'School', e.g. *Maths.* A volunteer says any word they associate with Maths, e.g. *numbers*, or *difficult*. Another pupil continues, saying any word they associate with the previous one. Continue round the class. If a pupil hesitates or says an inappropriate word, he/she is out!

Group work Groups of four use the internet at home or at school to research a school in another country. They present their school to the class.

Photocopiable 7.7 See teacher's notes p. 293.

Lesson 9

Lesson aims
To review the unit language with a game
To use the Picture dictionary

Revision language
Adjectives, school objects and subjects
Was it …? Were they …? / short answers; Did you have …? / short answers; I have finished.

Materials
Audio CD; Flashcards (Adjectives)

Optional activity materials
Active Teach; Digital Activity Book; Reading and Writing Booklet

Starting the lesson

- Ask two pupils to talk about the after-school activities they did last week. Encourage the class to ask them closed questions.

Pupil's Book page 80

24 Play the game.

- Give the class time to look at the pictures.
- Divide the class into groups of four and ask pupils to read the game instructions.
- Encourage the class to explain the rules of the game.
- Give pupils time to play. Circulate, monitor and help.

Picture dictionary

- Pupils can do the picture dictionary of the unit on Activity Book page 110.
- Ask pupils to look at the pictures and try to write the vocabulary on their own in their notebooks. Then ask them to look for the words they don't remember in the Pupil's Book.
- As they finish, ask pupils to exchange notebooks to check answers. (Notebooks can be collected for checking.)

Activity Book page 76

27 Circle eight school subjects. The letters that are left tell you the answer!

- Give pupils time to do the activity.
- Ask the class to say the answer in chorus. Count 1, 2, 3 … .

28 Find seven adjectives. Circle them. The letters that are left tell you the answer!

- Give pupils time to do the activity.
- Ask the class to say the answer in chorus. Count 1, 2, 3 … .

29 Make your own word search puzzle. Test a friend!

- Give pupils time to do the activity. Ask them to give their puzzle to a partner.

Ending the lesson

- Ask your pupils to solve the puzzles their classmates have invented (Activity Book Activity 29). Set a time limit. For Answer Key see p. 226. For Audioscript see p. 228.

OPTIONAL ACTIVITIES

Impossible sentences! Put all the unit flashcards together. Divide the class in two teams. Ask a confident pupil from each team to take three cards. Give them one minute to write a sentence on the board including the three words. The faster one wins the point.

Timetable In pairs, pupils ask and answer questions about last week at school. They can use their school timetables but mustn't look at them when they have to answer.

Reading and Writing Booklet p. 28 See answer key p. 284.

Lesson 10

Lesson aims
To personalise and assess efforts

Target language
Adjectives, school objects and subjects
Was it ...? Were they ...? / short answers; Did you have ...? / short answers
I have finished

Materials
Audio CD

Optional activity materials
Online World; Active Teach; Digital Activity Book; Grammar Booklet; Test Booklet; Grammar reference (PB); Unit review (AB)

Starting the lesson

- Invite the class to think of these activities as a way to assess their work, in order to find out if they need extra work in any of the unit contents.

Pupil's Book page 81

25  Listen and point.

- Give the class time to look at the pictures. Invite them to name the subjects in the table.
- Ask them to listen and point to the correct picture.
- Play the recording twice. The second time, pause for pupils to check the picture they are pointing to.
- Invite them to talk about the likes and dislikes with reference to the timetable that they heard.

26 Unscramble and say. Then choose the right answer.

- Ask the class to unscramble the first sentence. Encourage them to ask you, *Did you go into the cave?* Answer *Yes, we did. It was dark and wet.*
- Give pupils time to do the activity in pairs. Circulate, monitor and help.
- Then choose five pairs to check answers.

KEY
1 Did you go into the cave? – e
2 Were there any bats? – a
3 Was it a boring trip? – b
4 Was there a boat? – d
5 Did you go to any other places? – c

Activity Book page 77

30 Match.

- Give pupils time to do the activity.
- Divide the class in two groups and alternatively ask one group to read the definition and the other to say the correct word.

31 Write.

- Give pupils time to write *was* or *were*.
- Check the answers reading aloud.

32 Write.

- Give pupils time to read and write.
- Read aloud and stop for the class to say the answers in chorus.

33 Write about your favourite subject last year.

- Give pupils time to write. Pupils can do the activity in their notebooks.
- Ask volunteers to present their writing.

Ending the lesson

- Give pupils time to read the sentences in the *I can* section in the Activity Book (p. 77).
- Ask pupils to think carefully about whether they are able to do the *I can* points. Ask them what they found easy or difficult in the unit and why. For Answer Key see p. 226. For Audioscript see p. 228.

Online World Pupils can now go online to Ice Island and enjoy the fun and games.

	1 Monday	2 Tuesday	3 Wednesday	4 Thursday	5 Friday
1st class		ABC		ABC	
2nd class	ABC		1 + × % 2 − ÷ √	1 + × % 2 − ÷ √	
3rd class	1 + × % 2 − ÷ √	1 + × % 2 − ÷ √			1 + × % 2 − ÷ √
LUNCH					
4th class		1 + × % 2 − ÷ √			
5th class					ABC

26 Unscramble and say. Then choose the right answer.

1 go / did / into / you / cave / the
2 bats / any / there / were
3 boring / was / it / trip / a
4 boat / was / a / there
5 go / any / did / places / you / other / to

a Yes, there were. It was exciting!
b No, it was interesting.
c Yes, we went to a lake near the cave.
d No, there wasn't.
e Yes, we did. It was dark and wet.

OPTIONAL ACTIVITIES

Quiz Prepare a quiz in a PowerPoint presentation or on the board to assess the class as a group.

Grammar reference (PB p. 110) and Unit review (AB p. 102) You may want pupils to do the Grammar reference and Unit review activities for Unit 7 at this point.

Test Booklet You may wish to give the Unit 7 test at this time.

Grammar Booklet p. 28 See answer key p. 286.

Activity Book Answer Key

p. 68, Activity 1
1 easy **2** difficult **3** exciting **4** boring
5 interesting **6** funny **7** romantic **8** scary

p. 68, Activity 2
2 boring **3** scary **4** easy **5** difficult **6** exciting

p. 69, Activity 4
1 c **2** a **3** f **4** d **5** b **6** e

p. 69, Activity 5
1 How old were you?
2 Was your teacher kind?
3 Were there any scary things?
4 Were you happy?

p. 70, Activity 8
2 Geography wasn't easy. (True)
3 History and Music were fun. (True)
4 Maths wasn't interesting. (False)
5 Science and Computer Studies weren't difficult. (True)
6 Art was exciting. (False)

p. 71, Activity 10
Monday Computer Studies
Tuesday History
Wednesday Science
Thursday Art
Friday Music
1 Yes, he did. **2** No, he didn't. **3** No, he didn't.
4 Yes, he did. **5** Yes, he did.

p. 72, Activity 13
1 cave **2** see/isn't **3** Geography **4** thieves
5 got **6** too

p. 72, Activity 14
1 a (Rufus)
2 b (the treasure)

p. 72, Activity 15
1 good at **2** cave **3** late **4** statue **5** scary

p. 73, Activity 17
1 pen, leg, web **2** sit **3** hat **4** sock

p. 73, Activity 18
1 same, tale **2** make **3** ate, cake **4** wrote

p. 74, Activity 21
1 has **2** has **3** has **4** have

p. 74, Activity 22
1 taught, created **2** used **3** made up **4** followed **5** finished **6** helped

p. 74, Activity 23
1 club **2** competition **3** exam **4** glue **5** scissors **6** teacher

p. 75, Activity 25
Blog 1: friends, English, difficult, easy
Blog 2: Students, sports, Geography, subjects, activities
Blog 3: teachers, activities, homework

p. 75, Activity 26
I like music and science.

p. 76, Activity 28
Tom likes English.

p. 77, Activity 30
1 d **2** e **3** f **4** g **5** h **6** a **7** b **8** c

p. 77, Activity 31
1 Were **2** were **3** were **4** Was **5** was **6** wasn't **7** were **8** was

p. 77, Activity 32
1 Open (any subject) **2** English **3** Open (romantic, modern, scary, etc.) **4** Open (boring, difficult, etc.) **5** was **6** Open (great, fun, interesting, etc.) **7** PE/Sports **8** because **9** best/favourite **10** great/good/easy

Audioscript

PB Lesson 1 page 72

Lesson 1, Activity 1, p. 72 CD3:01

Emma = E Robbie = R

E There was a story-writing competition at school today.
R Were you the winner?
E No, I wasn't. Stories are difficult!
E Dan was the winner. His story, *The Green Hand*, was about a hand without a body.
R Was it scary?
E Yes, it was! The green hand went to people's houses and …
R/E Aaaarrrgggh!
E Dan! That wasn't funny!

Lesson 1, Activity 2, p. 72 CD3:02

1 interesting
2 boring
3 exciting
4 scary
5 funny
6 difficult
7 easy
8 romantic

AB Lesson 1 page 68

Lesson 1, Activity 1, p. 68 (AB) CD3:03

The first lesson at school was easy. The second and third lessons were difficult. There was an exciting game in the fourth lesson. Lunch was boring. The lessons after lunch were interesting. In the last lesson, we read some poems. Some were funny, some were romantic and some were scary.

Lesson 1, Activity 2, p. 68 (AB) CD3:04

1 Our school book last year was *Dinosaurs*. It was interesting.
2 My mum has got a book called *Pens and Pencils*. It's very boring.
3 Our school book in the summer was *Anna and the Aliens*. It was scary.
4 My first English book was *The First Book of Words*. It was easy.
5 Our teacher's favourite book last year was *Fun with Numbers*. It was difficult.
6 Our school book in the spring was *The Adventures of 009*. It was exciting.

PB Lesson 2 page 73

Lesson 2, Activity 4, p. 73 CD3:05

1 Were they exciting? Yes, they were. Story a and story c.
2 Was it exciting? No, it wasn't.
3 Were there any children in it? No, there weren't.
4 Was there an alien in it? Yes, there was.

PB Lesson 3 page 74

Lesson 3, Activity 7, p. 74 CD3:06

1 Computer Studies
2 Maths
3 Geography
4 Science
5 History
6 Art
7 Music
8 Sport
9 Design
10 Drama

Lesson 3, Activity 8, p. 74 CD3:07

Chorus:
Maths, Science, History, PE, Art, Geography.
A lot of subjects every day. Is school boring? No way!
Last year, Maths wasn't easy. The lessons weren't always fun.
But now I can do all my homework. Maths is for everyone!
Chorus
Last year, P.E. was boring. P.E. lessons weren't my thing.
But now it's my favourite subject. I can play football and swim.
Chorus

AB Lesson 3 page 70

Lesson 3, Activity 8, p. 70 (AB) CD3:08

Last week was fantastic! Sport and Geography are sometimes boring but last week they weren't boring. Geography was interesting but it wasn't easy. History and Music were fun. Maths was very interesting. Science and Computer Studies were both very easy. There was an Art lesson on Tuesday. I usually like Art but this week it was very boring.

PB Lesson 4 page 75

Lesson 4, Activity 10, p. 75 CD3:09

On Monday Robbie's homework was Maths and on Tuesday it was Music. Maths was easy but Music was difficult. On Wednesday his homework was Geography. Robbie likes Geography so the homework was interesting. Thursday and Friday's homework was easy. His homework on Thursday was English and on Friday it was History and Art.

Lesson 4, Activity 11, p. 75 CD3:10

1 On Monday Maddy had a lot of homework. Her English homework was easy but her Maths homework was very difficult.
2 Sometimes Science is her homework on Wednesday but this week she didn't have any. Her homework was drawing her friend's face for Art. It was fun.
3 Friday was Music homework. It wasn't difficult and it was interesting.

AB Lesson 4 page 71

Lesson 4, Activity 10, p. 71 (AB) CD3:11

On Monday Dan's homework was Computer Studies and on Tuesday it was History. On Wednesday his homework was Science. Dan doesn't like Science but the homework was interesting. Thursday's Art homework was easy and on Friday Dan had Music homework.

PB Lesson 5 page 76

Lesson 5, Activity 13, p. 76 CD3:12

Jenny = J Dylan = D Finn = F Dr Al = Dr

J	Here's the statue.
D	But where's the cave?
F	I can't see it! It isn't here.
Dr	Come on, Dylan. You're good at Geography. Where's the cave?
F	HEEEEELP!
D	Er, the cave's here.
D	Ooooh! That was scary!
F	No, it wasn't. It was exciting!
Dr	Be careful, kids!
J	Look, the thieves! And the treasure!
R	Ha, ha, ha! I've got the treasure!
I	WE! We've got the treasure.
J/D/F	We're too late!

PB Lesson 6 page 77

Lesson 6, Activity 14, p. 77 CD3:13

1 hat / hate
2 not / note
3 Tim / time
4 pet / Pete
5 kit / kite
6 Sam / same

Lesson 6, Activity 15, p. 77 CD3:14

1 name / flat
2 meet / bed
3 five / six
4 open / top
5 music / cup

Lesson 6, Activity 16, p. 77 CD3:15

1 That's the hat that I hate!
2 Please do not write me a note.
3 Tim is on time.
4 Pete has a pet.
5 This is a kit for a kite.
6 Sam has the same number.

Lesson 6, Activity 18, p. 77 CD3:16

I like to sing to music, it wakes me up!
But my favourite subject is Maths!

AB Lesson 6 page 73

Lesson 6, Activity 17, p. 73 (AB) CD3:17

1 pen leg web free
2 time five sit mine
3 take hat make date
4 rose note sock toe

PB Lesson 10 page 81

Lesson 10, Activity 25, p. 81 CD3:18

Monday
We study lots of subjects on Monday. The afternoon is difficult but all my classes in the morning are easy. I have Science, English and Maths.
Tuesday
Tuesday afternoon is difficult for me. The fourth class is Maths, then the fifth class is Sport. These are not my favourite subjects.
Wednesday
I like computers, so Wednesday morning is interesting because I have Computer Studies in the first class. In the third class I have Geography and then the last class of the day is History.
Thursday
The third class on Thursday before lunch is Music. After lunch, it's Music, too. Then for the fifth class I have Sport.
Friday
My first class on Friday is Computer Studies and my second class is Geography. My last class on Friday, after Art, is English.

8 All about us

Objectives

- ask and answer about where people come from
- talk about jobs and professions
- give extra information about people, things and places using relative clauses
- use time expressions
- properly pronounce –*ed* simple past /t/ /d/ or /ɪd/ endings

Language

Vocabulary

Nationalities: American, Canadian, Colombian, Brazilian, Argentinian, British, Spanish, Italian, Egyptian, Greek, Chinese, Irish, Japanese, Australian, Turkish, Polish

Jobs: artist, photographer, painter, astronaut, businessman, cook, firefighter, dentist, waiter, actor, engineer, mechanic, footballer, journalist

Structures

Is he from the United States?
Yes, he is. / No, he isn't.
Where's she from? She's from Argentina. She's Argentinian.
He's an artist. He likes playing the guitar. He's an artist **who** likes playing the guitar.
This is an American film. It's very famous. This is an American film **that** is very famous.
This is the gym **where** I go twice a week.
in/on/at (prepositions of time)

Revision

months of the year, seasons, telling the time (o'clock, half past, quarter past/to)
was/were

Receptive

autograph

CLIL and Wider world language

CLIL (Inventions): time, a.m., p.m., midday, midnight, hour, minute, date, year
Wider world

Phonics

- Simple past –*ed* pronunciation: /t/ /d/ /ɪd/

Topics

- nationalities
- jobs
- inventions
- time
- video games

Values

Be a good role model for others.

Stories

- Is Donaldo playing in the match?
- Island mystery: chapter 8

Song

Jobs

Socio-cultural aspects

- finding out about people's jobs
- talking about nationalities
- finding out about inventors and inventions
- working in pairs and groups

Learning strategies

- making use of prior knowledge
- following instructions
- recording new words
- creative thinking: inventing
- critical thinking: discriminating and classifying
- logical thinking: deductive reasoning
- using ICT resources to process and communicate information
- collaborative learning
- integrating contents: discussing and approaching new cultures
- reflecting on learning and self assessment

Cross-curricular contents

- Social Sciences: inventors and inventions; video games through history
- Music: song, pronunciation rhyme
- Language skills: reading a story, acting out, telling a story

Basic competences

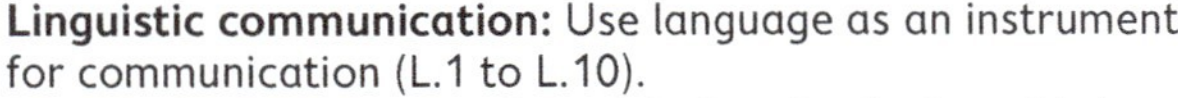

Linguistic communication: Use language as an instrument for communication (L.1 to L.10).
Knowledge and interaction with the physical world: Learn nationalities (L.1 to L.2, L.9 to L.10).
Mathematical competence: Talk about time (L.7).
Processing information and digital competence: Use Active Teach, Digital Activity Book and Ice Island Online World
Talking about the history of video games and new technology (L.8).
Social and civic competence: Talk about professions and skills (L.3). Be a good role model for others (L.5).
Cultural and artistic competence: Learn about inventions and inventors (L.7).
Learning to learn: Reflect on what has been learnt and self evaluate progress (L.10).
Autonomy and personal initiative: Use own judgement and ideas and further develop social skills (L.1 to L.10).

Skills

Listening
- can understand people talking about nationalities and jobs
- can understand a dialogue about nationalities and jobs
- can understand questions about nationalities and jobs
- can understand a song about jobs
- can understand a pronunciation rhyme

Speaking
- can talk about nationalities and jobs
- can use prepositions of time
- can sing the *Jobs* song
- can talk about inventors and inventions
- can talk about video games
- can use relative clauses
- can say the pronunciation rhyme

Taking part in conversations
- can ask and respond to questions about nationalities, jobs, inventions and video games
- can take part in a dialogue about nationalities, jobs, inventions and video games
- can ask and respond to factual questions about inventions and video games

Reading
- can read and understand information (about nationalities, jobs, inventions and video games) in sentences, short paragraphs and texts
- can read and understand a text about inventions and video games
- can read and understand a cartoon strip story, captions and speech bubbles
- can read and understand factual information about inventions and video games

Writing
- can write nationalities, job words and time expressions
- can complete sentences to write about nationalities, jobs, inventions and video games
- can write questions and answers about nationalities and jobs
- can use relative clauses in sentences, paragraphs and short texts
- can write about inventions
- can write a short text to prepare a presentation on video games

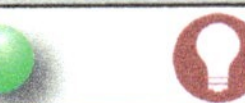

Classroom ideas

- Use the CLIL poster of the unit to decorate the class.
- Decorate the class with flags. Pupils can make their own flags.
- Ask pupils to bring photos of their parents working: they can describe their jobs, make posters or just talk about them.
- If you have pupils from other countries in your class, ask them to find out about an invention in their country.
- You or your pupils could use the websites below to access more information about inventors and inventions around the world: http://www.kidinfo.com/american_history/inventors_inventions.html
  http://www.kidskonnect.com/subject-index/15-science/86-inventors-a-inventions.html
- Play games from the Games Bank.
- Photocopiables 8.1–8.7

Take-home English

- Letters for parents. When you begin Unit 8, complete and give pupils a copy of the letter for the unit (Active Teach). This explains what pupils are going to learn in this unit.
- Home-School Link. Encourage pupils to talk to their family members about the different jobs they do. (L.5)
- Grammar Booklet and Reading and Writing Booklet. Pupils take these home to show their parents.
- Digital Activity Books
- Portfolios. Encourage pupils to take their portfolio files home to show their parents when they finish Unit 8.

Evaluation

Self assessment
- Pupils can ask and answer about events that happened in the past
- Pupils can talk about people's jobs
- Pupils can talk about where someone comes from
- Pupil's Book page 91
- Activity Book page 87
- Grammar reference (Pupil's Book page 111)

Resources
- Unit review (Activity Book page 103)
- Picture dictionary (Activity Book page 111)
- Test Booklet – Unit 8 (pages 34–37)
- Grammar Booklet (pages 29–32), Reading and Writing Booklet – Unit 8 (pages 29–32)

8 All about us

Lesson 1

Lesson aims
To learn and practise new vocabulary (nationalities)

Target language
American, Canadian, Colombian, Brazilian, Argentinian, British, Spanish, Italian, Egyptian, Greek, Chinese, Irish, Japanese, Australian, Turkish, Polish

Receptive language
autograph

Materials
Audio CD; Flashcards and Wordcards (Nationalities)

Optional activity materials
Active Teach; Digital Activity Book; Photocopiable 8.1

Starting the lesson

- Ask the class *What do you do in your free time?* e.g. *I watch TV. I play computer games*. Teach *entertainment*.
- Ask if pupils ever go to football matches. Ask *What's your team?* Ask *What countries are the football players from in your team* (or a team your pupils know)*?*

Presentation

- Present the vocabulary using the flashcards (nationalities). Hold up each flashcard in turn and say the word for pupils to repeat. Hold up the flashcards in a different order for pupils to repeat again.

Pupil's Book page 82

1 Listen and read. Is Donaldo playing in the match?

- Ask *Where are Robbie and Dan? (They are at a football match.)* Ask *Who are Dan and Robbie talking about?* (Pupils speculate.)
- Play the recording. Pupils listen, follow the text and find the answer to the question.

KEY No, he isn't.

2 Listen and repeat.

- Give pupils time to look at the pictures.
- Play the recording. Pause for pupils to repeat.
- Play the recording again, pausing after each word so that pupils can repeat.

3 Talk about famous people from different countries.

- Read the examples and ask pupils to tell you more. Give pairs time to do the speaking activity.
- Encourage pupils to self-correct if they make a mistake.

Practice

Activity Book page 78

1 Read. Then complete the crossword with the nationalities.

- Give pupils time to write the nationalities.
- Check before giving pairs time to do the crossword.

2 Think and write.

- Give pupils time to do the activity. If they have difficulty thinking of enough people, they could work in pairs.
- Volunteers read their famous people.

Ending the lesson

- Ask what jobs in entertainment pupils would like. Pupils mime their answers for the class to guess. For Answer Key see p. 252. For Audioscript see p. 254.

Pupils can now, or at the end of this unit, go online to Ice Island and find the boots that Penn and Gwyn are holding. They are on a shelf in the basement of Professor Ice's secret hiding place (his lair). The shelf is above the costume rack on the left-hand side of the basement. Once pupils click on the boots they are taken to a supplementary language game based on the vocabulary in this unit.

8 All about us

1 3:19 **Listen and read. Is Donaldo playing in the match?**

4
I am good. But look at my leg.
DONALDO
It's Donaldo! Can I have your autograph, please?

2 3:20 **Listen and repeat.**

1	American	2	Canadian	3	Colombian	4	Brazilian
5	Argentinian	6	British	7	Spanish	8	Italian
9	Egyptian	10	Greek	11	Chinese	12	Irish
13	Japanese	14	Australian	15	Turkish	16	Polish

3 **Talk about famous people from different countries.**

OPTIONAL ACTIVITIES

Action game Each pupil has a nationality card. They mingle to find a partner with the same nationality, asking *What's your nationality?* When they find a partner, they sit down and write a sentence using their imagination and their new nationality, e.g. *I'm a famous British football player.*

Pair work Pupils choose a nationality. Pairs take it in turns to ask and answer to guess their partner's nationality, e.g. *Are you Spanish? (No, I'm not.) Are you Indian? (Yes, I am.)*

Photocopiable 8.1 See teacher's notes p. 294.

Lesson 2

Lesson aims
To revise the vocabulary from Lesson 1; to learn and practise asking and answering questions about nationality

Target language
Is she from ...? Yes, she is. / No, she isn't.
Where is she from? She's from ... / She is ... .

Materials
Audio CD; Flashcards and Wordcards (Nationalities)

Optional activity material
Active Teach; Digital Activity Book; Grammar Booklet

Starting the lesson

- Pupils close their books. Write *Briebe nJstiu* and *áaKk* on the board. Pupils rearrange the letters to find the names of two famous people.
- Ask about Justin Bieber and Kaká in turn. *Where's he from?* (Pupils guess.) *What's his nationality?*

Presentation

- Display the flashcards (nationalities), learnt in Lesson 1, around the room and play *I spy* (see p. 300). Ask individual pupils to come and write on the board.

Pupil's Book page 83

- Ask the class to silently read the Look! box.
- Remind pupils we use the preposition *from* to ask for countries and nationalities.

  Listen and match. Then ask and answer.

- Give the class time to look at the pictures.
- Play the recording, pausing for pupils to find the correct picture.
- Play the recording again; pausing for pupils to say the full sentence, e.g. *She is from Colombia. She is Colombian.*
- Give pupils time to do the activity in pairs.

Practice

5 Play the game. *True* or *False*?

- Perform the example with a confident pupil.
- Give pupils time to do the activity in pairs.
- Ask your pupils to close their books and divide the class into two groups. Ask one pupil in each group to say one sentence to the other group, e.g. *Number 3 is from Spain, true or false?* The group that gives more right answers wins.

Activity Book page 79

  Listen and match.

- Give pupils time to look at the pictures.
- Play the recording. Pupils listen and draw lines to match the people with their nationality flags.
- Play the recording again, pausing to elicit and check each match.

4 Look at Activity 3 and write.

- Give pupils time to do the activity.
- Ask pupils to read the sentences.

Ending the lesson

- Ask pupils if there is someone in their family who comes from another country.
- Encourage him/her to talk about his/her family member, where he/she comes from, nationality and any other interesting information. For Answer Key see p. 252. For Audioscript see p. 254.

LOOK!

Is he from the United States?	Yes, he is.	No, he isn't.
Where's she from?	She's from Argentina.	She's Argentinian.
Where are they from?	They're from Australia.	They're Australian.

4 3:21 **Listen and match. Then ask and answer.**

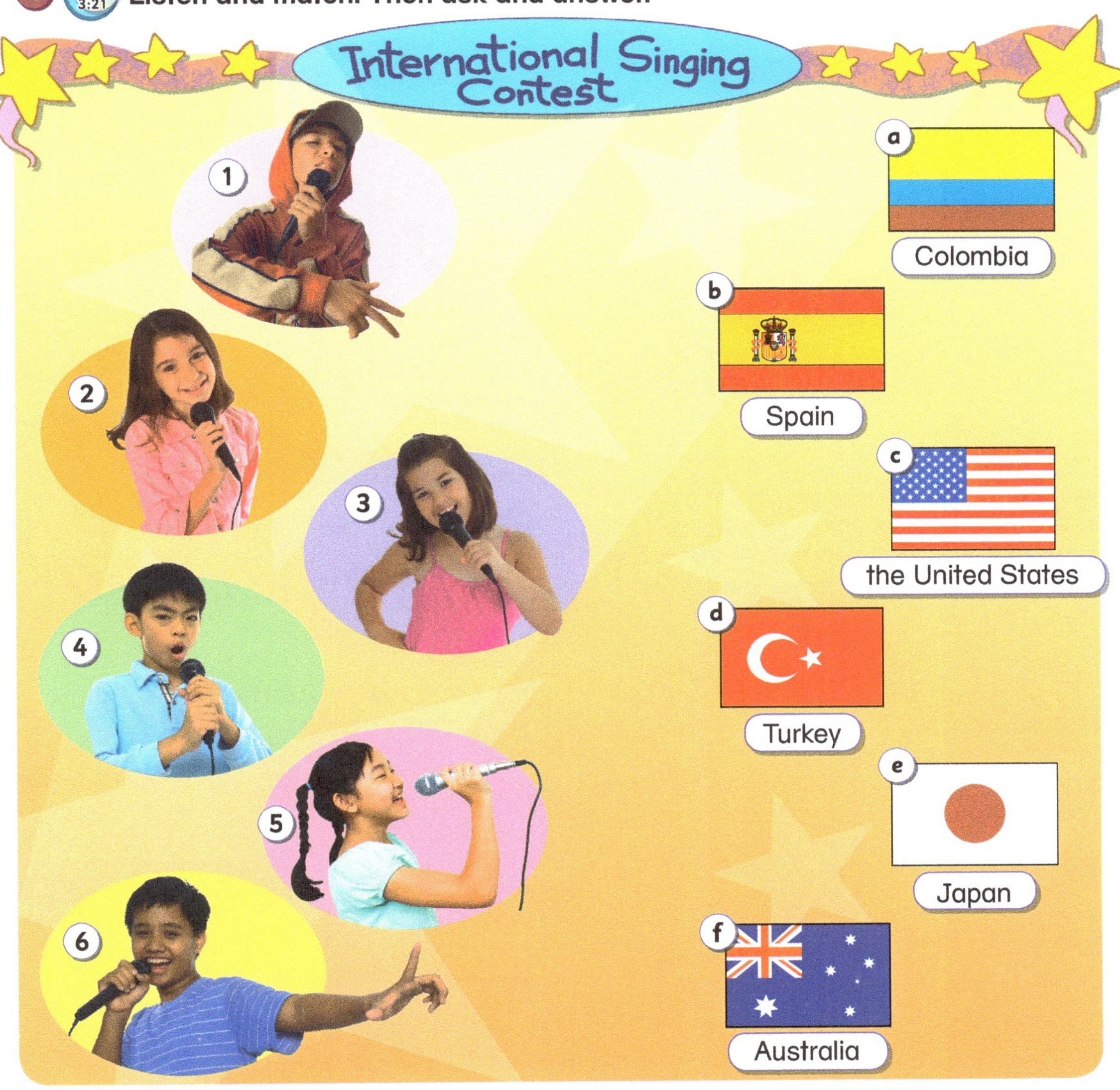

Number 1. Where's he from?

He's from Spain. He's Spanish.

5 **Play the game.** ***True*** **or** ***False*****?**

A: Number 1. He's from Brazil.
B: False! He's from Spain. He's Spanish.

A: The Colombian flag is red, yellow and green.
B: False! It's red, yellow and blue.

OPTIONAL ACTIVITIES

Guessing game Write on the board *country/ nationality/sport/description/good at.* Give pupils time to choose a favourite famous person. Invite volunteers to tell the class about their star, using the prompts on the board. Help with vocabulary where necessary. The class guess who it is, e.g. *He's from Switzerland. He plays tennis. He's tall and good-looking. He's very good at hitting. I think he's good at running, too. Who is he? (Roger Federer.)*

Roleplay Pairs imagine they are a famous person. They tell each other about themselves, e.g. Pupil A: *I'm British.* Pupil B: *Really? Me too.* Pupil A: *I went to the USA in 2010.* Pupil B: *Oh! I went to Australia.*

Grammar Booklet p. 29 See answer key p. 286.

Lesson 3

Lesson aims
To extend the unit vocabulary (jobs); to practise the vocabulary with a song

Target language
artist, photographer, painter, astronaut, businessman/woman, cook, firefighter, dentist, waiter, actor, engineer, mechanic, footballer, journalist

Materials
Audio CD; Flashcards and Wordcards (Jobs)

Optional activity materials
Active Teach; Digital Activity Book; Photocopiable 8.2; Photocopiable 8.3; Reading and Writing Booklet

Starting the lesson

- Play *Pictionary* with the class using jobs words. Divide the class into two teams. Ask one pupil from each team to choose one job they know in English and draw it on the board. The team that guesses the job first wins the point.

Presentation

- Introduce the new words using the flashcards. Hold them up and say the words for pupils to repeat.
- Put the flashcards on the board. Point to the different flashcards and ask the class to say the words.

Pupil's Book page 84

  Listen and repeat.

- Give pupils time to look at the pictures.
- Play the recording. Pause for pupils to find and say each word.
- Play the recording again. Repeat each word. Pupils repeat in chorus miming the jobs.

Song

  Listen and sing.

- Play the song. Pupils follow in their books.
- Play the song again. Encourage pupils to sing.
- Groups of four change the jobs words in one verse. If your class likes a challenge, suggest they change time expressions, days and years too!
- Fast finishers change words in a second verse.
- Groups sing their new verse(s) to the class.
- You can now play the karaoke song (Active Teach).

Practice

  Look and say. Then listen and check.

- Pupils look at the example while you read it.
- Pupils do the activity in pairs.

Activity Book page 80

5 Unscramble the words to find 12 jobs.

- Read the words as a class before pupils do the activity.
- Check answers in pairs.

6 Look and write their jobs and their countries.

- Give pupils time to look at the pictures. Ask them about their names.
- Ask a volunteer to do one example.
- Give pupils time to do the activity.
- Encourage pupils to ask and answer for the name and the country to check.

Ending the lesson

- Volunteers mime jobs for the class to guess. For Answer Key see p. 252. For Audioscript see p. 254.

6 3:23 **Listen and repeat.**

7 3:24 **Listen and sing.**

SONG

On Friday, I was a cook.
On Thursday, an engineer.
In June, I was a waiter,
I was an artist once last year.
CHORUS:
I'm an actor, yes, an actor.
Acting's the life for me.
I'm an actor, yes, an actor.
Acting's the life for me.

Last spring I was a journalist
And an astronaut. That was great!
I was a famous British footballer.
In two thousand and eight.
Chorus
I get up at five in the morning.
My days are very long.
But a life in films is exciting.
That's why I'm singing this song.
Chorus

8 3:25 **Look and say. Then listen and check.**

He is a businessman.
He is from Poland.

1 businessman / Poland
2 photographer / Brazil
3 mechanic / Ireland
4 cooks / Italy
5 painter / Greece
6 dentist / Egypt

OPTIONAL ACTIVITIES

Find the pairs
Play *Pelmanism* using jobs words.
Photocopiable 8.2 See teacher's notes p. 294.
Photocopiable 8.3 See teacher's notes p. 294.
Reading and Writing Booklet pp. 29–30 See answer key p. 284.

Lesson 4

Lesson aims
To revise the Lesson 3 vocabulary; to learn and practise the use of relatives *who* and *that*

Target language
Relatives who and that
He's an artist who likes playing the guitar.
It's an American film that's very famous.

Materials
Audio CD

Optional activity materials
Magazine images of famous people and places; Flashcards (Nationalities; Jobs) Active Teach; Digital Activity Book; Grammar Booklet

Starting the lesson

- Write on the board two sentences: *He's an artist. He likes playing the guitar.*
- Ask the class to think about joining the two sentences into one. Write *who* in big letters on the board. Invite them to try to join the two sentences into one using this word. He's *an artist* who *likes playing the guitar.* Write the single sentence on the board.

Presentation

Pupil's Book page 85

Skills

- Ask the class to silently read the Look! box.
- Remind pupils we use relative pronouns to give more information about a person *(who)*, about a thing *(which)* or about a place *(where)*. *That* can be used instead of *who* and *which*. Tell them that they are going to practise *who* for people and *that* for things.

9 Read and say using *who* or *that*.

- Ask five pupils to read the sentences.
- Remind them we use *who* for people and *that* for people, places and things.
- Ask a confident pupil to do the first sentence.
- Give pupils time to do the activity.

KEY **1** who **2** who **3** that **4** who **5** who

10 3:26 Listen. Then say.

- Give pupils time to read the names and the example.
- Play the recording and ask pupils to find the names first. Play the recording again pausing for pupils to say the sentences. Tell them that they have to use *who* to talk about these people.

KEY David is the dentist who is working now. Michael is the waiter who loves dancing. Sarah is the engineer who is making a road. Henry is the photographer who loves travelling and who is taking pictures in the jungle.

11 Play the game. Think of a famous person and give clues. Then your partner guesses.

- Pupils look at the example while you read it. *(Shakira)* Say *She is a Colombian artist who dances very well.* The pupil who guesses first takes the turn and continues giving hints about another famous person.
- Pupils play the game in pairs, two groups or the whole group.

Practice

Activity Book page 81

7 3:27 Listen and number.

- Ask pupils to look at the picture.
- Play the recording, pausing if necessary to allow pupils time to find and number the people in the picture.
- Play the recording again, pausing for pupils to say the right number.
- Now encourage them to remember the relative sentences to describe the scene. Ask *Who is a?*

8 Write. Then number.

- Give pupils time to look at the photos and read the text. Ask them to write. Then ask them to number the photo for each text.
- Pupils check and correct in pairs.

9 Write two sentences using *who* and two using *that*.

- Give pupils time to do the activity.
- Pupils check and correct in pairs.

Ending the lesson

- Show your pupils photos of famous people and ask them to use relative sentences to talk about them. Do the same with some famous monuments or objects that are popular in your country or in the world! For Answer Key see p. 252. For Audioscript see p. 254.

LOOK!

He's an artist.	He likes playing the guitar.	He's an artist who likes playing the guitar.
It's an American film.	It's very famous.	It's an American film that is very famous.

9 Read and say using *who* or *that*.

1 This film is about a Spanish astronaut. He went to Mars.
2 This book is about a Greek cook. He invented green pasta.
3 This magazine is about an Irish town. It is popular because there are beautiful landscapes in it.
4 This song is about a Turkish painter. He painted famous Turkish monuments.
5 This comic is about an Argentinian footballer. He scored lots of goals.

10 3:26 Listen. Then say.

Emma is the businesswoman who is in a meeting.

1

2
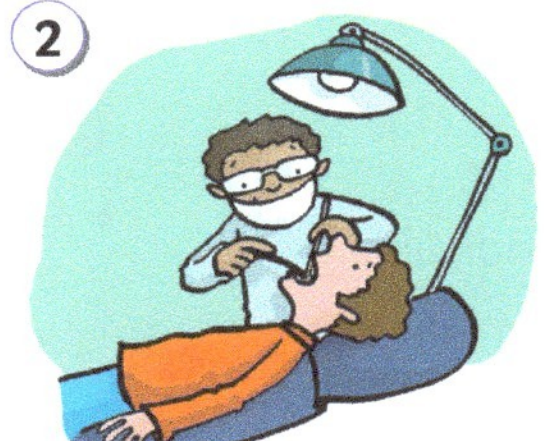

3

4

5

11 Play the game. Think of a famous person and give clues. Then your partner guesses.

She is a Colombian artist who dances very well.

Shakira.

OPTIONAL ACTIVITIES

Matching pairs for guessing

Put all the flashcards for nationalities in one pile and all the flashcards for jobs in another pile. Reuse the magazines with pictures of famous people and places. Divide the class into two teams and ask one pupil from each team to choose one person or place from the magazines and take two cards, one from each pile. They have to make a sentence using *who* or *that* and ask their teams to guess the person or place, e.g. *The Chinese monument that is the longest in the world.*

Grammar Booklet p. 30 See answer key p. 286.

Lesson 5

Lesson aims
To consolidate the unit language with a story

Values
Be a good role model for others

Materials
Audio CD

Optional activity materials
Questions about the Ice Island story so far, on separate slips of paper; Active Teach; Digital Activity Book; Photocopiable 8.4

Starting the lesson

- Stick the Ice Island question slips on the walls of your classroom. Groups of four circulate and note the answers. If your class needs support, let them look in their books. The first group to finish with all correct answers wins.
- Suggested questions: *Who likes studying the moon? (Dr Al.) Where does Captain Formosa live? (On a submarine.) What does Captain Formosa look like? (He's old, he's got one eye and a moustache.)* etc.

Presentation

Pupil's Book page 86

- Ask the class questions about each picture. Pupils answer or guess. Use the pictures to pre-teach *golden* and *rich*. Ask (Picture 1) *What have Rufus and Ivan got? (The treasure.)* (Picture 2) *What can you see?* (Pictures 3 and 4) Ask *What's happening?* (Picture 5) *Are Rufus and Ivan happy? (No.) Why not?* (Picture 6) *What can you see?*

12 Look at the pictures. Tell the story.

- Ask the class to look again at the pictures.
- Ask six volunteers to go in front of the class and tell the story just based on looking at the pictures, without reading. Each pupil tells the story of one picture.

Practice

  Listen and read. Then act out.

- Play the recording. Pupils listen and follow the story.
- Ask the class questions about the story, e.g. *Why are the thieves happy in Picture 1? (They've got the treasure.) What can they see in Picture 2? (A monster.)*
- Play the recording again. Pause for the class to repeat each line in chorus.
- Divide the class into six and allocate these parts: Rufus, Ivan, Jenny, Captain Formosa, Penn and Gwyn.
- Play the recording again. Pause for pupils to repeat their character's lines.
- Ask eight volunteers to act out the story.
- Take a class vote for the best actor/actress.
- Pairs predict what happens next.
- Volunteers tell the class their ideas. Take a vote to find the most popular idea.

Home-School Link

- Ask your pupils to talk with their family members about the jobs they do.

Values

- Ask the class why it's important to be a good role model for others, e.g. *Being punctual, tidy, a person that respects others, the rules,* etc.
- Groups of four discuss what being a good role model means to them and present their ideas to the class.

Activity Book page 82

10 Match.

- Pupils close their books. Ask questions 1–6. Volunteers guess the answers. Don't confirm if they are correct or not.
- Pupils do the matching activity.
- Pairs compare answers before you check.

11 Draw your favourite character and write about him/her.

- Ask *Who is your favourite character?* Encourage pupils to explain why, e.g. *I like Finn because I think he's cool. He's good at snowboarding, too.*
- Give pupils time to do the activity.
- Support pupils by writing prompts on the board, e.g. *He/She has ..., He/She's ... (adjective), He/She's (not very) good at ..., He/She likes ..., In my picture he/she's wearing ....*

12 What happens next? Imagine.

- Give pupils time to write.
- Ask volunteers to tell the class their ideas and take a vote to find the most popular idea.

13 Write about the characters using *who* or *that*.

- Give pupils time to do the activity.
- Ask fast finishers to play a guessing game with their drawings in Activity 13, e.g. *My character is someone who likes ....*
- Check the answers asking different pupils to read out.

Ending the lesson

- Ask the class if they liked the ending of the story (PB p. 86). Were they surprised? For Answer Key see p. 252. For Audioscript see p. 254.

12 Look at the pictures. Tell the story.

13 3:28 Listen and read. Then act out.

VALUES

Be a good role model for others.

HOME-SCHOOL LINK

PARENT

At home talk about the different jobs your family members do.

AB p.82

OPTIONAL ACTIVITIES

Spelling game
Pairs take it in turns to ask each other how to spell words from this episode, e.g. *treasure, grandfather, submarine.* The speller can't look.

Noughts and crosses
See p. 301. Prepare questions about Ice Island, e.g. *Is Captain Formosa dancing in Episode 1? (No, he isn't.) What was in Captain Formosa's sandwich in Episode 2?*
Photocopiable 8.4 See teacher's notes p. 293.

Lesson 6

Lesson aims
To identify the correspondence of the *–ed* suffix with the sounds /t/, /d/, /ɪd/

Materials
Audio CD; Phonics and spelling poster

Optional activity materials
Active Teach; Digital Activity Book; Photocopiable 8.5

Starting the lesson

- Give pupils time to look at the Phonics and spelling poster (see teacher's notes on p. 26). Read aloud the examples given in the eighth picture.
- Ask pupils to repeat after you some words. Write these words on the board.
- Encourage pupils to find a pattern.

Presentation

- State the goal of the lesson.
- Remind pupils that the simple past of regular verbs in English is formed by adding *-ed*.
- Explain that the *–ed* ending has three possible sounds /t/, /d/, /ɪd/. Agree upon a class sign to show each of these sounds.
- Make a web of ideas to explain the following rule: Find the final sound of the root/base word. Then you have three options.
  1. If the final sound is /t/ or /d/ (wanted, needed, decided), then the *–ed* ending is pronounced /ɪd/.
  2. If the final sound is other than /t/ or /d/, then hold three fingers to your neck and make that final sound. Do you feel a vibration? If you feel a vibration, the sound is 'voiced', and the *–ed* ending is said as /d/ (cleaned, dreamed).
  3. If there is no vibration, the sound is 'unvoiced' and the *–ed* ending is said as /t/ (walked, laughed).

Practice

Pupil's Book page 87

14  Listen and repeat.

- Give pupils time to read the sounds.
- Play the recording for pupils to repeat the sounds chorally.

15  Listen, point and say /t/, /d/ or /ɪd/.

- Give pupils time to look at the words.
- Play the recording. Pause for pupils to find, point and say.
- Play the recording again and walk around the class to make sure that pupils say the words as accurately as possible.

16  Listen and read. Then repeat.

- Read aloud the first sentence.
- Elicit whether *cooked* sounds like /t/, /d/ or /ɪd/ at the end (/t/)
- Play the recording.
- Ask the class to share their ideas for each sentence.

17 Read and practise with a partner.

- Model each sentence so that the class repeats chorally.
- Give pupils time to read and practise in pairs.

18  Listen and repeat.

- Give pupils time to look at the pictures.
- Play the recording. Then ask pupils to find the verbs ending in *-ed*.
- Play the recording again. Encourage the class to learn and repeat the rhyme.

Practice

Activity Book page 83

14  Listen and repeat. Then write /t/, /d/ or /ɪd/

- Read aloud the first sentence to provide another opportunity to recognise the sound in *cooked* (/t/).
- Play the recording.
- Give pupils time to do the activity.
- Correct the activity as a whole-group discussion.

15  Listen and circle. Which ending sounds different?

- Read aloud the first set. Ask the class to find the odd one.
- Play the recording.
- Check the activity as a whole-group discussion.

16 Read. Then complete the table.

- Read aloud the verbs in the box.
- Remind pupils about the rule for working out the ending sound.

17 Write four sentences. Use verbs from Activity 16.

- Encourage the class to make up their own sentences orally.
- Write some sentence prompts on the board to provide support for all learners.
- Give pupils time to do the activity.
- Ask volunteers to read their sentences. Elicit which words have each of the ending sounds /t/, /t/, or /ɪd/.

Ending the lesson

- Revisit the goal of the lesson and ask pupils to evaluate their own progress. For Answer Key see p. 252. For Audioscript see p. 254.

Simple past of regular verbs –ed

is pronounced /t/ after unvoiced sounds.
is pronounced /d/ after voiced sounds.
is pronounced /id/ after verbs ending –t or –d

14 3:29 **Listen and repeat.**

/t/ /d/ /id/

15 3:30 **Listen, point and say /t/, /d/ or /id/.**

1 mixed	2 turned	3 collected	4 reduced	5 recycled
6 landed	7 watched	8 cleaned	9 decided	10 reused
11 lived	12 painted	13 looked	14 helped	

16 3:31 **Listen and read. Then repeat.**

1 He cooked a nice meal.
2 The mechanic fixed my car.
3 The artist painted a picture.
4 An astronaut landed on the moon.
5 He played a good match.
6 They followed the signs.

17 **Read and practise with a partner.**

/t/	/d/	/id/
He liked the present.	He cleaned the room.	The plane landed on time.
We watched the show last night.	The teacher spelled the word.	We wanted to go.
They laughed so much.	It snowed yesterday.	The book ended well.
Anna hoped for the best.	I stayed at home.	You painted the fence.

18 3:32 **Listen and repeat.**

OPTIONAL ACTIVITIES

Poets' Workshop Add an *–ed* poem or rhyme to the class poetry book. Encourage the class to write their own poems.

Bingo Ask pupils to make their own Bingo cards with *–ed* verbs. Use the verbs from Activity 18.

Cumulative Game Continue the sentence *Yesterday I watched TV*, e.g. *Yesterday I watched TV and played basketball*, etc. This could be a chain activity around the class or a competitive game in which two teams alternate until someone makes a mistake.

Photocopiable 8.5 See teacher's notes p. 295.

Lesson 7

Lesson aims
To extend the unit vocabulary (times, dates); to learn and practise the use of relatives *where*, *which*

Cross-curricular focus
Social science: inventions

Target language
time, a.m., p.m., midday, midnight, hour, minute, date, year
This is the gym where I go twice a week.
Those oranges, which I bought yesterday, are delicious.
in/on/at; in – the morning, June, spring, 2008
on – Thursday, January 16th
at – five o'clock, night

Materials
Audio CD

Optional activity materials
Realia: alarm clock, blue jeans, basketball, ballpoint pen, digital watch; Active Teach; Digital Activity Book; CLIL poster; Photocopiable 8.6; Reading and Writing Booklet, Grammar Booklet

Starting the lesson

- Inventions are important – they have helped people discover new worlds, build communities, and cure diseases.
- Some inventors have created new things by thinking about solutions to a problem in a different way.
- Some inventions are a result of thinking about different uses for an object.

Presentation

- Ask the class to tell you about their favourite invention. Make a web of ideas.
- Before reading, give pupils time to look at the timeline on PB page 88. Ask *What can you see?* Compare the inventions: *What was invented first?*
- Use the Look! and Tip! boxes as well as the web of ideas to present the new structures. Make relative clauses to explain who invented it, where, its use, etc.

Pupil's Book page 88

19 Read and match. What are these inventions? Then find these words.

- Read the title and the introduction to the text.
- Remind the pupils how to read years in English (1787 = seventeen eighty seven).
- Set purpose for reading: *Let's find out which invention it is describing.*
- Read the whole text as a shared reading experience: use expression and intonation to model proficient reading.
- Ask pupils to follow your reading and find the words from the word bank.
- Ask volunteers to explain their meaning.

KEY
1 c alarm clock **2** d jeans **3** a basketball **4** e biro/ballpoint pen **5** b digital watch

Practice

20 Ask and answer.

- Complete the activity as a whole-group discussion.

KEY **1** American **2** Canada **3** hours, minutes, month or day **4** 1938

21 Talk to your partner. Which invention do you use the most?

- Allow some STT so that pupils talk in pairs about the inventions they use most.
- Ask one or two volunteers to share what they have discussed with the class.

Activity Book page 84

18 Read and match.

- Model how to complete this type of activity.
- Give pupils time to do the activity.
- Check answers as a whole-group discussion.

19 Read. Then complete.

- Review the new structure.
- Read aloud the first sentence.
- Give pupils time to complete the activity.

20 Write a description. Make up your own invention!

- Give pupils time to complete the description.
- Encourage fast finishers to add their own details to the text.
- Invite pupils to share their pieces of writing by reading aloud or exchanging with a partner.

Ending the lesson

- Revisit the objective of the lesson.
- Ask pupils to think of some recent inventions, e.g. the internet, the smartphone. Ask them to talk about these inventions as if it were 50 years in the future. For Answer Key see p. 252. For Audioscript see p. 254.

19 Read and match. What are these inventions? Then find these words.

time a.m. p.m. midday midnight hour minute date year

1 In 1787 an American inventor made a clock that he used to get up at 4 in the morning. 60 years later, a Frenchman invented a clock that people could set to any hour, AM or PM.

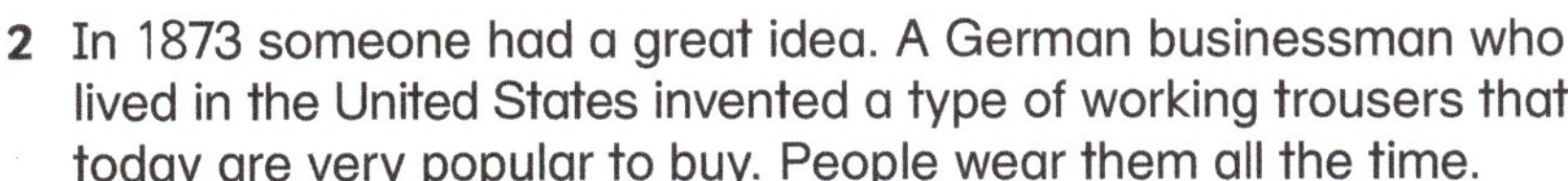

2 In 1873 someone had a great idea. A German businessman who lived in the United States invented a type of working trousers that today are very popular to buy. People wear them all the time.

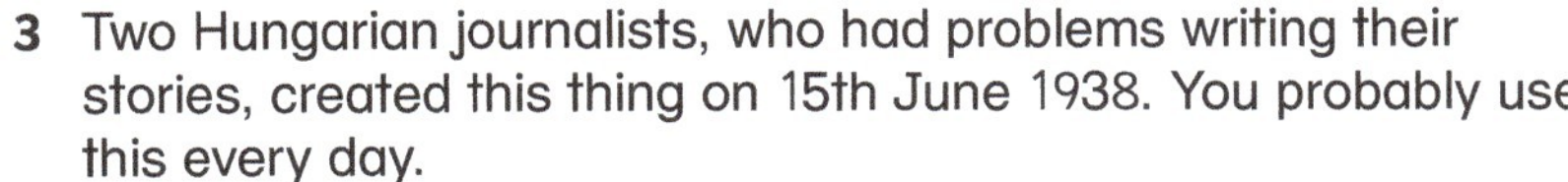

3 Two Hungarian journalists, who had problems writing their stories, created this thing on 15th June 1938. You probably use this every day.

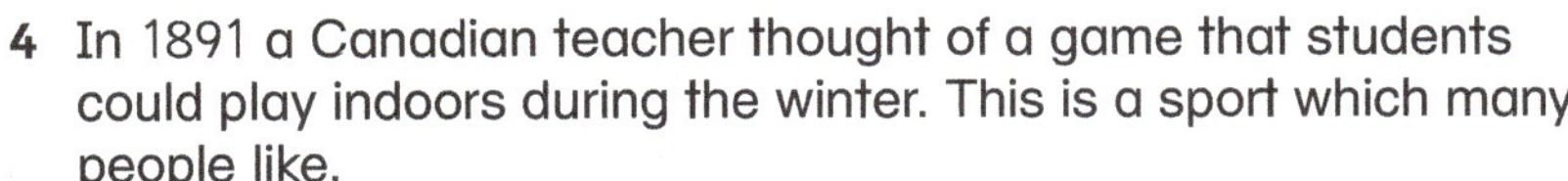

4 In 1891 a Canadian teacher thought of a game that students could play indoors during the winter. This is a sport which many people like.

5 This can show you the time: hours, minutes, the month or the day. It is there on your wrist at midday or even at midnight! American engineers made it electronic for the first time in 1957.

a 

b 

c 

d 

e 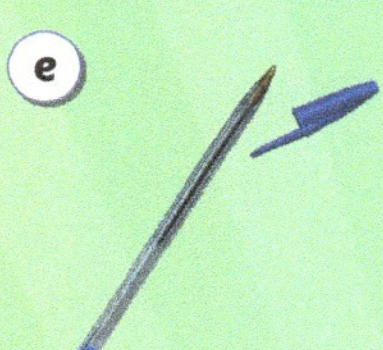

TIP!

in / on / at
in – the morning, January, spring, 1891
on – Thursday, 15th June
at – five o'clock, night, the weekend

LOOK!

This is the gym where I go twice a week.

These oranges, which I bought yesterday, are delicious.

20 Ask and answer.

1 What nationality was the person who invented the alarm clock?
2 In which country did basketball start?
3 What information can you see on a digital watch?
4 In which year was the ballpoint pen invented?

21 Talk to your partner. Which invention do you use most?

OPTIONAL ACTIVITIES

Researcher's Workshop
Find out more about a famous inventor from your country.
Write a mini biography about a famous inventor to practise prepositions of time.

Photocopiable 8.6 See teacher's notes p. 295.
Reading and Writing Booklet p. 31 See answer key p. 284.
Grammar Booklet p. 31 See answer key p. 286.

Lesson 8

Lesson aims
To learn about other cultures and respect cultural differences; to learn about technology – the history of video games

Materials
Audio CD

Optional activity materials
Active Teach; Digital Activity Book; CLIL poster; Photocopiable 8.7

Starting the lesson

- Ask *Do you like playing video games? What video games do you play?*
- Ask pupils if they've played any board games at home recently. Which one(s)?
- Ask *Do you prefer board games or video games? Why?*

Presentation

Pupil's Book page 89

22 Look, read and match.

- Give pupils time to look at the photos.
- Ask the class questions about each photo in turn. Pupils speculate. Ask *Do you know this game? Do you like it?*
- Give pupils time to read. Read again in groups and pause after each paragraph to check understanding.

KEY 1 c, **2** b, **3** a

23 Read again and answer.

- Ask pupils to read the questions.
- Give them time to read the text. They say the answers to a partner.

KEY
1 No, they were American.
2 No, it was expensive. (All video games used to be expensive.)
3 No, they were black and white.
4 Yes, they were very successful.
5 No, it wasn't.
6 Yes, you can.

Practice

24 Read and discuss.

- If your class likes reading aloud, ask volunteers to read the texts.
- Give pairs time to decide one good thing and one bad thing about playing computer games.
- Discuss pupils' ideas. Volunteers tell the class how many hours a day/week they play. They say if they think it's too much or about right.
- Discuss the importance of being self-disciplined and of not always doing what we want.

Activity Book page 85

21 Write *True* or *False*.

- Give pairs time to do the activity. They decide if each statement is true or false.

22 What do you think about video games? Do you have a favourite? Why?

- Give pupils time to write.
- Ask volunteers to read their work aloud.
- For the portfolio project activity, ask pupils to prepare a PowerPoint presentation about their favourite video game. If this is not possible for all of them, divide the class into two groups. Group one (those pupils who can do the PowerPoint) are the technicians and Group two (those who can't do the PowerPoint) are the journalists attending the presentation on 'The best video games'.
- Another possibility is to allow pupils to do the presentation at school, in groups. Ask them to read the project template on AB page 85 before they do the presentation.
- Encourage them to interact during their presentations.

Ending the lesson

- Ask pupils if they know what entertainment there was when older family members were children. For Answer Key see p. 252. For Audioscript see p. 254.

Wider world

Video games

22 Look, read and match.

The history of video games

Every year, there are new video games. But let's look at some of the old ones…

1 The first video games were American. Pong was new in 1972. Two small white rectangles went up and down and a small white square went left and right. What was the game? Computer table tennis!

2 The Game Boy was Japanese. It was first sold in shops in 1989. It was small and there were a lot of good games for it. The games were black and white. Games with the character Mario were very successful.

3 The Wii was new in 2006. In a lot of Wii games, you play with all your body and not just your fingers. Some sports games are very good exercise!

a

b

c

23 Read again and answer.

1 Were the first video games Japanese?
2 Was Pong cheap?
3 Were the first Game Boy games in colour?
4 Were the Mario games successful?
5 Was the Wii in stores in 2005?
6 Can you play Wii games with your whole body?

24 Read and discuss.

Hello! I'm Anna. I hate video games. I think they are very boring. I prefer playing outside with my friends. I like riding my bike every day after school. Don't you?

Hi! I'm Alex and I love my Play Station. I play every day and I have a lot of different games. Some of them are very interesting.

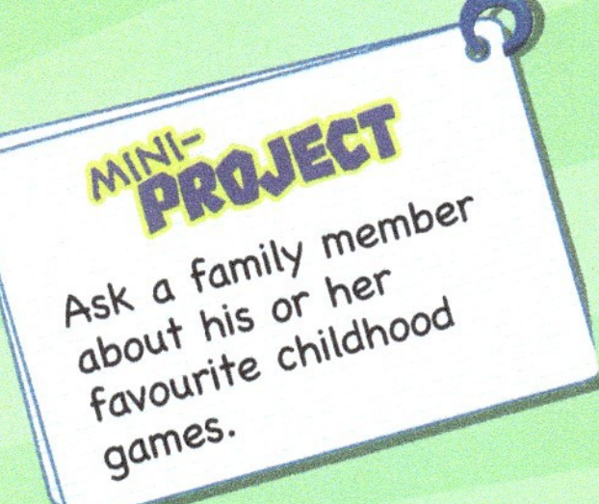

AB p.85

OPTIONAL ACTIVITIES

Class survey Pupils estimate how many hours a week they spend playing computer games. Write the number of pupils who play for one hour on the board. Continue until you have information about everyone in the class. Help pupils draw a graph or liaise with the Maths teacher.

Entertainment Quiz Pairs write five questions similar to those in the Technology Quiz (Activity Book Activity 23). They swap with another pair and answer.
Photocopiable 8.7 See teacher's notes p. 295.

Lesson 9

Lesson aims
To review the unit language with a game
To use the Picture dictionary

Revision language
Is she from ...? Yes, she is. / No, she isn't. Where is she from? She's from ... / She is ... Nationalities, jobs, Relatives who, that, where, which, in/on/at

Materials
Audio CD

Optional activity materials
Active Teach; Digital Activity Book; Reading and Writing Booklet

Starting the lesson

- Ask two pupils whose families are from different countries to talk about each other using *who*.
- Encourage the class to ask them about their parents' jobs and nationality.

Pupil's Book page 90

25 Play the game. Who did you meet?

- Give the class time to look at the game.
- Divide the class into groups of four and ask pupils to read the game.
- Encourage the class to explain how to play the game.
- Give pupils time to play. Circulate, monitor and help.

Picture dictionary

- Pupils can do the picture dictionary of the unit on Activity Book page 111.
- Ask pupils to look at the pictures and try to write the vocabulary on their own in their notebook. Then ask them to look for the words they don't remember in the Pupil's Book.
- As they finish, ask pupils to exchange notebooks to check answers. (Notebooks can be collected for checking.)

Activity Book page 86

23 Read. Then circle.

- Give pupils time to read and do the activity.
- To check, ask volunteers to read in turns.

24 Write. Who is the best role model?

- Give pupils time to read. Then do the activity orally, as a whole group.
- Ask pupils to make questions about the headings on the table, e.g. *Does Gwyneth usually arrive on time?* The class answer *Yes, she usually arrives on time.*
- Give pupils time to look at the table and think about the answer. Then say *The best role model is ...* and the class answers in chorus.

Ending the lesson

- Invite pupils time to discuss the four children from AB page 86 Activity 24. Ask them for themselves *Do you think you are good role models? Why (not)?* For Answer Key see p. 252. For Audioscript see p. 254.

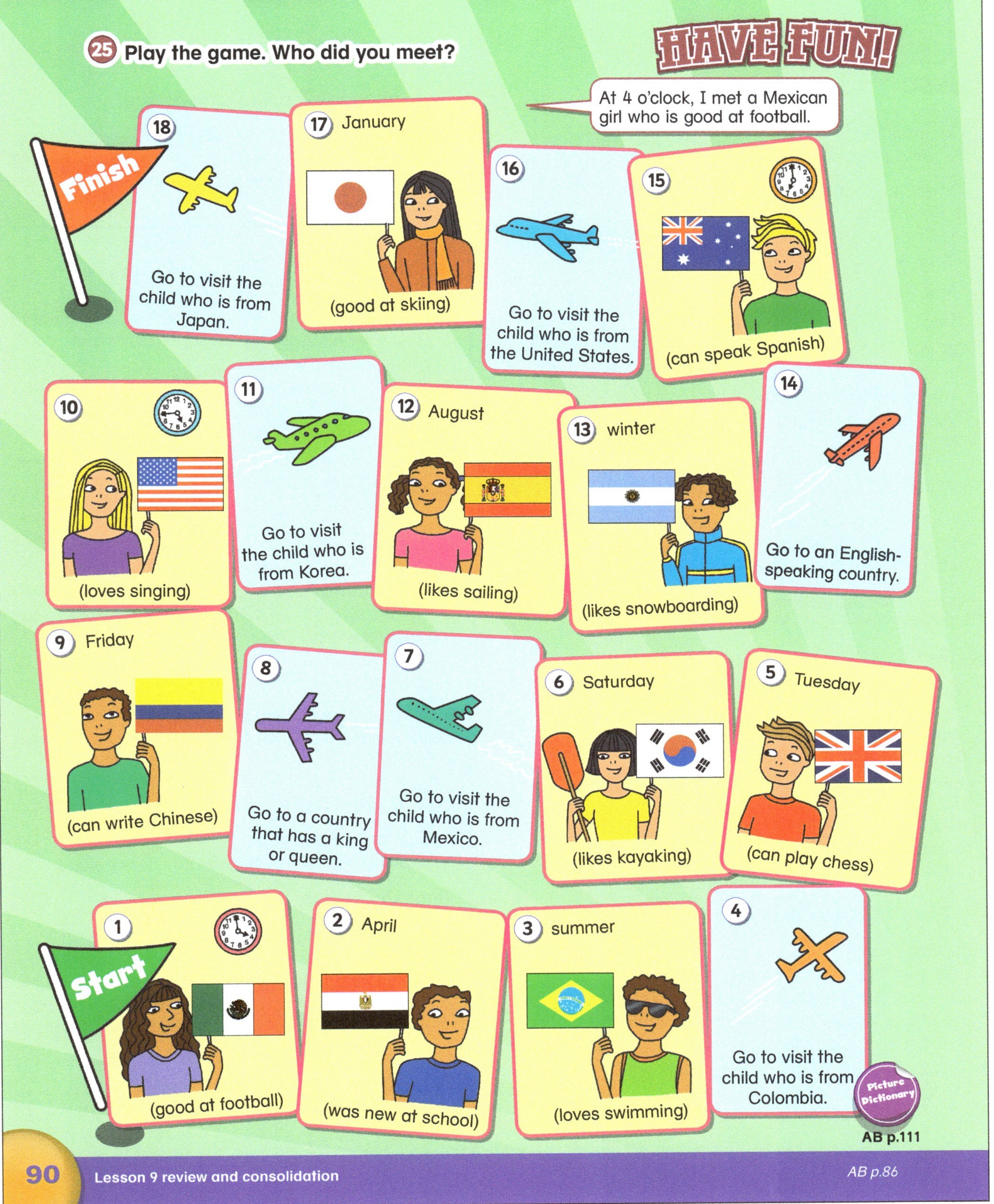

OPTIONAL ACTIVITIES

Dice game Pupils work in groups of four. They take it in turns to throw a dice or spin a spinner. They make a sentence with *in* if they roll one, *on* for two, *at* for three, *last* for four, *ago* for five and any of these words for a six. They score a point for each sentence the group thinks is correct. It's a good idea to have at least one capable pupil in each group.

Word game Play *Bingo* with one of the vocabulary sets from the unit, e.g. nationalities or jobs.

Reading and Writing Booklet p. 32 See answer key p. 284.

Lesson 10

Lesson aims
To personalise and assess efforts

Target language
Is she from ...? Yes, she is. / No, she isn't. Where is she from? She's from ... . / She is ... . Nationalities, jobs, Relatives who, that, where, which, In/on/at

Materials
Audio CD

Optional activity materials
Online World; Active Teach; Digital Activity Book; Grammar Booklet; Test Booklet; Grammar reference (PB); Unit review (AB)

Starting the lesson

- Invite the class to think of these activities as a way to assess their work, in order to find out if they need extra work in any of the unit contents.

Pupil's Book page 91

26 Read and say.

- Give the class time to read the sentence openers.
- Divide the class into two teams. One says the sentence opener and the other ends the sentence. Teams alternate.

KEY
1 Argentinian **2** Polish **3** Irish **4** Greek **5** Turkish **6** Canadian

27 Point to a flag. Ask and answer.

- Perform the example with a confident pupil.
- Give pupils time to do the activity in pairs.
- Ask your pupils to close their books. Ask two volunteers to perform the example again or a similar one. Then ask a pupil to say *He/She is the boy/girl who is from ....*

28 Read and link using *who* or *that*.

- Ask five pupils to read the sentences.
- Give pupils time to do the activity.
- Volunteers read the sentences again using *who* or *that* for linking.

KEY
1 He is the artist who created the famous statue in Central Park.
2 She is an astronaut who went to Mars in January.
3 This is the film with my favourite actor that I told you about yesterday.
4 They are the journalists who wrote the interesting article about video games.
5 I went to an Italian restaurant that was very good.

Activity Book page 87

25 Match.

- Give pupils time to do the activity.
- Divide the class into two groups and alternately ask one group to read the definition and the other to say the correct word.

26 Look at Activity 25 and write.

- Give pupils time to read and write.
- Read aloud and stop for the class to say the answers in chorus.

27 Write the sentences using *that* or *who*.

- Give pupils time to write.
- Ask volunteers to read their writing work aloud.

Ending the lesson

- Give pupils time to read the sentences in the 'I can' section.
- Ask pupils to think carefully about whether they are able to do the 'I can' sentences. Ask them what they found easy or difficult in the unit and why. For Answer Key see p. 252. For Audioscript see p. 254.

Online World Pupils can now go online to Ice Island and enjoy the fun and games.

26 Read and say.

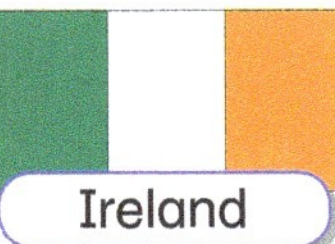

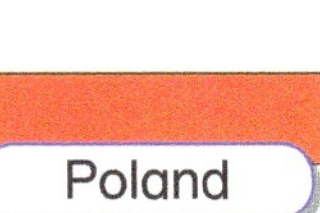

1 He is from Argentina. He is …
2 She comes from Poland. She is …
3 They're from Ireland. They're …
4 We are from Greece. We are …
5 I am from Turkey. I am …
6 You come from Canada. You are …

27 Point to a flag. Ask and answer.

28 Read and link using *who* or *that*.

1 He is an artist. He created the famous statue in Central Park.
2 She is an astronaut. She went to Mars in January.
3 This is the film with my favourite actor. I told you about it yesterday.
4 They are journalists. They wrote the interesting article about video games.
5 I went to an Italian restaurant. It was very good.

OPTIONAL ACTIVITIES

Quiz Prepare a quiz in a PowerPoint presentation or on the board to assess the class as a group.
Active Teach Pupils can watch the animated story Episode 4.
Grammar reference (PB p. 111) and Unit review (AB p. 103) You may want pupils to do the Grammar reference and Unit review activities for Unit 8 at this point.
Test Booklet You could give the Unit 8 test.
Grammar Booklet p. 32 See answer key p. 286.

Activity Book Answer Key

p. 78, Activity 1
1 British **2** Spanish **3** Colombian **4** Chinese
5 Australian **6** American **7** Mexican **8** Canadian
9 Irish **10** Brazilian **11** Egyptian **12** Argentinian
13 Greek **14** Italian **15** Polish **16** Japanese
17 Turkish

p. 79, Activity 3
1 f **2** c **3** a **4** b **5** d **6** e

p. 79, Activity 4
1 United Kingdom / British
2 Yes, he is. / Brazilian
3 No, she isn't. / Italy / Italian
4 China / Chinese
5 Yes, she is. / Argentina. / Argentinian
6 Egypt / Egyptian

p. 80, Activity 5
1 waiter **2** photographer **3** businessman
4 journalist **5** dentist **6** firefighter **7** cook
8 mechanic **9** engineer **10** painter **11** astronaut
12 artist

p. 80, Activity 6
1 dentist/UK
2 waiter/Italy
3 cook/Mexico
4 actor/Japan

p. 81, Activity 7
1 b **2** a **3** f **4** e **5** c **6** h **7** g **8** d

p. 81, Activity 8
1 Chinese/who/that
2 Egyptian/who/that
3 Brazilian/who/that

p. 82, Activity 10
1 c **2** d **3** e **4** b **5** f **6** a

p. 83, Activity 14
1 /t/
2 /t/
3 /ɪd/
4 /ɪd/
5 /d/
6 /d/

p. 83, Activity 15
1 fixed (/t/)
2 cooked (/t/)
3 followed (/d/)
4 landed (/ɪd/)

p. 83, Activity 16
/t/ liked, watched, laughed, hoped
/d/ cleaned, spelled, snowed, stayed
/ɪd/ landed, wanted, ended, painted

p. 84, Activity 18
midday → 12 p.m.
midnight → 12 a.m.
minute → There are 60 seconds in each of them.
year → There 365 days in one of them.
time → A unit to measure events.
months → There are 12 of them in a year.
AM → before midday
PM → after midday
hours → There 24 in a day

p. 84, Activity 19
1 who
2 when
3 which, where
4 who
5 which, when

p. 85, Activity 21
1 False **2** False **3** True **4** False **5** True

p. 86, Activity 23
1 In **2** at **3** Last **4** ago **5** playing **6** player **7** in **8** on

p. 86, Activity 24
Table:
Gwyneth u, a, u
Marcela n, s, n
Rob a, u, a
Harry u, s, s
Best role model: Rob

p. 87, Activity 25
1 b **2** d **3** e **4** f **5** g **6** c **7** a

p. 87, Activity 26
1 No, the actor is from Mexico.
2 The painter is from the USA.
3 The businesswoman is from China.
4 No, the cook is from Italy.

p. 87, Activity 27
1 He is a singer who sang last year in the Royal Albert Hall.
2 She is a firefighter who yesterday saved ten lives.
3 This is my favourite book that I showed to you yesterday.
4 They are waiters who work in a famous restaurant.

Audioscript

PB Lesson I page 82

Lesson 1, Activity 1, p. 82 CD3:19

Dan = D Robbie = R Donaldo = DL

D Where's Donaldo?
R Who's Donaldo?
D He's a famous Mexican player. He was in an American team in 2007 and in an Italian team last year. Now he plays here ... but he isn't playing in this match.
R Maybe he just isn't very good at playing football.
DL I am good. But look at my leg.
D It's Donaldo! Can I have your autograph, please?

Lesson 1, Activity 2, p. 82 CD3:20

1 American
2 Canadian
3 Colombian
4 Brazilian
5 Argentinian
6 British
7 Spanish
8 Italian
9 Egyptian
10 Greek
11 Chinese
12 Irish
13 Japanese
14 Australian
15 Turkish
16 Polish

PB Lesson 2 page 83

Lesson 2, Activity 4, p. 83 CD3:21

1 Where's he from? Is he American? No, he isn't. He's from Spain.
2 Is she Turkish? Yes, she is. She's from Turkey.
3 Is she Brazilian? No, she isn't. She's Colombian.
4 Is he from China? No, he's from the United States. He's American.
5 Is she from Japan? Yes, she is. She's Japanese.
6 Is he Australian? Yes, he is. He's from Australia.

AB Lesson 2 page 79

Lesson 2, Activity 3, p. 79 (AB) CD3:22

1 Where's she from? She's from the United Kingdom. The British flag is red, white, and blue.
2 Is he from Brazil? Yes, he is. He's Brazilian. The Brazilian flag is green and yellow with a blue circle and white stars.
3 Is she from Egypt? No, she isn't. She's Italian. The Italian flag has green, white and red stripes.
4 Where's he from? He's from China. His country's flag is red with one big yellow star and four small yellow stars.
5 Is she from Argentina? Yes, she is. The Argentinian flag is light blue and white.
6 Is he from Egypt? Yes, he is. He's Egyptian. The Egyptian flag has red, white and black stripes.

PB Lesson 3 page 84

Lesson 3, Activity 6, p. 84 CD3:23

1 artist
2 photographer
3 painter
4 astronaut
5 businessman
6 cook
7 firefighter
8 dentist
9 waiter
10 actor
11 engineer
12 mechanic
13 footballer
14 journalist

Lesson 3, Activity 7, p. 84 CD3:24

On Friday, I was a cook.
On Thursday, an engineer.
In June, I was a waiter,
I was an artist once last year.
Chorus:
I'm an actor, yes, an actor.
Acting's the life for me.
Last spring, I was a journalist
And an astronaut. That was great!
I was a famous British footballer
In two thousand and eight.
Chorus
I get up at five in the morning.
My days are very long.
But a life in films is exciting.
That's why I'm singing this song.
Chorus

Lesson 3, Activity 8, p. 84 CD3:25

1 He is a businessman. He is from Poland.
2 He is a photographer. He is from Brazil.
3 He is a mechanic. He is from Ireland.
4 They are cooks. They are from Italy.
5 She is a painter. She is from Greece.
6 He is a dentist. He is from Egypt.

PB Lesson 4 page 85

Lesson 4, Activity 10, p. 85 CD3:26

1 I am Emma. I am a businesswoman and I am in a meeting.
2 My name is David. I am a dentist and I am working now.
3 I am Michael. I am a waiter. I love dancing.
4 I am Sarah. I am an engineer and this is the road I am making at the moment.
5 My name is Henry. I am a photographer. I love travelling. I am taking pictures in the jungle these days.

AB Lesson 4 page 81

Lesson 4, Activity 7, p. 81 (AB) CD3:27

1 This is the girl who is walking her dog.
2 These are the girls who are playing badminton.
3 This is the boy who is catching a ball.
4 This is the boy who is throwing a ball.
5 This is the girl who is kicking a ball.
6 This is the boy who is running.
7 This is the girl who is wearing a big hat with her country's flag on it.
8 This is the Italian man who is selling ice cream.

PB Lesson 5 page 86

Lesson 5, Activity 13, p. 86 CD3:28

Ivan = I   Rufus = R   Captain = C
Jenny = J   Gwyn = G

I Fantastic!
R We're rich!
I Aaah! A monster!
R This is scary. What's happening?
C Hi, kids!
J It's Captain Formosa!
C It's the Golden Penguin of Ice Island! Well done, kids!
J Well done, penguins!
G I know this statue!
P It's the statue of King Penn. He was my grandfather. He was king of the penguins fifty years ago.

PB Lesson 6 page 87

Lesson 6, Activity 14, p. 87 CD3:29

/t/ /d/ /ɪd/

Lesson 6, Activity 15, p. 87 CD3:30

1 mixed
2 turned
3 collected
4 reduced
5 recycled
6 landed
7 watched
8 cleaned
9 decided
10 reused
11 lived
12 painted
13 looked
14 helped

Lesson 6, Activity 16, p. 87 CD3:31

1 He cooked a nice meal.
2 The mechanic fixed my car.
3 The artist painted a picture.
4 An astronaut landed on the moon.
5 He played a good match.
6 They followed the signs.

Lesson 6, Activity 18, p. 87 CD3:32

Yesterday, I reduced, reused and recycled in my flat.

AB Lesson 6 page 83

Lesson 6, Activity 14, p. 83 (AB) CD3:33

1 He cooked a nice meal.
2 The mechanic fixed my car.
3 The artist painted a picture.
4 An astronaut landed on the moon.
5 He played a good match.
6 They followed the signs.

Lesson 6, Activity 15, p. 83 (AB) CD3:34

1 played, followed, fixed
2 landed, painted, cooked
3 cooked, fixed, followed
4 followed, played, landed

Goodbye

Lesson 1

Lesson aims
To revise vocabulary and structures

Materials
Audio CD

Optional activity materials
Active Teach, Digital Activity Book

Starting the lesson

- Ask pupils to talk about the end of the story. Ask *Did you like it?* Encourage them to think of another ending for the story and tell the class. Take a class vote for the most popular ending.

Practice

Pupil's Book page 92

1 Listen and point.

- Play the recording. Pupils listen and point to the pictures of the story.
- Play the recording again. Pause for the class to check they are pointing to the right picture.
- Ask nine volunteers to tell the story, one pupil describing each picture.

2 Read. Ask a friend.

- Give pupils time to do the activity in pairs.
- Check answers.

Activity Book page 88

1 Read and circle.

- Give pupils time to do the activity.
- Check answers.

2 Read and circle.

- Give pupils time to do the activity.
- Check answers.

Ending the lesson

- Ask if pupils would like to live an adventure like this. *Why (not)?*
- For Answer key and Audioscript see p. 264.

Goodbye

1 3:35 Listen and point.

2 Read. Ask a friend.

1 What was your favourite scene in the story? Why?
2 Who was your favourite character in the story? Why?
3 What was your favourite song in this book? Can you sing it?
4 Which 'Have Fun!' page was the best in this book?

OPTIONAL ACTIVITIES

True or false? Pupils say true or false sentences about the pictures of the story and ask a friend to say if they are True or False, e.g. *Jenny is eating pizza.* (False.)

Tell the story! Divide the class into eight groups, one per unit. Each group has to silently read one chapter of the story and then, in turns, give the class a summary.

Guessing the story chapter Divide the class into eight groups, one per unit. The groups prepare some clues for their classmates to guess the chapter they have read.

Lesson 2

Lesson aims
To revise vocabulary and structures

Materials
Audio CD

Optional activity materials
Active Teach, Digital Activity Book

Starting the lesson

- Ask pupils to talk about the units they liked the most and the least. Why?

Practice

Pupil's Book page 93

3 What unit are these pictures from? Say.

- Give pupils time to look at the pictures of the story.
- Ask five volunteers to talk about each picture and say which unit it comes from.

KEY
1 Unit 3 **2** Unit 5 **3** Unit 7 **4** Unit 8 **5** Unit 2

4 Who said this?

- Give pupils time to do the activity in pairs. Set a time for every sentence. The member of the pair that finds the answer first wins the point.
- Check answers.

KEY
1 Jenny **2** Captain Formosa **3** Dylan **4** Finn **5** Dylan

5 Quiz. Answer the questions.

- Give pupils time to read the questions.
- Divide the class into two teams. The two teams ask each other questions alternately.
- Check answers.

KEY
1 Snow Mountain **2** Ivan **3** Rufus **4** Captain Formosa
5 Rufus and Ivan **6** Yes, she can
7 mischievous/cheeky and helpful **8** Yes **9** the moon
10 give some fish to the penguins and read the map

Activity Book page 89

3 Read and write.

- Give pupils time to do the activity.
- Check answers in pairs.

4 Read and circle.

- Give pupils time to do the activity. Set a time limit.
- To check answers divide the class into two teams.

Ending the lesson

- Ask pupils about their favourite story with Kipper and his friends. Ask them if they have got pets.
- For Answer key and Audioscript see p. 264.

3 What unit are these pictures from? Say.

1 

2 

3 

4 

5 

4 Who said this?

1 'Look! He's dancing!'

2 'Yes! There's a forest…'

3 'The thieves were in their boat!'

4 'I can't see it! It isn't here.'

5 'He's watching polar bears.'

5 Quiz. Answer the questions.

1 What was the name of the mountain in the story?

2 What's the name of the thief who is fat?

3 What's the name of the thief who is thin?

4 This is a name from the story. Who is it?

t r n a f o a c o p s m i a

5 Who took the treasure map from the submarine?

6 Can Jenny snowboard?

7 What are the penguins like?

8 Is Dylan good at Geography?

9 What does Dr. Al look at in the middle of the night?

10 What does Captain Formosa do after breakfast?

OPTIONAL ACTIVITIES

True or false? Pupils say sentences to the class looking at the chapters of the story, e.g. *In chapter 1 there is a man on the submarine. True or false? In chapter 2 the thieves escape riding a bicycle. True or false?*

The story line Divide the class into two groups. Write the story line on the board and write *Welcome* at one end and *Unit 8* at the other. Write all the other units in between. Then say a brief sentence about something that happens in one of the chapters. Choose two pupils, one from each group. They have to say the chapter you are referring to and point at the unit on the story line. Each correct answer is one point. The group with the most points wins!

Lesson 3

Lesson aims
To revise vocabulary and structures

Materials
Audio CD

Optional activity materials
Active Teach, Digital Activity Book

Starting the lesson

- Ask two different pupils to talk about their nationality, a member of their family and a friend. Invite the class to ask them questions.

Practice

Pupil's Book page 94

6 My family, friend and country. Read, then say.

- Give pupils time to read and do the activity in pairs.
- Ask three pairs to talk about each topic.

7 Say a sentence from each unit to practise the language you have learnt.

- Give pupils time to do the activity in pairs. Ask them to make the sentence include as much information from the unit as possible.
- Ask volunteers to say their sentences. Pupils can write these sentences in their notebooks. The one who gets the longest correct sentence wins.

Activity Book page 90

5 Listen and write.

- Ask volunteers to read the dates and the countries before they listen.
- Play the recording. Pupils listen and write. Give pupils time to write.
- Play the recording again. Pause for the class to check.
- Ask volunteers to read their answers.

6 Complete your school timetable. What do you think about each subject?

- Give pupils time to do the activity.
- Ask volunteers to read their timetables. Encourage pupils to compare in pairs.

7 Write about your daily routine.

- Give pupils time to do the activity in pairs.
- Ask volunteers to read out. You could hold a vote for the best role model.

Ending the lesson

- Ask pupils to talk about the daily routine of a family member.
- For Answer key and Audioscript see p. 264.

6 My family, friend and country. Read, then say.

My family	My friend	My country
Choose a family member.	What is your friend good at?	Where are you from?
What can they do?	What is he/she like?	What is your nationality?
What can't they do?	What does he/she look like?	What is interesting about your country?
What does he/she like?		

7 Say a sentence from each unit to practise the language you have learnt.

OPTIONAL ACTIVITIES

Guessing game

Ask pupils to talk about someone in the class using the information model in PB Activity 6, e.g. His/her family, his/her friends, his/her country. The pupil who guesses who he/she is talking about goes next.

Sentence game

Write a few sentences from the different chapters of the story. Write each sentence in two halves on different pieces of paper. Give pupils the halves and ask them to find a partner to complete their sentences.

Lesson 4

Lesson aims
To revise vocabulary and structures

Materials
Audio CD

Optional activity materials
10cm x 10cm sheets of paper – one per pupil; Active Teach; Digital Activity Book

Starting the lesson

- Ask pupils to say the countries they remember and then the nationality associated with each country.

Practice

Pupil's Book page 95

8 Point to a flag and say.

- Point to a flag and say *This is a country that is very far from Spain. (China)* Encourage pupils to guess.
- Ask pupils to do the activity in pairs.
- Ask volunteers to say their sentences.

9 Say three rules for home and three rules for school. Use *must* and *should*.

- Give pupils time to think and say their rules.
- Take a class vote for the most popular rules and write them on the board.

10 Make a Golden Penguin farewell card for your classmates to sign.

- Give pupils time to do the activity. Circulate, monitor and help.
- Give pupils time to walk around and sign their classmates' Golden Penguin cards.

Activity Book page 91

8 Write.

- Give pupils time to do the activity.
- Check answers.

9 Draw your favourite place. Then write.

- Give pupils time to do the activity.
- Pupils swap answers and volunteers describe their partner's work.

10 Draw or stick a picture of your favourite famous person here. Then write.

- Give pupils time to do the activity.
- Volunteers read their answers aloud.

Ending the lesson

- Ask pupils to talk about their favourite places and famous people.
- For Answer key and Audioscript see p. 264.

8 **Point to a flag and say.**

9 **Say three rules for home and three rules for school. Use *must* and *should*.**

My rules

10 **Make a Golden Penguin farewell card for your classmates to sign.**

First, get some paper and cut out a square.

Second, fold Line A.

Third, fold down Line B.

Fourth, turn it over.

Fifth, fold Line C, fold Line D.

Sixth, fold back Line E.
Fold back Line F.

Seventh, fold down Line G.

Eighth, draw eyes on the penguin.

It's a Golden Penguin! Well done!

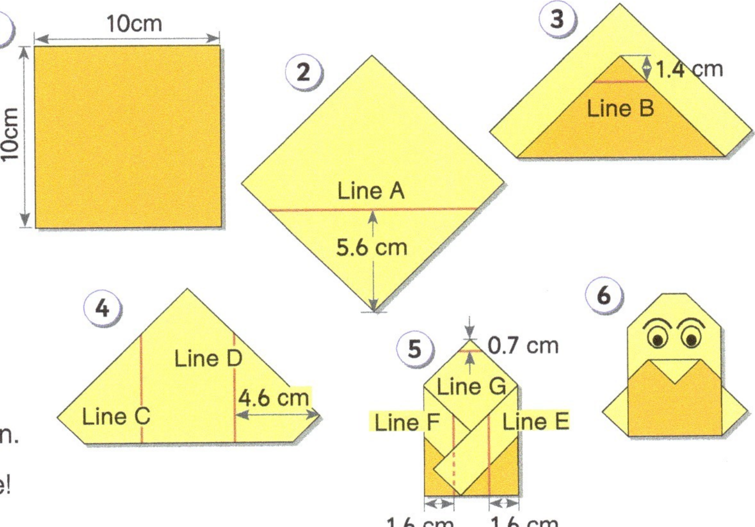

OPTIONAL ACTIVITIES

Spot the difference
Ask two pupils to come to the board. Divide it into two parts. They have to draw a place following the instructions they hear from the class. Then get the pupils to spot the differences between the two drawings.

Researcher's Workshop
Ask pupils to find out about the origin of origami.

Activity Book Answer Key

p. 88, Activity 1
1 F **2** T **3** F **4** F **5** T **6** F

p. 88, Activity 2
1 Dr Al's **2** Captain Formosa **3** the thieves **4** a shop **5** Finn **6** Dylan **7** Captain Formosa's **8** treasure map

p. 89, Activity 3
1 Yes **2** Yes **3** No **4** No

p. 89, Activity 4
1 clever but lazy **2** doing her homework **3** kicking balls **4** playing computer games **5** straight **6** jacket **7** £124 **8** reading a book **9** catching birds **10** brown **11** green **12** football **13** Donaldo **14** Spanish

p. 90, Activity 5
the United Kingdom, 23rd March, Italy, the United States, 6th May, 27th May, China, 2nd July, Greece

p. 90, Activities 6–7, p. 91, Activities 8–10,
Pupils' own answers

Audioscript

Lesson 1, Activity 1, p. 92 **CD3:35**

1 The story has finished. The treasure is safe so now this man is looking through his telescope.
2 They didn't get the treasure and are not at the dinner party. They are in jail.
3 Wow! What a great dinner. This boy loves eating chicken and drinking lemonade.
4 This man is leaving Ice Island. He's leaving in his submarine.
5 She is the only girl who is at the dinner party. She's happy.
6 He is at the party, too. He likes the food and drink. He loves the pizza.
7 They're happy. They're dancing around the statue of their king.

Lesson 3, Activity 5, p. 90 (AB) **CD3:36**

Captain Formosa went around the world in his submarine. He started from the United Kingdom on the 1st of March and sailed to Spain. He got to Spain on the 23rd of March. Next, on the 30th of March he went to Italy and then he had a long trip to the United States. He got to the United States on the 29th of April. He sailed down from the United States to Mexico on the 6th of May and then down to Argentina on the 27th of May. To end his tour he went to China, then Korea, then Greece. He visited China on the 21st of June, Korea on the 2nd of July, and Greece on the 8th of July.

Halloween

Lesson aims
To provide pupils with insights into how British people celebrate Halloween

Target language
dress up, apple bobbing, pumpkin bread, caramel corn, devils, ghost story

Materials
Audio CD

Optional activity materials
Active Teach; Digital Activity Book

Starting the lesson

- Ask *What do you know about Halloween?* Pupils tell you their ideas.

Presentation

Pupil's Book page 96

1 Listen and read. What food can you eat at Halloween?

- Pupils predict the answer. Accept their suggestions without saying if they are right or wrong, so they still have a reason to listen.
- Play the recording. Pupils follow the text and find the answer to the question.
- Play the recording. Pupils listen and point to the food in the text as they listen.

KEY You can eat pumpkin bread and caramel corn.

2 Read again and answer.

- Ask pupils to read the questions before they do the activity.
- Ask pupils to close their Pupil's Books. Ask the questions one by one and encourage pupils to give the answers. Write them on the board.
- Ask them to read the text again to check their answers.

KEY
1 Yes, she does.
2 They dress up and play traditional Halloween games.
3 Pumpkin bread and caramel corn.
4 Singing and telling scary stories.

Practice

3 Ask a friend.

- Give pairs time to do the activity.
- Volunteers read out the questions. Elicit answers from the class.

Activity Book page 92

1 Listen and colour. Then draw and write.

- Give pupils one minute to look at the picture. Ask them to describe it. Explain to them that they will have to complete the picture colouring, drawing and writing using the information they hear.
- Play the recording. Pupils listen and colour.
- Play the recording. Give them time to draw and write.
- Walk around and choose two pupils with different answers. Divide the class into two groups. Ask pupils from the two groups to compare the two pictures, e.g. *In our picture there is a ... but in your picture there is a ... .* Give them one point for every accurate sentence.
- When you are checking answers, ask different pupils to describe their pictures.
- Give pupils time to correct their pictures.

Ending the lesson

- Take a vote for your pupils' favourite Halloween costume.
- For Answer key see p. 273. For Audioscript see p. 274.

OPTIONAL ACTIVITIES

Guessing game
In groups of four, each pupil chooses a well-known celebration in their country. They don't say what it is. Pupils take it in turns to ask one group member *yes/no* questions about their celebration to identify it, e.g. *Is it in December? (No, it isn't.) Do we eat cakes on this day? (No, we don't.) Do we eat fish? (Yes, we do.) Is there any school? (No, there isn't.) Is it (the name of the celebration)?* The pupil who correctly guesses gets a point.

Roleplay
Pairs imagine Janie is going to visit their school. They prepare five questions to ask her about Halloween. They role play the conversation, taking it in turns to be Janie. Fast finishers could role play another conversation with Janie. This time, Janie asks questions about a celebration in your country.

Halloween

Lesson aims
To provide pupils with insights into how British people celebrate Halloween

Target language
gravestone, spooky food

Materials
Audio CD

Optional activity materials
Active Teach; Digital Activity Book

Starting the lesson

- Ask *Have you ever been to a Halloween party?* Pupils tell their experiences.

Presentation

Pupil's Book page 97

4  **Listen to find out. What do you need to prepare for a Halloween party?**

- Pupils predict the answer. Accept their suggestions without saying if they are right or wrong, so they still have a reason to listen.
- Play the recording. Pupils follow the text and find the answer to the question.
- Play the recording again. Pupils listen and point to the pictures again.

5  **Listen, point and repeat.**

- Ask pupils to look at the pictures.
- Play the recording. Pupils point and repeat.
- Play the recording again pausing for pupils to check they are pointing to the right picture.

KEY
decorations, party games and activities, invitations, jack-o-lanterns, spooky food, treats ideas, Halloween costumes

Practice

6 What is your ideal Halloween party? Think and say.

- Give pupils time to think.
- Volunteers explain their ideal Halloween party. Give pupils time to do the activity in pairs.

7 Play the memory game.

- Pupils look at the example dialogue while you read it. Ask a pupil to continue the game, adding a new item.
- Pupils play the game in pairs, two groups or whole group.

Activity Book page 92

2 Read and match.

- Give pupils time to read the definitions. Ask them to write the correct words.
- To check answers, ask half the class to read the definition and the other half to give the correct word alternately.

3 Write an invitation to a Halloween party. Decorate it with a scary drawing!

- Give pupils time to do the activity.
- Ask some pupils to read out and show the drawing to the class. Encourage the class to talk about the drawings.

Ending the lesson

- Ask your pupils if they would like to have a Halloween party in the class. Ask them *What do we need to prepare for a Halloween party in the class?* Write on the board their ideas.
- For Answer key see p. 273. For Audioscript see p. 274.

OPTIONAL ACTIVITIES

PowerPoint Presentations
In groups of four or five, ask pupils to do a PowerPoint presentation on the following titles: Group 1: Origin, Group 2: Different countries, different ways of celebrating Halloween, Group 3: Halloween costumes, Group 4: Halloween parties. Once they are finished, pupils can invite other classes to show them their presentations on Halloween.

Guessing game
Mime a ghost, the pupil who guesses first continues miming Halloween scary characters!

Halloween design contest
Ask pupils to design a Halloween costume or scene. Take a vote for the most ... (scary, black, bloody, etc.).

Christmas

Lesson aims
To provide pupils with insights into how people celebrate Christmas around the world

Receptive language
Christmas tree, Father Christmas, mistletoe, Christmas cards

Materials
Audio CD

Optional activity materials
Internet/magazine photos of Christmas and winter celebrations around the world (see PB page 98 Activity 3); Active Teach; Digital Activity Book

Starting the lesson

- Ask *Did you know that Christmas is celebrated around the world in many different countries and in many different ways?* Encourage pupils to give examples. If you have pupils from different origins, ask them to explain how Christmas is celebrated at home.

Presentation

Pupil's Book page 98

1 Look, listen and read. Did you know …?

3:41

- Play the recording. Pupils listen and follow the text. Ask them to underline any words they don't know.
- Explain that the photos will help them understand the unknown words. They should also look carefully at the surrounding words. Give pairs time to look at the photos and ask *What is a Christmas tree?* Ask a confident pupil to answer.
- Play the recording again, pausing for pupils to explain each word: Christmas tree, Father Christmas, mistletoe and Christmas cards.

Practice

2 Read again and think about winter celebrations in your country. Then make up your own 'Did you know …?'

- Ask pupils to read the text again. Then talk with them about winter celebrations in your country to give them ideas to make up their own 'Did you know …?'
- Give pupils time to do the activity. Ask volunteers to read their 'Did you know …?'

3 Read again and answer the questions.

- Draw attention to the winter celebrations in Question 1. Ask pupils if they know something about them.
- Volunteers share their ideas and experiences.
- Ask pupils to read the questions before they do the activity.
- Give pupils time to do the activity in pairs.

Activity Book page 93

1 Answer.

- Give pupils time to write the answers but ask them to do it with the PB closed.
- For checking answers, divide the class into two groups and ask two pupils, one from each group, each question. Every right answer is one point for their teams.

Ending the lesson

- Ask pupils to look for information about the winter celebrations in PB Activity 3 that they don't know, and write about them in their notebooks. Read them out for starting next Christmas lesson.
- For Answer key see p. 273. For Audioscript see p. 274.

OPTIONAL ACTIVITIES

Pair work
Pairs ask and answer the 'Did you know …?' sentences in PB and others they invented.

Guessing game
Divide the class into four teams. Show pupils a photo of a winter celebration. Pupils from each team take it in turns to either guess what the celebration is, or to ask a question, e.g. *Is it in (name of a country)?* The first team to guess correctly wins a point.

Christmas

Lesson aims
To provide pupils with insights into how British people celebrate Christmas

Target language
stocking, turkey, Brussels sprouts, Christmas pudding

Materials
Audio CD; Christmas songs/carols

Optional activity materials
Active Teach, Digital Activity Book, internet/ magazine photos of a British Christmas; six known objects wrapped in paper like Christmas presents so they aren't visible/identifiable

Starting the lesson

- Ask volunteers to read the information they found about the winter celebrations in PB page 98 Activity 3.
- Encourage the class to ask questions to these pupils.

Presentation

Pupil's Book page 99

4 Read to find out. How does Alesha celebrate Christmas?

- Give pupils time to read the text on their own. Remind them to look for the relevant information as they read.
- Ask *How does Alesha celebrate Christmas?*

KEY She sings Christmas songs, receives presents and eats Christmas food with her family.

5 Listen and read. Then look and say.

- Play the recording. Pupils listen and follow the text. Ask them to underline any words they don't know.
- Explain that the photos will help them understand the unknown words. They should also look carefully at the surrounding words. Give pairs time to look at the photos and say, e.g. *Picture d is a Christmas pudding*, etc.

KEY
a stockings **b** turkey **c** Brussels sprouts
d Christmas pudding

Practice

6 Read again and say.

- Ask pupils to read the questions before they do the activity.
- Give pupils time to do the activity. Remind them to underline the relevant information as they read. They say the answers to a friend.

KEY
1 Yes, she does. **2** The stocking goes in the living room. **3** It's got presents in it. **4** Yes, she does.

Activity Book page 93

2 Read and write the missing words.

- Give pupils time to write.
- When you are checking answers, ask different pupils to spell the words aloud to give them extra practice at saying the alphabet.

3 Write a Christmas greetings card to a friend.

- Ask the class to write a Christmas greetings card to a friend or classmate.
- Pupils give their AB to a classmate who reads the greetings card to the class.

Ending the lesson

- Play a Christmas song and ask pupils what they like most about Christmas.
- For Answer key see p. 273. For Audioscript see p. 274.

OPTIONAL ACTIVITIES

Pair work and poster
Pairs write down two questions they would like to ask Alesha about Christmas in Britain. They exchange their questions with another pair. Pupils do internet research at school or at home to answer the questions they have been given. They tell the pair whose questions they have answered what they have found out. You could make a class poster, using pupils' questions, answers and pictures.

TPR game
Divide the class into two teams. Show pupils a 'present' you have wrapped and brought. Pupils from each team take it in turns to either guess what the present is, or to ask a question, e.g. *Is it a toy? Is it for children?* The first team to guess correctly wins a point.

Pancake Day

Lesson aims
To provide pupils with insights into how Pancake Day is celebrated in many countries

Target language
Shrove Tuesday, recipe

Materials
Audio CD

Optional activity materials
Active Teach, Digital Activity Book, internet/ magazine photos and recipes of pancakes in different countries

Starting the lesson

- Ask your pupils *Have you ever tried pancakes? When? Where? Did you like them? Why?*

Presentation

Pupil's Book page 100

1 Listen. Then read. What does Josh prefer?

- Pupils predict the answer. Accept their suggestions without saying if they are right or wrong, so they still have a reason to listen.
- Play the recording. Pupils follow the text and find the answer to the question.
- Play the recording again. Pupils listen again and read. Ask pupils to try to explain the meaning of new words.

KEY Banana and chocolate pancake.

Practice

2 Ask and answer.

- Give pupils time to do the activity in pairs.
- Volunteers read out the questions. Elicit answers from the class.
- If there is no day of thanks for food in your country, ask pairs to invent one, e.g. *Our new festival is Sardine Day! Sardine Day is on June 30th. On Sardine Day we eat a lot of sardines and we have a holiday!*

KEY
1 Pancake day
2 40 days before Easter
3 eggs, flour, milk and butter
4 last year

3 Read again and say *True* or *False*.

- Ask pupils to read the sentences before they do the activity.
- Pupils do the activity.
- They check their answers with a friend.

KEY
1 True
2 False (40 days before Easter)
3 True
4 False
5 False

- Divide the class into four groups. Ask groups to look for information about pancakes (give them the magazines and recipes you have prepared). Be careful to give each group different recipes. They have to make a poster on A3 paper (or similar) copying the recipe and highlighting the relevant information about this particular pancake recipe, e.g. ingredients, country, etc. They can decorate the poster.

Ending the lesson

- Ask the groups to explain their posters to the class.
- For Answer key see p. 273. For Audioscript see p. 275.

OPTIONAL ACTIVITIES

Crazy food
Keep the groups and ask them to invent crazy dishes. They have to write the ingredients, the recipe and draw the dish on their notebooks. Each member of the group writes his/her own recipe. They have to take a vote for the craziest. The four groups present their craziest dishes and the class takes a vote for the super-craziest one!!

Cooking
If cooking is possible at your school, this is a great opportunity for cooking with your students.
Each group cooks the pancake recipe they made the poster about. Then they can try four different pancakes recipes ... mmm!

Pancake Day

Lesson aims
To learn how to cook a pancake

Target language
pour, beat, batter, heat, toss, syrup, topping, mashed

Materials
Audio CD

Optional activity materials
Active Teach; Digital Activity Book

Starting the lesson

- Ask your pupils if they can cook at home. Invite the class to talk about their favourite food and their experience in the kitchen.

Presentation

Pupil's Book page 101

4  Listen to find out. What ingredients are needed to cook a pancake?

- Pupils predict the answer. Accept their suggestions without saying if they are right or wrong, so they still have a reason to listen.
- Play the recording. Pupils follow the text and find the answer to the question.
- Play the recording again. Pupils listen again and read. Ask pupils to point to the pictures of these ingredients as they listen again to the recording.

KEY milk, eggs, flour and butter

5 Read and say. How do you cook a pancake?

- Ask pupils to read the recipe again before they do the activity.
- Give pupils time to look at the pictures and encourage them to explain the steps, looking at the pictures.

Practice

6 Can you cook? Think of a recipe you can cook and tell the class.

- Ask pupils to think of a recipe they can cook.
- Volunteers tell the class how to cook those recipes step by step.

Activity Book page 94

1  Listen and write.

- Give pupils time to read the questions and answers they have to complete.
- Play the recording for pupils to write. Play it again pausing for checking answers.

2 Complete the recipe.

- Give pupils time to do the activity.
- Ask a pupil to start reading for checking. The class pay attention to possible mistakes. When a pupil thinks the pronunciation or intonation was not right he/she should put his/her hand up and give the correct pronunciation or intonation. If it is better, he/she continues reading.

3 Write or invent a recipe. Give it a name.

- Give pupils time to write.
- Ask volunteers to read their inventions.

Ending the lesson

- Invite the class to talk about who cooks at home, when and what.
- For Answer key see p. 273. For Audioscript see p. 275.

OPTIONAL ACTIVITIES
Whose is this recipe?
Collect the Activity Books and read some of the invented recipes in Activity 3. The class guesses the inventor.

April Fools' Day

Lesson aims
To provide pupils with insights into how British people celebrate April Fools' Day

Target language
contest, prize

Materials
Audio CD

Optional activity materials
Active Teach; Digital Activity Book

Starting the lesson

- Ask *Do you know what a 'contest' is? Have you ever participated in any contest? What was it about?*

Presentation

Pupil's Book page 102

1 Listen to find out. What is the contest about?

- Pupils predict the answer. Accept their suggestions without saying if they are right or wrong, so they still have a reason to listen.
- Play the recording. Pupils follow the text and find the answer to the question.
- Play the recording again for pupils to check.

KEY Writing

2 Read. Then answer.

- Ask pupils to read the questions before they do the activity.
- Ask pupils to close their Pupil's Books. Ask the questions one by one and volunteers give the answers.
- Ask them to read the text again to check their answers.

KEY
1 a newspaper article
2 London
3 a writing contest
4 free admission to all the amusement parks in UK for one year
5 answers may vary

3 Read and say *True* or *False*.

- Give pairs time to do the activity.
- Five pairs read and say.

KEY
1 True **2** True **3** False **4** False **5** True

4 Listen to find out. Was the writing contest *True* or *False*?

- Pupils predict the answer. Accept their suggestions without saying if they are right or wrong, so they still have a reason to listen.
- Play the recording. Pupils follow the text and find the answer to the question.
- Play the recording again for pupils to check.

KEY False (it was a prank)

Practice

- Tell the class they are going to participate in a similar contest held this year in your country. Explain to them that the prize is a school trip to a very popular place for children in your country, or near it.
- Ask pupils to open their notebooks and do a piece of writing of one hundred words approximately. They can write about anything they want.
- Collect the notebooks at the end of the lesson.

Ending the lesson

- Volunteers can read their writings.
- For Answer key see p. 273. For Audioscript see p. 276.

OPTIONAL ACTIVITIES

Reading contest
Ask one pupil to read their writing. The class pay attention to possible mistakes. When a pupil thinks the pronunciation or intonation was not right he/she should put his/her hand up and give the correct pronunciation or intonation. If it is better, he/she continues reading the classmate's writing. If a pupil is able to read the writing with no mistakes set a prize and give the prize to him/her.

April Fools' Day

Lesson aims
To provide pupils with insights into how people celebrate April Fools' Day in many countries

Target language
prank, practical joke

Materials
Audio CD

Optional activity materials
Active Teach; Digital Activity Book

Starting the lesson

- Start the lesson by telling the class that, starting today, school finishes two hours later because they need to learn more things and the usual timetable does not provide enough practice in the different areas.

Presentation

Pupil's Book page 103

5 Read. Then answer.

- Ask pupils to read the questions before they do the activity.
- Ask pupils to close their Pupil's Books. Ask the questions one by one and volunteers give the answers.
- Ask them to read the text again to check their answers.

KEY
1 1st April.
2 28th December
3 jokes and pranks
4 April fool!
5 answers may vary

Practice

6 Ask a friend.

- Give pairs time to do the activity.
- Ask five pairs to ask and answer.

Activity Book page 95

1  Listen to Elizabeth. Answer using the short form.

- Give pupils time to read the questions and answers they have to complete.
- Play the recording for pupils to write. Play it again pausing for checking answers.

2 Answer the questions to write about April Fools' Day.

- Give pupils time to do the activity.
- Circulate, support and help. Read some examples for checking.

3 Write about the last prank or joke you played on a friend.

- Give pupils time to write.
- Ask volunteers to read their pranks or jokes.

Ending the lesson

- Say *April fool! April fool!* Explain to the class that the writing contest and the new timetable were a joke.
- For Answer key see p. 273. For Audioscript see p. 276.

OPTIONAL ACTIVITIES
The best joke!
In groups of four, each pupil invents a joke. Pupils take it in turn to tell their jokes to the group and decide which the best joke is. Then they explain the joke to the class.
Role play the jokes
Instead of explaining, pupils can role play their jokes to the class.

Activity Book Answer Key

Halloween

p. 92, Activity 1

three orange Jack-o-lanterns, black spider biscuits, red brain cakes, label says 'Halloween Party', spider web in one of the corners, girl in ghost costume wearing red shoes and boy in bat costume wearing blue trainers

p. 92, Activity 2

1 decorations
2 Jack-o-lantern
3 invitations
4 Halloween costumes
5 spooky food

Christmas

p. 93, Activity 1

1 put in houses to ensure good crops for the coming year
2 answer may vary
3 acceptance and reconciliation
4 in the United Kingdom

p. 93, Activity 2

on, of, at, at, in, but, on, at, in, from, on, and, for

Pancake Day

p. 94, Activity 1

1 300ml milk
2 2 eggs
3 125g flour
4 25g butter

p. 94, Activity 2

milk, two, beat, flour, pour, butter, 1–2, pancake, batter, golden brown, put a topping on

April Fool's Day

p. 95, Activity 1

1 Yes, it was.
2 No, they didn't.
3 Yes, they were.
4 Yes, they did.

p. 95, Activity 2

1 First of April.
2 At home, school, work.
3–5 answers may vary

Audioscript

Halloween, Activity 1, p. 96 — CD3:37

Hello! My name is Janie and I'm from England. The 31st of October is Halloween! It's my favourite celebration. We celebrate it every year. At school we sometimes dress up and play traditional Halloween games such as apple bobbing.
My grandmother cooks pumpkin bread for us and my mum makes some caramel corn for me and my brothers. They learnt the recipe from my Aunt Sarah, who lives in the USA. We all dress up as monsters, ghosts, skeletons, witches, or devils and go from house to house, asking for treats such as sweets or sometimes money, with the question, 'Trick or treat?'
But my favourite thing about Halloween is when we have to sing a song or tell a ghost story to earn our treats because I love telling scary stories!
Do you celebrate Halloween in your country?
Love, Janie

Halloween, Activity 4, p. 97 — CD3:38

For a fun and scary Halloween party you need ...
Decorations such as spider webs, gravestones, bats, etc. Try to make them on your own. A few Halloween party games and activities. Halloween party invitations for your friends. Don't forget to decorate them, too! Some jack-o-lanterns. Delicious spooky Halloween food: fingers, green jelly ...
Lots of ideas for Halloween treats!
Halloween costumes for everybody. How about ending your party with some fancy dress prizes?
All this will help your party to be a spectacular Halloween celebration!

Halloween, Activity 5, p. 97 — CD3:39

decorations
party games and activities
Halloween party invitations
Jack-o-lanterns.
delicious spooky Halloween food
Halloween treats ideas
Halloween costumes

Halloween, Activity 1, p. 92 (AB) — CD3:40

There are three big orange Jack-o-lanterns on a table.
There is a plate with delicious spooky food on the table in front of the Jack-o-lanterns. The spider biscuits are black and the brain cakes red.
There is a party banner in the room and it says 'Halloween Party'.
There is a spider web in one of the corners. It is scary ...
The children are playing Halloween party games and are dressed up in Halloween costumes! The ghost costume is a girl with red shoes and the bat costume is a boy wearing blue trainers.
I like this Halloween party!

Christmas, Activity 1, p. 98 — CD3:41

1 Did you know that ancient cultures put trees indoors and decorated them to ensure a good crop for the coming year? This was the origin of our modern Christmas trees.
2 Did you know that Santa Claus is the patron saint of children and sailors? He is also known as Saint Nicholas and Father Christmas. What do you call him in your country?
3 Did you know that a kiss under the mistletoe symbolises love?
4 Did you know that the first Christmas cards were invented in the United Kingdom to reduce the time spent in writing greeting letters? There was someone lazier than me!

Christmas, Activity 5, p. 99 — CD3:42

Christmas Day is on the 25th of December and there are two weeks of school holidays. My favourite thing about Christmas is the music. I'm in a music club at school and in the evenings before Christmas we sing Christmas songs outside the shops. It's cold and dark, but we love it.

On the 24th of December, I hang a stocking in the living room. In the morning, it's got presents in it. Some children think the presents are from Father Christmas.

We eat a big lunch on Christmas Day with Granny and Grandad: turkey, potatoes and Brussels sprouts. Then we eat a fruit pudding called Christmas pudding. After the meal, there are presents for everyone.

Pancake Day, Activity 1, p. 100 CD3:43

Hello! My name is Josh and I'm from Scotland. I'm cooking pancakes because today is Pancake Day in my country. This celebration is also known as Shrove Tuesday and it is held all over the United Kingdom. There are many other countries around the world where Pancake Day is celebrated too: the USA, Australia, Canada, Ireland, Poland and many other places.

The date is different every year because it is celebrated forty days before Easter.
Do you know what I really like about this festival? Yes! Cooking and eating lots of pancakes with my family!

A pancake is a delicious dish made of eggs, flour, milk and butter. The traditional pancake is served with sugar and lemon but my favourite recipe is banana and chocolate pancake because I love chocolate and bananas are my favourite fruit.

Last year, it was the first time my mum let me cook my own pancakes, but not alone! She's always ready to help me. It isn't difficult but you need some practice. As you can see, this year I am an expert! Can you cook pancakes?

Pancake Day, Activity 4, p. 101 CD3:44

Pour 300ml of milk into a jug and add 2 eggs – beat well.
Add 125g of plain flour into a bowl. Now, pour the egg and milk mixture into the centre of the flour, beating just in the centre as you pour.
Beat 25g of melted butter into the batter.
Heat the frying pan and add a bit of butter.
Then pour 70 ml of batter for each pancake and leave to cook for 1–2 minutes.
To check if the pancake is ready to be turned give it a little shake – it should move in the pan.
Toss the pancake over.
When your pancake is a golden brown colour, you must be ready to put a topping on it! Try to put some chocolate syrup and mashed bananas on top ... and Happy Pancake Day!!

Pancake Day, Activity 1, p. 94 (AB) CD3:45

Pour 300ml of milk into a jug and add 2 eggs – beat well.
Add 125g of plain flour into a bowl. Now, pour the egg and milk mixture into the centre of the flour, beating just in the centre as you pour.
Beat 25g of melted butter into the batter.
Heat the frying pan and add a bit of butter.
Then pour 70 ml of batter for each pancake and leave to cook for 1–2 minutes.
To check if the pancake is ready to be turned give it a little shake – it should move in the pan.
Toss the pancake over.
When your pancake is a golden brown colour, you must be ready to put a topping on it! Try to put some chocolate syrup and mashed bananas on top ... and Happy Pancake Day!!

April Fools' Day, Activity 1, p. 102 CD3:46

Woodford School in London is one of the finalists of the writing contest held this year in the United Kingdom. Ms Smith, one of the teachers at this school, who was interviewed yesterday by our reporters, explained to us that the children participating in the contest didn't know about it yet. 'It will be a wonderful surprise for them!' She said. Contests are a great way to get children starting to write. 'I thought they were doing very well in our class work, so I decided to present their work for this contest,' she said.
Of course, it will be a great surprise for them because the contest has this incredible prize: free admission to all the amusement parks in the United Kingdom for one year! Well done everyone!

April Fools' Day, Activity 4, p. 102 CD3:47

Hello! My name is Elizabeth and this is my class. This was the clever prank Ms Smith played on us last year on April Fools' Day. It was really good fun and we enjoyed it a lot but, actually, we were very disappointed when she told us it was an 'April Fool'! We all knew that the 1st of April is April Fools' Day in our country but nobody in the class thought it was a joke! The newspaper looked authentic!

After playing this prank on us, Ms Smith explained to the class that this celebration is shared by many other countries such as Poland, Italy, Brazil, Canada, Australia and the United States. She also told us that in Mexico and Spain there is a similar celebration on the 28th of December. There, people also play all kinds of jokes and pranks on each other and usually end them by calling their victims, 'Inocente! Inocente!' It was a fun and interesting April Fools' Day!

April Fools' Day, Activity 1, p. 95 (AB) CD3:48

See audioscript in previous exercise.

Extensive reading

Unit 1 Pupil's Book page 104

1 Look and say *True* or *False*.

- Give pupils time to look at the picture. Ask *What can you see?* Elicit pupils' answers. Review vocabulary to *describe people*.
- Ask pupils to read the sentences and think about the answers independently.
- Read each sentence aloud and discuss the answers. If the answer is *False*, encourage pupils to explain why.

KEY **1** F **2** T **3** T **4** T **5** F **6** F **7** T

2 Look and read.

- Ask pupils to make predictions about the text by looking at the picture. Tell them that good readers and test takers look at the pictures to get a better understanding of texts.
- Ask pupils to read the text independently. Tell pupils to use context clues to figure out unfamiliar words.
- After reading, develop a discussion about the text. Ask *Who is bored? Why? What does he decide to do? What are the children going to do? What does the TV presenter look like? What is he like? What are their favourite members of the group? Why?*

3 Read and choose the best answer.

- In pairs or as a whole group, pupils read the sentences and choose one of the three options. Model test-taking skills, e.g. Pace yourself! Don't rush!
- Check answers as whole-group discussion.

KEY **1** b **2** a **3** a **4** c

4 Choose the best title for the story.

- Ask pupils to make a summary about the text. It can be oral or written.
- Pupils read the options and choose the title that is the best fit.

KEY C

5 Find these words or phrases in the text. Explain their meaning.

- Ask pupils to work in pairs to read the phrases and find them in the text.
- Discuss the meaning as a whole-group discussion to check answers. Pupils can check or copy the meaning from the board or as a dictation activity in their notebooks.

Unit 2 Pupil's Book page 105

1 Look and say *True* or *False*.

- Give pupils time to look at the picture. Ask *What can you see?* Elicit pupils' answers. Review *adverbs of frequency and expressions* before they read the sentences.
- Ask pupils to read the sentences and think about the answers independently.
- Read each sentence aloud and discuss the answers. If the answer is *False*, encourage pupils to explain why.

KEY **1** T **2** F **3** F **4** F **5** T **6** F **7** F

2 Look and read.

- Ask pupils to read the text independently. Tell pupils to use context clues to figure out unfamiliar words.
- After reading, develop a discussion about the text. Ask *What is the alien like? What does he look like? What does he usually do on Mondays? And on Saturdays? What time does the alien make his bed? Why? Would you like to be this alien?*

3 Read and choose the best answer.

- In pairs or as a whole group, pupils read the sentences and choose one of the three options. Model test-taking skills, e.g. Finding a key word in the text and in the question.
- Check answers as whole-group discussion.

KEY **1** a **2** c **3** c **4** c

4 Choose the best title for the story.

- Ask pupils to make a summary about the text. It can be oral or written.
- Pupils read the options and choose the title that is the best fit.

KEY C

5 Find these words or phrases in the text. Explain their meaning.

- Ask pupils to work in pairs to read the phrases and find them in the text.
- Discuss the meaning as a whole-group discussion to check answers. Pupils can check or copy the meaning from the board or as a dictation activity in their notebooks.

Unit 3 Pupil's Book page 106

1 Look and say *Yes* or *No*.

- Give pupils time to look at the picture. Ask *What can you see?* Elicit pupils' answers. Review *hobbies*.
- Ask pupils to read the sentences and think about the answers independently.
- Read aloud each sentence and discuss the answers. If the answer is *No*, encourage pupils to explain why.

KEY **1** Yes **2** No **3** No **4** Yes **5** No **6** No **7** Yes

2 Look and read.

- Ask pupils to read the text independently. Tell pupils to use context clues to figure out unfamiliar words.
- After reading, develop a discussion about the text. Ask *Why does Henry like the sports camp? What are his favourite activities? Why? What are his friends good at? What is he good at? What does he really like about this camp?*

3 Read and choose the best answer.

- In pairs or as a whole group, pupils read the sentences and choose between *right, wrong* or *it doesn't say*. Model test-taking skills, e.g. Rereading the text.
- Check answers as whole-group discussion.

KEY **1** c **2** c **3** b **4** c

4 Choose the best title for the story.

- Ask pupils to make a summary about the text. It can be oral or written.
- Pupils read the options and choose the title that is the best fit.

KEY C

5 Find these words or phrases in the text. Explain their meaning.

- Ask pupils to work in pairs to read the phrases and find them in the text.
- Discuss the meaning as a whole-group discussion to check answers. Pupils can check or copy the meaning from the board or as a dictation activity in their notebooks.

Unit 4 Pupil's Book page 107

1 Look and say *True* or *False*.

- Give pupils time to look at the picture. Ask *What can you see?* Elicit pupils' answers. Review vocabulary about *places* before they read the sentences.
- Ask pupils to read the sentences and think about the answers independently.
- Read aloud each sentence and discuss the answers. If the answer is *False*, encourage pupils to explain why.

KEY **1** F **2** F **3** T **4** T **5** F **6** F **7** T

2 Look and read.

- Ask pupils to read the text independently. Tell pupils to use context clues to figure out unfamiliar words.
- After reading, develop a discussion about the text. Ask *Do you go on holiday with your family? Where do you usually go on holiday? What is your favourite country? Why? Would you like to visit the places described in the advertisement? Which ones? Why?*

3 Read and choose the best answer.

- In pairs or as a whole group, pupils read the sentences and choose one of the three options. Model test-taking skills, e.g. Read the whole sentence carefully.
- Check answers as whole-group discussion.

KEY **1** b **2** a **3** c **4** b

4 Choose the best title for the story.

- Ask pupils to make a summary of the text. It can be oral or written.
- Pupils read the options and choose the title that is the best fit.

KEY B

5 Find these words or phrases in the text. Explain their meaning.

- Ask pupils to work in pairs to read the phrases and find them in the text.
- Discuss the meaning as a whole-group discussion to check answers. Pupils can check or copy the meaning from the board or as a dictation activity in their notebooks.

Unit 5 Pupil's Book page 108

1 Look and say *True* or *False*.

- Give pupils time to look at the picture. Ask *What can you see?* Elicit pupils' answers. Review vocabulary about *clothing and accessories* before they read the sentences.
- Ask pupils to read the sentences and think about the answers independently.
- Read aloud each sentence and discuss the answers. If the answer is *False*, encourage pupils to explain why.

KEY **1** T **2** F **3** T **4** F **5** F **6** T **7** T

2 Look and read.

- Ask pupils to read the text independently. Tell pupils to use context clues to figure out unfamiliar words.
- After reading, develop a discussion about the text. Ask *What does she want to buy? Why does she try a different colour? Where does she go to try on the swimsuit? Why doesn't she buy the swimsuit? Do you go shopping on your own? Why (not)?*

3 Read and choose the best answer.

- In pairs or as a whole group, pupils read the sentences and choose one of the three options. Model test-taking skills, e.g. If you have extra time, look over your test.
- Check answers as whole-group discussion.

KEY **1** c **2** a **3** c **4** c

4 Choose the best title for the story.

- Ask pupils to make a summary of the text. It can be oral or written.
- Pupils read the options and choose the title that is the best fit.

KEY C

5 Find these words or phrases in the text. Explain their meaning.

- Ask pupils to work in pairs to read the phrases and find them in the text.
- Discuss the meaning as a whole-group discussion to check answers. Pupils can check or copy the meaning from the board or as a dictation activity in their notebooks.

Unit 6 Pupil's Book page 109

1 Look and say *True* or *False*.

- Give pupils time to look at the picture. Ask *What can you see?* Elicit pupils' answers. Review the words *bonfire, ground and fireworks* before they read the sentences.
- Ask pupils to read the sentences and think about the answers independently.
- Read aloud each sentence and discuss the answers. If the answer is *False*, encourage pupils to explain why.

KEY **1** T **2** F **3** F **4** T **5** F **6** T **7** T

2 Look and read.

- Ask pupils to read the text independently. Tell pupils to use context clues to figure out unfamiliar words.
- After reading, develop a discussion about the text. Ask *Where did the story happen? Who was the king of England? What did the group of Catholic men plot? Why? What was Guy Fawkes's job in the plot? What happened to him? When was the first Bonfire Night in England? How do people celebrate it nowadays?*

3 Read and choose the best answer.

- In pairs or as a whole group, pupils read the sentences and choose one of the three options. Model test-taking skills, e.g. Double check that you answered all the questions.
- Check answers as whole-group discussion.

KEY **1** b **2** b **3** c **4** c

4 Choose the best title for the story.

- Ask pupils to make a summary about the text. It can be oral or written.
- Pupils read the options and choose the title that is the best fit.

KEY B

5 Find these words or phrases in the text. Explain their meaning.

- Ask pupils to work in pairs to read the phrases and find them in the text.
- Discuss the meaning as a whole-group discussion to check answers. Pupils can check or copy the meaning from the board or as a dictation activity in their notebooks.

Unit 7 Pupil's Book page 110

1 Look and say *True* or *False*.

- Give pupils time to look at the picture. Ask *What can you see?* Elicit pupils' answers. Review the words *opposite, modern, main, pots, inside* and *playground* before they read the sentences.
- Ask pupils to read the sentences and think about the answers independently.
- Read aloud each sentence and discuss the answers. If the answer is *False*, encourage pupils to explain why.

KEY **1** F **2** T **3** F **4** T **5** F **6** F **7** F

2 Look and read.

- Ask pupils to read the text independently. Tell pupils to use context clues to figure out unfamiliar words.
- After reading, develop a discussion about the text. Ask *What type of school is Skyline School? Why has it got only twenty-five students? What do you have to do to go to this school? What type of books do they use? Is it necessary to speak English to go to this school? How many experimental schools are there in the world?*

3 Read and choose the best answer.

- In pairs or as a whole group, pupils read the sentences and choose one of the three options. Model test-taking skills, e.g. Keep your eyes on your test! Don't get distracted.
- Check answers as whole-group discussion.

KEY **1** b **2** a **3** b **4** b **5** a

4 Choose the best title for the story.

- Ask pupils to make a summary of the text. It can be oral or written.
- Pupils read the options and choose the title that is the best fit.

KEY B

5 Find these words or phrases in the text. Explain their meaning.

- Ask pupils to work in pairs to read the phrases and find them in the text.
- Discuss the meaning as a whole-group discussion to check answers. Pupils can check or copy the meaning from the board or as a dictation activity in their notebooks.

Unit 8 Pupil's Book page 111

1 Look and say *True* or *False*.

- Give pupils time to look at the picture. Ask *What can you see?* Elicit pupils' answers. Review the words *inside, in front* and *behind* before they read the sentences.
- Ask pupils to read the sentences and think about the answers independently.
- Read aloud each sentence and discuss the answers. If the answer is *False*, encourage pupils to explain why.

KEY **1** T **2** T **3** F **4** F **5** T **6** F **7** F

2 Look and read.

- Ask pupils to read the text independently. Tell pupils to use context clues to figure out unfamiliar words.
- After reading, develop a discussion about the text. Ask *Do you know any other astronaut? What do you like about astronauts? Do you know what NASA stands for? What is the difference between a shuttle, a rocket and a spaceship? What is the most popular career among astronauts? Would you like to be an astronaut?*

3 Read and choose the best answer.

- In pairs or as a whole group, pupils read the sentences and choose one of the three options. Model test-taking skills, e.g. Read your answers again starting from the end.
- Check answers as whole-group discussion.

KEY **1** a **2** a or b **3** a b or c **4** a **5** a

4 Choose the best title for the story.

- Ask pupils to make a summary about the text. It can be oral or written.
- Pupils read the options and choose the title that is the best fit.

KEY A

5 Find these words or phrases in the text. Explain their meaning.

- Ask pupils to work in pairs to read the phrases and find them in the text.
- Discuss the meaning as a whole-group discussion to check answers. Pupils can check or copy the meaning from the board or as a dictation activity in their notebooks.

Review

Welcome and Unit 1 AB p. 96

1 Write about you.
Pupils' own answers.

2 Use the words in Activity 1 to invite your friends.
Pupils' own answers.

3 Read and write.
1 I'm ...ing
2 What is she doing now?
3 What are they doing now? They are drinking milk.

4 Look at your classmate and answer. What does he/she look like? What is he/she like?
Pupils' own answers.

5 Think and compare.
1 taller/tallest **2** more interesting/most interesting

Unit 2 AB p. 97

1 Give orders or advice.
must do your homework, tidy your bedroom, revise before a test, take notes in class
should eat vegetables, drink a lot of water, do sports, be on time

2 How often do you ...?
Pupils' own answers.

3 Look at the answers of a classmate and write what he/she says.
Pupils' own answers.

4 Read and answer.
1 to play.
2 I go to the United States to learn English.
3 I buy lemons to make lemonade.

Unit 3 AB p. 98

1 Write about you.
Pupils' own answers.

2 Read, think and answer.
Pupils' own answers.

3 Ask a classmate the questions in Activity 2. Then write the answers.
Pupils' own answers.

4 What would you prefer to do? Complete.
1 sing/acting
2 playing chess/playing football
3 rather go to the cinema/have dinner

Unit 4 AB p. 99

1 Write about your country. Use *there is/isn't* or *there are/aren't*.
Pupils' own answers.

2 Use these words in plural to make sentences.
1 volcanoes **2** pyramids **3** statues **4** lakes
5 cities **6** people

3 Classify these nouns: *water, lake, air, cave, pyramid* and *city*.
countable cave, pyramid, city, lake
uncountable water, air

4 Look at Activity 3 and write sentences using *much* or *many*, *few* or *little*, *a lot* and *any*.
1 much/little/a lot **2** many/a lot, many
3 much/much **4** many/any

5 Complete.
books many, some, any, not many, a few, a lot of
water much, some, any, not much, a little, a lot of

Unit 5 AB p. 100

1 Write and ask a friend.
Pupils' own answers.

2 Answer.
1 Betty's **2** Carlos's **3** teacher's **4** children's

3 Complete.
1 mine **2** your **3** his **4** hers **5** our **6** theirs

4 Complete. *Going to* or *will*?
1 am going to buy **2** will save **3** is going to fall
4 Are you going shopping?

Unit 6 AB p. 101

1 Classify these verbs.
regular listen/listened, play/played, study/studied, practise/practised
irregular make/made, have/had, come/came, give/gave, see/saw, sing/sang, bring/brought, meet/met, eat/ate, get/got, fall/fell, take/took, be/was, were

2 Write the questions.
1 Where did you go? **2** When did you travel?
3 What did you see? **4** Who did you meet?

Unit 7 AB p. 102

1 Complete.
1 was, **2** weren't, **3** was, **4** weren't, **5** were

2 Write the questions.
1 Did you revise for the text?
2 Did you tidy your bedroom last night?
3 Were they interesting?
4 Did they come home yesterday?
5 Was it a funny film?
6 How many lakes are there in your city?
7 Are there any volcanoes in your country?
8 Are those her glasses or yours?

3 Look at your timetable. Then ask and answer *Yes* or *No*.
Pupils' own answers.

Unit 8 AB p. 103

1 Write the questions.
1 Are you from Colombia?
2 Are you British?
3 Where are you from?
4 Are you from Greece?
5 Where are you from?

2 Write sentences using *who*, *which* or *where*.
1 She is the firewoman who is Australian.
2 My brother is a painter who likes painting landscapes.
3 This is the famous statue that is from China.
4 This is my grandmother's house where I was born.
5 Shakira is the popular singer that is from Colombia.

3 Complete.
1 at/in/on **2** on/in **3** in/in/in/at

Reading and Writing Booklet

Answer key

Unit 1

1 Pupils' own answers
2 A good friend is kind and understanding. (A good friend is not bossy.)
3 **1** F **2** F **3** T **4** T **5** T **6** F
4 **1** shows/good **2** understanding **3** kind **4** bossy **5** clever
5 **1** There are six boys in the class. **2** There are four girls in the class. **3** 'Kind' has got the highest number. **4** 'Bossy' has got the lowest number. **5** 'Clever' (only) has one vote.
6 **1** bossy / c kind **2** sporty / a lazy **3** shy / b talkative
7 best, excellent, sporty, lazy, clever, kind, friendly, talkative, excited, bored
8 **1** ✗ intelligent **2** ✓ **3** ✗ excited **4** ✗ lovely **5** ✓
9 **2** sporty **3** friendly **4** young **5** kind **6** helpful **7** excited **8** bored

P	A	T	V	U	N	F	M	A	V	D	C
D	W	F	A	O	T	R	S	P	H	B	F
E	Z	R	Y	D	L	I	G	B	D	O	H
X	U	U	C	U	T	E	E	A	W	R	E
C	S	N	P	B	J	N	H	B	A	E	R
I	H	P	F	C	E	D	I	V	Q	D	S
T	K	G	O	S	Z	L	A	U	T	N	J
E	Q	I	R	R	D	Y	O	U	N	G	X
D	G	B	N	K	T	O	C	I	F	R	M
C	E	B	W	D	T	Y	Y	Y	B	A	Y
C	H	D	H	E	L	P	F	U	L	J	K
I	O	A	X	M	K	T	D	L	S	A	L

10 Pupils' own answers

Unit 2

1 Pupils' own answers
2 Pupils' own answers
3 **1** b **2** b **3** c
4 **1** T **2** F F **4** T **5** F
5 **1** b **2** a/c **3** d **4** c/a
6 **1** How often does Tim get pocket money? **2** When does Tim get his pocket money? **3** How much (pocket money) does Tim usually get (on Saturdays)? **4** What must Tim do to get extra pocket money? **5** When is Tim tired?
7 **1** snack/f **2** chocolate/d **3** sugar/b **4** flour/a **5** butter/e **6** salt/c
8 **1** my bed **2** washing up **3** out the rubbish **4** my homework **5** a test
9 **1** Fiona usually tidies her bedroom. **2** Fiona never does the washing up. **3** Fiona always makes her bed. **4** Fiona sometimes meets her friends.
10 **1** gett, get **2** usualy, usually **3** somtimes, sometimes **4** lissen, listen **5** breckfast, breakfast **6** shoping, shopping **7** alweys, always **8** frends, friends
11 Pupils' own answers

Unit 3

1 Pupils' own answers
2 They are writing about their hobbies and interests.
3 **1** c **2** d **3** a **4** b
4 **1** c **2** a **3** b **4** a **5** b **6** a/c
5 **1** They often play football in the park. **2** She wants to write a book (one day). **3** He can play the drums and the piano. **4** She usually goes shopping at the weekend.
6 **1** d **2** b **3** c **4** a **5** f **6** e
7 **1** singing karaoke/e **2** rollerblading/c **3** acting/f **4** diving/b **5** running races/d **6** playing video games/a
8 **1** score/c/B **2** graph/b/A **3** team/d/D **4** calculate/a/C
9 Pupils' own answers
10 Pupils' own answers

Unit 4

1 Pupils' own answers
2 **1** Mira is in Bogota, Colombia, South America. **2** Johnny is in Cairo, Egypt, Africa. **3** Lucy is in Athens, Greece, Europe.
3 **1** Lucy **2** Mira **3** Johnny **4** Mira
4 **1** d **2** a **3** b **4** c
5 **1** b **2** c **3** a **4** a
6 South America: Colombia, the Andes, spicy food, Caribbean, Bogota
Africa: crocodiles, Cairo, Egypt, Alexandria, River Nile
Europe: Samos, swimming, Greece, Athens, noisy
7 **1** factory/d **2** pyramid/a **3** volcano/f **4** cave/e **5** city/c **6** statue/b
8 **1** air **2** hills **3** lakes **4** sky **5** planet
9 **1** Korea **2** Australia **3** Mexico **4** Poland **5** Egypt **6** Argentina **7** China **8** Italy
10 **1** ✗ the River Nile **2** ✗ the Andes in Colombia **3** ✗ the Pyramids of Egypt **4** ✓
11 Pupils' own answers

Unit 5

1 Possible answers: in magazines, on the internet …
2 Pupils' own answers
3 **1** b **2** e **3** f **4** g **5** d **6** c **7** a
4 **1** g **2** e **3** b **4** d **5** c **6** f **7** a
5 **1** b **2** b **3** a **4** c **5** b **6** c
6 **2** belt **3** swimsuit **4** gloves **5** watch **6** umbrella **7** wallet **8** bracelet
7 **1** expensive/c **2** old-fashioned/b **3** tight/a
8 **1** shopping/department **2** assistant/change **3** much/label

9 Pupils' own answers
10 Pupils' own answers

Unit 6

1 Pupils' own answers.
2 The party was last weekend.
3 **1** c **2** a **3** d **4** f **5** e **6** b
4 **1** a **2** c **3** b **4** c **5** b
5 **1** T **2** F **3** F **4** T
6 **1** Emily wrote the email. **2** They played (water) volleyball in the pool. **3** They ate veggie burgers and vegetable kebabs. **4** They wrote the cards and blew up the balloons.
7 **1** went **2** met 3 came **4** brought **5** gave **6** made **7** gave **8** ate **9** had **10** had **11** sang **12** had
8 **2** thirtieth of September **3** twenty-third of February **4** twenty-fifth of August **5** first of July
9 winter: January, February
autumn: November, October
spring: April, March, May
10 Pupils' own answers

Unit 7

1 Pupils' own answers
2 Yes, she does.
3 **1** a **2** a **3** b **4** c
4 **1** rules **2** classroom **3** outside **4** Maths
5 **1** c **2** a **3** b
6 **1** Everyone can work together safely when there are rules. **2** Learning about life outside school and learning what we can and can't do. **3** Yes, they do. **4** Talking and playing around in class.
7 **1** boring/b **2** difficult/c **3** scary/a
8 **1** Sports **2** History **3** Geography **4** Maths **5** Art **6** Science
9 **1** c 2 **d** **3** a **4** b
10 Pupils' own answers

Unit 8

1 Pupils' own answers
2 It's about this year's International Day
3 **1** b **2** c **3** a **4** a
4 **1** F **2** F **3** T **4** F **5** T **6** T
5 **1** c **2** a **3** d **4** b
6 **1** Why is International Day special? **2** Who takes/took part in International Day? **3** When was International Day this year? **4** Where was the food? **5** What did younger children have? **6** What was there in the hall?
7 **1** ✗ Argentinian **2** ✓ **3** ✗ Australian **4** ✗ Korean **5** ✗ Polish 6 ✓
8 **1** dentist **2** journalist **3** cook **4** mechanic **5** actor **6** astronaut
9 **1** minute **2** hour **3** day **4** weekend **5** week **6** month **7** season **8** year
10 **1** painter **2** waiter **3** firefighter **4** photographer **5** footballer **6** engineer
11 Last week we went on a school trip to the Tower of London. We left school at 9.15 and arrived at Tower Bridge at 10.30. The coach journey took a long time because there was a lot of traffic on the road. We were really excited when we arrived at the tower.
12 Pupils' own answers

Grammar Booklet

Answer Key

Unit 1

1 **1** c **2** b **3** c **4** b
2 **1** e **2** Are they tall and handsome?/c **3** Has he got blue eyes?/b **4** What do they look like?/d **5** What does he look like?/a
3 **1** He's clever and kind. **2** She's talkative and helpful. **3** They're hard-working and shy. **4** He's friendly but helpful. **5** I'm sporty and clever!
4 Pupils' own answers.
5 **1** He is the tallest in the group. **2** Anita is younger but taller than Julia. **3** Julia is older than Tom. She is the oldest in the group. **4** Anita and Steve are the youngest. **5** Julia and Tom are the oldest.
6 **2** the deepest **3** faster than **4** bigger than **5** the longest
7 Pupils' own answers.
8 **1** Tom is my best friend. **2** He has got short spiky hair and blue eyes. **3** I think that he is taller than me. **4** He is more intelligent than me. **5** He is the cleverest boy in our class. **6** My grandad is the oldest person in my family. **7** My friend Tom is lazy at home but hard-working at school / lazy at school but hard-working at home.
9 **1** shorter **2** the shortest **3** the longest **4** bossier then **5** the bossiest **6** more hard-working **7** more intelligent than

Unit 2

1 **1** c **2** d **3** e **4** f **5** b **6** a
2 **1** I must remember to practise the piano. **2** I should study every day. **3** Mark does not have to learn English. **4** He must not be late for his lesson.
3 **2** Pupils' own answers.
4 Pupils' own answers.
5 **2** often brush my teeth **3** sometimes make my bed **4** never set the table **5** always take out the rubbish
6 **1** b **2** c **3** c **4** c **5** a
7 Pupils' own answers.
8 **2** should **3** never **4** should **5** shouldn't **6** always **7** shouldn't **8** must
9 **2** You should brush your teeth. **3** You should always do your homework (before dinner). **4** You should always help to tidy your house. **5** You should always make your bed.

Unit 3

1 **1** Tom isn't good at catching. **2** Sam is good at throwing. **3** They are good at singing **4** We aren't good at acting. **5** I am good at English!
2 **1** hitting **2** Are you good at diving? **3** Are you good at throwing? **4** Are you good at catching (a ball)?
3 **2** was kicking **3** was practising **4** was reading **5** were chatting
4 **1** What were you doing (yesterday) at seven o'clock (yesterday)? **2** Were you watching a DVD yesterday afternoon? **3** What were your friends doing at eight o'clock? **4** Were they playing volleyball? **5** Were they going to school on Saturday morning at 8.00? **6** Were your parents playing chess at nine o'clock? Plus pupils'own answers.
5 **2** I prefer dancing to singing. **3** I prefer playing football to playing volleyball. **4** I prefer playing video games to going shopping. **5** I prefer throwing to catching.
6 **1** singing **2** cooking **3** watch **4** sing **5** playing
7 **1** play **2** trampolining/playing **3** playing/running **4** meet/do
8 **2** What was Sara doing at 9.00? She was playing football. **3** What was Sara doing at 11.00? She was meeting friends. **4** What was Tom doing at 15.00? He was climbing trees. **5** What were Tom and Sara doing at 14.00? They were having lunch.
9 **1** skateboarding **2** to **3** at/play/than **4** playing

Unit 4

1 **1** There aren't any crocodiles in Canada. **2** There isn't a rainforest in Greece. **3** There is a waterfall in England. **4** There aren't any penguins in Spain. **5** There isn't a Great Wall in Brazil. **6** There are some beautiful beaches in Australia.
2 **1** Are there any hippos in Poland? No, there aren't. **2** Are there any spiders in Australia? Yes, there are. **3** Are there any mountains in Mexico? Yes, there are. **4** Is there a Great Wall in Japan? No, there isn't. **5** Are there waterfalls in Egypt? Yes, there are. **6** Is there any rainforest in Brazil? Yes, there is.
3 **2** No, there isn't. **3** Yes, there is. **4** No, there aren't. **5** Yes, there is.
4 Yes, there is. **2** No, there isn't. **3** Yes, there are. **4** No, there isn't. **5** Yes, there are.
5 **2** Is there a desert in the United Kingdom? No there isn't. **3** Are there any forests in Mexico? No, there aren't. **4** Are there any caves in China? Yes, there are. **5** Are there any cities in Spain? Yes, there are. **6** Are there any statues in Turkey? Yes, there are.
6 **2** much **3** many **4** much **5** many **6** many
7 **2** a **3** a **4** a **5** c **6** c
8 **2** Yes, there are. **3** No, there isn't. **4** No, there aren't. **5** Yes, there is. **6** Pupils' own answer.
9 **1** much **2** many **3** are **4** is **5** much **6** some **7** is **8** are **9** many

Unit 5

1 **1** How much is that watch? It's £30 **2** How much are those gloves? They're £18 **3** How much is that bracelet? It's £49 **4** How much are those sunglasses? They're £97
2 **2** it **3** those **4** They **5** expensive **6** how **7** are **8** them **9** eighty-five pounds **10** Here **11** change
3 **2** Whose trainers are these? **3** Whose watch is this? **4** Whose books are these? **5** Whose glasses

are these? **6** Whose tracksuit is this? **7** Whose bracelet is this? 8 Whose gloves are these?

4 **2** These umbrellas are yours. **3** This ball is Tom's **4** These kittens are hers. **5** This watch is his. **6** These trousers are yours. **7** This hat is Sara's.

5 **1** my **2** his **3** her **4** our **5** theirs **6** your **7** hers

6 **1** What are you going to do (today) after school (today)? **2** What are you going to watch on TV this evening? **3** What are your parents going to do at the weekend? **4** What are your friends going to do tomorrow? Plus pupils' own answers.

7 **2** won't rain **3** will be **4** will go **5** will look for **6** will have to **7** will go **8** won't be

8 **2** What are you going to do at the weekend? **3** I think I will go to the film at six o'clock. **4** Me too! I'm going to see the latest Superman film. **5** Really? Maybe I will see you at the cinema!

9 **1** are going to / our / yours **2** mine **3** these / yours **5** his **6** mine / them

Unit 6

1 **2** have **3** came **4** can **5** ate **6** gave **7** brought **8** meet **9** saw **10** go

2 **2** had **3** was **4** helped **5** played **6** was **7** was **8** came **9** sang **10** were **11** started **12** practised **13** took **14** sang **15** played **16** made

3 **2** He didn't come today, he came yesterday. **3** We didn't go to Spain, we went to Argentina. **4** She didn't meet Tom, she met me. **5** They didn't see a giraffe, they saw a hippo. **6** She didn't buy a present, she bought a cake.

4 **1** Where did you go on holiday last year? **2** Who did you go with? **3** Who did you meet? **4** What did you do? **5** What did you see? **6** What type of food did you eat?

5 **2** I must/have to finish my story. **3** I must/have to do my homework. **4** I must/have to write to granny. **5** I must/have to tidy my room. **6** I must/have to practise the piano.

6 **2** I have to buy a present for grandad. **3** I must finish my homework. **4** I have to meet Sara after school. **5** My parents say I must go to bed before nine o'clock.

7 **1** I have to meet my friends on Friday. **2** Did you go to the cinema last weekend? **3** I must write to my grandad. **4** Who did you meet at the party? **5** When did you see the film? **6** You should meet your friends at five o'clock.

8 **2** I couldn't play the violin last year. **3** He watched TV yesterday evening. **4** My friends didn't come to my house yesterday. **5** We met Tom and Sara after school. **6** She didn't make a cake for his birthday yesterday afternoon.

Unit 7

1 **1** Was there any Maths homework yesterday? **2** Were there any computers in class yesterday? **3** Was your last class interesting? **4** Were you late to class?

2 **2** Was the poem boring? Yes, it was. **3** Were school lessons difficult? No, they weren't. **4** Was your/the homework easy? No, it wasn't. **5** Was the book interesting? Yes, it was.

3 **1** c **2** d, **3** a, **4** b, **5** e

4 **2** Did you see ... ? (open) **3** Did you go... ? (open) **4** Did you... ? (open)

5 **1** Did the scary film have an alien? **2** Did Maddy have Maths homework on Monday? **3** Were your Drama lessons interesting last Monday? **4** Was there anything exciting in your last Science class?

6 **1** e **2** d **3** c **4** b **5** f **6** a

7 **2** Have your friends played a football match? No, they haven't. **3** Have you revised for your Maths exam? Yes, I have. **4** Has Tom chosen a title for his new book? No, he hasn't. **5** Has Sara been at the museum? Yes, she has.

8 **2** Yes, it was. **3** No, there weren't. **4** Yes, there was. **5** No, they didn't. **6** Yes, there were.

9 **2** been **3** went **4** went **5** didn't know **6** didn't hear **7** tried **8** was **9** didn't have **10** stayed **11** slept **12** went camping **13** had to **14** weren't **15** had **16** rains **17** got **18** wanted **19** haven't been

10 1 finished **2** Have/visited **3** Has/helped **4** Has/studied

Unit 8

1 **2** We're Chinese. **3** They're Spanish. **4** He's Canadian. **5** She's Turkish.

2 **1** Spanish **2** Thai **3** Brazilian **4** Poland **5** the United Kingdom

3 A: Where are you from? B: I'm from Mexico. A: Are they from Argentina? B: Yes, they are. A: So you are Mexican and they are Argentinian.

4 **2** He is the teacher who teaches P.E. **3** Karen is the friend who beats me in the tennis match! **4** They are the film stars who were in the park. **5** They are the Australians who taught me how to surf.

5 **2** Australian/She's an Australian singer who sings all over the world. **3** the United Kingdom/This is a car that is made in the United Kingdom. **4** Greek/He's a Greek sailor who tried to sail across the Atlantic Ocean. **5** Japan/These are the computers that were made in Japan. **6** the United States/He's a famous astronaut who is from the United States.

6 **1** In **2** at **3** in **4** in **5** In **6** in **7** at **8** On **9** at **10** In **11** at

7 **2** Carnival is usually in February. **3** My birthday is on 26th November. **4** My aunt won the lottery in 1970. **5** It's always cold in winter. **6** I get lots of presents on Christmas Day.

8 **1** where **2** who **3** which **4** which **5** who **6** where

9 **2** This is a special celebration which is celebrated on 25th December. It's Christmas! **3** This is an important person in England who lives in Buckingham Palace. It's the Queen! **4** This is a very big place where you watch your favourite football team. It's a stadium! **5** This is a famous festival which is celebrated on the last day of October.

Photocopiables notes

Unit 1 Friends

1.1 Find each word in the dictionary. Write the meaning in the box. (Lesson 1)

- Give pupils time to do the activity.
- Read the definitions aloud. Encourage pupils to say their own definition. Model and practise dictionary skills.

1.2 Unscramble the words. (Lesson 3)

- Give pupils time to unscramble the words.
- Encourage them to describe the picture. Tell pupils that they can use the words in the box in Activity 2.

KEY bossy, clever, hard-working, kind, shy, friendly, sporty, talkative, lazy, helpful

Read and classify

- Ask pupils to read the words in the box. Give them examples of the grammatical categories using words from the box. Remind them to put the word in the right position, e.g. *spiky hair* so it is an adjective/noun.
- Give pupils time to do the activity. Read out or write on the board to check.

KEY

Adjectives:	bald, handsome, good-looking, cute
Nouns:	friend, sister, face, eyes, hair, beard, moustache

1.3 1:17 Listen and complete. (Lesson 3)

- Ask pupils to read the song.
- Play the recording so that pupils read and complete the missing words.
- Play the recording so that pupils check their answers. Pupils can also look at their Pupil's Books to check their answers.

1.4 Complete the speech bubble. (Lesson 5)

- Ask pupils to look at the picture.
- Give pupils time to write a speech bubble.
- Ask volunteers for checking.

Draw your favourite character. Then describe. What is he/she like? What does he/she look like?

- Give pupils time to do the activity.
- Ask volunteers for checking.

1.5 Listen and write the words. Then check your answers. (Lesson 6)

- Ask pupils to listen as you read the words on the photocopiables. The sheet is folded during the dictation. The part with the words remains hidden while pupils write the words they hear on the other part with the blank spaces. After the dictation, pupils unfold the paper to check their answers.

1.6 Read. Then write *True (T)* or *False (F)*. (Lesson 7)

- Ask pupils to visualise as you read the text aloud. Ask pupils to share out loud who is in Chrissie's family. Ask the class *Who is Chrissie? How do you know? (It's a cat.)*
- Give pupils time to do the activity at the bottom of the photocopiable.
- Discuss the answers. Encourage pupils to say the true sentence when it is false.

1.7 Find someone who ... (Lesson 8)

- Tell pupils that they're going to complete a survey. Read aloud the questions to check understanding.
- Model how to circulate and ask the questions. Pupils need to write the name of those pupils that they found that matched the idea. Tell pupils that they need to ask all the questions in the given time.
- Discuss pupils' experiences.

Unit 2 My Life

2.1 Write a sentence using each phrase. (Lesson 1)

- Give pupils time to do the activity.
- Read aloud the sentences. Encourage pupils to say their own sentence.

2.2 Unscramble the words. (Lesson 3)

- Give pupils time to unscramble the words.
- Tell pupils that they can use the words in the box in Activity 2.

KEY never, usually, often, sometimes, always

How often do you ...?

- Give pupils time to do the activity.

Read and classify.

- Ask pupils to read the words in the box. Give them examples of the grammatical categories using words from the box. Remind them to put the word in the right position.
- Give pupils time to do the activity. Read out or write on the board to check.

KEY

Nouns:	salt, chocolate, butter, cooker, fridge
Verbs:	brush, wash, tidy, revise, taste
Adverbs:	usually, never, always, often, sometimes

2.3 Listen and number the lines in order. (Lesson 3)

- Ask pupils to read the song.
- Play the recording so that pupils read and order the lines.
- Play the recording so that pupils check their answers. Pupils can also look at their Pupil's Books to check their answers.

2.4 Complete the speech bubbles. (Lesson 5)

- Ask pupils to look at the pictures.
- Give pupils time to write the speech bubbles.
- Ask volunteers for checking.

Choose a character from the story. Write about their daily routine. Use the words in the box.

- Give pupils time to do the activity.
- Ask volunteers for checking.

2.5 Cut and play. (Lesson 6)

- Use the word cards for matching games. Before playing, read all the words and ask pupils to make up sentences with them. Review the different endings. Consider incorporating some visual support, e.g. colour-coding the cards so that pupils remember the sound or writing the phonetic symbol.
- Pupils cut out the cards to play in pairs. Each pupil stacks their half of the cards putting both groups together. Pupils take turns to take two cards from both stacks and read the words. If the /s/ sound is the same, they keep them. The pupil with more pairs wins the game. The FREE cards allow pupils to say any verb in the third person that has the same sound. They are also allowed to repeat the same word.

2.6 Read and complete. (Lesson 7)

- Give pupils time read the clues, write the words and label the pictures.

KEY **1** butter **2** fridge **3** flour **4** sugar **5** cooker **6** salt **7** piece **8** chocolate **9** nose **10** mouth

2.7 Find someone who… (Lesson 8)

- Tell pupils that they're going to complete a survey. Read aloud the questions to check understanding.
- Model how to circulate and ask the questions. Pupils need to write the name of those pupils that they found that matched the idea. Tell pupils that they need to ask all the questions in the given time.
- Discuss pupils' experiences.

Unit 3 Free time

3.1 Write a sentence using each phrase or word. (Lesson 1)

- Give pupils time to do the activity.
- Read aloud the sentences. Encourage pupils to say their own sentence.

3.2 Unscramble the words. (Lesson 3)

- Give pupils time to unscramble the words.
- Tell pupils that they can use the words in the box in Activity 2.

KEY trampolining, playing chess, acting, playing the drums, running races, singing karaoke, rollerblading, reading magazines

What are they doing ?

- Give pupils time to do the activity.

Read and classify.

- Ask pupils to read the words in the box. Give them examples of the grammatical categories using words from the box. Remind them to put the word in the right position.
- Give pupils time to do the activity. Read out or write on the board to check.

KEY

Nouns:	snowman, bicycle, snowball, score, sledge, programme, ski, team, player, swing
Verbs:	hitting, kicking, throwing, catching, go out, telling jokes, reading poetry, playing golf, trampolining, acting, rollerblading

3.3 Listen and complete the lines. (Lesson 3)

- Ask pupils to read the song.
- Play the recording so that pupils read and complete the end of the lines.
- Play the recording for pupils to check their answers. Pupils can also look at their Pupil's Books to check their answers.

3.4 Complete the speech bubbles. (Lesson 5)

- Ask pupils to look at the pictures.
- Give pupils time to write the speech bubbles.
- Ask volunteers for checking.

Draw your favourite character doing a different activity for each day of the week. Then describe.

- Give pupils time to do the activity.
- Ask volunteers for checking.

3.5 Read and answer. Then practise the intonation with your partner. (Lesson 6)

- Review the intonation skill before completing. Give pupils time to answer the questions independently. Ask volunteers to read and answer the questions out loud.

3.6 Ask your friends. Then graph the results. (Lesson 7)

- Pupils ask and answer the questions. Then they use the data to make a graph.

3.7 Find someone who ... (Lesson 8)

- Tell pupils that they're going to complete a survey. Read aloud the questions to check understanding.
- Model how to circulate and ask the questions. Pupils need to write the name of those pupils that they found that matched the idea. Tell pupils that they need to ask all the questions in the given time.
- Discuss pupils' experiences.

Unit 4 Around the world

4.1 Draw the flag in the box next to the country. (Lesson 1)

- Give pupils time to do the activity.
- Read aloud the countries and check each flag as a whole-class discussion.

4.2 Unscramble the words. (Lesson 3)

- Give pupils time to unscramble the words.
- Tell pupils that they can use the words in the box in Activity 2.

KEY desert, pyramid, statue, city, cave, volcano, forest, lake

Read and classify.

- Ask pupils to read the words in the box. Give them examples of the grammatical categories using words from the box. Remind them to put the word in the right position.
- Give pupils time to do the activity. Read out or write on the board to check.

KEY

Adjectives: big, small, far, interesting, close

Nouns: desert, statue, cave, lake, pyramid, volcano

4.3  Listen and number the paragraphs in order.

- Ask pupils to read the song.
- Play the recording so that pupils can order the paragraphs.
- Play the recording for pupils to check their answers. Pupils can also look at their Pupil's Books to check their answers.

4.4 Complete the speech bubbles. (Lesson 5)

- Ask pupils to look at the pictures.
- Give pupils time to write the speech bubbles.
- Ask volunteers for checking.

Choose a character from the story and draw him/her travelling around the world. Then write questions about those countries and places and ask a classmate.

- Give pupils time to do the activity.
- Ask volunteers for checking.

4.5 Cut and play. (Lesson 6)

- Use the word cards for matching games. Before playing, read all the words and ask pupils to make up sentences with them. Review some of the matching pairs.
- Pupils cut out the cards to play in pairs. They should put the contractions in one pile and the other cards in another pile. Pupils take turns to take one card from each stack and read the words. If the cards match, they keep them. The pupil with more pairs wins the game.

4.6 Read and calculate. Then circle the answer. (Lesson 7)

- Review previous knowledge on planets. Read and discuss what gravity is. Pupils use calculators or paper and pencil to calculate their gravity on different planets. Check the answers that they circled.

Complete the sentences.

- Give pupils time to do the activity. Read out some sentences.

4.7 Find someone who... (Lesson 8)

- Tell pupils that they're going to complete a survey. Read aloud the questions to check understanding.

- Model how to circulate and ask the questions. Pupils need to write the name of those pupils that they found that matched the idea. Tell pupils that they need to ask all the questions in the given time.
- Discuss pupils' experiences.

Unit 5 Shopping

5.1 Find these words in the dictionary. Write the meaning in the box. (Lesson 1)

- Give pupils time to do the activity.
- Read aloud the definitions. Encourage pupils to say their own definition. Model and practise dictionary skills.

5.2 Unscramble the words. (Lesson 3)

- Give pupils time to unscramble the words.
- Tell pupils that they can use the words in the box in Activity 2.

KEY modern, cheap, tight, expensive, baggy, old-fashioned

Read and classify.

- Ask pupils to read the words in the box. Give them examples of the grammatical categories using words from the box. Remind them to put the word in the right position.
- Give pupils time to do the activity. Read out or write on the board to check.

KEY

Adjectives:	tight, modern, baggy, cheap, old-fashioned
Nouns:	watch, umbrella, gloves, belt, tracksuit, receipt

5.3 2:23 Listen and complete. (Lesson 3)

- Ask pupils to read the song.
- Play the recording so that pupils read and complete the missing words.
- Play the recording so that pupils check their answers. Pupils can also look at their Pupil's Books to check their answers.

5.4 Complete the speech bubbles. (Lesson 5)

- Ask pupils to look at the pictures.
- Give pupils time to write the speech bubbles.
- Ask volunteers for checking.

Draw your favourite character wearing your favourite clothes. Then describe.

- Give pupils time to do the activity.
- Ask volunteers for checking.

5.5 Read and match. (Lesson 6)

- Pupils use scissors to cut along the dotted line. In pairs, they match the situations with the exclamations. Ask volunteers to act out the exclamation cards.

5.6 Read and match. (Lesson 7)

- Before reading, draw attention to the picture. Ask pupils to make predictions about the dialogue. Review the words *receipt, pence, pounds* and *shop assistant*.
- Ask pupils to read the dialogue and find the missing sentences underneath.
- Check answers. Ask the class *Have you ever returned something at a department store?*
- Encourage pairs to act out the dialogue.

KEY C, A, B, F, D, E

5.7 Find someone who ... (Lesson 8)

- Tell pupils that they're going to complete a survey. Read aloud the questions to check understanding.
- Model how to circulate and ask the questions. Pupils need to write the name of those pupils that they found that matched the idea. Tell pupils that they need to ask all the questions in the given time.
- Discuss pupils' experiences.

Unit 6 Party time

6.1 Find these verbs in the dictionary. Write the meaning in the box. (Lesson 1)

- Give pupils time to do the activity.
- Read aloud the definitions. Encourage pupils to say their own definition. Model and practise dictionary skills.

6.2 What is the date? (Lesson 3)

- Give pupils time to look at the pictures and dates. They say what special date each one is.

Read and classify.

- Ask pupils to read the words in the box. Give them examples of the grammatical categories using words from the box. Remind them to put the word in the right position.
- Give pupils time to do the activity. Read out or write on the board to check.

KEY
Adjectives: foggy, horrible, dangerous
Nouns: month, diary, piece of cake, balloon, card, candle
Verbs: make, came, saw, sing/sang, brought, meet, get

6.3 Listen and number the lines in order. (Lesson 3)

- Ask pupils to read the song.
- Play the recording so that pupils order the lines.
- Play the recording so that pupils check their answers. Pupils can also look at their Pupil's Books to check their answers.

6.4 Complete the speech bubbles. (Lesson 5)

- Ask pupils to look at the pictures.
- Give pupils time to write speech bubbles.
- Ask volunteers for checking.

Choose a character from the story. Then invent what he/she did yesterday. Use the verbs from the box.

- Give pupils time to do the activity.
- Ask volunteers for checking.

6.5 Cut out and match. (Lesson 6)

- Pupils use scissors to cut along the dotted line. In pairs, they match the questions and answers to practise intonation. Ask volunteers to share.

6.6 Read and match. (Lesson 7)

- Review the objects and their meaning. Draw attention to the pictures.
- Give pupils time to read and match the Thanksgiving words and the descriptions.
- Check answers. Ask the class about other situations when they might use these things, e.g. you need to use a thermometer in a science experiment about temperature, etc.

KEY **1** C **2** D **3** A **4** E **5** B

6.7 Find someone who... (lesson 8)

- Tell pupils that they're going to complete a survey. Read aloud the questions to check understanding.
- Model how to circulate and ask the questions. Pupils need to write the name of those pupils that they found that matched the idea. Tell pupils that they need to ask all the questions in the given time.
- Discuss pupils' experiences.

Unit 7 School

7.1 Find each word in the dictionary. Write its meaning in the box. (Lesson 1)

- Give pupils time to do the activity.
- Read aloud the definitions. Encourage pupils to say their own definition. Model and practise dictionary skills.

7.2 Unscramble the words. (Lesson 3)

- Give pupils time to unscramble the words.
- Tell pupils that they can use the words in the box in Activity 2.

KEY dictionary, Drama, Art, Computer Science, Maths, P.E., Music, Design, History, subject, Geography, language

Read and classify.

- Ask pupils to read the words in the box. Give them examples of the grammatical categories using words from the box. Remind them to put the word in the right position.
- Give pupils time to do the activity. Read out or write on the board to check.

KEY
Adjectives: exciting, romantic, difficult, scary
Nouns: Geography, language, Drama, scissors, flag, History
Verbs: study, teach, bring, learn

7.3 Listen and complete the lines. (Lesson 3)

- Ask pupils to read the song.
- Play the recording so that pupils read and complete the end of the lines.
- Play the recording for pupils to check their answers. Pupils can also look at their Pupil's Books to check their answers.

7.4 Complete the speech bubbles. (Lesson 5)

- Ask pupils to look at the pictures.
- Give pupils time to draw, colour and write a new or similar story.
- Ask volunteers for checking.

Choose a character. Which subject do you think is the character's favourite? Explain why.

- Give pupils time to do the activity.
- Ask volunteers for checking.

7.5 Read and sort the vowels. Write them in the correct column according to the vowel sounds. (Lesson 6)

- Pupils read the words and classify them into long and short vowels.
- Check answers and point out the pattern with the 'magic e' at the end. Ask volunteers to make up sentences with the words.

KEY
Short: pig, hat, not, Tim, leg, Sam, bed
Long: cake, hate, note, time, Pete, same, meet, race

7.6 Beat the clock word search! (Lesson 7)

- Pupils complete the activity in the given time. Then they complete the sentences using the present perfect.

Complete a sentence.

- Give pupils time to complete the sentences. Read out for checking.

7.7 Find someone who ... (Lesson 8)

- Tell pupils that they're going to complete a survey. Read aloud the questions to check understanding.
- Model how to circulate and ask the questions. Pupils need to write the name of those pupils that they found that matched the idea. Tell pupils that they need to ask all the questions in the given time.
- Discuss pupils' experiences.

Unit 8 All about us

8.1 Write the country for each nationality. Then write the language spoken there. (Lesson 1)

- Give pupils time to do the activity.
- Read aloud the countries and the nationalities. Encourage pupils to talk about the answers they have written.

8.2 Unscramble the words. (Lesson 3)

- Give pupils time to unscramble the words.
- Tell pupils that they can use the words in the box in Activity 2.

KEY waiter, photographer, actor, painter, artist, mechanic, astronaut, cook, dentist, journalist, engineer, footballer, businessman, firewoman

Do the crossword.

- Ask pupils to complete the crossword, using the picture clues.

KEY **1** photographer **2** cook **3** engineer **4** waiter **5** astronaut **6** mechanic

8.3   Listen and number the paragraphs in order. (Lesson 3)

- Ask pupils to read the song.
- Play the recording so that pupils order the paragraphs.
- Play the recording for pupils to check their answers. Pupils can also look at their Pupil's Books to check their answers.

8.4 Complete the speech bubbles. (Lesson 5)

- Ask pupils to look at the pictures.
- Give pupils time to write the speech bubbles.
- Ask volunteers for checking.

Give a job to each character of the story. Then explain why you think this job is good for him/her.

- Give pupils time to do the activity.
- Ask volunteers for checking.

8.5 Cut and play. (Lesson 6)

- Review the unit's phonetic skill.
- Ask pupils to cut out the words and stack in two groups. In pairs, pupils take turns picking up and reading a word from each stack. If they have the same ending sound, they keep them. The pupil that ends the game with more cards wins the game. The FREE cards allow pupils to say any verb with any ending that has the pattern. Consider colour-coding the cards to facilitate the sound correspondence.

8.6 Read and complete. Then answer the questions. (Lesson 7)

- Give pupils time to read and complete the text with the missing words.

KEY American, in, where, which, year, on, at, in
True, False, False, True

Read and write (T = *True*, F = *False*)

- In pairs, pupils read the sentences and decide if they are true or false. Then pupils work independently to write their sentences about the text.
- Challenge the class to calculate how long the first flight was.

Write one true sentence and one false sentence about the Wright brothers.

- Give pupils time to do the activity. Ask volunteers to read for checking.

8.7 Find someone who ... (Lesson 8)

- Tell pupils that they're going to complete a survey. Read aloud the questions to check understanding.
- Model how to circulate and ask the questions. Pupils need to write the name of those pupils that they found that matched the idea. Tell pupils that they need to ask all the questions in the given time.
- Discuss pupils' experiences.

Festivals

F.1 Complete the Festivals' Research Corner about Halloween! (Halloween)

- Brainstorm ideas and knowledge about the festival. Write them down on the board.
- Ask pupils to look at the Festivals' Research Corner table. Encourage pupils to talk about the five entries they are going to write. Give pupils the opportunity to research the magazines and cut outs. If you have a computer in your classroom or an ICT room at school, pupils can visit it to find out about the festival on the internet.
- Give pupils time to write.
- Read and display pupils' work. Discuss the different information they have found and recorded.

F.2 Complete the Festivals' Research Corner about Christmas! (Christmas)

- Brainstorm ideas and knowledge about the festival. Write them down on the board.
- Ask pupils to look at the Festivals' Research Corner table. Encourage pupils to talk about the five entries they are going to write. Give pupils the opportunity to research the magazines and cut outs. If you have a computer in your classroom or an ICT room at school, pupils can visit it to find out about the festival on the internet.
- Give pupils time to write.
- Read and display pupils' work. Discuss the different information they have found and recorded.

F.3 Complete the Festivals' Research Corner about April Fools' Day! (April Fools' Day)

- Brainstorm ideas and knowledge about the festival. Write them down on the board.
- Ask pupils to look at the Festivals' Research Corner table. Encourage pupils to talk about the five entries they are going to write. Give pupils the opportunity to research the magazines and cut outs. If you have a computer in your classroom or an ICT room at school, pupils can visit it to find out about the festival on the internet.
- Give pupils time to write.
- Read and display pupils' work. Discuss the different information they have found and recorded.

Answer Key

PLACEMENT

Reading

1 **1** makes/make **2** are/are **3** is/am **4** Is/He's
2 **1** Tomorrow **2** Yesterday **3** ago **4** Now
3 **1** He's going to go swimming **2** On Friday evening **3** No, he isn't. (He's going to play football on Saturday morning / He's going to the beach on Sunday) **4** After the game (on Saturday afternoon) **5** He's going to learn to sail.
4 **1** T **2** F **3** T **4** F

Writing

1 **1** C **2** B **3** D **4** A
2 **1** We walked to school this morning. **2** I played football on Saturday afternoon. / On Saturday afternoon I played football. **3** They lived in Colombia three years ago. / Three years ago they lived in Colombia. **4** She's funny because she tells jokes. **5** She doesn't want to be a singer.
3 **1** skiing **2** cooking **3** leaves **4** snorkelling

Listening

1 Tony: **1** solving **2** evening **3** problem **4** watching **5** TV **6** sitting down **7** doesn't like **8** running **Sue:** **1** skiing **2** Every winter **3** fast **4** slowly **5** swimming **6** diving **7** like
2 **1** evening **2** cinema **3** CDs **4** played **5** walk **6** morning **7** chess **8** living
3 **1** ✓ **2** ✓ **3** ✓ **4** ✗ **5** ✓ **6** ✓ **7** ✗

UNIT 1

Reading and writing A

1 **1** Thursday, October 6th **2** Tuesday, October 4th **3** Monday, October 3rd
2 **2** On Tuesday, Tom watched a DVD. **3** On Wednesday, Tom played tennis. **4** On Thursday, Tom went swimming. **5** On Friday, Tom went to the cinema.
3 **1** intelligent **2** dark **3** face **4** today **5** played **6** listened **7** helpful **8** studied **9** ago **10** problems

Reading and writing B

1 **1** Monday, September 2nd **2** Saturday, August 31st **3** Tuesday, August 27th Friday, August 30th
2 **1** On Monday Tina studied English. **2** On Tuesday Tina watched a DVD. **3** On Wednesday Tina chatted online. **4** On Thursday Tina went swimming. **5** On Friday Tina had music lessons. **6** On Saturday Tina went running. **7** On Sunday Tina went to the cinema.
3 **1** sporty **2** played **3** month **4** Tomorrow **5** spiky **6** red **7** beautiful **8** helpful **9** shy **10** ago **11** went **12** practised **13** helped

Listening and speaking A

1 **1** F **2** F **3** T **4** F
2 **1** friendly **2** talkative **3** talkative **4** sporty

Listening and speaking B

1 Thomas: **1** nine **2** like **3** don't like **4** like **5** every day Ian: **1** ten **2** black **3** like **4** tidying my bedroom **5** lazy Georgia: **1** ten **2** long **3** tidy **4** talkative **5** I'm not Paula: **1** eleven **2** tall **3** dark **4** love **5** never **6** are **7** bossy
2 **1** most **2** more intelligent **3** shortest **4** is

UNIT 2

Reading and writing A

1 **1** f **2** h **3** e **4** c **5** g **6** d **7** b **8** a
2 **1** I always tidy my bedroom at the weekend. **2** I should listen to my parents. **3** I sometimes eat unhealthy food. **4** I usually brush my teeth after lunch. **5** I must wear my uniform at school. **6** I never go to bed after ten o'clock.
3 **1** You should/must study. **2** you should eat. **3** You should go running. **4** You should/must tidy it (your room). **5** You should/must go to bed early. **6** You must take your swimsuit.

Reading and writing B

1 **1** my bed **2** my homework **3** for a test **4** my teeth **5** the rubbish **6** my face
2 **1** I never tidy my bedroom at the weekend. **2** I always listen to my parents. **3** I sometimes eat healthy food. **4** I often wash my hands before lunch. **5** I must get to school before half past eight. **6** I should go to bed before ten o'clock.
3 **1** You should have a drink. **2** You must/should buy some food. **3** You should/must ask the teacher. **4** You must/should be on time. **5** You should open the window. **6** You must/should study.

Listening and speaking A

1 **Helen:** messy room, hasn't got a bin, tidies on Saturday. **Victor:** can't study, can't sleep, listens to quiet music, eats more healthy food, eats one vegetable a day has pizza one day a week
2 **1** e **2** f **3** d **4** c **5** a **6** b

Listening and speaking B

1 **1** c **2** d **3** a **4** b
2 Girl: 1, 3, 8, 9, 10 Boy: 1, 2, 4, 5, 6, 7

UNIT 3

Reading and writing A

1 **1** good at kicking **2** not good at catching. **3** not good at diving. **4** good at telling jokes. **5** good at playing video games. **6** not good at throwing.
2 **1** playing / d **2** running / e **3** singing / c **4** writing / b **5** meeting / a
3 **1** play **2** playing **3** taking **4** afternoon **5** practise **6** at **7** Last **8** was **9** singing **10** prefer

Reading and writing B

1 **1** Is Sam good at (playing) football? **2** Is Sue good at telling jokes? **3** Is your mum good at trampolining? **4** Is your grandad good at diving? **5** What are you good at?

2 **1** Are you good at acting? **2** Are you good at playing chess? **3** Are you good at drawing? **4** Are you good at rollerblading? **5** Are you good at skateboarding? (Plus pupils' own answers.)

3 **1** prefer / at **2** rather **3** watching / don't / cold **4** sailing / than

Listening and speaking A

1 **1** b **2** b **3** a **4** a

2 **Betty:** Rollerblading **Jed:** Drawing **Val:** Singing Karaoke **Todd:** Playing the drums

Listening and speaking B

1 **1** b **2** d **3** e **4** c **5** a **6** f

2 **1** F, (He was walking home at 4.30pm) **2** T **3** F (Ben went to the stadium too.) **4** T **5** T **6** F (She doesn't learn quickly.)

UNIT 4

Reading and writing A

1 **many:** volcano, pyramid, rainforest, statue, lake **much:** water, space, sky, air, time

2 **1** How many lakes are there in Egypt? / There are a lot. **2** How much air is there on Mercury? There isn't any air on Mercury. **3** How many deserts are there in Italy? / There aren't any (deserts in Italy). **4** How many pyramids are there in Spain? / There aren't (any pyramids in Spain). **5** How much water is there on Neptune? / There isn't any (water on Neptune) **6** How many cities are there in China? There are a lot/lots of cities in China).

3 **1** cities **2** volcanoes **3** statues **4** lakes **5** forests

Reading and writing B

1 **Much:** space, environment, air **Many:** planet, hill, statue, forest, cave, city

2 **1** Are there any pyramids in Australia? No, there aren't. **2** Are there any lakes in the UK? Yes, there are. **3** Are there any caves in Spain? Yes, there are. **4** Are there any volcanoes in Mexico? Yes, there are.

3 **1** are **2** some/a lot of **3** aren't **4** are **5** aren't **6** much

Listening and speaking A

1 **1** a **2** b **3** b **4** a **5** b **6** b

2 **1** T / T / F **2** T / F / F **3** T / F / T **4** T / F / F

Listening and speaking B

1 **1** e **2** d **3** b **4** c **5** a

2 **1** F **2** T **3** T **4** F **5** F **6** T

UNIT 5

Reading and writing A

1 **1** 60 **2** 1000 **3** 350 **4** 315 **5** sixteen **6** five hundred **7** one hundred and five **8** nine hundred and ninety-nine

2 **1** trousers/jumper **2** trousers **3** bracelet **4** jeans (Plus pupils' own answers.)

3 **1** Harry's **2** hers **3** Ben's / his **4** your / yours

Reading and writing B

1 **1** five hundred and five pounds. **2** one hundred and ninety six pounds. **3** thirty seven pounds **4** eighty three pounds **5** nine hundred and fifty three pounds. **6** one thousand pounds

2 **1** How much are those baggy trousers? They're sixty pounds. **2** How much is this old-fashioned wallet? It's sixteen pounds. **3** How much is that modern watch? It's eight hundred and eight pounds. **4** How much is this tight tracksuit? It's fifty three pounds.

3 It's his **2** It's hers **3** It's his **4** It's hers

Listening and speaking A

1 **1** £60 **2** £10 **3** £50 **4** £15

2 **1** green and brown and white / stripes **2** beautiful / old-fashioned **3** baggy / different coloured / **4** tight / leather pocket

Listening and speaking B

1 **1** £85, leather (expensive) **2** £20 for **2** (£10 each), black / dark blue (bargain) **3** £260 / gold (too expensive, cheaper bracelets in shop next week) **4** £16 / purple stripes

2 **1** new jeans, look at the prices in the different shops, jeans with the best price **2** trainers, to check the prices, good and strong, £43.50

UNIT 6

Reading and writing A

1 **1** third **2** fifteenth **3** eleventh **4** eighth **5** fifth **6** sixteenth **7** first **8** thirteenth

2 **1** b **2** e **3** f **4** a **5** c **6** d

3 **1** have to **2** must **3** have to **4** have to **5** must

Reading and writing B

1 **1** The second of August. **2** The fifteenth of May. **3** The fourteenth of April. **4** The eighteenth of November. **5** The fifth of June. **6** The ninth of September. **7** The first of July. **8** The twelfth of January.

2 **1** Who did you go with? **2** When did you go? **3** What did you do? **4** Could you...? **5** Where did you go? **6** How did you get there?

3 **1** have to **2** must **3** must **4** have to **5** must

Listening and speaking A

1 Pupils' own answers. (Balloons. Barbecue, sandwiches, sausages, potatoes, salad, cakes, biscuits, jelly, ice cream, guitar)

2 **1** h **2** d **3** a **4** j **5** k **6** f

Listening and speaking B

1 A: **1** F **2** F **3** T **4** F **5** F **6** F **7** T B: **1** F **2** T **3** T **4** F **5** F **6** F

2 **1** Ireland **2** August **3** hiking **4** caught **5** dancing **6** storytelling

UNIT 7

Reading and writing A

1 **1** b **2** a **3** d **4** c

2 **1** were / I was four years old. **2** Were / Yes, I was very excited. **3** was / It was very hot and sunny.

4 Was / It was a very interesting holiday
3 1 have 2 has 3 have 4 have 5 has 6 has

Reading and writing B

1 1 Yes, I was. 2 No, he / she wasn't. 3 No, they weren't. 4 Yes, it was. 5 Yes, I was. 6 No, it wasn't.
2 1 How old were you? / I was three years old. 2 Were you excited? / No, I wasn't. 3 What was the weather like? / It was very cold and raining. 4 Was it interesting? / No, it wasn't.
3 1 have read 2 has written 3 have seen 4 have learnt 5 has created 6 has made

Listening and speaking A

1 1 school 2 scary 3 kind 4 History 5 museums 6 plays 7 horrible 8 intelligent 9 boring 10 Science 11 exciting
2 Monday / M: Computer Studies / Monday / A: Music Tuesday / M: Science / Tuesday A: Sports Wednesday / M: Computer Studies / Wednesday / A: Drama Thursday / M: Guitar lessons Thursday / A: Science Friday / M: Computer Studies / Friday / A: Geography

Listening and speaking B

1 A: 1 c 2 b 3 e 4 a 5 d B: 1 a 2 f 3 d 4 c 5 e 6 b
2 1 page 5 / Geography 2 page 7 / Language 3 page 10 / Science 4 page 4 / Dictionary 5 page 6 / History 6 page 2 Computer Studies

UNIT 8

Reading and writing A

1 1 c 2 d 3 a 4 f 5 e 6 b
2 1 e, actor 2 f, waiter 3 a, astronaut 4 d, cook 5 c, dentist 6 b, journalist
3 1 who 2 where 3 which 4 who

Reading and writing B

1 1 Are you from Brazil/Brazilian? 2 Are you Irish? 3 Are they Thai? 4 Are they Canadian? 5 Is he Mexican? 6 Is she Italian?
2 1 d, artist 2 b, photographer 3 a, engineer 4 c, footballer
3 1 They are the children who are Chinese. 2 Camels are animals which are African. 3 This is the library where I found the wallet. 4 This is the shop where I bought my bracelet.

Listening and speaking A

1 1 Mexican 2 Chinese 3 Japanese 4 Italian 5 Greek 6 Spanish
2 1 football player/e 2 journalist/a 3 cook/d 4 dentist/f 5 mechanic/b 6 actor/c

Listening and speaking B

1 1 Pablo: Bogota / Colombian 2 Anton: Krakow / Polish 3 Val: Montreal / Canadian 4 Ruth: Washington / American 5 Marco: Venice / Italian 6 Cristobal: Seville / Spanish 7 Anna: Beijing / Chinese 8 Ryan: Dublin / Irish
2 1: 4 2: 3 3: 8 4: 1 5: 5 6: 0 7: 1 8: 10 9: 4

END OF TERM 1

1 1 a 2 g 3 h 4 f 5 c 6 d 7 b 8 e
2 1 I was watching TV. 2 I'm good at playing chess. 3 She's got long straight hair. 4 She's sporty. 5 She's reading a book. 6 I should brush my teeth every day.
3 1 I was playing tennis. 2 I am good at football and basketball. 3 No, I'm not. 4 I am kind and sporty. 5 She's got straight blonde hair. 6 I love rollerblading and trampolining.
4 Suggested answers: **Should do:** brush my teeth, wash my face, do my homework, take the rubbish out, tidy my bedroom, set the table **Want to do:** practise the piano, play in a band, play video games, read books **Both:** go shopping

END OF TERM 2

1 1 b 2 e 3 f 4 a 5 g 6 d 7 h 8 c
2 1 Are there any volcanoes in your country? / f 2 Is there a cave in the mountains? / e 3 How much is the jacket? / c 4 Whose is this brown wallet? / d 5 Who won the swimming competition? / b 6 Those trousers are very tight! / a
3 1 No, there is not (isn't). 2 Yes, there are. There are lots. 3 I usually bring a present. 4 It's Les' book. 5 My birthday is on the 1st of May. 6 I went shopping two days ago.
4 Clothes: gloves / bracelet / sunglasses / swimsuit / helmet Adjectives: old-fashioned / expensive / baggy / cheap / tight

END OF TERM 3

1 1 d 2 f 3 a 4 c 5 h 6 g 7 e 8 b
2 1 Yes but it was scary. 2 They are both Egyptian. 3 Yes, there were lots. 4 No but there were three sailors. 5 Yes, we did some exciting tests with water and salt. 6 At quarter to four in the morning.
3 1 Where's your teacher from? 2 Did you visit America last year? 3 Did you watch a film on TV last week? 4 Was the film scary? 5 Were you in a school competition last year? 6 Did you have Maths on Tuesday?
4 1 h 2 b 3 e 4 a 5 d 6 f 7 g 8 c (Plus pupils' own answers)

FINAL

Reading A

1 1 c 2 a 3 a 4 b 5 a/b

Reading B

1 1 F 2 F 3 T 4 F 5 F 6 T

Writing A

1 1 went 2 love 3 are 4 am 5 snowboarding 6 In 7 played 8 singing
2 1 three hundred 2 two hundred and seventy eight 3 six hundred and fifty nine 4 one hundred and fourteen
3 Suggested questions: 1 Are you from Egypt? Are you Egyptian? 2 Where did you go last summer? 3

What are they good at? **4** Was the film interesting?

4 **1** In **2** on **3** at **4** in **5** in

5 **1** Why are you excited? / c Because tomorrow it's my birthday. **2** How often do you tidy your room? / d Every Saturday at midday. **3** Where did you go last summer? / b I went to Ibiza.

Writing B

1 **1** got **2** gave **3** had **4** sang **5** came **6** played **7** ate **8** helped

2 Suggested questions: 1 Are you Egyptian? Are you from Egypt? **2** Where did you go last summer? **3** What are they good at? **4** Whose book is this? **5** When did she come home? **6** Did you watch the TV last night?

3 **1** Are there any mountains in your country? **2** She is the tallest in her family. **3** You should go to the doctor. **4** He couldn't come to the party.

4 **1** birthday **2** storyboards **3** glue / scissors **4** scissors / glue **5** characters **6** midday **7** snack **8** chocolate **9** sang **10** score

Listening A

1 **1** watched **2** basketball **3** was **4** difficult **5** practised **6** went **7** a quarter past eleven **8** at **9** tired **10** watched **11** chatted **12** telling

2 **Sue:** Australian / surfing / every day after school / beach next to her house **Tony:** Argentina / diving / spring and summer / lakes

3 **1** expensive/c **2** lovely/a **3** cheap/e **4** tight/d **5** baggy/b **6** old-fashioned/f

4 **1** exciting **2** scary **3** boring **4** funny

Listening B

1 **1** watched **2** violin **3** exciting **4** difficult **5** practised **6** went **7** finished **8** midnight **9** didn't do **10** must **11** met **12** Mexican

2 **Stephanie:** Greece / diving / spring - summer – autumn / cave near home. **Rob:** Canada / climbing – skiing / climbing in summer – skiing in winter / mountains near his house

3 **1** cheap / belt **2** expensive / candle **3** mechanic / helmet **4** label / umbrella **5** baggy / trousers **6** birthday present / bracelet

4 **1** chess **2** poetry reading **3** drum-playing **4** joke-telling **5** karaoke

EXAM PREPARATION

Reading and writing A

1 **1** b **2** a **3** f **4** c **5** d **6** e

2 **1** Yes **2** No **3** Yes **4** No **5** Yes **6** No

3 **1** b **2** c **3** a

4 **1** walked **2** was **3** climbed **4** had **5** started **6** weren't **7** got **8** made

5 **1** Yes, there are. **2** Lots of statues. **3** On the islands. **4** No, there aren't.

Listening A

1 In order from left to right: Nick, Harry, Clara, Frankie, James, Susie

2 **1** Help mum tidy the house. **2** Go shopping. **3** Meet cousin Gary in London. **4** Meet Sally and her family for a birthday tea in a café. **5** Watch Dad's team play football. **6** Swimming competition.

3 **Bob** b **Mandy** d **David** c **Angela** a

4 **a ✗ b ✓ c ✗ d ✓ e ✓ f ✗ g ✓ h ✗**

5 Check with picture.

Reading and writing B

1 **1** f **2** d **3** e **4** a **5** c **6** b **7** h **8** g

2 **1** Yes **2** No **3** No **4** No **5** No **6** Yes **7** No **8** No

3 **1** b **2** c **3** a

4 **1** had **2** were **3** came **4** started **5** finished **6** was **7** didn't **8** made

5 **1** T **2** F **3** T **4** F

Listening B

1 In order from left to right: Jack, Michael, Tony, Helen, Vicky, Cynthia

2 **1** Pat **2** 16 North Street, Little Troddick **3** school bag **4** school books, train ticket, pursem new mobile phone **5** on the train **6** 0452 78993

3 **1** c **2** b **3** d **4** a

4 **1** c **2** c

5 Check with picture.

Games

Introduction

Games are an entertaining way for pupils to revise, practise and consolidate language. Fun is a great motivator, allowing pupils with different skills and abilities to learn in a stress-free environment.

Most of the games and activities described here can be played by the class as a whole, or by dividing it into small groups or pairs. However, you should bear in mind that the smaller the number of pupils in a group, the more talking time they will have in their group. Also, pairing is important; if you pair confident and shy pupils together, the latter will not have much chance to produce a lot of language.

It's a good idea to decide beforehand how many groups you want to divide your class into and what materials you will need for all the pupils. Also, it will save you time if you have a clear idea of the pupils' seating arrangement before starting the activity.

Setting clear rules and a time limit from the beginning keeps games competitive and fun. Finally, during the game, you might want to move around the class unobtrusively, monitoring and noting down good language usage and mistakes/errors so that after the game you can have a brief feedback session. This session is better kept impersonal, not mentioning who produced either the instances of good language or the mistakes. This will prevent pupils from feeling singled out and will allow them to focus on communication more freely rather than accuracy.

Games and fun activities

Vocabulary

Hangman

This game can be played in pairs, small groups or with the teacher against the whole class. A pupil from group A comes to the board and chooses a word from a secret pool of words that you have decided upon and writes as many dashes as the word has letters on the board. The pupils from group B try to guess the word by calling out possible letters. Incorrect letters are written on the board to help pupils remember which letters have already been chosen.

Hot seat

This is useful to revise/consolidate vocabulary or as a warmer/finisher. Play as a whole class. A volunteer sits on a chair at the front facing the class so they can't see the board. Write a word on the board. Different pupils say individual words associated with the word on the board to help the volunteer guess it. The pupils can't mime, make noises or say sentences!

I spy

This is useful to revise vocabulary. Play as a class or in groups. Choose an object pupils can see. Say *I spy with my little eye, something beginning with, e.g. P.* Invite guesses, e.g. *pupil, pen.* The first pupil to guess correctly starts a new round of the game saying *I spy ....*

Pictionary

On small blank cards write words or phrases you want pupils to revise. Divide the class into two groups. A pupil from group A takes a card from the pack and draws a picture of the word/phrase on the board within a set time limit. His/Her partners must guess the word to score a point. Then it's the turn of the other group. The winner is the group who has scored the most points.

Whispers

This is useful to consolidate/revise vocabulary and practise listening. Play as a whole class or in teams to make it competitive. Whisper a word/short sentence to a pupil. They whisper the word to the person next to them. Continue until all pupils in the row/class have whispered the same word. The last pupil tells the class what they think the word/sentence is.

Word snakes

Pupils make word snakes by joining together different vocabulary and writing them in the form of a snake. To make it more difficult pupils could also add extra letters between words. Pupils swap their snakes with another pair or group and have to identify all the words in the snake. The winners are the pupils to identify all the words.

Grammar and Lexical-Grammatical games

Alphabet tennis

This is useful to consolidate/revise a lexical set or as a warmer with no specific vocabulary focus. Play with the whole class. Divide the class into two teams. Decide which team/pupil will begin. 'Serve' a word from the lexical set, e.g. say *b.* The pupil says any word from the set beginning with *b.* Any pupil from the other team says another word beginning with *b*, without hesitating or repeating. The final team to say a word wins a point. 'Serve' a different letter and start again.

Bingo

This is useful to consolidate/revise a lexical set or grammar. Play with the whole class. Pupils draw a grid on a piece of paper with three columns and three rows. Choose a lexical or numeric set, e.g. sports. Pupils individually write one word or number from the lexical set in each square.

Read out a word/number and note it. Pupils cross it out if they have it. Continue. Pupils shout *Bingo!* when they cross off all their words. Check the winner's card against your list.

Guessing game

In pairs, pupils write five sentences about members of their family and what they are doing at that particular moment. Their partners try to guess. This game can be adapted to be used with many different tenses and can practise the affirmative, questions and short answers, e.g. *Your father is working right now. Yes, he is. / No, he isn't. Is your father working? Did your father work yesterday? etc.*

Happy families

This is useful to practise *have got*, family members and possessive *'s*. Play in groups of four. Give four blank card-sized pieces of paper to each pupil in the class. They each draw someone from their family on each card and write their name and relationship, e.g. *(name)'s granny.*

One pupil in each group of four shuffles and deals the cards so each pupil has four. The aim of the game is to swap cards in order to collect one family. Pupils take it in turns to ask each other questions, e.g. A: *Have you got (name)'s dad?* B: *Yes, I have.* If the answer is positive, Pupil A can ask for another card, e.g. *Have you got (name)'s grandad?* When they get a negative response, it is the next player's turn. The winner is the first to collect one family.

Noughts and crosses

To play the game draw a grid of two parallel horizontal lines and two parallel vertical lines crossing at right angles on the board. This should give you nine squares. In each square write, e.g. the infinitive of an (ir)regular verb. Divide the class into two groups and give one group the symbol **O** and the other the symbol **X**.

Group **O** choose a square and a pupil provides the past form. If they are correct, they write their symbol in the square. Then group **X** choose a square and repeat the procedure. The first team to get three consecutive **O** or **X** across, down or diagonally is the winner.

Pelmanism (pairs)

This is useful to consolidate/revise a lexical set. Play in groups of three or four.

Choose a lexical set. Each group draws a different target word on each of twelve small pieces of blank paper. Each group writes twelve matching word cards.

Pupils place the cards face down. They take it in turns to turn over two cards at a time. If they turn over a matching pair they keep it and have another turn. The pupil with the most pairs wins.

Teacher says

Play the game as a whole class. You give pupils orders in the imperative and pupils must obey you **only** if you precede your order by saying *Teacher says ... (e.g. jump/ don't close your books, etc.).* If pupils obey orders which are not preceded by this utterance, they lose and are out of the game. The winner is the last player to stay in the game.

Trivial pursuit

Divide the class into small groups and hand a pack of small blank cards to each group. Ask them to write a question and an answer on each card using a variety of vocabulary and structures you want them to revise. Shuffle the cards, divide the class into new groups and hand a pack of the written cards to each group to play. They play individually in their groups asking and answering questions. The winner is the player who has answered the most questions correctly.

TPR games

Touch and guess

This is useful to consolidate/revise a lexical set. Play with the whole class. Put 6–8 objects connected to a topic/ lexical set in a non-transparent bag.

A pupil comes to the front. Blindfold them. They take an object from the bag, feel it and guess what it is.

How to use classroom language

Using classroom language is a good way to get pupils to react in English rather than in L1. The more they use these new phrases and expressions, the more confident they become and the less they will need to rely on L1 to communicate with the teacher. If classroom language is used consistently, it becomes a natural part of pupils' vocabulary. It is important to teach both the classroom language the pupils have to understand as well as language they need to produce. The following is a list of common English expressions that could easily be introduced in the classroom and used on a daily basis. It's best to begin with a few expressions and increase the number gradually.

Greeting the class

Hello. Hi!
Good morning/afternoon.
Come in.
Come in and sit down quietly. You're late!
Sit down/stand up, please.
What day is it today?
How are you today?
Is everyone here?
Is anyone away today?
Where is (John)?

Starting the lesson

Are you ready?
Let's begin.
May/Can I have (Tuesday's) homework, please?
Listen (to me).
Look (at me/at the board).
Take out your books/notebooks/coloured pencils.
Where's your book? Please share with (John) today.
Give this/these out, please.
I'm going to give you all a worksheet.
(John,) can you give out these worksheets, please?
Have you got a (pencil)?
Open your books at page (4).
Turn to page (6).
Open/close the window/door.

Managing the class

Be quiet, please.
Come to (the front of the class/to the board).
Come here, please.
Put your hands up/down.
Who's next?
Queue/Line up!
Repeat after me.
Wait a minute, please.
Hurry up.

During the lesson – instructions

Hold up your picture.
Show me (the class) your picture.
Draw/Colour/Stick/Cut out … .
Look at the pictures at the top/bottom of the page.
Listen and read.
Listen and read the speech bubbles.
Listen and repeat after (me/the recording).
Write the answer on the board/in your book.
Turn your book over.
Close your books, please.
You can speak, but only in English.
Can you write the word on the board, please (John).
How do you spell (mountain)?
Let's check the answers.
Let's sing.
All together now.
It's break time/lunch time.
Wait a minute, please.
Be careful.
Sorry, guess/try again.
Next, please.
Again, please.

During the lesson – questions

Do you understand?
What do you think?
Anything else?
May/Can I help you?
Are you finished?
Who's finished?
Who would like to read?
What can you see?
Any questions?

Words of praise

Well done!
Excellent!
Fantastic!
That's nice.
Much better.
Congratulations.
That's correct!
Great work!
Good luck!
Thank you.

Pair work/Group work

Find a partner.
Get into twos/threes.
Who's your partner?
Work in pairs/groups.
Make a circle.
Work with your partner/friend/group.
Show your partner/friend/group.
Tell your partner/friend/group.
Now ask your partner/friend/group.
Change roles with your partner/friend/group.

Language used for playing games

It's my/your/his/her turn.
Whose turn is it?
You're out.
Shuffle/Deal the cards.
Pick up a card.
Put down a card.
Don't look.
No cheating.
Turn around.
Shut your eyes.
Pass the (ball, cup, etc.)
Wait outside.
Spin the spinner.
Move your/my counter (3) spaces.
Miss a turn.
Go back (2) spaces.
Spin again.
I've won!
You're the winner!

Online language

Move your mouse to the left/right/up/down.
Go left/right/up/down.
Go to (Scene 2, the school).
Enter/Exit (the chatroom).
Jump (on the roof).
Click to collect (the card).
Click on the speech bubbles.
Click on the (Ticket Inspector).
Use your Picture dictionary in your backpack.
Put on./Take off.
Pick up./Put down.
What's this/that?
Let's play a game.
Try again.
Come back later.
I'm busy now.
Bus stop.
Joy stick.
Map.
Costumiser.
Report card.

Active Teach language

Click on the tick/CD/game icon.
Find the sticker.
Look and sing.
Who wants to play a game?
You're in Team 1.
Spin the spinner.
Move the counters.
Let's start again.
You're out of time.
Team 1 get ready!
Team 1 wins!
It's a draw.
What's this in English?
Mime or act the word.
Make the sentence/question.
Move the wheel.
Find the pairs.
What's the answer to (number 2)?
I need a volunteer!
Touch the picture.
Compare your answers.
Are you right?
Is it right?

Ending the lesson

Put your books/notebooks/coloured pencils away.
Tidy up.
Put that in the bin/rubbish bin, please.
That's all for today.
Collect the stickers/cards/spinners/scissors, please.
(John,) can you collect everyone's books/worksheets, please?
The lesson is finished.
Goodbye!
See you tomorrow.
Have a nice weekend/holiday.

Useful phrases for the pupils

May/Can I go to the toilet?
I understand. I don't understand.
Excuse me. Pardon me?
I'm sorry.
I'm sorry I left my book/homework at home.
Can you help me?
I'm finished.

Pearson Education Limited
Edinburgh Gate
Harlow
Essex CM20 2JE
England
and Associated Companies throughout the world.

www.islands.pearson.com

First published 2012
Third impression 2015
ISBN: 978-1-4082-9073-6

Set in Fiendstar 10.5/12pt
Printed in Great Britain by Ashford Colour Press Ltd